A
Celebration
of
American
Family
Folklore

Tales and
Traditions from
the Smithsonian
Collection

Steven J. Zeitlin
Amy J. Kotkin
Holly Cutting Baker

Pantheon Books
New York

A
Celebration
of
American
Family
Folklore

Grateful acknowledgment is made to the following for permission to
reprint previously published material:

MARYLAND ARTS COUNCIL FOLKLIFE PROGRAM: Excerpt from "Family
Folklore: A Model Course Outline." Copyright © 1977 by Amy. J.
Kotkin, Holly Cutting Baker, and the Maryland Arts Council Folklife
Program. Reprinted by permission of the Maryland Arts Council Folklife
Program, Baltimore, Md.

SANGA MUSIC INC.: Excerpt from "The Ranger's Command" by Woody
Guthrie. Copyright © 1960 by Sanga Music Inc. All rights reserved.
Used by permission.

SATURDAY REVIEW: Ballad by Frank Warner, quoted in "Growing Up in
Greenwich Village." Copyright 1943 by *Saturday Review*. All rights
reserved. Reprinted by permission.

TEMPLE UNIVERSITY PRESS: For permission to adapt material that appeared
originally in *Children of Strangers: The Stories of a Black Family* by
Kathryn L. Morgan.

THE WASHINGTON POST: Excerpt from "Interview with Maria Katzenbach"
by Kevin Scott, *Book World,* January 15, 1978. Copyright © 1978 by The
Washington Post. Also for excerpt from "Fifty Ways to Meet Your Lover"
by Michael Kernan, *Washington Post,* December 29, 1976, p. B-3.
Copyright © 1976 by The Washington Post. Reprinted by permission of
The Washington Post.

Library of Congress Cataloging in Publication Data
Main entry under title:
A celebration of American family folklore.
collected from the Family Folklore Program of the Smithsonian's Festival
of American Folklife.
Bibliography: p.
1. Family—United States—Folklore.
2. United States—Social life and customs.
3. Festival of American Folklife. Family Folklore Program.
I. Zeitlin, Steven J. II. Kotkin, Amy J.
III. Baker, Holly Cutting, 1949–
IV. Festival of American Folklife. Family Folklore Program.
GR105.C34   1982   398.2'7'0973   82-47873
ISBN 0-394-52095-5 AACR2
ISBN 0-394-71223-4 (PBK.)

BOOK DESIGN: ELISSA ICHIYASU
Manufactured in the United States of America
First Edition

For our parents:

🌿

Irving Zeitlin
Shirley Stein Zeitlin

🌿

David Kotkin
Eve Goldfeld Kotkin

🌿

Dick Cutting
Ruth Murray Cutting

*My grandfather mentioned that
his ancestors had been, perhaps, for the
most part honest — traveling peddlers
and merchants — but perhaps with a
little bit of piracy. They were in Latvia
and Lithuania on the Baltic Sea.
I'd like to think they were pirates, but
when I think about it seriously, they **were**
probably all hard-working people,
to be perfectly honest.*

JOHN BISHOP

*The history of my family is like the
history of the country: good people, and
bad people, and famous people, and
people nobody ever heard of.*

SUSAN BERRYMAN BOBROW

*I remember my relatives talking and
talking and talking, and yet as a kid,
I didn't listen. I'd love to go back
now and listen.*

WAYNE DIONNE

CONTENTS

ACKNOWLEDG-
MENTS

Since the first family folklore tent was erected at the Festival of American Folklife on the National Mall in 1974, we have been the grateful recipients of scholarly guidance, encouragement, and sound advice from many distinguished folklorists, colleagues, and friends. That the tent appeared at all is a tribute to Dr. Robert Byington, former deputy director of the Smithsonian's Office of Folklife Programs. His acceptance of the idea and support for our collecting and early publications has enabled us to gather a rich corpus of folklore and to begin to interpret its meaning. We are deeply grateful to him.

A special thanks is also owed to Sandra Gross. As a founding member of the Family Folklore Program, her perspectives on the material and her creativity enabled us to communicate our findings to the public through exhibitions and publications. She helped to edit our earlier publications, and, in that way, helped to shape this one. We value her insights; they are very much a part of this book.

We would also like to thank the Office of Folklife Programs, Smithsonian Institution which sponsored this project, and its director, Ralph Rinzler, for his encouragement throughout the years and his advice on our exhibitions and presentation techniques. We would also like to thank Barbara Strickland who cheerfully responded to thousands of inquiries for our earlier pamphlets and Richard Derbyshire for organizing the collection of photographs. The Smithsonian's Office of Fellowships and Grants also deserves thanks for Steven Zeitlin's predoctoral fellowship during which portions of this book were written. Our sincere appreciation also goes to the National Institute on Aging for its support of our continuing research on the folklore of older Americans.

Dr. Kenneth Goldstein, Department of Folklore and Folklife at the University of Pennsylvania, has also been a long-time supporter of the program and an invaluable resource for fieldwork methodology. We are likewise indebted to Bess Lomax Hawes, director of the Folk Arts program at the National Endowment for the Arts for her enthusiasm and advice on the program through its many incarnations.

Folklorists Margaret Yocom, Karen Baldwin, and Kathryn Morgan were pioneers in the field of family folklore. Their thought-provoking and detailed research on their own families provided us with new methods of inquiry and, most importantly, an understanding of the ways in which folklore evolves and functions in family life.

A number of other people have been generous with their support and encouragement at crucial times over the past seven years. Wilton Dillon and Charlene James of the Smithsonian Institution gave us opportunities to test our ideas in workshops across the country and at related programs in Washington; Suzanne Roschwalb helped us to collect the photos from local residents which were used in our exhibits and this book; Ethel Mohamed showed us how family memories could be beautifully embroidered on cloth, and graciously allowed us to use her works in our exhibitions and our publications; John Baker and Dan Berger were very supportive during the endless days of preparation for the festivals; Jeff Warner endured constant revisions of the manuscript, and lent his advice on each successive draft.

We would also like to acknowledge our gratitude to Wendy Wolf, our editor at Pantheon, for seeing the potential in this collection and encouraging us to undertake this project. Her enthusiasm and ability to give new expression to our familiar thoughts is much appreciated. We would like to thank Nan Graham at Pantheon for taking over the book when Wendy departed on her trip around the world. Thanks also to Milly Daniel for copyediting the book and Elissa Ichiyasu for designing it.

Finally, our deepest thanks goes to the many hundreds of families who interrupted their summer holiday to share their stories and traditions with us. This book is a tribute to their heritage.

Family folklore collectors: Deborah Autorino, Holly Cutting Baker, Linda Burack, Robert Clayton, Susan Davis, Lorrie Gross, Sandra Gross, Amy Kotkin, Carolyn Mitchell, Jack Santino, Rosemary Scanlon, Amy Schuman, Andrea Shelton, Paul Wagner, Linda Watson, Mark Workman, Steven Zeitlin.

Assistant editor: Amanda Dargan.

A
Celebration
of
American
Family
Folklore

Family Folklore: The Creative Expression of a Common Past

Families travel light. As the greater part of our experience slips beyond our reach, we clasp a mere handful of stories, expressions, photographs, and customs. Our photo albums, attic trunks, even our memories can only hold so much: Aunt Ida's fading wedding photo or a pair of unused tickets for the fateful voyage of the Titanic may be all that remain of whole generations in a family. From countless incidents, families choose a few stories to pass on, the funniest or perhaps the most telling. From all of the garbled baby talk, a single utterance may become a family expression. Yet these time-honored images do more than recall scattered people and events; they come to represent the unremembered past, the sum total of a family's heritage.

Like the folktales collected by the brothers Grimm, or the songs collected by Cecil Sharp in the Appalachian Mountains, family stories, expressions, customs, and photographs are examples of folklore, the informal and expressive traditions of close groups.[1] These traditions spring up whenever Americans gather their kinfolk together to talk, to celebrate, or to play. For every famous literary and photographic work, there are hundreds of thousands of stories and snapshots in which Americans have invested a large portion of their creative genius. Family tradition is one of the great repositories of American culture. It contains clues to our national character and insights into our family structure.

For an individual family, folklore is its creative expression of a common past. As raw experiences are transformed into family stories, expressions, and photos, they are codified in forms which can be easily recalled, retold, and enjoyed. Their drama and beauty are heightened, and the family's past becomes accessible as it is reshaped according to its needs and desires.

A family's folklore differs from its history. Its stories, photographs, and traditions are personalized and often creative distillations of experience, worked and reworked over time. When a family tells of that glorious moment when a relative just missed the sailing of the Titanic, or a great-grandmother held off a band of outlaws, or a grandfather tricked a border guard on his departure from the old country, the lore is precisely that: a glorious moment carefully selected and elaborated through the years, tailored to the demands of the present. Even photographs are not unbiased slices of life.

We look at a picture of a child in the family, and we think, "that is it, this is the way it was," but it is simply the way the world looked for a single moment through a mother's or a father's eye.

This is a book about those stories, expressions, keepsakes, and customs which characterize family life. It is a book about Uncle Velvl, the horse thief, lynched according to one yarn in "Lynchburg," Virginia; about Max Blum, pictured in a photograph as "One Gun Blum the Jewish Cowboy"; about Ethel Mohamed who embroidered her memories of great storms and her peddler husband's pushcart in cloth; about the Janneys who invented their own holiday, "St. Grunes Day."

But it is also a book about some prominent themes in American culture. The interviews we conducted with more than two thousand family members at the Smithsonian's Festival of American Folklife from 1974 to 1977 can help us understand how Americans interpret their history, the subjects they celebrate in their stories, photographs, and customs. General patterns emerge. Americans like to photograph themselves in front of their new cars or in pastoral settings, but rarely in their daily routine. They tell stories about eccentric rather than conventional souls; about up-

HOLLY CUTTING BAKER

PROGRESSIVE PHOTOGRAPHS

AT ONE YEAR

AT MAJORITY

AT THREE YEARS

AT FIFTEEN YEARS

AT FIVE YEARS

MARY GOODWIN

heavals, natural disasters, migrations, supernatural occurrences, not ordinary events. And they are especially fond of
tales which tell of how their ancestors lost a great fortune
which would otherwise have gone to them.

This is also a book about five particular American families. Following our collection of stories and traditions, folklorists from different backgrounds reminisce and contemplate the lore which shaped their family lives. One talks
about the proverbs told to him by his great-grandmother,
passed down from slavery times, another tells of a Russian
dance still performed at his Jewish family weddings. One
focuses on storytelling at Pennsylvania German weddings
and funerals. One centers on the expressions of small children growing up in a Greenwich Village family in the forties,
while yet another concentrates on the "characters" in a rural
South Carolina clan. At the end of the book, a brief interviewing guide and sample questionnaire offer suggestions
for starting one's own family folklore project.

The past is a dark screen occasionally lit by vivid images.
Families perpetuate only a few of the radiant scenes from
their histories — jubilant weddings, hilarious practical jokes,
terrifying earthquakes and fires — bright, flashing images
indeed. We think the ones we've assembled here come together like the frames of a film which expresses the artistic
side of family life, and hope that the reader will be able to
watch it like a dazzling and yet familiar home movie, a
chronicle of what American families choose to remember
and preserve about themselves.

The Forms of Family Lore

Man has been called the time-binding animal. The development of language, the invention of writing, and the advent of photography have each altered man's relationship to his past. Language gave him oral tradition; now he had the ability to tell another person what happened to him in a story or reminiscence. Writing made it possible for him to record his own account of his past; now his experiences could be transmitted across the generations in his own words. Photography and taping made it possible to record the past at the moment of its occurrence, to record the present at the moment of its transformation into the past.

Families make use of all of these. We tell stories, write letters and memoirs, take pictures to document our shared experience and later to relive it. In the same way that we take a different kind of vehicle—automobile, luxury liner, jumbo jet—depending on that portion of the globe to which we wish to travel, so the varied forms transport us to different segments of our past, for different purposes.

Birthdays, for instance, are a common scene preserved in American family pictures. A collection of these images can be a fascinating record of a person's growth. A story about those experiences, however, might fall below the threshold of interest: "first they brought out the cake, then they blew out the candles. . . ."

Oftentimes, a photograph just can't convey what a story can. The birthday party with its sweetness and its fragile hold on time makes a good subject for a picture. Yet one woman remembers and tells a story about only one birthday, an embarrassing party where her family ran out of spaghetti. Appropriately, that is the birthday at which no photos were taken. Stories are most often told about out-of-the-ordinary events, those which harbor some excitement and conflict. Photos are more idealized, and would not have served to preserve this incident in her past. How does one communicate running out of spaghetti in a snapshot?

Each form of family lore can convey only one portion of the family's past. It skews reality in a particular way. For instance, on looking through the Williamson family photographs, we might figure that they lived in a snowy northern climate. The truth is that all of the family's pictures were taken on those rare occasions when it snowed on their tobacco farm in sunny South Carolina. That is when they were inspired to take out their camera.

We have met a number of women who, like Ethel Mohamed of Belzoni, Mississippi, have begun to stitch their family history into cloth. They discover that their thread moving through cloth cannot convey scenes with the detail of a photograph or the movement of a family story. Their work becomes symbolic: family background is symbolized by a coat of arms, occupations by a shovel or a pushcart. In Mrs. Mohamed's work, the symbolism becomes quite elaborate, with the happiness she found in family life represented by her children pouring out of a treasure chest. Stitched into cloth, a family's past seems far more impressionistic and dreamlike than in their photographs and stories.

Events like the Civil War live on outside the history books in the traditions and remembrances of countless individual families. Yet each form of folklore conveys a different perspective. In one southern family, for instance, the photographs of grey-clad soldiers serve to unravel mysteries of family resemblance, while a single surviving story focuses not on a soldier but on an ironic incident that befell a well-intentioned great-aunt. Apparently, this ancestor felt sympathetic towards the Union soldiers starving in a nearby prison camp. She brought them greens and a dish called clabber, a kind of sour milk. Soon afterwards the soldiers began to die in great numbers. Some claimed they starved to death, but in the family the legend persists that their great-aunt's clabber

JOAN BERNICK

killed them, and that, inadvertently, she killed more Union soldiers than her husband and the rest of the family together.

Diaries and letters from the Civil War often record the everyday, discuss such issues as the quality of the army's food, the weather, an amusing incident; the tales in oral tradition pay little attention to dates, places, or ordinary events and center on character, particularly on heroes and cowards; a family's memorabilia, swords, uniforms, and medals suggest only the heroics; an ancestor who was court-martialed may be a fine subject for a family story, but his dishonorable discharge papers are unlikely to be hung on the wall.

Folklore represents one of the important ways we give life meaning beyond the immediate present. If we were simply to list all the events of a person's life in chronological order, it would look as much like a shopping list as a lifetime. Using the forms of folklore, we order our lives into eras, and organize and dramatize incidents within them. We become able to both understand and communicate our experiences through our photo albums, our stories and celebrations, the objects we have collected.

One of the most telling uses of the past came in a set of stories made up by a father for his young son. Each night before going to bed, Saul wanted to hear a story. After trying a number of formulas, the father discovered that his son's greatest preference was for a recounting of his own day. So the father began each evening: "Once there was a little boy named Saul, and he woke up in the morning and had a bowl of Cheerios. . . ." Then he told of this young child's activities throughout the day.[2]

For this boy, the goings-on of his last twelve hours became wonderfully pleasing when recast in story form. Certainly the events were not the source of the appeal; the magic was in the telling, in the transformation of a daily history into story, of life into art.

Many of the episodes in a family's past are exciting and memorable; still, much of their magic derives from the forms in which the past is expressed — stories, photographs, celebrations. They hold secrets — about the past, of course, but also about the way we choose to think of ourselves, about the dreams we project backwards on our ancestors concerning what we would like them to have been, and what we need from them now.

1903.

JOAN BERNICK

Family Stories

A man is like a phonograph with half a dozen records," George Bernard Shaw once said, "You soon get tired of them all; yet you have to sit at a table while he reels them off to every new visitor." We like to think of family tales as those narratives which we don't mind hearing over and over again. For this book, however, we have considered a family story any incident retold by one family member about another over a period of years.[1]

A family generally believes its stories to be true, at least in part, for they are a rendering of history in which it has a definite stake. One person suggested that as we grow older our yarns are more likely to be accepted as fact:

That's one of the privileges of age. You get that old and you get to have all your stories be true. You could have been a liar all your life, but when you get old enough, all your stories become true. My grandfather lived by that privilege as he got older.[2]

Family stories are usually based on real incidents which become embellished over the years. They are relevant to American history not only because they convey some factual information, but because they often capture the ethos of an era.[3] A family story may epitomize a certain time period even if the details are false. They also tell us much about the storytellers and how certain episodes in our national history bear upon their lives today.

By combining fact and fiction expressively a family can shape its own history. Consider these contrasting anecdotes about the Civil War:

I have a great-great-grandfather who did not fight in the Civil War. He lived in Boston, and he looked just the way someone who fought in the Civil War would have looked, but his mother had bought him out. For three hundred dollars she got somebody to take his place. My mother used to tell me that when she was a little girl and they had the Memorial Day parade, in Boston, when all the old veterans who were alive were honored, my great-great-grandfather who had a little goatee and who looked like Colonel Sanders, but skinnier, used to have to hide in the house. And they would close the shutters and lock the door to hide their shame because he had not fought in the Civil War.[4]

A gentleman in Portland, Oregon, told quite the opposite story. His great-great-grandfather had not only fought in the Civil War, but had apparently been wounded so that he was remembered as having walked with a limp for most of his adult life. In fact, he started a long tradition of military heroism in the family. His grandson had fought in World War I; his great-grandson, in World War II; and his great-great-grandson, whom we interviewed, in Vietnam. All had been decorated soldiers.

Recently, this young man became inspired to do some research into the history of his family only to discover that his great-great-grandfather had been bought out by his mother for three hundred dollars—just like the great-great-grandfather in the earlier tale! Rather than face closing the shutters on Memorial Day, he simply relocated out west, walked with a limp, and passed down heroic stories.

The first story contains useful information for historians about the process of buying exemptions for military service, and the pressures on those who had done this once the war was over. The second, though patently false, is historically important because of the way it shaped subsequent events; the military history of the family is incomprehensible without knowledge of this story—regardless of its inaccuracy!

ANN HAWKINS

Until recently, folklore collectors were interested more in traditional folktales than in family stories. They gathered the legends and jokes which appeared in only slightly altered forms in many different locales, and were not grounded in the actual experiences of the tellers and their families. They set down the classic American tall tales about the giant killer mosquitoes of Texas, for instance, and the legends about our heroes such as Jesse James and Davy Crockett. These were often told in families, but did not concern the family's past.

Occasionally, traditional tales of the sort gathered by these well-known American collectors such as Vance Randolph and Frank C. Brown are told about members of one's own family. Jokes, floating legends, and traditional folktales sometimes appear as family stories. A grandfather, for instance, may tell a joke about a numbskull; when his grandchildren retell it, he may well become the numbskull. A traditional joke is thus transformed into a family story.

When we first collected this next story we thought it had no currency outside of one particular family:

My great-grandfather lived in Scotland, and he had a habit of going into a little pub or tavern in the evening and getting a little messed up and then he'd come home. One night he got to talking to this barmaid and she went with him over to the field and they had a little sport and then he passed out. She wanted to tell him how much she had enjoyed it and she couldn't talk to him so she took a blue ribbon from around her hair and tied it on his tool and left his kilt rolled up. My great-grandmother waited for several hours and he didn't come home. So she started toward the tavern in town and found him lying on the hillside with his kilt rolled up and the blue ribbon on his tool. And she said, "I'll not be knowing where you've been or what you've been doing, but I'm proud to see that you won the first prize."[5]

The folklorist who transcribed this tape for us was a young lady unfamiliar with the risqué meaning of "tool", and she transcribed it as "toe". Even with this alteration, she felt the story was funny. Sometime later she retold it at a dinner party at her parents' home in a different part of the country where an elegantly dressed woman told her, "Oh, you don't have to say the word 'toe.' We all know what you mean. We've heard that story before." This was an education for our interviewer, but reminded us, too, that traditional folktales can be told as family stories.

Despite such exceptions, family stories are usually particular to individual families. Hearing many different narratives about courtships or great fortunes lost in the family, members may mold their stories and memories to fit a traditional pattern. But for the most part tales are created anew in every family, and only occasionally travel between them.

America's diversity shapes its folklore: stories told in New England have their own distinct style and subject matter, as do the tales of Texans or Jewish-Americans. Whereas third-generation Americans often tell of perilous escapes from the old country, westerners recall their ancestors' journeys across the Oregon trail. Appalachian families often tell stories of long-standing feuds, black Americans of heroic action taken against oppression, and urban dwellers of poverty-stricken lives in ghettoes and tenements. There may be individual topics which recur in particular ethnic groups and regions; yet the general patterns and themes—around which we've organized our stories here—are national. As citizens of this country we share many similar experiences—immigration, the Great Depression, Vietnam. We also share a common language, and, along with it, similar ways of telling a story, certain ideas about what sorts of episodes are humorous or dramatic.

Grace McDonald lost her memory like a person losing a set of keys. She was an old lady, a grandmother, and after one of her bouts with sickness, she couldn't recognize her children or remember the narrative flow of her past. Through all her trials, however, she remembered one incident, one that seems distinctly forgettable. Twenty years before she had given her grandson some cookies. He didn't want to eat them at the time, so he hid them in the attic. Several days later she discovered his stash and chided him. When she took sick and her memory faded, that incident, that family story was the part of the past she held on to. Using such stories as

SOPHIE PARKMAN

clues to help her identify each of her children and grandchildren, her memory slowly returned.

Now she remembers each of them with a single story. Neal is the one who would not pull the weeds when she asked him to. Jay left the cookies in the attic. "Every time she sees me she'll say that," Jay said. "You can tell all she has to do is remember one thing like that and then she gets a whole flood of things. But you know that's how she remembers you. . . . It's easier to remember if she has these things as keys.

"She used to remember everything about you," he went on. "She used to be real sharp, and she used to really take care of us and she used to be a fantastic cook and a fantastic baker, bringing up a family of seven people. Now it's almost like she only has room in her head for one thing."[6]

If an aging woman only has room in her head for one thing, why would it be a family story? Grace McDonald's thought process, even in old age, delineates our own. Family stories are part of the way we remember. They enable us to simplify the complexities of a family member's personality into an easily remembered, easily communicated narrative.

Incidents which describe a character, which pinpoint personality are remembered in family tradition; we call this the *character principle* in American family stories. One man told

SUSANNE BENDA

us that his grandfather once asked his dad to help out a man whose horse was having trouble pulling a cart up a hill. His dad helped the man, and then lived by the principle of helping others. For the grandson the incident is "the sum total of things, it shows the kind of life he tried to perpetuate through me and my brother. . . . This is just one story," he told us, "it's just one incident, it's the sum total of things."[7]

Occasionally, family stories can pinpoint the subtleties of a personality with astonishing accuracy. We asked Grace McDonald's grandson and his wife if they thought her incidents or "keys" were well chosen.

"Neal is not lazy," Jay's wife said, referring to the story in which Neal put off pulling the garden weeds. Then she thought about it for a moment: "but he is sometimes."

And Jay agreed: "He is, Neal's extremely lazy. I'm sort of sneaky," he added, suggesting that the incident about hiding the cookies harbored a certain truth.

As we read these family stories and contemplate our own, we become aware of a certain irony. If the stories seem to pinpoint character, they simultaneously stereotype it.[8] Simplifying a personality into a single incident automatically reduces it to a character type as well; we must beware of what is lost as well as captured in these incidents. For example, in our collection of stories about memorable relatives, the most common protagonists are mischief makers, heroes, villains, and innocents. All of these celebrated family members must have been complex individuals in their own right. Their lives were probably filled with mundane events and contradictory acts; our innocents may even have been vicious on occasion. But their personalities linger in our memories and family stories in a simplified though satisfying way.

Along with characters, families hold on to episodes which mark the upheavals and sharp changes in their history. Families, like individuals, have a life cycle marked by stages of transition which are often celebrated in story. These include courtships, great fortunes lost in the family, migrations, catastrophes like fires and earthquakes, and family feuds. We call the tendency to retain incidents surrounding radical changes in our history the *transition principle* in family stories.

Sometimes, significant turning points are subtle and hardly seem dramatic at the time. One folklore student, for instance, related a tale about her ancestor Elizabeth and a confrontation she had with her Grandmother Astel on their farm in Wisconsin:

Grandma Astel lived with the family and ruled it with an iron will and a north country accent. Lizzie was something of a tomboy and her grandmother didn't approve of this. As one of her chores, Lizzie was supposed to collect the hens' eggs every morning. One day her grandmother came around to the henhouse and realized that the eggs hadn't been collected. She went looking for Lizzie and found her up in a tree. Grandma Astel extended her arm to the sky and then pointed to Elizabeth and said, "May ye never have a hen!"[9]

Surely this story seems far too insignificant to be passed down across three generations, yet it persisted. As the student explained, the incident marked a turning point in her family's history. Elizabeth left farming and lived in cities all her life; she never did have a hen. "The fact that she left farming was . . . important, because if one were to trace my family back through my matrilineal descent line, Lizzie was probably the first woman to leave farming in perhaps a thousand years." Thus, even this simple exchange between a grandmother and a granddaughter about the morning chores becomes a resonant tale in the context of a family's evolution.

Families, then, are selfish in what they choose to remember and pass on. They are willing to remember incidents which come to epitomize the character of a particular family member; and they are willing to remember an occurrence which marks a turning point in their own life or their family history. In this way, each narrative becomes not a rehash of an event, but a distillation of experience. A single episode comes to represent the entirety of a relative's personality; a whole family history is symbolized by a few dramatic turning points. The stories stand for much larger quantities of experience, and families have at their disposal a heightened form of communication which holds the family together and acts, in one person's words, "as a kind of glue."[10]

In talking about his own family, Donald Collins touches on an important aspect of storytelling—the setting.

*Usually we all get together on Thanksgiving and Christmas.
Relatives come in from Chicago, Florida — we've got some that
come in from New Mexico. And you should see that house on
the holidays. We'll have forty or fifty people come in there. All
the women cook and all the men sit out on the porch and booze,
you know. And that's when you really hear the stories. When
you get them all together like that, you sit back and you hear
them. Some of them I've heard so many times, it's just as if I
was there.*[11]

Meals are common settings for storytelling. They seem to
be the time when family members are most at home with
each other both physically and psychologically; perhaps it is
not a coincidence that we satisfy our emotions along with
our appetites. A quintessential family ritual, dinner involves
the "ceremonial use of leisure,"[12] often with a ceremony of
carving a main course, tossing the salad, and serving. It is
often set apart from other meals by the use of more formal silverware and dishes, and often by prayer. As this example
suggests, storytelling at the table is often, like the rest of the
eating ritual, quite patterned and ceremonial:

*My family is Sicilian and we also have a tradition of sitting
around a table telling stories. But you can't tell stories except*

at certain parts of the meal. . . . We have a saying, "when you eat you don't talk." And any of us who talked during the first or second course of the meal were always chastised by grandma and grandpa. . . . After those courses were over, things came out like the artichoke which was not considered a course exactly, but it was kind of something that followed the real meal. Or the chestnuts, or what in Italian families we call the "frutte, dolce, caffè"—the fruit, the sweets, and coffee.

And that part of the dinner would begin with my grandfather eating a chestnut or eating an artichoke, and all of a sudden he would begin to laugh to himself. And inevitably, somebody would say, "Grandpa, why are you laughing?"

And that would begin the storytelling time. And he said, "I'm just remembering the time when. . . ." And that's how one began to tell stories at dinner time. And it happened in the same way almost every night.[13]

Storytelling in American families takes place at family reunions, at holidays, across the table at the evening meal. The very predictability of these occasions helps render them relaxing and enjoyable. Yet the subjects for stories contrast sharply with these recurring activities. Whereas dinners, reunions, and holiday celebrations tend to be peaceful and pleasurable occasions, stories told at those times are often about the unpredictable. They signal disruption or disaster.

Consider this example. During the Depression a grandmother scraped together a meal which consisted of vegetable soup and a salami. Uncle Bill, then a small boy, was alternately throwing a dirty ball against the wall and tossing it to his dog, King. On a misthrow the ball splashed into the vegetable soup. The grandmother was so enraged that she threw the hunk of salami at the young boy. King, mistaking the salami for the ball, leaped up, caught it in his teeth, and ran outside to savor it. The Depression meal was ruined.[14]

The episode is interesting because it marks such a sharp break in the storytelling routine. Ironically, the tale recounts an incident which may have ended a tale-telling session in the past; if any stories were to be told around the table that night they certainly wouldn't be after the dog ran off with the dinner. It is the same with countless similar tales which refer not to the day-to-day routine but to dramatic occasions which disrupt it—ruined meals, burnt turkeys, not the usual fare.

Transformed into story form, the incident of the dog and the salami was occasionally repeated as part of the evening's activities in the Martin family. It became part of the recurring dinner and after-dinner rituals, part of the very routine it disrupted. Through storytelling, the faux pas, the cooking disasters, the Depression traumas, and all the other misfortunes celebrated in family stories become institutionalized; they become part and parcel of holiday gatherings, of long rides in the car or of the evening meal. In this way family stories serve as a way of making the unexpected, the unforeseen, and the disastrous part of the smooth and routine functioning of the family.

We seem to acknowledge this function of storytelling when, after a harrowing or traumatic experience the remark is heard, "at least it will make a good story," or "we'll look back on this and laugh." Our family stories make it possible to laugh over incidents which were anything but funny at the time, and the laughter signals that the trauma has been incorporated into the daily round of family life. At its worst, a bout with poverty in the Depression, or outlaws in the west, or an earthquake or flood might have torn the family asunder. But transformed into stories these incidents become part of the smooth, day-to-day flow of family activities.

Storytelling is part of a number of family rituals and in many ways partakes of their functions. It stimulates healthy family interaction, it provides a technique for influencing and managing family members, it serves as a "family engineered canal" through which culture flows from one generation to the next.[15] Yet storytelling serves one function apart from other traditions.

In the family, as in every community, members gather on certain occasions to share in their leisure. The emotional investment often transforms these recurring activities into a set of binding traditions. Storytelling is a particularly meaningful part of these because it serves to make the critical, the disturbing, the tragic breaks in the cycle of rituals part of the smooth, ongoing life of the family.

HEROES

Tales of heroic action are plentiful in family stories. Their virtuous protagonists triumph over malicious opponents, with wit and wisdom or a decisive physical stroke. These stories are especially common among minorities such as blacks and Mexican-Americans. Many are also told about women who exhibit great courage defending their families, their plots mirroring the lines from a Woody Guthrie song about a cowgirl in the wild west:

When the rustlers broke on us
In the dead hour of night
She rose from her warm bed
A battle to fight.

She rose from her warm bed
With a gun in each hand
Said come all of you cowboys
And fight for your land.[1]

Katherine Morgan in her essay, "Caddy Buffers: Legends of a Middle Class Black Family in Philadelphia" writes about the stories surrounding her great-grandmother Caddy in slavery and in the years following the Civil War. She suggests that they were a "buffer," an antidote against the oppression of white society. One story tells how Caddy would run away from her masters, then get caught and whipped with a cat-o-nine-tails. "Do you think she would cry?" the story goes. "Not Caddy. It would take more than a cat-o-nine-tails to make Caddy cry."[2]

This next story about Caddy, and the examples from our own collection which follow, suggest our fascination with women and other oppressed groups who will not yield to the pressures and conventions of society:

Caddy got married to a Mr. Gordon. Getting married in those days wasn't like getting married today. Caddy never bothered to go to a preacher or anything. It was enough for two people to want to be married. Anyway, Caddy wanted a last name for her children and Mr. Gordon was willing to give them his. It's important for children to have an honest last name. Now Mr. Gordon was not a very good man, but he did have an honest last name and he let Caddy have it for the children. So Caddy

*put up with his laziness and didn't say too much. Finally
though, he left Caddy and got himself another wife. . . . Caddy
worked hard and saved her money. One day she heard that Mr.
Gordon had gotten himself in some kind of trouble and was
going to be sent to jail. Caddy went to the bank. She marched
herself right up to the courthouse, marched right up the middle
aisle. Stood before that judge. She reached down under her
skirt and put the money on the table. She said, "Judge, I don't
want no man with my children's name to go to jail so I'm here
to bail him out." Now everybody respected Caddy, even the
judge, so he let Mr. Gordon go. Caddy was that kind of a
woman. Respectable.*[3]

MIDGE HEIMER

: THE PAISLEY SHAWL :

*My grandmother had an uncle who was the captain of a schoo-
ner out of Norfolk and she would go there to visit him. One
time she had been down there for an extended stay and she had
cast very envious eyes at a paisley shawl which was in one of
the stores in Norfolk. Unfortunately, it was far too expensive
for her to buy. So she talked about it and mooned over it and finally, when my uncle took her aboard ship, he said to her,
"Sarah, you see that yardarm?" And she said, "Yes, Uncle
Joe." "If you climb the main mast and touch the yardarm," he
said, "I'll buy you the shawl." He thought for sure that she
would never think of doing such a thing. After all, she would
have to climb up in her dress which in those days had long
trains on them. But she just looped her dress up as best she
could, climbed the yardarm, and got her paisley shawl!*

GERARD E. SHELTON
Vienna, Virginia

: IF IT WEREN'T FOR THAT
DAMN LITTLE GIRL :

*My grandmother grew up in Shepherdstown, West Virginia,
where she lived with her grandfather. He was the head teller of
the bank in Shepherdstown and they lived in a brick house
right next to the bank. One night — this was in 1885 probably —
she heard a noise and looked out the window. She could see*

some men trying to break into the bank. She woke up her grandfather—which was a gutsy thing to do, I guess, considering that he was like a bear. He took his horse pistol out of his bedside table, pointed it out the window, and fired at the bandits and they ran away. He didn't hit any of them. The bank, in gratitude, gave my grandmother a Smith and Wesson .32 pearl handled special.

She used to take it out into the country in the fall—this is how she tells it—and she'd stand on a bridge. As the leaves blew off the trees she'd go bang! bang! bang! She claimed to be a good shot.

After she got the gun she was again woken up by a noise in the bank next door. This time she skipped her grandfather, the middleman, and just leaned out the window herself. Like roota-toot-toot! It's the bandits!

This lot, I think, got caught at the ferry trying to cross the Shenandoah River. And according to her story, at the trial—when they were tried and sentenced to twenty-five years in jail or whatever—they said, "If it hadn't been for that damn little girl, we would have gotten away clean."

BENJAMIN THOMAS
Exeter, New Hampshire

RUTH COYNE

: THE TRIALS OF AUNT LUCY :

My grandfather was a lawyer, and all it meant to be a lawyer in those days was to pass a test, not to have an education per se. And so he was teaching both his sons to be lawyers, and my aunt Lucy pestered him to teach her. And he couldn't deny her anything, so he did. And everybody was in an uproar over that.

When a family feud broke out Lucy's mother insisted that she not fight, even though she had logged with the boys, and hunted with the boys, and been treated like a son. She apparently wore overalls long after the time it was cute. And Aunt Lucy stood it until the night that Ballard got shot. When that happened and she saw her mother holding her father and knew her father was badly wounded, she grabbed a gun and ran out in her nightgown into the middle of the front yard and just shot at everything and just cursed and sweared and carried on. And the Bakers stopped shooting for a moment, because they thought *this was a good time to make fun of her. And as my aunt Neva says, "They called her everything vile and shameful on the face of this earth." But she still stood there and shot at them and wounded two men. Finally they started firing back, and my uncle Andy got the wherewithall to go out there and drag her back into the house so she could at least shoot from beyond the door. And from that point on she fought with them. She would go out in men's clothing.*

When she hit about, I guess, twenty, she wanted to set up a law office, so her father helped her set up a law office, but unfortunately no one would come to a woman lawyer. So her father gave her money to buy a farm in southern Indiana. She wanted to leave the area, because she felt so bitter about all these things. And she left with a woman friend of hers and farmed there the rest of her life until she died chasing a cow around a cow lot. Died of a heart attack.

MARY GOODMAN

BEVERLY LEE HOWARD, AGE 24
Washington, D.C.

: Escape from Ignorance :

My father, Junius Taylor, born a slave, escaped ignorance. He escaped not by the underground railroad, but by the big house. My paternal grandmother, a maid of the slave mistress, took her infant son Junius to "the big house" each day—the slavemaster's home was called "the big house." To secure the baby, grandmother placed the child under the kitchen table and used his long shirttail to tie him to the leg of the table. In that manner, she always knew where he was. So Junius grew up at the big house, playing with the master's boys his age and older. When the tutor came and gave the boys lessons, the boys always taught Junius reading, writing, arithmetic, and everything else they learned. That went on quietly for years.

Then one day, rushing through the house, the slavemaster asked his boys playing on the floor, "What time is it?" His boys ignored the question.

Junius looked up at the clock and answered, "It is 10:30, Sir." Running back into the room, the slavemaster demanded, "Junius, didn't you answer that question?"

"Yes, Sir."

TOM THOMPSON

"*If you can tell time, you can read!*" *Grabbing and opening the Bible, he shoved it into Junius' small hands and shouted, "Read!" His face was blood red.*

Junius noted that the Bible was open to John 1:5, so he read, "And the light shineth in darkness, and the darkness comprehended it not."

The slavemaster snatched the Bible, and ran to the door calling his wife, "Vinnie, Vinnie, come quickly—I've got a nigger that can read!"

This violation of the anti-reading law had to remain a deep family secret, but one can no more unteach the ability to read than one can overcome and return yesterday's windstorm.

MANIE T. GEER, AGE 78

Durham, North Carolina

: RISING FROM THE RUBBLE :

Uncle Walter who lived down in Waldorf, Germany, was the descendant of Huguenots that had run away from France during the persecution of the Protestants in the 1600s. During the war he wanted to build himself a house, but all the materials for the house, of course, were defense important. You couldn't build a house for yourself. And to a German middle-class guy your house is the most important thing in the world; building your house and getting in it, getting out of apartments, is the crucial thing. And nothing—the world was turning upside down—nothing would deter him from this. . . .

He built a house and he hid it under a junk pile. He bought a lot, and loaned it out for people to throw junk on it. And then he would go there at night and build, layer by layer of brick, and cover it up with junk. When the end of the war came, there was a big pile of junk, but there was a house practically built. All it needed was a roof. In 1946, when the war was over, he raised the roof like a madman. And he was jubilant. He said, "I beat the Nazis, goddamn it, I beat them. I got my house." But the American army took it from him and quartered officers in it for two years, so it was a little delayed in his occupancy of it.

This story always appealed to me because it's an average person's story of what happened during the war. I like it because it's an example of how indomitable certain kinds of selfishnesses are even in the midst of great patriotic struggles. This guy refused to give up middle-class ideals.

CARLTON FLETCHER, AGE 26
Washington, D.C.

: Beating the Wrap :

There's another one of these narrow escape stories that my father always tells. My sisters and I would always make him tell these stories, and now that I am an adult I know that it was painful for him to have to relive this by telling these stories, but we would insist and insist on his telling us. Here's one. Jews weren't allowed to carry over a certain amount of cash on the streets in Prague. This was before the war. And my father was out on the street one day with what he knew was more than the amount of cash in his pocket that he was supposed to have. And he was stopped and picked up. The cops took him into the police station, and he was supposed to empty out his pockets. So he's desperate, but he got this brain wave. He took his handkerchief which he had in his pocket and he wrapped it around the money and pulled it out and blew his nose, and the money was in the handkerchief. Then cleared his pockets out, and it was okay. They didn't look in his hand, but the money was in his handkerchief. He just stuck it back in his pocket and walked out free. So he was very quick on his feet.

MARIANNE ROSS, AGE 41
Bethesda, Maryland

: Cold Feet :

As a child growing up, I didn't know much about my paternal grandfather. He had died before I was born. The only thing I knew was that he had been a bartender, which didn't exactly give me much reason to think very highly of him. But the one story that was told about him meant more to me than I think anything else could have. One day he was working at the bar and a tramp came in without any shoes. My grandfather served him, and the tramp said he had far to go still, and it was a cold day. So my grandfather said, "Would you like to have my shoes?" And the tramp said, "Yes." He took off his shoes, gave

HOLLY CUTTING BAKER

them to the tramp. And in return the tramp said, "I'll draw your picture for you." So he did a beautiful charcoal drawing of my grandfather, nearly life size. We still have it in the family.

Shortly thereafter my grandfather developed what they then called consumption, which it is felt was really pneumonia, and died as a result. I have reason to think that perhaps it was from giving his shoes away, and tending bar for the rest of the day and part of the night in his stocking feet. But it really endeared my grandfather to me because I felt if he was nothing more than a bartender, at least he was very loving and very kind and very giving. And that to me is important.

SONDRA GORDON BLAZER, AGE 39
Franklin, Ohio

: Jesse James Robs a Stagecoach :

This is a story that my grandmother and my great-aunt Patty used to tell us about one of our great-great-uncles, Alexander Gregg. Aunt Patty had this portrait of him dressed in his bishop's robes in her dining room. He was the first Episcopal bishop of Texas, and of course everybody in the family thought he was just a wonderful man. And they told a story about how, when he was out in Texas, he was riding in a stagecoach and the stagecoach was held up by Jesse James and his gang and they stole Alexander Gregg's gold watch. Later Jesse James realized who he had stole the watch from, and realized what a wonderful man Alexander Gregg was. And so he returned the watch, with apologies.

AMANDA DARGAN, AGE 31
Darlington, South Carolina

: In the Nick of Time :

I had no father, so my grandfather was like a father figure in our home. He lived with us from the time I was age ten until he died when I was not quite twenty-two. His name was Edmund L. Faringhy, and his grandfather's name was John Forsythe, and he had fought in the Civil War. John Forsythe was half Indian, and because he was half Indian when he got out of the

Civil War he didn't have the rights and privileges that the white man had. The only work that he could get was in a cavalry post. During that time they were fighting the Indians. He was kind of an Indian scout, from what I understand from grandfather.

The Indians had captured their captain. So, he took and put flour sacks on the feet of the horse, and he rode into the Indian encampment just as they were getting ready to kill the captain. They had him tied and were going to burn him at the stake. As my grandfather tells me, he rode in and got him off the stake, and rode out while they were having a war party. For doing that he was given the Congressional Medal of Honor. My grandfather still has the pistol he used.

LOU CAMPBELL
Washington, D.C.

ROGUES

Outlaws and horse thieves shoot their way through countless family stories; Americans like to relate to their grandparents, their great-grandparents, and ancestors as notorious characters. John Bishop got to the heart of the matter when he said:

My grandfather mentioned that his ancestors had been, perhaps for the most part honest—traveling peddlers and merchants, but perhaps with a little bit of piracy—they were in Latvia and Lithuania on the Baltic Sea. I'd like to think they were pirates, but when I think about it seriously, they were probably all hard-working people, to be perfectly honest.[1]

The baddest man we encountered in all of our interviews was an ancestor of a Portland, Oregon, family. This rogue migrated west, blotting out his past so well that the genealogical efforts of his descendants proved fruitless. He made one trip back east, chasing after the wife who abandoned him for his cruelty; he tracked her down and shot her in a cheap hotel. In an effort to put a stop to his wanton violence, or at least to give it some direction, he was made sheriff of a frontier town. The brutality continued, only now on the side of the law. Before he died he had gone mad, and he insisted that the family place his deathbed out in the middle of the town square. Then he demanded that his holster and two pistols be brought to him. Sitting in bed, the dying man began shooting leaves off the big tree that shaded the town square. As each leaf split from the tree he called out the name of a man he had killed.[2] This violent, cruel man is removed from the teller by a number of generations—rarely do we find such non-heroic behavior attributed to close relatives.

The Prohibition laws, however, proved a great boon for family storytellers. In 1933 when the law was repealed families could suddenly glorify the illegal act of bootlegging because the sale and purchase of liquor was now perfectly legal. They now had an ideal "notorious deed" by which to memorialize their fathers or grandfathers. As Prohibition began to seem pointless in hindsight, bootlegging qualified an individual as an outlaw when he had never really done anything wrong.

Women are rarely depicted as true outlaws in family stories, but bootlegging was an activity considered honest enough for them. Vera Pratt, for instance, is remembered in her family for smuggling bottles on the Pullman car from Montreal to New York:

She would line the bottles all up and down her body and the customs officers would come around and ask her if she had anything to declare. Since she'd be in bed, nude, they wouldn't want to check her sheets or anything like that, so she'd say, "of course not," and she'd hand them her passport.[3]

As William Humphreys said in his novel, *The Ordways*, the ancestors of a family go "beyond good and evil."[4] Families have a way of accepting their renegades; the black sheep remain part of the flock. As Susan Bobrow put it, "The history of my family is like the history of the country: good people, and bad people, and famous people, and people nobody ever heard of . . ."[5] We pass no judgment on the rogues who follow, except to note that their shadiness, their cowardice, their drunkenness were sufficient to earn them a place in tradition.

PATRICIA BEACH

: LET ME TELL YOU ABOUT MY UNCLE VELVL :

My mother is famous in our family—in fact all of her sisters are—for telling bobe-mayse. *A* bobe-mayse *is a Yiddish expression for grandmother's tale, so they're all, you know, a little hairy. My favorite one has always been one about her Uncle Velvl.*

Uncle Velvl was a horse thief. After he came to this country from the old country, which was presumably Russia, he continued to practice his trade down in the hills of Virginia. One day, they caught him at it. And you know what they used to do with horse thieves. So they found a nice tall tree, and they did it to Uncle Velvl.

Some time later, a town grew on this site, and there was a lot of dissension over what they should call it. Then someone remembered that a long time ago a horse thief had been tied to a tree there, and they decided to name the town after the occasion of my uncle's hanging. They named the town Lynchburg, Virginia.

Now it just so happens, apparently, that there really was a great-great-uncle in the old country—who never got to this country—whose name was Velvl and who apparently really was a horse thief. But how this story ever grew up about Lynchburg, I don't know. But the assumption is that Burg, being a Jewish name, would fit the story.

ELINOR ABRAMSON
Washington, D.C.

: IT HAPPENED QUICKLY :

We're related to General Porterfield, who was the first southern general to be court-martialed. He lost a big Civil War battle at the beginning of the war. He had been in some of the battles in Texas, and had gone to the military academy. He was one of the few people with military experience at the beginning of the war, and was quickly made general, and quickly lost a big battle, and was quickly court-martialed.

ANNE SAUNDERS GREENFIELD
Alexandria, Virginia

: ELEVEN TO ONE :

*I should probably tell you about my great-great-grandfather being killed by the Indians. There were about eleven Texas Rangers—he was one of the rangers—and one Indian. The Indian got about six or seven of them before they finally got him. So that's one of the not-so-brave things in the family.**

: MY NOTORIOUS RELATIVE :

My great-grandfather was Italian. His wife came over here with his daughter and they lived in the United States for awhile and while they were here, he died carousing over in Italy. He died by jumping out of his mistress's balcony window and missing his horse. That was my notorious relative.

CATHY TIEF, AGE 18
Camp LeJeune, North Carolina

*At the request of several contributors, we have reprinted this story and all other unattributed stories anonymously.

: THE RAID :

Grandmother had lotto games. All the old ladies from the neighborhood and the parish had lotto games. They took turns having the games in their houses. For prizes, they'd have hand-tatted pillowcases or handkerchiefs, and their home canning, their jellies and their jams and things. And once in a while, a great prize would be a quilt or a jackpot of twenty-five dollars or something. We kids would be allowed to play a little bit but mostly we went around and collected the pot money.

But in those years, St. Louis cracked down on what they called vice. There was a ban on all kinds of gambling, supposedly including gambling in your own home. The ladies at the lotto club were raided by the police! There wasn't a lady under seventy-five there, but they were all herded into the paddy wagon and down to the police station! That was the talk of the town. They thought it was the greatest fun. Of course, they resumed their games the very next week.

SHARON BABER, AGE 42
Arlington, Virginia

: LET US PRAY :

The church meeting was the only place people had to go, and so that's where your courting and your meeting of all sorts went on. My aunt Neva tells me about walking seven miles to Bernan Springs School and walking seven miles back and then eating supper and walking seven miles to the Bernan Springs Church of God. The whole big gang of them would go, and she said they could care less what was said in church. And [she] said there wasn't really any place else for the drunkards to go either, because that's the only place where they'd have a crowd and any audience for their antics.

One evening this boy, Jake — I think his name was — came in and sat down next to my aunt Neva and aunt Lucy, and he was drunk and carrying on. And they were ashamed, so they told him to go outside. So he up and left. Well, he got into the vestibule of the church, and he ran into Bobby. Bobby was dating Jake's sister, Lena. Jake didn't think that Bobby was worthy of Lena. And pretty soon Jake had a knife in Bobby's stomach. And the next thing you knew there was shooting all in the ves-

MARY GOODWIN

tibule of the church; all these drunks that had been sitting out in front of the church and all these boys started fighting.

So the preacher raised the window in the back of the church, and everybody started crawling out through the back. And they were in a single file, and everybody was pressing, and as Aunt Neva says, "There was more screaming going on than a midwife would hear in a lifetime." And she got up to about where the altar was, and Sister Ann Hall, Sister Ann Hall Jones, that's her name, was on her knees there praying, paying no more mind to anybody coming and going. And she looked up when she saw Neva, and she said, "Neva, why do you worry? We're in the Lord's house. Whatever could happen to us here? Why, you may well know that I for one am not surprised. This is just a sign of things to come. Now get down here on your knees and pray with me for these poor souls that are marked to die." Neva said, "Thank you kindly, Sister Hall. I do believe I'll go along here for the ride." And so they crawled out the window and went to a couple of houses nearby.

Bobby was taken up to the local doctor, named Daddy Doc, who said it was only due to his belt buckle that he was alive. The knife had caught him in the belt buckle. So then they went back home, and the next evening they were all back in church at meeting time. I mean, you just accepted the violence along with everything else.

BEVERLY LEE HOWARD, AGE 24
Washington, D.C.

: WE ALL KNOW THE TRUTH :

This is something my father told me about once. I can't remember if it's my great-grandfather or great-great-grand-father. He'd been a Civil War veteran and after the war he went back to Massachusetts where he was, I think, a minor official of the town. One day they had a large fire at the town hall and it burned down. In the course of it burning down, my great-great-grandfather apparently rushed back in and came out with several things in a bag. Later on they declared him a hero for running into the burning building and supposedly looking to save somebody or something like that. But the story is passed down in the family that he remembered at the last

*minute to get a bottle of whiskey in his desk drawer. He ran
back in to get it, and he was proclaimed a hero. But we all
know the truth.*

DENISE COOK, AGE 24
Washington, D.C.

: THE SAGA OF ABRAHAM CLARK :

*This is a story that I seem to have gotten from my grandfather,
Frank Kapple, before I was six years old, because he died
shortly after that. I asked him about my middle name, which is
Clark. He told me I was named for Abraham Clark, who was
one of the signers of the Declaration of Independence. And then
grandfather, without any comment, told me this story.*

*Each of the thirteen colonies had to have three members
there for the Congress to participate in whatever was going on.
And the Declaration of Independence was one piece of business
that had to have at least three delegates who would be willing
to sign it. Well, the story went that when they went around
counting heads for the signatures, they were missing one person
from New Hampshire. And they were frantic because they had
to have every colony represented. So they went out into the
street, "Anybody from New Hampshire? Anybody from New
Hampshire?" Down the street comes Abraham Clark about
three sheets to the wind. And he says, "I'm from New Hampshire." So they grabbed him, pulled him in, gave him a pen,
and said, "Sign here." So he signed. And if you look at the signatures, you'll see that his is one of the two or three shakiest signatures on the entire document.*

*Recently I did some research to find out about the signers of
the Declaration of Independence. We couldn't find much in our
library, but finally we found out that Abraham Clark was not
even from New Hampshire; he was from Elizabethtown, New
Jersey. His nickname was "Congress Abraham," because he
served several terms.*

*I've always wondered who the toads were who were so tight
that they wouldn't put up any money for Washington's troops at
Morristown and at Valley Forge and then back at Morristown.
As it turns out, the leader of the tightwads was Abraham
Clark. That's true.*

DAVE KAPPLE, AGE 41
Littleton, Colorado

MISCHIEF MAKERS

Each society and each culture," writes psychologist Erik Erikson, "institutionalizes a certain moratorium for the majority of its young people. . . . The moratorium may be a time for horse stealing and vision quests, a time to go out west, or a time for pranks."[1] America is no exception. We expect our young, particularly men, to "raise Cain," to "sow their wild oats." We even institutionalize rambunctious, rowdy behavior in mischief night and fraternity rituals.

Parents love to tell their children about their youthful antics—even while discouraging them from the same behavior. One person, for instance, remembered his father warning him not to play with firecrackers while in the same breath telling about the fun *he* had with firecrackers as a boy. Family storytelling often reinforces the mischief-making traditions of the next generation.

Pranks and practical jokes make especially good family stories and are extremely widespread. After all, the tales in their essence depict characters in conflict, A getting the better of B, B sometimes turning the tables and getting the better of A.[2] All family narratives share in this structure, but none fits as snugly within it as the practical joke.[3] The pranks are usually directed towards figures of authority—parents, teachers, drill sergeants, priests, preachers, rabbis—and have, by their very nature, a build-up, a conflict, and a

EARL HIGGINS

climax which can be transformed into a family story with little effort. Turning over an outhouse, for instance, was not only a tempting practical joke, but made for a good story which is told in numerous American families.

DAN BERGER

: THE OUTHOUSE :

I can't lend any authenticity to this story at all, but it has been told a hundred thousand times in the family. Grandpa Hatch was one of the first attorneys in South Dakota. He went to some kind of Methodist college. People are always talking about how rebellious youth are these days. But apparently, one Halloween they were going around dumping over outhouses and being particularly belligerent, and they dumped over the dean's outhouse. Unfortunately, the dean was sitting in the outhouse at the time. The dean identified them and they were about to be expelled from school and they pleaded and carried on and finally the powers that be decided that if they would buy the dean a new outhouse and put it up and build it with their own hands, then they would be reinstated in school. So they built the outhouse and they decided to have a dedication ceremony on campus. And they made a very large deal out of it and probably half the campus was there. They had a prayer and a little speech and then they decided to sing a hymn. And the hymn that they chose was a good Methodist hymn called "I Need Thee Every Hour" and they were expelled from school!

WILLIAM HATCH
Alexandria, Virginia

: THE BEARD I :

My grandfather and many of his brothers and perhaps some sisters emigrated to this country from the northern part of the Ukraine. When they were going to school in the old country they didn't have public schools. They had religious schools if they had any at all, and they went to a Jewish school somewhere in a town in the northern part of the Ukraine.

This school was run by a rabbi who had a long white beard. This old fellow had gone through many generations of young kids, tutoring them in their studies. So it got to a point where he

PAUL REIMERS

got kind of bored with the stuff. *My grandfather, his youngest brother, and several other kids from the village were sitting around a very large, round heavy oaken table studying from their prayer books or doing whatever they were doing. As the kids would drone on with their prayers [the rabbi] had a habit of resting his chin on his doubled-up fists so that the beard sort of fell onto this table. My great-uncle said that one late afternoon when it was quite dark and the room was lit by candlelight, the kids got an idea. While one was droning on with his prayer book, another kid picked up a candle and allowed the molten wax to drip on this old fellow's beard till there was a good solid bond between beard and table. Then at the appointed time they all banged on the table, made a lot of noise, and the old fellow picked his head up but left part of his beard on the table. Every boy in the village got punished that night.*

SHELDON LIPSON, AGE 42

: THE BEARD II :

My grandfather was the youngest of the three brothers. They were being taught their lessons by a rabbi with a very long beard. And the three boys were really rambunctious. And one day, the rabbi, while he was on a break or something, fell asleep. His beard touched the table. (It hurts to think about it!) The boys dipped tar, and attached his beard to the table. And then they banged the table, and the rabbi jerked up!

The story has got to be at least fifty, sixty years old.

JEFF FRANKEL, AGE 25
Silver Spring, Maryland

: ANYTHING YOUR HEART DESIRES :

When my father was going to college, it was the middle of the Depression. He was very poor and had to work to put himself through college. One of the jobs he had was at the student union which was run by a little Jewish fellow by the name of Goldheimer. Mr. Goldheimer was about five feet two and his arms were about four feet long. He looked like an ape. He walked sort of bowlegged with his arms swinging to and fro.

At that time the student center had a blue plate special, like a twelve-course dinner for sixty-five cents. The advertisement was *"Anything Your Heart Desires."* So one of those hot shot college kids came in and he happened to be from Newark. And he ordered the blue plate special. He went through all the courses and came to dessert. And the waiter said, *"Now what will you have for dessert?"* The guy looked at the menu and said, *"Well, it says 'Anything your heart desires' and my heart desires a corned beef sandwich."* The waiter was a little taken aback and said, *"Well, I don't know if we can serve you that for dessert. After all, you've just had four corned beef sandwiches for dinner. I'll have to check with the boss."* So he went to Mr. Goldheimer and said, *"This character wants a corned beef sandwich for dessert."* Mr. Goldheimer was outraged. He came back to the table and said, *"What's this about your wanting a corned beef sandwich for dessert?"* And the guy said, *"Well, on the menu it says 'Anything your heart desires' and my heart desires a corned beef sandwich."* Goldheimer threw up his hands, after he had paddled down the aisle like an ape. *"All right, you're going to get the corned beef sandwich. Where are you from, son?"* And he said, *"Newark."* And Goldheimer said, *"Well, let me tell you something. You may be a big shot in Newark, but in Philadelphia, you're a big peeg!"*

DAN BERGER, AGE 28
Philadelphia, Pennsylvania

TOM THOMPSON

: BUTTER I :

My father loves to eat. He likes good food and good cooking. Of course, during the war, certain foods were in limited supply, particularly on board ship where you could only carry so much; not only that, it was also very expensive. One day my father was eating at officer's mess and he was having a great time. He loved butter, and he was putting butter on everything, and the captain was watching. Finally the captain couldn't stand it, and he stood up and he said, "Cutting, do you know that butter costs two dollars a pound?" And my father reportedly looked at him and said, "Yes sir—and worth every damn cent!"

HEATHER CUTTING RAYL, AGE 24
Fall River, Massachusetts

: BUTTER II :

My grandfather told a joke which was repeated so many times that it got to be a tradition. The joke was that the family was sitting around the dinner table one evening, and an uncle was visiting. The uncle kept taking huge hunks of butter and spreading it on his corn. This was many years ago when it was very expensive. So my grandfather said, as sort of a gentle hint, "Butter is fifty cents a pound." And the uncle reached out and took another huge amount of butter and said, "Well worth it!"

JAN MAILON, AGE 28
Falls Church, Virginia

: HELL'S A POPPING :

The story that my grandchildren like most is the one about church a long time ago. We were Baptists, and they had no activities in church then at all; the children just had to sit and be still. That got very, very tiresome, so the boys would walk out of the church occasionally and try to find something to amuse them. One time they went to the church of the white people. There were great big cracks in the old fashioned church, and one of them noticed that a dog's tail was right by one of the cracks. He took a forked stick and pulled it out. He got a hold of the dog's tail, and he put his foot against the wall of the church, and he hollered, "Mad dog!" as he pulled back on the dog's tail. The dog started howling, and he kept it up and hollered, "Mad dog!" Well, the house just emptied itself.

That was so funny they decided that they just had to have some more fun. The church of the white people was completely empty, so they went down to the colored people's church, and they tried to find some meanness to get into down there. They noticed that every time the pastor'd make a good point, he'd say, "Now if I'm lying to you tonight, I hope I go to hell a-poppin'." And so the next week they went in and made the pulpit into a trap door. The next Sunday night they were ready to have their fun. They were listening to the preacher preach, and he made a real good point, and he said, "Now, if I'm lying to you tonight, I hope I go to hell a-poppin'." And so they jerked the trap door and under the pulpit he went. That was down in Louisiana, and the houses were built up high because of flooding. Under the pulpit he went and people went out of the windows and doors and everything saying, "I knew that preacher was lying, and now He's caught him at it!"

It was a crowd of boys, a lot of them. One of my uncles was in the crowd. They were not going to tell it, but it was so funny they had to tell it. So their fathers were the judges, and their fathers got together and decided these boys had to be punished. So they made the boys pick cotton for thirty-five cents a hundred until they made enough money to repair that pulpit and buy an organ for the black people.

CATHERINE NELSON, AGE 83
Little Rock, Arkansas

STEVEN ZEITLIN

: FIVE CARD DRAW :

My dad was always a nonconformist. He and his brothers worked in the oil fields during the oil boom days. One day my dad got hurt on the job and as a result, he said he couldn't bear to put any weight on his heels. The doctors, however, said it was all in his mind, and they sent him to a psychiatrist. This irked him, so my dad said, "If they want to think I'm crazy, I'll make them think I'm crazy." So he goes to the doctor's office, and the doctor brings out the Rorschach ink-blot tests. The doctor laid these cards down in front of my father, and dad reached over, picked them up, shuffled them and dealt them out for a

DALE BROWN

hand of Five Card Draw and said, "I'll open for a dollar." This was enough to prompt the psychiatrist to report to the company lawyers, "He's a good old boy, but he's crazy as hell."

DANIEL W. HUMPHREY, AGE 28
Holdenville, Oklahoma

: SUNDAY SUPPLEMENT :

When my father was working construction, he became an amateur photographer, and a pretty good one too. They were building something in Providence, Rhode Island, and there was a news photographer on the scene. They wanted to do a feature story in the Sunday supplement on this building, and the news photographer wanted to have an aerial shot, but he was scared to death of heights. So my father, being my father, said, "Well, give me the camera, and I'll take the picture for you." "Well, where are you going to take the picture from? There's no bridge; there's nothing you can look down from." And my father pointed to this crane which was several hundred feet up in the air. So my father said, "I'll take it from up there." And the guy said, "You're crazy!" But my father climbed up to the top of his crane, not thinking anything of it. And he took a picture of the site, and in doing so he missed, and he took a picture of his foot. And so my father's foot made it on the front page of the Sunday supplement.

HEATHER CUTTING RAYL, AGE 24
Fall River, Massachusetts

: THE HABERDASHER'S CON :

My grandfather worked for a haberdasher for awhile when he came here. He was a good salesman and a good hustler. I don't know if this joke about haberdashers really happened to him. He said one day, a woman in her late forties came in and said, "My husband has just passed away. He needs a suit to go to the hereafter. He never had a decent suit in his life." Apparently, according to my father, he sold her a suit with two pairs of pants.

MYRON BRETHOLZ, AGE 21
Baltimore, Maryland

: One Last Fling :

I never heard a cross word out of either one of my parents. I've never seen such a couple get along in my life. Dad died just before I was nine years old and prophesied his own death. He prophesied his own death in 1904. He told mother at Christmas—he didn't drink then—he said, "I'm gonna get just full enough to have a little fun." She said, "No, you're not." He said, "Yes, I am. This will be my last Christmas. I'll never live to see another." And he was only a young man, only thirty-six years old, when he died. He said, "I'm gonna die before next Christmas, and I'll never see another, so I'm gonna enjoy life."

Well, he was so serious, that she agreed to go along with it. So the first thing he did—he had a quart of whiskey hidden in the kitchen—he called his next door neighbor and said, "Come on in, let's have a drink." He said "Drink fast now, before the old lady catches us." So old man Jolly, he uncorked the bottle and threw a big drink down, and it came right back. And mother had to mop the kitchen, because she had found the bottle and had exchanged it for a quart of vinegar.

So then dad went downtown, and the first thing he did, he threw a big firecracker under the chief of police, and the chief took after him and right through a store they went. Dad squatted down behind a counter, and the chief ran out the back door when the clerk pointed to it. And when the chief got tired afterwards, he told his deputy, he said, "Don't chase Dick Smith, because that's enough, because he's having fun off of us." Well, that took the fun out of the game.

So dad, he bought about a quart of torpedoes, you know, the kind you throw down, that pop? He bought about a quart of them and he paid nine dollars for nine firecrackers. And in 1904 a dollar firecracker was some firecraker. Dynamite wasn't anything. They didn't have taxis then, so he hired a horse-drawn surrey home. He got home and lit one of those big crackers and threw it on the front porch of the sawmill shanty where we lived; it blew the door open, blew out a window, scared the hackman's horse, and he scattered that hack a mile back to town. Dad was really celebrating. Mother confiscated the crackers and put them away before he blew up the house, but he had that quart of torpedoes. He went up and took a double handful and threw them up on the roof and burned all of us kids until mother put him to bed with a broom handle.

C. O. BURNS

Well, he got up next morning, and he was feeling just as good as ever. A few of the neighbors came over to get a drink off him, and Santa Claus had brought me a little steam engine about that long. Dad was trying to fire that up and get steam to run that. Well everything was going just fine until he spilled alcohol on his hands. It caught them on fire, and he wiped his hands on his Georgia knit socks real good and got his socks on fire, tried to beat the fire out with a broom, and said, "Now get out of here and bring me some water." And, "Go bring me some stove wood." So he ran out and the next thing she knew, he had the stove round full of Roman candles. Well those Roman candles had the fuse first, you know, they shot out of the old wood burning cook stove. We didn't have any screen doors. Some of them went out in the yard and shot the chickens out from under the house, shot the cats from under the beds, through the bedrooms. It was a whoopee time. Mother was fit to be tied by then.

But the next June, his picture came off the wall. No frayed string, no broken wire, or anything, it just fell from above the mantle right on the pine floor, a 16 by 20 picture. It was an enlarged photograph and the old gilt frame must have been as big as this table top. It didn't even scar the frame, didn't break the glass. So dad told mother, "Old lady," he said, "see that. Well that means I'm going before the end of the year." "Oh," she said, "Maybe not." "Yeah," he said, "I am, too," and sure enough, he went on and insured his life. He paid one premium, that was all. He died December the eighth, 1905.

ERNEST A. SMITH, AGE 80
Pine Bloom, Georgia

: VOTING FOR SHERIFF :

Dad dropped off the train in his overalls one day, and he found a voting booth set up on the station platform. Wearing his greasy overalls, he went in and voted for the man of his choice, who was the chief of police running for reelection. Then he took the train out of town, went home, came back down again, and he voted again. He'd cleaned up, and they didn't recognize him. Then he went to the barbershop, had his handlebar mustache shaved off, and bought him an overcoat and a derby hat, and he came back and voted again. That time the sheriff, I mean the police, caught him. He said "Dick, don't you think you've voted enough times?" "Well," he said, "What are you kicking on? I voted for you every time." Well, the chief got reelected all right, and he went on from there to become the high sheriff of the county.

ERNEST A. SMITH, AGE 80
Pine Bloom, Georgia

: DOMINOES :

I don't know just how true this is. My father related it one way, my mother contradicted. My great-grandmother was Catholic and the rest of the family was Protestant. My great-grandfather wouldn't let her practice her religion. And on her deathbed she of course begged to see a priest. And he finally said OK, it was all right for her to be buried in a Catholic church.

He had to get loaded to go to the church. And supposedly the priest was up there saying his funeral mass and you know they say "Dominus vobiscum." And he misunderstood, being drunk and in the back of the church. And he goes staggering up the aisle and he says "I'll have a game of dominoes."

Like I said, my father was a notorious exaggerator.

JEAN BOURASSA, AGE 50
Oxon Hill, Maryland

: CHECKERS :

My dad has a really famous story about the first day the Golden Gate Bridge was open. He was about seventeen years old, and he and a friend thought they would be the first people to cross it, so they went down early in the morning. Well, when they got there, they found out that there were five thousand people there, and some of them were in track suits all ready to cross the bridge. My father and his friend thought, "Ah, we'll never make it." So what they did is they went into town, into San Francisco, and they bought a checkerboard. And they went out to the middle of the bridge and they sat down and they began to play. So now they can say they were the first people to play checkers on the Golden Gate Bridge.

ANN REYNOLDS, AGE 22
McLean, Virginia

: THE PIGS :

My mother's uncle Leo always had to feed the pigs when he was a boy, but he didn't like it. Whenever his dad asked him if he had fed the pigs, he said he did when he really didn't.

One day Leo went outside and noticed that two of the pigs were dead. They died of starvation. Leo ran away and didn't come back till dark. Then he started pretending to feed the pigs. Each day he moved the dead ones into a different position so that when his mom and dad looked out the window they wouldn't get suspicious. Since rigor mortis had set in, the pigs were stiff, and their eyes bulged out. Because of the eyes, Leo had to make the pigs face in the opposite direction.

One day when Leo was sick, his dad went out to feed the pigs for him. . . . He called the pigs and when the two dead ones didn't answer, he went to investigate. He tapped one of them, and it fell over. The same happened to the other. Leo was lucky that he was sick because he couldn't get that much of a beating.

JEFF MAJTYKA, AGE 15
Purcellville, Virginia

SURVIVORS

Family members who triumph over poverty and hardship are often remembered in family traditions. Stories about struggles for food, shelter, or clothing are told in every generation, but become especially common with the Great Depression. For all of their needs, Depression children were not to want for good stories with which to discipline their children. "My father," said Sherry Lynn Cocheres, "has always told us about his youth during the Depression. He always tells about his worn blue pants with the green patch, or was it his green pants with the blue patch?"

More often than not, these stories have women protagonists who hold the family together through desperate times. Some believe that whereas men do well in emergency situations, women are more successful in coping with longterm stress. They are celebrated for this quality in family tales.

One person we interviewed suggested that people like to reminisce about their hard times because it makes them feel as if they have accomplished something with their lives. They made it through. They earned the right to look back with laughter and nostalgia on their trials, and tell good stories from hard times.

: THE SHEEP SHED :

This is about my favorite aunt, Caroline. She's had a hard life over the years. When she had probably given birth to about her sixth child, there was a promise from her husband's side of the family of a section of land that they moved to. With that section of land there were already farm buildings but no house. They arranged for a house to be moved down from a county two counties north of there. Well, this was during the Depression, during the early 1930s, and they were just dirt poor. Of course, Caroline, with these six kids, couldn't go up to look it over, but Ed went up and looked over the house and said it was fine. It had linoleum floors, and it was wallpapered, and it had, I think, three bedrooms and a front porch, which at that time was a fairly good house. It was a house they could live in.

There was another old house at this farm, which had been used as a sheep shed. The movers got confused, and they moved the sheep shed down, drove into the yard with the wrong house, with sheep shit all over it and cobwebs. You can imagine the stench which must have accompanied it. And they simply could *not afford to have the right house moved down. It would've been another $250, and they couldn't make the workers undo their mistake.*

Caroline and her sister Millie helped clean up the worst. She actually scooped it out. It being a sheep shed of course, there were no closets or anything, so the kids would just have to keep their clothes in boxes under the bed. Eventually Ed got hold of some lumber, and he did build closets and raised the roof, in order for the kids to sleep upstairs. But they lived in that house, in a sheep shed, for twenty years.

LOUISE KROESE, AGE 29
Washington, D.C.

TOM THOMPSON

: FAIRY TALE :

There is sort of . . . it's almost like a fairy tale the way it happened to work out when some relatives came over around 1880. Two families settled next to each other. One was very wealthy and had five handsome sons, and the other had sort of a drunken father that no one would talk about and they had a daughter. This daughter went to clean house, to be the maid for the rich family, and she married one of the boys. And these are my great-grandparents. But it's very interesting because it's sort of like Cinderella and the prince.

My parents are now fairly well off, not really rich or anything, but they own an apartment building. They could afford to have someone come in and do the domestic work, like cleaning the stairways, but to this day my mother insists on doing the scrubwork. And we've talked about how it's perpetuated, this thing that she thinks she's just a scrubwoman even though she really is very comfortably well off.

SUZANNE GIBSON, AGE 30
Alexandria, Virginia

: DOWN IN ALABAMA :

In Alabama—Talladega, Sylacauga, Goodwater—in the late thirties, early forties, people worked very hard. Farming was their way of life. It was difficult because, being black, a lot of them were sharecroppers; my dad was a sharecropper. When I was born, he didn't have the money to pay for the delivery which was thirty dollars, so he gave the doctor a suckling pig and fifteen dollars. Doctors and lawyers were accustomed to taking something in trade in those days.

I was born the year that Joe Louis defeated Max Schmeling; many black parents named their male children "Joe Louis." My father dubbed me Joe Louis Thomas, but the man he sharecropped from, Mr. Fred Burroughs, who ran a jewelry store in town, insisted that I be named after him, so I was named Fred Louis. He didn't have too much of a choice; he didn't want to alienate the man.

I don't know if it was a black-only kind of thing, but I do remember that by the time my grandfather harvested his crop and went in town to sell the cotton and things like that, he ended up owing the man money. And he would have to go into debt to get enough seeds to go start all over again. It was a very traumatic experience to see a man who you consider stalwart stand and cry and have to swallow it.

That's all they did—they worked. They worked and went to church every Sunday. One would carry one's shoes over one's shoulders till you got to the church, because the roads were not covered, so you got a lot of dust. And what you did was use Vaseline to polish your shoes, give 'em a high gloss. Some of the guys would slick their hair down with a pomade, but use soot from the chimney or the stove to make it very black and shiny.

Part of the tradition was to teach us how to survive under white domination. So you were taught little expressions, "If you're white, you're all right/ If you're brown, hang around/ If you're black, stay back." And you begin to accept that as part of your lifestyle. "Don't mix in white folks' business," we were told all the time. "Mind your tongue around white folks." It was almost like an eagle teaching their young ones how to feather their nest, you know.

The fireplace was a gathering place at night. It was the greatest source of light because we only had kerosene lamps. And the older people would sit around and tell stories. They were primarily ghost stories or stories of black people running into trouble with white people—the time they really saw the Ku Klux Klan, how they came and got this or that person. Sometimes there were stories about how the Klan would come in and there would be a standoff.

I remember I lived with an Indian doctor in Talladega—his name was Dr. Peavy—and he ended up getting most of the patients in town who were not able to be helped by trained physicians. He cured a lot of people using roots and herbs. I was one of them, 'cause I had a serious case of athlete's foot when I was a child, and I couldn't walk. The doctor at Talladega College was giving me a treatment, but it wasn't working and the root doctor made a salve out of roots and in three or four days I was back on my feet again.

But one of the stories was that the Klan came after him one time. I don't know for what reason. He was sitting on his porch with a shotgun, knowing that they were coming. They were threatening to kill him, but he didn't back down; he just said that he had a doublebarreled shotgun, and the first one that moved to try to take him—well, he would take a few with him. He was ready to die. And they finally said, "Oh, he's crazy!" and they left him alone.

And that became part of instilling some kind of pride, you know, here was a man who stood them off. But it didn't help you overcome the basic fear. I remember once, after having moved to Brooklyn, New York, going back on a vacation to a place called Tallapoosa, Georgia, which was just across the Alabama line. I had forgotten the racial fears. I was walking down the streets with some former childhood schoolmates, and I bumped into this elderly white man by accident. And he turned and he drew back to hit me (but he didn't)—he just ver-

bally threatened me. And all of a sudden the fears came back. And I said, "My God, now I remember it all." And I promised I'd never go back again.

FRED THOMAS, AGE 38
Washington, D.C.

: Pride from the Soles Up :

The story that's on my mind is on my mind because I just got word that my great-uncle Jim died. His name was Jim Cobb and this is a story he used to tell me about looking for work in the Depression. He'd been out of work like everybody else for months and months and pounded the pavement and wore out the soles of his shoes — his shoes were threadbare and so forth. And finally he got hired and the man who hired him, as he told the story, said, "I want you to know why you got this job, because there were twenty or thirty other applications. I hired you because you polished around the soles of your shoes, you polished the edges of your shoe soles." And the man said, "I think that's a sign of somebody who'll take pride in his work." And I polish the soles of my shoes to this day.

WARREN CORBETT, AGE 30
Washington, D.C.

: Scrap Metal Days :

When I was growing up in St. Louis during World War II, the kids in the neighborhood would get together and go en masse to the neighborhood theater. We'd have our ten cents to get in and our five cents for popcorn, and we'd go, six or eight or ten or twelve of us, at ten in the morning and stay till six at night. During the war, there was such a shortage of gasoline, rubber, and metal. One way to encourage people to get scrap metal was to have kids bring it to the movies on Saturday. We'd each have to bring a piece of metal and that was our entrance fee. If you didn't have your piece of metal, you would have to pay a dime to get in. The metal would be piled up in a parking lot and then they would send it down to be melted down for airplanes and whatever else was needed. I once donated my pair of roller skates and then I cried afterwards, wishing I still had them. A couple of kids took their mothers' good pots and pans from the kitchen and some took their fathers' tools out of the tool chest... anything to get metal so that we could get into the movies.

SHARON BABER, AGE 42

Arlington, Virginia

: DOWN TO THE LAST DOLLAR :

There were times, you know, when we were right down to the last dollar. I remember once we had started off to travel around, sort of mixing vacation with my father's selling to keep the family together in the summer. I think they were down finally to about eight dollars, and before the end of the day they had about a dollar and a half left. My dad had gone into general delivery at the post office to pick up some things that would have come from his mother who was watching our home and supervising the business that was being run out of the basement. There was a letter asking for a dollar and a half as a refund for something. My dad said, "Well, if I send a dollar and a half, that's the last money we've got." And my mother said, "Well, just go ahead, Charles, the good Lord will take care of us some way." So he went in to make out a money order to pay the dollar and a half and got to talking with the woman who was making out the money order. And before they were through, she had asked to see some of his things. And he sold her about forty dollars worth, and she brought in some other friends. So before the day was out, we were back in business again and going. But I don't know how many kids today had their families down to the last dollar they have.

CHARLES BERGUN, AGE 46

Lafayette, California

INNOCENTS

Family stories are peopled with characters in conflict; heroes shoot outlaws, jokers play pranks, immigrants outsmart border guards. But there is a particular kind of family character who is not bent on getting the better of another, nor is he a victim or the butt of a joke. He simply gets the better of himself.

It's the innocent who, in a characteristic episode, gets into the wrong car, drives away with the wrong wife, talks to her all the way home, and doesn't notice the difference. William Humphrey writes about Giles Ordway who rode his horse and buggy to Knoxville on business. By accident he took the train home. About a week later he remembered the horse and buggy. He went to the depot to buy his ticket, and purchased a round trip![1]

These family stories are related to many traditional tales and jokes found around the world. "The Stupid Man" is even a category in folktale indexes. Oftentimes, they are told about children in the family. A child's solution to a problem often seems comical to us, yet forgiveable and charming because it makes perfect sense from the young person's point of view. In one family, a child gently sat on an egg, hoping to hatch it like a mother hen. In another, a child was told by her sister that they should split a diet soda which had only two calories, that way they would only consume one calorie apiece. The young child asked how her sister could be so sure that the two wouldn't end up in the same glass.

We spoke to one family which told about an incident which happened when the mother was pregnant, and her two children were suggesting names for the baby.

"Well, if it's a boy," said the oldest child, "can we name him John?"

"Maybe," said the mother.

"Well, if it's a girl," she went on, "can we name her Mary?"

"Maybe."

Finally, the youngest child, anxious to prove her intelligence, piped up, "Well, if it's a dog, Mom, can we name it Lassie?"[2]

Sometimes these stories are told to teach a lesson, to tease a child or an absent-minded adult into changing his behavior, and thus resemble moral or cautionary stories. But perhaps more often, the celebrated mistake is so much the product of a child's stage of life, or an adult's established way of thinking, that the tales are just playful and forgiving. We don't laugh at these innocents derisively, but gently. Perhaps we understand that the simple day-to-day tasks of going to work, keeping track of money, or finding our car in a parking lot aren't all that easy. We all do them, succeeding most of the time, but failure is inevitable. And if one person fails a little more often, a little more flagrantly than another, he deserves some affection along with our laughter; perhaps we're laughing at a small part of ourselves.

NANCY CHISUM

: THE FOGGY MUSICIAN :

We've always been a musical family. When my grandfather was old, he elapsed into a complete fog. He wouldn't say a sensible word, week in and week out. But his nurse would bring him to the dinner table and he'd sit there and he'd eat. The night boat to Norfolk from Baltimore would come by every night at eight o'clock and it would go "Boooooooaaah" as it went by the house. One night, out of this total fog he had been in for months, grandfather stood up, went over to the piano, poked it, and said, "E Flat." Then he sat down and went right back into the fog.

: INNARDS I :

My mother's family are emigrants from Sweden and one of my great-uncles was well-known as a storyteller in the town that he came from. He used to declare that he had a next door neighbor named Henrik who was over seven feet tall. He was an enormously strong man. He only cut his hair and shaved once a year, and only bathed once a year. He was quite a character. People would just tell stories about how Henrik would just take a whole fish and gulp it down, bones and all. . . . One of the stories they tell is that Henrik always used to go to the butcher's and buy, or actually he was given, all of the innards of the animals, because he loved to eat them. He'd bicycle over and they'd be wrapped up in brown paper and he'd put the brown paper inside his coat and button it up to keep the sack next to his body and he'd bicycle home.

Well, one day when he was bicycling home, there was a drunk motorist coming the other way. He got very close to Henrik and Henrik swerved and he went down into a ditch and his bicycle crashed. The motorist stopped and he got very frightened because Henrik's jacket had come open and the bag had broken and all of the entrails were all over his chest. And the motorist, who was very drunk, said, "Oh, no! Get an ambulance!" And Henrik at that point stood up and said, "No, no!" And the motorist fainted and Henrik had to get help for him instead.

: INNARDS II :

I bought a secondhand bicycle with the money I had saved over a period of years and got a job in a meat shop delivering meat. The man I worked for had a big saloon business. In those days the saloons had what was called a free lunch counter. There would be a place in the back of the bar where you could go and eat whatever you wanted, included free when you paid for the price of the beer. My job was to deliver the liver. They always bought large quantities of it. If they'd buy fifty pounds of liver, I couldn't put that much on my bicycle, but I could make two twenty-five pound trips. The liver was always wet and messy so he always wrapped it in double thicknesses of butcher paper. Then I'd quickly put it in the carrier basket of my bicycle and I'd run down to the saloon. I'd carry it in and by that time the paper would be soaked.

Well one day when I had twenty-five pounds of liver in the basket, the fellow said, "Look. There's a delivery over on Orchard Lane. The woman's in a hurry. Go there first and then go to the saloon." So I did, but this was a slight delay and the moisture from the liver got into the paper a little deeper. Just as I turned to come up to the front door of the saloon a woman came along in a car and hit the front wheel of my bicycle. I was sent sprawling into the street. The liver had been in the paper just long enough to soak through so that when it spilled into the street, there was all this bloody liver laying in the street and me laying in the street. She looked at me and she said, "Oh, are you all right?" I guess she thought the liver was me spread all over the street.

TED F. SILVEY, AGE 71
Washington, D.C.

: Four Twenty-fives :

My grandmother had a younger brother who was a funny guy. He had been living on the farm until it was time to go to college. When he was ready to leave home, his father gave him a one hundred dollar bill. And you know that was the most money he had ever seen. Before that he had never seen anything bigger than a five. So he went down to the bank to get it broken down. To the bank teller he said, "Can I have change for this one hundred dollar bill?" And the teller asked, "How would you like it?" He replied, "Just give me four twenty-fives."

: Up from the Dead :

The grandfather after whom I was named was David Herman. He was blind in one eye, and he was once hit by a hearse. The two drivers, two young gentlemen, figured they'd just pick him up and take him to the hospital. So they picked him up and put him in the back of the hearse. When he woke up, he found he was in the back of the hearse. So he decided that no one was going to bury him! He opened the door when they stopped at a traffic light, and he started to run, and they started to run after him, but they couldn't catch him. Eventually the whole story came out in the newspaper about how they ran after this man jumping from a hearse.

DAVID CAREY
New York, New York

WENDY WOLF

: ON THE WINGS OF A TURKEY :

This is about my great-grandfather. He would have died around 1910, or so. His name was Frank, and he was supposed to have been a real small guy, very short, very slight. He was out in the woods running his turkey traps one day. He was very lucky that day, and he got something like eight or ten, maybe a dozen turkeys. Now a wild turkey's a pretty big animal. I don't know if you've ever seen one. He had all of them collected, and he was holding a half dozen in each hand by the feet, and he swung them over his shoulder to carry them. Then a wind came up and caught in the turkey's wings as he swung them over his shoulder, and supposedly carried him up in the air. He had to let go of a few turkeys before they let him down.

And this is my dad's addition to the story—that his grandfather, the son of the man this was supposed to have happened to, always said that if their grandpa had been smart, he wouldn't have let go of them, but would've held on until they flew him over the house and then let go of a few, and he would've been home, and he wouldn't have to carry them all.

DENNIS F. SIEVERS
Vincennes, Indiana

LOUISE TIRANOFF

: To Life! :

Well, my grandfather came from Poland, and he just died here about a year ago, at the age of ninety-five. I remember one thing he said. He was a very wise man, but he was kind of a boozer all his life. My grandmother was also from Poland, and she didn't approve of alcohol, and so they had kind of a going battle all their lives about him drinking. On his birthday or something like that I'd take him a bottle of bourbon. And he told me one day when I brought him a bottle of bourbon for his birthday—I think he was ninety-two at the time—he said that he had given up alcohol, that alcohol had killed two of his brothers and so he thought that it was time for him to quit, because he wasn't old enough to die yet. So I asked him about the brothers it had killed. And he told me it had killed his brothers Collin and Stanley. I checked up on it and found that Collin was ninety-two when he died and Stanley was eighty-nine.

ROBERT KOSMICKI, AGE 36
Washington, D.C.

: The Walrus Story :

This is a story about my younger sister Ann. She was probably about seven years old and I was probably about twelve. Her birthday happened to fall on Easter Sunday, and true to family tradition, you got to pick what you wanted to do on your birthday. She decided that she wanted to go to the Coney Island Aquarium, so after church on Sunday the family packed up to go. Everybody was still dressed in their Easter finery, including an old Easter hat that my mother had stayed up until the wee hours of the morning putting a new velvet ribbon and a new flower on, so it would look pretty and new for Ann to wear to church on Easter Sunday on her birthday.

So we went to Coney Island, walked around, looked, and then it was time to go home. And being a family of four women and one man, three of the women had to go to the bathroom, and I stayed with my father. We wandered around a little bit, and then it's time to meet at the walrus exhibit, which is an outdoor exhibit. We get there and all of a sudden there's this huge crowd around the exhibit, and we're wondering what's going on. So we nose our way up and look around and everyone is laughing hysterically. And we look at the walrus, and here's the walrus diving and jumping in the water wearing an Easter bonnet — my sister's Easter bonnet! Then we saw this one bright red, shrieking, hysterical little girl crying because her Easter bonnet is being worn by the walrus. The zoo keeper is yelling at my mother about how the animal is going to eat this hat and choke and die, and she will be responsible for this eight-hundred-dollar walrus.

Well, finally the zoo keeper got the hat away from the walrus and handed it back to my sister, who didn't look too pleased about getting it back at all. And we packed up in the family station wagon and went home. And that's the end of the walrus story. Every time the family gets together we tell it.

CAROL BIGELOW RIGGS, AGE 25
Arlington, Virginia

: HOW MOTHER LEFT HER MARK :

When we moved into our house in 1935, it still had an outhouse. Being a large house, it had two doors with two holes in each door so you could seat four comfortably. We had plumbing, too, but there were nine in our household and mother kept up the outhouses because there were times when everyone had to use the bathroom at the same time. She had shellacked the wooden seats one day and a week or more had gone by, and she went out and sat down and realized that she was not going to be able to get up. The shellac was still sticky. So she contemplated the various alternatives, one of which seemed to be to holler for help, and another one not to holler for help and she realized that the eventual outcome would be that one way or another she was going to have to get up and leave part of her attached. So she finally did it alone. The ring around her backside took several weeks to heal!

MIDGE HEIMER
Germantown, Maryland

: NAPOLEON :

One of my ancestors had once driven a carriage for Napoleon when he was fleeing Russia because the czar had made a bargain with Napoleon to provide transport through Germany, which is where my family came from. Later on, the family came to the United States to live.

This ancestor was a very old man. He was poor of eyesight, he was hard of hearing, and he had no sense of smell whatsoever. They lived out in the woods and he didn't recognize many of the animals here or how they lived.

So one day he was strolling there with his walking cane and his Sunday best, and he came upon a skunk. The skunk of course had a nice big stripe up his tail and a great plume and it reminded him of Napoleon whom he had driven in his carriage. And he said, "Well, Napoleon, what are you doing here?" He took his cane and gave the skunk a big smack and of course the skunk retaliated. The old gentleman was completely unaware of it because he had no sense of smell and he returned home but no one would let him in the house. They made him go to the barn where they burned the Sunday clothes which he had brought all the way from Germany.

CAROL MAAS, AGE 27
Greenbelt, Maryland

: A STUDENT TILL THE END :

My grandmother was married to a rabbi who apparently was not much of a worker. As a rabbi, he was a perpetual student, but he decided that what he really wanted to do of all the things in the world was to be a farmer — never having farmed in his life. He had about five or six children at that point, and off he went to a communal farm, my grandmother protesting all the way. They discovered that this was not for them, and they moved into another farm with a person who was an extremely shrewd businessman, and when he milked the cows he added a considerable amount of water to the milk. And my grandfather, who in addition to being a poor businessman, was also terribly honest, decided that that wasn't for him. So off they went to St. Louis, where my grandmother opened a small grocery store, and my grandfather spent all his time in synagogue praying. And it was there that my mother was born.

The early stories about my mother in St. Louis are mostly about the staunch bravery of my grandmother, and the flitting around of my grandfather from city to city. He never had any money. And he died in San Francisco when he was reading a book crossing the street. He was hit by a car. He was a student till the end.

HELEN ABRAMS
New York, New York

: THE VIEW FROM THE TRANSOM :

I had a dog named Shane. My niece and nephew called him Shame, but that's another story. When I went off to boarding school, my mother hired a neighborhood kid named Stevie to walk Shane. One February morning my mother had overslept when she heard Stevie knocking at the door. So she threw on a flimsy housecoat and rushed downstairs and grabbed the dog and there was Stevie happily retreating toward his house through the backyard. She called him back and he begrudgingly took the dog for a walk — and my mother found she was locked out.

It was lightly snowing, not real cold, but snowing, and there was my mother in her baby doll pajamas and a housecoat. She rang the doorbell, tried to wake my father, but nobody would awake. She pounded at the door, but nobody would awake. She decided, "Ah! The kids get in by going in the milk chute next to the back door." You could reach in through the outer door and unlock the inner door and get in. She tried that, but just about two months before we had put in a top latch because my grandmother, who was in her seventies and living with us, was afraid of rapists. My mother couldn't reach the top latch, so she went to the garage and got a log; she stood up on it, shimmied herself through, and reached up to get the top latch. And just as she was unlocking it, the log slipped out, and she went lurching forward and got herself wedged halfway in and halfway out of the milk chute! Her backside was sticking out and it was just about time for the milkman to come and try with some difficulty to deliver the milk or for Stevie to return and see Mrs. LaRiche in this precarious position.

So she decided to shout, and started screaming "Bill, Bill," but my father keeps the air conditioner on summer and winter to drown out bird sounds. My grandmother heard her and said, "Betty, Betty, what is the matter?"

And my mother said, "Get Bill, I'm stuck in the milk chute and I hurt!"

"The clothes chute," said my grandmother, "what the hell are you doing in the clothes chute?"

"Not the clothes chute, damn it, the milk chute!"

"Bill, Bill, Betty's stuck in the clothes chute" — by this time my grandmother is looking down the chute — "and I can't see her anywhere!"

"Not the clothes chute, damn it, the milk chute!"

"What the hell is she doing in the clothes chute?" said my father.

"Not the clothes chute, damn it, the milk chute!"

So my father comes down and sees her and says, "What the hell are you doing in there?"

"Never mind, just get me out." So he started fiddling with her legs and she says, "Stop fiddling with my legs, get me a chair!"

And my grandmother is saying, "Oh, I thought the house was on fire!"

So my father got her a chair and mother got herself out with some difficulty just moments before Stevie returned and the milkman came. Grandmother screamed again, "I thought the house was on fire. I think I'm going to have a heart attack."

"If you are going to have a heart attack," said my father, "go to your room and have it!" They forgot about my mother, they were so upset with one another!

But the clincher of the story is that friends of theirs told the local [Cleveland] Plain Dealer *gossip columnist about the incident and the columnist wrote about it with this poem appearing underneath:*

There was a lady quite handsome
Who got wedged in her bedroom transom.
Cry as she might, they ignored her plight
Reasoning the view was worth more than the ransom.

JEFFREY LARICHE, AGE 34
Cleveland, Ohio

MIGRATIONS

In nineteenth-century Norway a well-to-do governess fell in love with a poor farmer. The caste system discouraged marriage, but the governess was determined. In a burst of rebellious exuberance and a blue wedding dress, she married the farmer and sailed for America the same day, May 17, 1843. It was Norway's independence day.

Their ship, the *Tricolors,* arrived in New York harbor on July 4, America's Independence Day. Here, as their great-granddaughter Miriam Fors tells it, "they were free to love each other."

They moved from New York to Wisconsin where they built a log cabin. When the Civil War broke out, the farmer went to fight for the Union. His wife and young son longed for a flag to fly above their home, but American flags were scarce and there was little cloth to be had. So the mother and son took unbleached muslin flour sacks and made the white portions of the flag. Others were dyed red with Indian berries. But blue cloth was almost impossible to acquire.

When there seemed no alternative, she took her blue wedding dress out of the large wooden trunk she had brought from Norway. And with tears in her eyes, she cut out the blue background for the white stars. Her son cut down a sapling tree, and the Norwegian immigrant family had an American flag to fly above their home.[1]

Beyond the circumstances and coincidences of this crossing-over narrative lies one of the great human stories. It is, like the epic of Moses, a migration story. As Moses struggled against the pharaoh and escaped across the desert toward the promised land, so the family member escapes from a home riddled with hardship and oppression, making his way across ocean and land to establish himself in a new home. The only difference is, as William Humphreys was to put it in his novel, *The Ordways,* for the ordinary family "the waves were not to part."[2]

Like the story of Moses, the family migration story has three parts: a reason for departure, a journey, and a struggle for survival in a new home. Although there may be a dramatic narrative about only one of the three parts, all three are often touched on by the family storyteller. In the story of the Norwegian migration, for example, the oppression of the rigid Norwegian social system marks the first; the Independence Day journey, the second. Finally, the sewing of an American flag symbolizes their assimilation into a new home. The three-part structure helps to explain why the episode of the flag, taking place two decades after the actual migration, is still part of one continuous narrative. The assimilation of the family into its new home, however long that takes, is an integral part of the migration.

East coast dwellers, particularly those whose ancestors migrated to this country in the past three generations, frequently tell a crossing-over story as one of their most basic and furthest back family tales. Families who have been in this country longer often replace the immigration saga with a story about the westward migration as their oldest tale, their story of origins.

The reasons for a family's departure from their old home are often depicted in a dramatic incident. In the slave experience this is the moment of capture. In Alex Haley's family, the story is told of the ancestor Kunta Kinte who went out to chop wood for a drum when he was captured and brought into slavery.[3] That single piece of detail—that Kunta Kinte was chopping wood—was not a random scrap of remembrance. It was passed down through the generations because it was part of the dramatic moment at which the destiny of a family was transformed. A number of family stories handed down in black families center on the moment of capture, and suggest that some Africans were lured by slave traders onto ships through the use of red cloth. This example was told by a college student, and had been passed down from "granny's grandmother":

MARIAN PATTEN

She told granny that one day she and some other children were playing in Africa. They sighted a red flag flying at a distance from them. They became curious as to what the red flag was and ran to it. On approaching they were grabbed by some white men and put on a ship. This ship brought them to Virginia where they were sold. She always hated anything red because that was the color that attracted her from home and people whom she never saw or heard from. She is referred to as often saying, "Oh that red rag, that red rag brought me here."[4]

Westward journeys were often embarked on in episodes as dramatic and at times as violent as those of the immigrant or the slave. In "The Family Saga as a Form of Folklore," Mody Boatright offers this example:

In 1846 when Jim Dandy was a youth in Tennessee, there were in the community in which he lived two factions: the mountain boys and the valley boys, or the hill boys and the plantation boys. They crashed each other's parties and dances and had numerous fist fights. Then the valley boys brought knives into action, and the arms race was on. The mountain boys went to a valley boys' dance on a river boat with hickory clubs concealed in their pants legs. The fight began on signal. A valley boy drew a pistol and shot a mountain boy in the knee. But the clubs were more effective than the single pistol, and many a valley boy was knocked off into the river. Some climbed back in their wet clothes and reentered the fight, but when it was over, thirteen were missing. A mob formed and began rounding up the mountain boys. But not Jim and his brother Watt. They hid in a cave where an old fisherwoman brought them food. They eventually got to Texas after shooting two of their pursuers.[5]

Few families are driven to embark on such harrowing, difficult migrations on the basis of a single incident; these stories are often a dramatic summation of years of oppression.

On their journey across the ocean or the Great Plains, the perils Americans most remember come from human rather than natural forces—from Indians and border guards, not hurricanes and storms. We have, however, heard occasional stories of storms at sea, even of an ancestor who fell off the Mayflower.

At times, humorous incidents attach themselves to one of the parts of the migration story, incidents which would have been long buried had they not taken place in that sensitive period. On one family's migration to Iowa by train, for instance, the family horse and cow were on one end of the railroad car and the furniture on the other.

And I do remember my folks telling this, when my dad opened his office desk a very weak cat got out of the area where the typewriter ordinarily is put and I have no idea how long the cat had been en route. It came from St. Paul—just no idea how long it had been en route. That poor cat was pretty weak.[6]

As families journeyed westward they often kept diaries and journals in which were recorded items of interest as well as

PAUL REIMERS

their day-to-day routines. Yet Francis Haines, Sr., who studied travelers' accounts of journeys on the Oregon Trail, notes that these memoirs do not mention one episode which is frequently retold by their descendants. He calls this apocryphal story "Goldilocks on the Oregon Trail."[7] In these tales, Goldilocks, described as a three-year-old dimpled darling (or in some versions as a twelve-year-old redhead) is found to be unbearably attractive by a tribe of friendly Indians who stop the wagon train and offer to trade a number of ponies in return for this fair child. The white pioneers never surrender her, although in one version "Goldilocks'" father offers the chief her braid, and the Indians go on their way begrudgingly. In "Suny," the story from our collection, the woman is a red-haired beauty about to be married, and the chief offers forty horses (see p. 72). The historian Haines suggests that these stories are based on some Anglo-Saxon misconception that all other people on earth envy their children and their women. He also notes that similar stories were current in the folklore of England a century ago with the Gypsies as the dark-skinned people who wanted the blond English offspring.

The third part of the migration saga explains how an immigrant or a pioneer establishes a new home. The central thrust of many adjustment stories is the problem, comical to all but those involved, of having time-honored customs viewed as eccentric in a new place; oftentimes accents, outmoded beliefs, and a lack of familiarity with new lifestyles become a source of humor and of family stories. There is also a distinct group of tales about misunderstanding objects and customs in "modern America" (see pp. 79–82). A number of stories are also told about name changes (see pp. 78–9). For the immigrant arriving in America these changes were often the work of an inconsiderate, ignorant, or harried immigration inspector at Ellis Island; for the slave they were the deliberate work of a master imposing an American name in an effort to crush the slave's African identity; for the westward traveler they may have been an intentional effort to disguise his identity; a number of drifters west are said to have taken a new name off a tombstone.

Storyteller and ballad singer Maggie Hammons tells a good example of a family migration saga. The story goes that her great-grandfather was friendly with an old Indian who would visit him every day. They would swap tales and jokes. He liked the old Indian. One day the Indian came to him and said, "I had a dream last night." And he went on to say that an Indian's dreams always come true. Maggie's great-grand-father had a beautiful gun that was one of his most prized possessions, and the Indian told him that he had had a dream about owning that gun. So out of fear, her great-grandfather gave the Indian his weapon.

A few weeks later the great-grandfather came up with a plan to reclaim his possession. He went to the Indian and said, "I dreamed I had my gun back. Not only did I have my gun back, but I also had one of your ponies."

The Indian thought for a while. At last he said, "Take it, paleface, but dream no more."

Afraid that the Indians would kill him now, Maggie's great-grandfather rounded up his ponies, his family, and his possessions and left the area with the Indians in pursuit. They crossed the Newcon River, swimming across with the horses, escaped the Indians, and finally settled in a new home.

LOUISE TIRANOFF

The Hammons family originally came from Great Britain, and Maggie is a folksinger. Folklorists often stress the British origin of many of her ballads. But as far as she is concerned, her history begins with the story of her great-grandfather's journey across the river.[8]

Families often tell a migration saga as the first real narrative in the history of a family. One reason for this is practical. The great blank wall which separates an individual from his past before his ancestors arrived in America or before they journeyed west was, in part, intended to be that way. The poverty and hardship left behind was often painful and immigrants wanted to become Americans quickly. Those who moved west often did so for unsavory reasons, leaving behind broken hearts, unpaid debts, and dead men—and they were damned if they wanted those to come down in oral tradition.

Migrations also make ideal origin stories: they explain why the old world ended and how the new world began. The three-part origin sagas have a foot in both worlds, and suggest the way in which an ancestor steps out of the amorphous flow of European or American history and into the oral history of a particular family.

Family stories, of course, are not myths. The family is a social grouping but it is not a tribe. Family tales are peopled with ordinary men and women, not gods. The stories seldom go back more than a hundred years, and they do not begin, "In the beginning . . ." Still, there is often a migration saga which serves a mythological function for the family. It introduces a dramatic beginning, a dynamic sense of origins, and a patriarch or matriarch who brings future generations to a promised land.

: THE CZAR'S ARMY :

We're Jews and my grandfather was a Jew in Russia in the army under the Czar, which of course wasn't a good place for a Jew to be at all. But he had no choice being drafted. All I know is he had done something to aggravate his senior officer, or the officer wanted to make times difficult for him. So he was told that he was supposed to clean this officer's horse. The officer didn't like how he had done it, and he ordered my grandfather to lick the sweat off the backside of the horse. It's a double indignity because it violates Jewish laws. He was forced to do it,

*so he did it and that night he left, he just split from the army. I
don't know the rest of the details except that was the point at
which he left Russia. He made his way to the United States.*

GERRY RUGEL, AGE 29
Washington, D.C.

: FISHBOK :

*My father's side of the family came from Hessia, a little town
called Fishbok, and they migrated to this country in about
1850. The basic story that runs along the line is that my great-
great-grandfather was in Hessia, in the little town of Fishbok,
going to a grocery store, and another young man came in the
store after he did. At the same time, a Prussian officer also
walked into the store. The young man who had followed him in
didn't give him the proper respect, didn't salute him, or whatever he had to do, so the man, the Prussian officer, took out his
saber and slashed him across the face, cut his [face] open. At
which point my great-great-grandfather said, "Well that's
enough, I've had it with this country," and decided to emigrate
which he did.*

ALAN LUDWIG, AGE 24
Erie, Pennsylvania

: THE CORN SQUEEZERS :

*The Amish side of my family was named Blank, and they got
kicked out of the [Amish country], according to the stories that
have been told, because they had this bad habit of making
"corn squeezings." The way the story goes is that in the Revolu-
tionary War the Hessian soldiers were gotten drunk by drinking the "corn squeezings" of the Blanks, and the church never
forgave the family for this. But, because they contributed to
winning the war and securing American independence they
were sort of forgiven for that particular piece of business.*

    *Then when the Civil War came along, and they had all the
troops going into the battle of Gettysburg, my great-grandfather was a little bit ticked off because he was a restless youth
and kind of wanted to get involved in this but he wasn't allowed
to. So he and his brothers went out and started selling their
corn squeezings to the northern troops. And [when] the Union*

*troops came in they found the corn squeezings—and they stayed
a day too long, so they were unable to satisfy the need for re-
placements in Pickett's charge! So my great-grandpa's dad and
mother were kicked out because that was the second time they'd
been involved with physical violence, and war, and booze. As a
result of that they were [strongly] encouraged to move west!*

NANCY RIGG

Denver, Colorado

: THE LORD'S DAUGHTER :

SUSAN: *I guess the first story I would tell is the one about my
great-great-grandfather, who was a very poor peasant on a
farm in Ireland. His last name was McCarthy. I'm not sure of
his first name. And he fell in love with Kathleen O'Brien, the
daughter of the big lord of the neighborhood.*

CHRISTOPHER: *And the lord didn't like him; he didn't want her
to marry him. So one night he put a ladder up to her window,
and they both came down. And they went into her father's stable and got the fastest horses in almost the world. The next
morning when the father woke up, he saw that his daughter was
missing, and he got so furious, he said, "No matter how fast
they run, I can sure catch them." And he went to the stable, and
his horses were gone. So he had to run by foot, and by the time
he got to the boat station, they were already to America.*

SUSAN: *They came to this country, and he became a landscape
gardener, and evidently they did very well, because they made
enough money to go back and snoot it up in Ireland for awhile.*

SUSAN MEEHAN, AGE 38, AND CHRISTOPHER MEEHAN

Washington, D.C.

: THE TRUNK BUSINESS :

*My dad and my uncle had a leather store in Rumania where
they made trunks and harnesses and saddles. Apparently they
were pretty good artisans because the local dignitary, the
prince or whatever, asked them to make him a special trunk
with secret drawers and things of that nature. They finished the
trunk, and when the prince and his men came to collect it, my
father and my uncle only charged him for the labor, since they*

felt that it was quite an honor to have been asked to make the trunk. The prince's men slapped them and spat on them for having the affrontery to charge even for labor. A local ordinance was then passed that applied to my father and uncle only. They could no longer throw water into the street which was the only way to dispose of water in that community. So they had no way to operate their business and that's why they both decided they had to leave. In addition to religious oppression, they couldn't make a living.

My dad had a relative fairly near the border of Rumania who was a miller. He figured out a way to get my dad over the border. He went to the border guard with a wagon and a horse, my dad, and a large sack of flour. He called the guard out and asked him to help my father carry the sack of flour across the border. When he got it across the border my dad just kept walking.

In several of the other countries he got by because he had a birth certificate written in Rumanian which looked very official, rolled up in a metal tube. When anyone would challenge him for his credentials he would take this certificate out. Of course, no one could read it outside of Rumania, so he kept going.

When my father, and later my uncle, got to the United States they opened one of the first and largest trunk manufacturing businesses in Cleveland. They made trunks for people all over the world, shipping them as far away as India, and they actually made the first automobile trunk. Instead of a car having a trunk that you could lift up, it had a trunk that you strapped on to the back. It was made to fit the back of a Pierce Arrow body.

They also designed the first trunk made exclusively for clothing. You see, traveling salesmen didn't have automobiles and when they would have to sell clothes in another community, they would have to ship the clothes by train. In baggage handling, a regular rectangular trunk could be stowed upside down, which means that the clothing samples would arrive all disheveled. So my father and uncle designed a trunk which could only be stood on its end. Now you see clothing trunks with a hump on the top. They designed that so that hangers would go into that hump. You couldn't stand it any other way than on its bottom and that was the start of the clothing trunk.

MORTIMER L. FEIGENBAUM, AGE 57
Washington, D.C.

LORRAINE ARDEN

: SUNY :

This is the story as I heard it. My great-great-grandmother Suny was very young and very, very, very beautiful — and, as a matter of fact, she was. I have photographs of her. And she had beautiful bright red hair, and she was always dressed in the height of the latest fashion of that year. And she had some — not a great many — beautiful things, china and silverware, that she was very proud of.

Well my great-great-grandfather arrived in Boston to take her west with a group of other people, to make this very long, rigorous journey. Some place in Iowa or Nebraska they ran into a band of Indians who wanted to buy her because she had such beautiful red hair. I can remember very clearly my father's aunt, who is my great-aunt, telling me this story over and over again, about how horrified she was by those Indians and how marvelous they thought she was with this big pompadour sort of pile of red curls that she had and her bright blue dress. They offered my great-great-grandfather forty ponies for her, and somehow he got out of this difficult situation politely without offending anybody, and she made it out to Denver. My aunt Catherine always used to finish the story by saying that forever after she was deathly, deathly afraid of Indians.

SUSAN DAVIS, AGE 24
Philadelphia, Pennsylvania

: BORDER BALLAD :

My grandfather was a teacher in Russia and consequently, he was quite distinguished — had a mustache, spoke High Russian, and didn't have a Jewish accent or anything like that. One day he went out to teach, and two Russian soldiers attempted to rape my grandmother, who was a redhead of Dutch extraction, and somebody went and called my grandfather. He came back and he practically beat the two Russian soldiers to death.

Now this was unheard of in Russia and immediately there was a warrant out for his arrest. About the same time, his brother-in-law had been called to service. Jews never wanted to go into the Russian army, so the two of them decided to leave the country.

When they reached the border there was a guard with a rifle there, and my grandfather — who appeared like a Russian —

gave all his baggage to my grand-uncle and told him, "Now look. I'm going to distract the guard, you sneak across the border."

So what happened was this. He's busy talking with the guard, and they're talking about the large number of Jews who tried to get across the border. The guard says that if he sees them, he shoots them. My granddad says that that's absolutely the right thing to do. And they go on with it. Somehow or other, the guard realizes something's happening, and sees uncle, and starts to raise his rifle. My grandfather grabbed it—"Please, please! You're here all the time, let me have the gun and let me...." The guard gave it to him, and he hit the guard over the head with his own gun, and that's how they crossed the border.

ROBERT FREED

Bethesda, Maryland

: THE LAST COVERED WAGON :

I had a relative who rode on the last covered wagon going west. She just died a year or so ago. Her father came from a very fancy family in England, who disinherited him because he had married an American woman. He became a Baptist preacher and a musician and had lots of children. His wife came down with tuberculosis and died, and he was told that he would have to go west to save the children, so they made and loaded a covered wagon, and in 1910 they rode west. They had a box with coals down below in which they would cook all their food, gently, as they went. By the way, they walked, they did not ride in their covered wagon.

At one point they were riding down in Kansas, and there was an awful snowstorm for three days and nights. The twelve-year-old walked barefoot with her ten-year-old sister for three days and nights, trying to get help for the rest of the family, and they lived to tell about it. They used to earn their money by playing music as they got into each town. There were about seven or eight sisters and brothers and the father; he would preach, and then afterwards they would all play music and take up a collection. And in that way they would earn their way to the next town. Eventually, they got to Oklahoma.

SUSAN MEEHAN, AGE 38

Washington, D.C.

: Crossing-over Melodrama :

My grandfather came to America in about 1906 or so. Apparently he came either on a freighter or in steerage on a passenger ship that came from Germany to New Orleans. There was a big storm at sea and he was washed overboard by one wave, but almost before he knew what was happening, another wave came and washed him back. That's what my grandmother says. I don't know if that actually happened or not.

FREDERICK L. KEPPLER
Washington, D.C.

: Tiny Feet :

There's just two stories I know about my great-great-grandmother, Nancy. She was Irish, and she came across during one of the potato famines. Apparently she cried so loud on the boat that the captain threatened to throw her overboard. The other story is that her feet were so tiny that she could do an Irish jig on a silver platter.

When I was about five or six I asked, "How did I get the name Nancy?" And this is what they told me. And that's all I know about her.

NANCY KILCZEWSKI, AGE 35
Herndon, Virginia

: One Last Goodbye :

My grandfather didn't tell stories, but my grandmother still does, and she tells them over and over so many times that you remember them. When she left Russia during the Russian Revolution, they had soldiers out after her and my grandfather. They had just gotten married, and most of his older brothers and sisters had been in this country for a while, so he wanted to come here.

They escaped one night with my grandfather's father. The way she explained it it's very hard to visualize, but they ran across the military lines, and they were shot at. And when they were at their destination, my grandmother decided that she didn't like the way she left. She wanted to go back to say goodbye to her family, because she knew she wouldn't be seeing them again, so she ran back through these military lines, and they shot at her again. She said her goodbyes. Then she came back through, and they got on the boat, the three of them, and came over.

VICKI PERLER, AGE 29
Gaithersburg, Maryland

JOAN BERNICK

: TWIST OF FATE I :

My great-grandfather, Moses Erlich, was apparently a very important man in Springfield, Massachusetts. The story was that Moses had actually come to Hartford and set out as a very young man, about fifteen, to go to Boston to make his fortune. The train goes from Hartford to Springfield to Boston. He was an orthodox Jew, so I assume he must have been wearing a black long coat and a black hat, with long paiss *on the side. At Springfield, a man got on the train dressed like him and sat down next to him. The train apparently had a twenty-minute stop or so, and [the man] said, "Where are you going?"*

He said, "I am Moses Erlich. I am going to Boston to seek my fortune."

"Well, why don't you seek your fortune in Springfield?"

He said, "What would I do in Springfield?"

"The Jewish community has sent me to the train, because we're trying to get thirteen Jews to settle in Springfield so we can have a minyan. *If you get off the train with me here, I'll get you a job."*

So he said, "Fine!" and he got off, and he said, "What's the job going to be?"

"You meet all the trains from Hartford to Boston, try to get 'em to come off and settle in Springfield."

LYNN CHAITOWITZ, AGE 39
Kensington, Maryland

: TWIST OF FATE II :

Probably the oldest story that the parents on my mother's side passed on comes from the time they were settling Louisiana before the Civil War. Our family history extends back into Tennessee in the 1750s. And the stories that are told are mainly about the migration that they made apparently from there into northern Louisiana, before the land was settled and cultivated. There's one story about my great-grandparents, or their grandparents who were in northern Louisiana, just passing through. But the winter had [started] and she was very pregnant, so they were forced to stop. Since the weather was getting pretty bad they had to look for shelter, and they found this old hunter's cabin. There was no hunter but there was firewood and they had some provisions so they stopped with the idea they would just stay there until the storm ended and move on, and hoped that whoever built it and maintained it wouldn't mind too much. As it turned out, the guy never returned so they simply stayed there and decided to claim the land and built their own house right there at the cabin site. That's how they got their start in northern Louisiana.

ANDREW GRIFFIN
Washington, D.C.

: TWIST OF FATE III :

One of my forebears came as an eighteen-year-old farmboy from Brunswick, which was under the rule at that time of the Prince of Hesse who was selling mercenaries to George the Third to fight [with] the British. This poor kid didn't know anything about the war and was drafted off the farm and sent over here to America, down in Pennsylvania. The story was told that once he stopped to light his pipe. You had to use a flint, and oftentimes it took a while to light it. So, by the time he got his pipe lit his troop was a half mile off and he was all alone out there in Pennsylvania. And it looked like home, so he just took off into the woods and got a job on a farm. After a while he saved up enough to buy his own farm and that's how part of me got here.

S. ZIMMERMAN, AGE 44
Springfield, Ohio

: BREAKFAST WITH THE INDIANS :

I wanted to tell a story about my family — my aunt and uncle and their ranch. He went to Wyoming after the Civil War and started a ranch, my uncle did, in the late 1860s or early 1870s. This was on a river called the Cheyenne, and this was an incident that happened there.

The Indians used to travel between the Black Hills and the Bighorn Mountains in Wyoming, so they went through my uncle's ranch as they went back and forth. On this occasion, the cowboys were all out, everyone was away from the ranch except for my aunt and her son. This was just in the morning after everyone had left to go to work, and the door opened and three Indians came in. They didn't say anything. And my aunt's story of this is very movielandish—she just motioned to the table for them to sit down and she cooked pancakes for them—a lot of pancakes—and she gave them coffee. And they thanked her, they nodded, and left then.

And sometime after that these same Indians came by and gave her a really lovely buckskin dress, really fantastic, it is just beautiful and it's still in the family, for remembering.

ALBERT HERMAN, AGE 47
Bethesda, Maryland

: O Lucky Man! :

There's a story on my father's side of the family about how the family got its name, which is Glickman. Evidently when my great-grandfather, or a relative of his who came over to the States maybe a few years earlier, was passing through Ellis Island sometime around 1904, he was asked by some official what his name was. He was standing in the line there and he didn't understand what was being asked; he didn't have any English at all, just probably spoke Russian and Yiddish. And he said something like, "I'm licht man," which means "lucky man." His name was written down as Glickman.

RALPH GLICKMAN, AGE 28
Silver Spring, Maryland

: Miller :

I'd like to tell the story of how my last name got to be what it is. When my great-grandfather came to this country as a draft dodger from Russia, his last name was twenty-eight letters long with no English vowels in it. The story of how to pronounce it died with him. When he got here on the boat, right around the turn of the century, there was this man about five up in the line who was an American. His name was Miller. The customs of-

*ficials asked him his name and he gave it. The customs man
knew how to spell it, so he wrote it down and passed him right
through. Most of these immigrants were going through a lot of
trouble because they didn't know how to speak English. So
when my great-grandfather got up there, he just said, "My
name is Miller." And they passed him right through. He wrote
back to the old country and told them that if any of them immigrated to this country, they should immediately change their
name to Miller so that they could get through.*

ROBERT MILLER

Charlotte, North Carolina

: ON THE JOB TRAINING I :

*My family tells a story about a distant cousin who had been a
rabbinical scholar in Europe. But you can't earn a living in
America being a rabbinical scholar, so he decided he would be
a tailor. He went to the first tailor's place, where they were
doing some manufacturing, and the manufacturer said to him,
"Well, where's your scissors?" He said, "I don't have any." He
said, "You can't be a tailor if you don't have a scissors." So he
said, "Well, what kind of scissors should I have?" And he told
him. So the next day he went out and bought that kind of scis-*

LOUISE TIRANOFF

sors, and he applied for another job. Well this time he brought the right kind of scissors. And the boss said, "Well, all right, cut this." And he said, "Well, how do you want me to do it?" So the first day he got the scissors, the second day the boss showed him how to cut it. But he said, "If you don't know that, you're not a tailor," and my cousin lost his job. Each day after he got a different job, until several months went by and he really had a job—and he was *a tailor.*

ELAINE GURALNICK, AGE 48
Baltimore, Maryland

: ON THE JOB TRAINING II :

My grandfather had been an apprentice shoemaker in Latvia. He sewed the upper part of the shoe to the soles and he decided that was the logical job for him to do after he got here. So he took a bag lunch and went out in search of work. The first place he went to was a walk-up where each flat was a different factory. He went to the first one and they said, "Have you any experience with electrical equipment?" And he said, "Sure, sure." He had never seen an electrical machine before. So he starts sewing with this thing and it goes wild. He ruins one shoe

*and he ruins two shoes and he ruins three and he stuffs them in
his lunch bag and gets out of there in a hurry. Then he goes
up to the second floor, another factory, and he pulls the trick
again. And then the third floor. Each time he goes out on the
street and dumps out his wasted shoes. By the time he got to the
fourth floor he was an expert, and he got the job. I like the story
because it says something about on the job training and about
having a little bit of gall in getting a job.*

BETTY-CHIA KARRO, AGE 35

Washington, D.C.

: On the Job Training III :

*During the Depression, grandfather saw a job advertised for
an elevator repairman. Really, they wanted two. So he and a
good friend from college whom he had studied engineering with
applied for the job. The man asked them if they knew anything
about elevators. "Oh, yes," they said, "we know all about elevators." "Okay, you're hired." So as soon as they were hired,
grandfather and his friend went up to the top, to the little house
on the top of the building, and locked the door, took the whole
thing apart and put the whole thing back together, and then
they knew all about elevators. They didn't know a thing before,
but they weren't going to tell him that. He's seventy-five now,
and he'll still tackle anything.*

MIDGE HEIMER

Germantown, Maryland

: Banana I :

*When he first came to America, my grandfather said he had
heard of bananas but he didn't quite know what they were. So
his cousins who had been here awhile — a grand total of about
three months — and who were wise to the ways of the world,
decided to pull a joke on him. They gave him a banana, and
speaking in Yiddish they used the word that has kind of two
meanings. It can either mean, "bend it" or "do you like it?"
And they set him up by asking him to bend it gently because he
didn't want to break it. And it snapped. Then he realized that
they were playing a joke on the green cousin from the old*

country. And he said, "Oh, this is a banana, everybody knows how you break them and you eat them." And then, he proceeded to eat it — skin and all — saying every last bit was delicious. Thinking back on it — every time my granddad saw bananas he'd crack up.

MARVIN SAKOLSKY, AGE 30
Riverdale, Maryland

: BANANA II :

My grandfather was an émigré from Latvia and he came over when he was a little older than thirteen. His first time out of that area was this trip. When he got to London, there was a layover between boats. He was stuck in the street and he bought this banana which he had never seen before and wanted to eat it. He ate the skin and threw the banana away — well, you eat a peach that way!

BETTY-CHIA KARRO, AGE 35
Washington, D.C.

: UNCLE SAM WANTS YOU :

My great-grandfather had come from Poland, or right near Poland, and he came to this country during the Spanish-American War. There was one of those Uncle Sam posters saying "We Want You" and he thought it meant him! "Why me?" he wondered. "What's so special about me? I just came to America." And he went and he joined the army!

DAVID NACHAMANOFF, AGE 10½
Arlington, Virginia

Americans love to tell stories of how an ancestor, a grandparent, or a parent lost the fortune which would otherwise have gone to them. Often our forebears owned an insignificant plot of land—which they lost through a quirk of circumstance—and which now sits smack in the middle of a downtown city block, spilling its revenues to everyone it seems, except the storyteller and his family. As one professional genealogist told us, whatever city our ancestors were from, their farms always seemed to have graced what was soon to become the biggest intersection of the busiest section of town. Our nineteenth-century forebears, writes folklorist Mody Boatright, often missed their chance for untold wealth by failing to find a lost mine or buried treasure.[1] Nowadays, we lose our fortunes in the stock market, real estate ventures, or entrepreneurial gambles.

According to folklorist Stanley Brandes, who first wrote about this category, these kinds of stories are told almost exclusively by whites, particularly those from working and lower middle class backgrounds. In Europe and Latin America, he suggests, success is often considered to hinge on luck, and local stories often tell of winning the lottery or receiving an unexpected gift.[2] Americans, on the other hand, are imbued with the Protestant ethic. Failure or success is viewed as a direct reflection of our personal virtues or flaws. This is a terrible burden, Brandes writes, "the knowledge that we will be measured by our degree of success, a success over which we are supposed to have virtual control but over which in actuality we do not."[3] Confronted with failure, a family misfortune story somehow consoles us. We can absolve ourselves by blaming our ancestors, by telling often humorous stories of how our forebears lost their wealth by letting themselves be victimized by relatives, by failing to capitalize on a rare opportunity, or by losing their legitimate inheritance.

: CADILLAC SQUARE :

My father's great-grandfather ran a station of the underground railroad in what is now Cadillac Square in downtown Detroit, Michigan. When the Civil War came they were trying to carry supplies down into the southern areas to northern troops, and at one point the whole wagon train was captured. This destroyed

LOST FORTUNES

·ALICE TAYLOR

my grandmother's father financially, and apparently they never recovered. They lost the farm in Cadillac Square, and so now we are poor Americans like everybody else and don't own Cadillac Square in Detroit.

GERTRUDE LEE AIKEN, AGE 37
Washington, D.C.

: AN EVEN SWAP :

My father's father left Farmington, Missouri, in 1893 heading for southwestern Oklahoma. At that time, land was being parceled out by lottery. He and his brother registered and eventually found some land in Indian territory and established a hog farm. There's an interesting story which is supposed to be true that when my grandfather owned the hog farm, a man who owned a hotel in a small, nearby town offered to trade him the hotel and four square blocks of downtown real estate for the hog farm—an even swap. Grandpa told him, "I can make a better living out of the hog farm. I know nothing about running a hotel. Besides that town will never amount to anything. I mean, who ever heard of a town named 'Tulsa'?"

DANIEL W. HUMPHREY, AGE 28
Holdenville, Oklahoma

: THE WAR OF THE WIVES :

The Cuttings were apparently very wealthy at one point. There's still a very prominent New York family called Cutting. That is one branch of it, very far removed. In order to justify the lack of money in my family, the story goes that my great-grandfather was married to a woman for twenty years, got itchy feet, divorced her, and then he decided he wanted to marry some more women. And, depending on who tells the story, it's six wives, seven wives, at one point it went up to twenty-four wives, that this gentleman had. On his death bed, he was in the process of divorcing one wife and marrying another one. His will had not yet been changed, and his divorce papers had not yet been filed, or maybe it was that the will had been changed, but the divorce papers had not been filed, but his last wife and his next wife fought over the money until it was all gone. Gobbled up in legal fees.

HEATHER CUTTING RAYL, AGE 24
Fall River, Massachusetts

: How About Vending Machines? :

My father and his friends were sitting around one night, and they came up with the idea to use vending machines for everything. They figured that the retail merchant of the future would be the vending machine. And for a long time they were thinking of things that could be sold in vending machines, like Coke and all. But they never got to do it, and now you know you see so many vending machines. They sell everything under the sun in them. He wishes he had done it.

JOSEPH DEMARIA, AGE 17
Lakewood, New Jersey

: The Stubborn New Englander :

My grandfather's grandfather was pretty stubborn, like your typical crusty New Englander. When the family came over from Ireland, some of them went to New England and some of them went to South America. And the part of the family that went down to South America apparently became quite wealthy. When the last relative in South America died, he left no heirs, and a lawyer from South America spent years trying to find someone who could inherit the property. Eventually, he came to my great-great-grandfather's farm in Chicopee and said, "You're the relative of so-and-so in South America, and you can inherit a lot of land. And I can set it up for you, but I spent a long time looking for you and I'm not going to tell you how to do it unless you give me half of it." At that point my great-great-grandfather said, "Half of it, you crook!" and got his gun and chased him off the farm and never inherited any of it. He'd rather have none of it than give half of it to that lawyer. He was just that stubborn.

GREGORY F. FARRELL, AGE 22
Rockville, Maryland

MARIAN PATTEN

: A BET ON DECATUR :

My grandmother was born in Germany, in Pomerania. It doesn't exist any longer. She came to this country at the age of three months. Her father was a soldier, of course; everyone in Prussia at that time was a soldier. Poor man, every time he got his little shoemaking business going, the kaiser would start another war and he'd have to pack up and off he'd go. So finally, after about the third war, he decided that was enough. He packed up mom and the kiddies and they came to this country and went out to the middle west and settled in Iowa. And at that time the railroad was driving west and the information was it was either going to go through Omaha or Decatur. He bet on Decatur. Right. He lost.

MARTHA L. SWARTWOUT
Wheaton, Maryland

: TUCKER AND FOX :

My father's uncle had a hotel right in the city called Tucker's Hotel. That was his name, Dan Tucker. He always played cards and one night he played with this guy named Fox—Fox by name and nature. He came down to the last thing he had left, which was the hotel. He said, "I'm on." And he signed it away. He lost the game. In the morning he nearly went crazy, but he was crazy for doing it. He lost everything. And to this very day it's called Fox's Hotel.

MARGARET TUCKER, AGE 35
Arlington, Virginia

: GREAT-UNCLE HORACE :

My great-uncle Horace died before I was born; he lived up in Maine where everybody worth legending about lived. He was very frugal and he was very attached to his mother, my great-grandmother. The story about him was that he was a drummer boy in the Civil War and he came back shell-shocked. He was never quite right in the head after that. After my great-grandmother died, he kept her house just the way it had been. He never threw anything away.

After he died they were clearing the house out and on the second floor they found hogshead after hogshead full of empty shredded wheat boxes which he had been unable to throw away. They started building a bonfire and threw them in and when they got about half way through they found money in some of them and realized that he hadn't trusted banks either! So they never knew what they had burned up.

Horace was a very queer coot. He used to repair watches for free, and it seems that he forgot to return them because there's a safe up in that house in Maine, full of neatly repaired watches. There are traces of him everywhere.

JOAN RADNER
Washington, D.C.

: MOUTHWASH :

About a year after my grandfather died I took a trip across the country and stopped in St. Louis to see my grandmother. It turned out that they had a lot of money tucked away here and there—money under the mattress, in different banks, fifties here and there. It all added up to close to one hundred thousand dollars.

When I stopped again on the way back, I went into the house and my grandmother says, "Oh Leslie, I have something for you, upstairs. I had thought about giving it to you on your way across country."

And here I was, old greedy me thinking that maybe she had found a hundred dollar bill under the mattress and was thinking of giving it to me. So I followed her upstairs, toward the bedroom when she all of a sudden makes a cut into the bathroom, and she opens the cabinet and pulls out these two huge bottles of mouthwash and she says, "Your grandfather was going to use these but he didn't get the chance."

LESLIE HALL, AGE 25
Washington, D.C.

: THE COMSTOCK LODE :

My great-grandfather was a great traveler. He'd go off for years for a time, and my great-grandmother would never see him. She'd just be suffering along trying to make do until one day he'd walk in and say, "I'm home!" "Yes, I see that," she'd say. But he went out west with two other men, and they bought a small claim. And they didn't have enough money to try it out. So they had to sell it for fifty dollars. The man who bought it tried it out, and it later became very famous. It was known as the Comstock Lode. And now it's a great symbol of remorse in our family.

SUZANNE MACKENZIE, AGE 17
Brewster, Massachusetts

: THE BIG ONE GOT AWAY :

Summitville was one of those turn-of-the-century boom towns where they found a couple of motherlodes and people became very wealthy. When the war came and the war effort demanded more attention, the town became a ghost town.

In 1955 my father, through some bit of business, acquired the lease [to mine for silver and copper]. My mother used to pan for gold in the water from our clothes after we'd go out there and roll around in the dirt. And she has three or four gold buttons from the gold that she got out of our clothes.

But anyway, what happened was, back in 1974—yeah it was seventy-four, after we had released our lease on this particular

CAROL DANDY

part of the property—a man was bulldozing the roads. This guy wasn't a miner, he was just a bulldozer operator and a rock hound. And he was just tooling along the road there and all of a sudden he saw this little glimmer in the distance. He took a look, and it was about three feet by three feet and weighed eight to nine hundred pounds—not what you would call a dainty gold nugget! It had been there for years and years and years and it took several harsh, harsh winters to work its way up to the top and then roll out on to the road.

And he got back into his bulldozer and went back down to see the geologist and the foreman [and] they said, "Why don't you show us what you've got." And the guy said, "Bring your truck." They all almost had a heart attack.

It turned out that that particular sample of rock is the largest sample of high grade gold ore that's been found in North America! It's worth over a million dollars—and the rock now stands in the Museum of Natural History in Denver.

And when (we) heard about the rock everybody in the family had to go see it. We took pictures of my nephew on the rock, and sent them out to everybody in the family.

Boy! Talk about the one that got away!

NANCY RIGG
Denver, Colorado

MARTHA SWARTWOUT

COURTSHIPS

American family storytellers wax poetic over tales of courtship, and are especially enamored of the seemingly serendipitous first meetings of husbands and wives. Romance inevitably transforms reality. Two persons meet as a result of some meaningless combination of circumstances. If they died the next day the encounter would have little significance, but if they take to each other and finally marry, a sort of "alchemy of mind" transforms the incident into a rendezvous with destiny and the deepest sort of romance.

The family storyteller typically reshapes reality in a number of ways when narrating a courtship. To begin, any dramatic or memorable episode in the early stages of dating is likely to be remembered as a first encounter, "the first time I met your dad." Further, selective remembering and after-the-fact interpretation often add an element of love at first sight, as in this romantic Civil War story:

My great-grandfather, Alan Taylor Sherman, came to Washington with the Union army during the Civil War. He stopped at my great-grandmother's house to get some water and she was the one who handed him the glass of water. He put his hand over hers as he took the glass of water, and then he got off the horse, and after that, they got married.[1]

Is it plausible that General Alan Taylor Sherman fell in love with a woman because she brought him a glass of water? Probably not. After the fact, the storyteller imbues his courtship with romance by postulating instant attraction. Marriage bonds seem to be strengthened by the memory of a romantic, passionate courtship, of love at first sight. By the same token succeeding generations, exaggerating the romance still more, can look back at their progenitors as having been linked by mysterious and powerful passions.

First encounters are also made to seem predestined in families. In one story, for instance, two persons who had the same initials, M. A. B., accidentally took each other's luggage when they arrived in this country. They met when clearing up the confusion and went on to get married. If they had not wed, the incident would not have been worth remembering. Instead, the chance encounter is imbued with meaning. In this sense, Americans think in reverse, revising the past on the basis of what happened later, replacing coincidence with destiny.

In "Fifty Ways to Meet Your Lover," part of his "Heirs" series in *The Washington Post*, Michael Kernan retells a courtship story he collected from a couple married five years. It combines two chance encounters, and illustrates this metamorphosis once again.

A college radical leader, he had written an angry manifesto that was circulated around the campus. One day after a rally, as he was walking away in his uniform of jeans, blue plastic windbreaker, and uncombed hair, this girl accosted him.

"Did you write that crap?" she demanded. For twenty minutes they wrangled about politics there on the path while people walked around them. Finally she snapped, "Man, you are a bad trip" and stormed off in her jeans, blue plastic windbreaker, and uncombed hair.

The next summer which he spent with his wealthy parents on Long Island, he was a guest at a flossy wedding. He was milling around, champagne glass in hand, in the big striped tent overlooking the Sound. Suddenly he saw a big picture hat, with a face under it that he knew from somewhere.

"You!" he said.

"You!" she said.[2]

A second coincidental meeting introduces a variation on the destiny theme. The aura of predestination is doubled. A man and a woman are taken with each other but lose touch. Years later, against all odds they are brought together for a second chance. This time they have no choice but to blame fate.

Storytellers effect a final transmutation in their courtship romances by adding or emphasizing details from fiction. When snatches of popular love stories are suggested in the family tales, they take on some of the aura of romantic fiction. The story about General Sherman proposing to a young lady who brought him a glass of water suggests *Gone With The Wind* and a host of other romantic tales.

Storytellers are also familiar with fairy tales, and on different occasions will use them to establish the tone, to supply details, or to structure their courtship story. One lady quoted earlier even began by saying, "It's almost like a fairy tale the way it happened" as she told of a handsome son who married

ALICE TEMPLE

JAY BURG

a scrubwoman tyrannized by a drunken father. "But it's very interesting," she said, "because it's sort of like Cinderella and the prince."[3]

One of the oldest and most widespread themes in folktales from around the world concerns a suitor who must pass a test to win a true love's hand in marriage. He may be forced to climb a mountain, slay a dragon, start a princess laughing; perhaps she must detect a pea beneath a mattress. A number of family tales also tell how a grandmother or a mother chose between her suitors by putting her lovers to the test. They illustrate once again how folk and fairy tales influence family tradition. Here, novelist Maria Katzenbach tells an interviewer about a favorite family courtship story:

One [story] I like best is how my grandmother chose between the two finalists of all the men who were courting her. She had them to dinner, one Monday night, the other Tuesday night. She had the same dinner served both nights; she played the same songs on the piano; she told the same jokes. After dinner she asked each beau out into the garden behind her house in Georgetown. "What beautiful cherry blossoms," she said to the first beau. He nodded, "Yes, they are beautiful." The next night she said the same thing to her other suitor. He leapt up on the fence and broke off a twig from the cherry tree and brought it to her. Then and there she agreed to marry him. Now, I can't be sure that a story like this isn't just a tall tale. It's been told so many times. But then a little imagination is required to bring the past back to us.[4]

In still another example, a grandmother was said to have chosen among her suitors by taking them for a carriage ride. When she got the horses galloping at top speed she would drop the reins. She married the man who did not jump from the cab in fright.[5]

The family storyteller, then, takes the iron rod of reality and bends it a number of ways in the courtship story. Any early dating episode is likely to be recalled as a first encounter, mixed emotions are transformed into love at first sight, coincidence is changed to destiny, and motifs, themes, and details from fiction romanticize reality. The result is a sort of charter for the family's life together, the family romance.

: The Test I :

My mother was dating my father and another man, and she couldn't decide which one to marry. And she had dates with both of them two days apart. For the first one they went for a walk in the park and he wore a sweatsuit, only he called it his "perspiration trousers." And she decided that he wasn't for her. So the great test was she took my father for a walk in the same park. And she said, "Let's run down the hill." And he took her hand and they ran down the hill together. And that's how she decided that was going to be the one.

NANCY KILCZEWSKI, AGE 35
Herndon, Virginia

: The Test II :

My grandmother tells this story. So that her sons would be able to tell if the prospective bride would be industrious and diligent, they took a long string and tied it into many knots very tightly, and then they would give this tightly-knotted string to the prospective bride. If she was very careful and diligent about untying it and didn't go into tantrums or anything like that, then she would be a good, industrious wife. If she had tantrums and was impatient and didn't finish it, then she wouldn't be good enough for her son.

: On the Balcony :

[During World War II] my mom was living in Thuringia, which is all the way east, up in the mountains [of Germany]. One summer's night at some very late hour she was walking with her girlfriend. Naturally the whole city was blacked out because of the attacks. Out of the darkness these two soldiers approached them. At first they were getting kind of scared because it was so black, and there was nobody around them. But these two young guys had lost their way and just wanted to know how to get back to the house where they were staying. And the two girls said, "OK, we know where that is, we'll walk you over."

So they walked them over to the house, and said, goodnight, and the two soldiers said, "Now we really can't let you go home by yourselves. We have to walk you back to where you live."

My father, I guess, liked my mother very much, and he said that she would hear from him and he said—he was a pilot—said that tomorrow morning she should stand out on her balcony and watch for him. She naturally said to herself, "What does he want, how can I see him, coming down in a plane?"

But, next morning she went out on her balcony, looked out, and she was brushing her hair—she had very long hair she told me—and suddenly out of the sky emerged two planes. They started circling around the city, like they always do before they start to climb. But then one of them stayed, I think, instead of circling around and banked its wings, yeah, and she knew that was my father, the young gentleman, and she waved.

Somehow my father, through all kinds of friends, found out where she lived, and started writing her, and on his next vacation from the front they were engaged. It was one of those quick war things; it took only a few hours. They got married in 1947.

They never had a honeymoon. The only luxury they had at the wedding was, my mother, somehow, found somebody who had a coach, a white coach—in that devastated city with hardly any houses standing, and nothing to eat, and nothing to wear except old clothes. No wedding dress, no flowers, nothing—and so that's what they had, they drove the horse-drawn carriage to the church. It was the only thing they had, it was something very romantic.

MARIAN BRAUNSHAUSEN, AGE 19
Washington, D.C.

: THE FERRIS WHEEL :

We have a story about a set of grandparents who got stuck on a ferris wheel at Coney Island way back when. It was their first date and they got stuck on the top of the wheel—that's pretty high up—and supposedly my grandfather proposed marriage to her. There was no way she could get out of it unless she jumped off or something.

: THE WALLET MAKER :

My grandfather was a wealthy wallet maker during the height of the Depression. In 1930 he advertised for a secretary, and since jobs were almost nonexistent, two hundred women lined

DONNA CHAPPELL

up outside his office for interviews. *Many of these women had held jobs before the Depression, and had all of the secretarial skills they needed. My grandmother was nineteen, just out of high school, and could barely type. She was about the seventy-fifth person he saw, and it was love at first sight. When she told him that she couldn't take shorthand, he said, "Don't worry, I'll buy you a dictaphone." He spent more on a dictaphone than her salary would have been for two months.*

Three weeks later they were married.

BARBARA LAUTMAN
Washington, D.C.

ANN HAWKINS

: DOWN TO THE WIRE :

There's some story about Arac, my great-great-grandfather. He had two wives. His first died as they often did in those days. He had been living alone for about seven years since she died, and he wanted to find himself a new wife. So he drove in a buckboard, a wagon, into Bedford, Indiana, the county seat. He went up to this widow's house that he knew, and he said, "I'm going into town to buy a few bales of wire, and when I come back, I want you to decide whether or not you'll marry me." She was stunned. And he went in and bought the wire, came back, and she had decided to marry him. That was their courtship.

PHILIP LINNEMEIER, AGE 23
Bloomington, Indiana

: ONLY YOU :

This is a love story. This is a gay love story. Kitty and I met in college and after we got together we started to go to this one gay bar in downtown Atlanta. They had a singer that used to come around and sing "Only You," the old 1950s song by the Platters. There weren't that many places to go, so we would keep going to the same bar and she would be there singing "Only You," and we adopted it as our song.

After we'd been together about a year I moved to Europe. We missed each other a lot so after about three months Kitty decided to come over and meet me, and we would go to Paris for Christmas. We fooled around like tourists for about a week and on Christmas day we woke up and didn't have anything to do. There was nobody on the streets, everybody was home doing their Christmas thing; we were just tourists. We were walking up and down the streets and finally came to an old kind of run down cafe. There wasn't anything to do but eat, so we went in and ordered omelets and sandwiches and everything else there was, and sat there and ate a lot. Then a group of teenage boys came in and they all sat down and started to get really rowdy. They put a couple of francs in the juke box and "Only You" came on right there in Paris.

: SURE OF HIMSELF :

My grandfather was a courier on the train, and he was sent up to Frederick with a message. While he was there he met a woman, and the next time he was sent up, he went to New York, went to Tiffany's, and had a diamond ring made, a cluster that I wear. Almost a year and a half later, he was sent up to Frederick again, and when he saw this woman, he went up to her and proposed to her, and she said, "Yes," so he opened a pocket and took out the ring. Later she said, "If I had known he was that sure of himself, I'd have never said, 'Yes.'"

MARGARET SAYLOR, AGE 69
Silver Spring, Maryland

: PEARL'S COURTSHIP :

My great-grandmother Rebecca had six daughters. Pearl was the most beautiful one: blonde hair, blue eyes, fair skin, and a beautiful figure. The rest of them got fat fairly early, but Pearl never did, and she was always very vain. Pearl went to work in a real estate firm, and one of the young fellows there was very attractive. She liked him a lot, but he was not Jewish, and the family was not very happy about this relationship. They went out together, taking one mother or the other with them. He knew they were traditional, and his parents were also. They tried to be as nice as they could about how the families felt, and they never really had any physical relationship. They had a platonic one. Finally, the family said, "Pearl is not getting any younger, and we must introduce her to a nice Jewish boy and get her married." So this was arranged, and she thought, well, she liked her friend John very much, even though he's not Jewish, but nothing would ever come of it. So she went ahead and entered into this marriage that was somewhat arranged by the family. And it turned out that this fellow was a drunk, and no one knew it. Not all Jewish boys are as nice as people think. Pearl couldn't put up with this, so she went ahead and had a nervous breakdown.

My great-grandmother Rebecca then called in the non-Jewish fellow, John, and said, "We don't know what to do with Pearl. For months and months, this is what she's been through." Well, he was very upset and said, "Of course I'll come and see if I can help." So he came to the hospital and gradually got her over the nervous breakdown. His visits and his attention were what brought her out of it.

Well, this marriage had never been consumated, so it was annulled, and my great-grandmother decided that part of Pearl's problem was that she was still a virgin. She was probably thrity-five or thirty-six by that time, so my great-grandmother, in her humanness, called John in and said, "You know how I always liked to travel. Well, I just decided I need to take about a six-week trip, and while I'm gone, I want you to take very good care of Pearl and help her in every way, because she has some needs that are not being met." He was obviously the only person she really loved, but she herself didn't realize how much she did. All the years he had never married another girl either so it was apparent they belonged together.

When my great-grandmother returned, John and Pearl had their physical relationship going strong, and they got married. And they had a very beautiful marriage with no children, because she was beyond the age where she could have children. And they were married thirty-two years, and she passed away this winter. This all came out after my great-aunt Pearl passed away last winter. My mother told me all these things that happened.

REBECCA COFMAN
Bethesda, Maryland

MITZI WERNICK

: TAKE CARE OF NINA :

My aunt Nina—we called her Aunt Nina, even though she was my father's second cousin—used to speak about her first husband. There's a picture over the desk, and it was her husband and her first husband standing in front of a Model A Ford. She said, "That was my first husband Jack, and there's Louis." So I asked my mother, "Why does Aunt Nina talk about her first husband Jack in front of Uncle Louis like that?"

And she said, "Well, this is how they got together." Uncle Louis and Jack were best of friends, and they were in a bar one night in Mississippi, and one of the hands came in and shot Jack dead. And while he was dying, he said, "Louis, take care of Nina!" So he married her.

LESLIE BARDEN, AGE 32
Bethesda, Maryland

JAY BURG

: ONE POINT TELLS YOU :

My mom's a practicing pharmacist, and my dad's a professor in pharmacy. They met in pharmacy school and got married right after school. When they both took the state board exam, he got a ninety-nine, and she got a ninety-eight out of a hundred, which are damn good scores. Whenever mother would come home from one of the drugstores saying, "Well, I gave him 500 milligrams of tetracycline," dad would jump on her saying, "No, it should have been 250 mils," and they'd argue back and forth. He'd say, "One point tells you that it's this way." And she'd whine.

About ten years ago, this old prof of theirs came down, a guy named Straley. At dinner he said, "Well, how long have you guys been married?" "Twenty-five years." And he says, "Well, I think we can tell you. You know we graded your exam up there, and, well, we knew you two were getting married, and we knew we didn't want any trouble. And to tell you the truth, Elizabeth here got the ninety-nine, and you got the ninety-eight." My mother had taken fifteen years of crap from my father. She was flabbergasted, and soon came a chance for her to bellow at the top of her lungs, "One point tells you."

RICHARD MILLER, AGE 32
Washington, D.C.

: Dumb City Kid :

My mother grew up in Memphis, and my father says that the way she managed to trap him was she told him that her father owned a plantation. And when he asked what kind of plantation it was, she said, "Well, it's a sardine plantation." And he was such a dumb city kid that he believed her!

ELINOR ABRAMSON
Washington, D.C.

: Late to the Wedding :

When they got married, my dad, being a great mountain climber, was late to the wedding because he couldn't get off Mount Rainier. Mount Rainier's about fourteen thousand feet tall, with a nice steamboat prow glacier which had come apart, and he had no way to get across the son of a gun. He marched up a thousand feet and sat down on his big mountaineering pants and just started sliding on this ice. He must have been going about forty miles an hour. He went, "Wheoo," and sailed right over this ten-foot crevasse. Finally he got off the mountain, ran to his wedding, and got married.

RICHARD MILLER, AGE 32
Washington, D.C.

SUSAN DAWSON

: APHRODITE :

We didn't have a car when I was little, but my husband courted me in an automobile and that automobile was called Aphrodite. Aphrodite was fantastic. I remember every inch of it. It was a green Rambler, and it had a real personality — a very dynamic car, not static at all. When it was coming to pick me up, its blinkers went on and off and they were placed in such a way that it looked like it was smiling through the grill work.

That car wasn't sold; we would have never parted with it willingly. One day its brakes died when my husband was in it and it crashed into a pole because he averted hitting a group of school children. It wrapped itself around the pole and he got a fine of twenty dollars for destroying public property. He thought that it would be best to just leave the car, walk away from it, and never go back. That's what he did. It was beyond its time at that point and it had obviously let us down.

The second automobile we got was called Eusephelus. Things were breaking down already and it was not so exciting. The third one was called Demon. We skipped Cupid somewhere along the way. Demon is the contemporary, it's the car we've got now. But Aphrodite was the mythic automobile.

SUSANNE ROSCHWALB
Pittsburgh, Pennsylvania

Families enjoy gossiping about their relatives and many tell full-blown stories about squabbles and feuds. Recent family arguments and divorces, of course, are usually talked about in hushed tones, not with the dramatic flair reserved for stories. Only with time can the irony, the pathos, even the humor begin to emerge from the bitterness. As one woman said about her mother's broken marriage, "It's just looking back on something that's very, very far away. It just takes time, and then it's just history, and you can live with it and work with it."[1]

By the time families are telling stories about the young married lives of their grandparents and great-grandparents, much of the pain has dissipated. Once tragic stories like this odd tale sound humorous to later generations:

Notorious? Yes! This is a little strange, but one of my great-grandfathers lived in the bathroom. In Germany, the bathroom was large—it was more than just a bathroom. And he couldn't stand his wife. So he moved into the bathroom. He brought his bed in there and he lived there.[2]

Of course people also fight with relatives other than their spouses, and in the most surprising ways. Bill Howard told how his cousin Mr. Rick woke up early each morning to visit his sister's house where he would build a fire, put on water for hominy, and then wake her up. Once Mr. Rick was returning from his sister's, when he met Bill and breathed a long sigh. "I do my part," he said, "and speak to my sister on Monday, Wednesday, and Friday, but she won't do her part and speak to me on Tuesday and Thursday."[3]

Dividing up inheritances, as many of us know, often leads to bickering if not bitter disputes and, years later, to tales. In one, the death of a flamboyant, moderately wealthy aunt precipitated an argument among four nieces over who should inherit her mink coat. One claimed it fit her perfectly, another that she had often borrowed it in years past, one that she was most in need, and still another that it had once been promised her in conversation!

Some of the most elaborate family feud stories we collected are set in the Appalachian Mountains. In a distinctive storytelling style, they unfold pitched battles between two branches of a large extended family. Feuding families of this

FAMILY FEUDS

kind are part of our literature and lore. The Hatfields and McCoys are celebrated in song, and in the course of his adventures, Huckleberry Finn suddenly finds himself caught in the crossfire between clans of Shepherdsons and Grangerfords. He has never heard of such feuds before, and his friend Buck explains it to him this way:

. . . a feud is this way: A man has a quarrel with another man, and kills him; then that other man's brother kills him; *then the other brothers, on both sides, goes for one another; then the cousins* chip in—*and by and by everybody's killed off, and there ain't no more feud. But it's kind of slow, and takes a long time.*[4]

Our first story, "Die with It in You, Frankie," is a particularly striking example of a feud tale. It recounts an episode memorialized in the folksong "Frankie and Johnny," and is well known in the region. The narrative comes from a cultural setting where large, extended families comprise a community, and where the most dramatic episodes in the history of the area are likely to come down in the traditions of various branches of the family.

: "DIE WITH IT IN YOU, FRANKIE" :

Well, my great-great grandfather was a first cousin to Charlie Silvers that got his head cut off. Charlie's wife, Frankie, cut his head off, cut his body up, and burned it all night. Hid part of his remains in a log—his lights, the guts, the parts that won't burn, under a rock. He was buried in a little family cemetery up on the ridge above where she killed him, what was left of him, what they could find. And she was the first woman ever hanged in North Carolina, or legally anyway. My mother was raised just about a half a mile from where that happened. Oh Lordy, I've heard that all my life. Well, I tell you, it's even been put in books.

    I tell it to you like my uncle At told me because he told it different than anybody else. He said it wasn't Frankie that started it, it was her daddy. I don't know what they had against Charlie, but he was a trapper. This was way back before the Civil War, a long time ago. It was nearly Christmas and

Charlie had been out cutting wood all that day to burn all during Christmas. There was a big snow on the ground. They lived in a little shantylike cabin that just had two rooms, a kitchen-livingroom where the fireplace was, and a back bedroom. And they had a daughter—she couldn't have been more than a year old; she was still crawling.

So anyway, my great-great-uncle At told me that her daddy was down to supper that night and Charlie had got through cutting that tree down. He had piled up the wood and come in and eaten supper. And they said that when Charlie got in, he said, "I'm beat, I think I'll lay down." And Frankie said, "Well, I fixed a pallet for you by the fireplace. I thought you might want to take a nap before you got ready to go to bed." [laughs] I don't know why he wanted to take a nap before he got ready to go to bed to sleep again. But anyway, he got the baby and laid down there in front of the fireplace and went to sleep. And when he got to sleep, my great-uncle said that her daddy said, "Now's your chance, Frankie."

And they said she went and laid the baby in the back room. Then she took the ax that Charlie had brought in and come back in there. Charlie was laying on his back, and they said everytime she'd come back to take a swing at him, he would smile at her in his sleep. And she swung about three times and her arm about give out. "Well," she said, "I just can't do it. I can't kill him like this." And her pap said, "If you don't kill him, I'll kill you and him both." So I reckon she figured she better go ahead. And they said that finally she come down and give one hit in the head. They claim that he jumped up and screamed, "God bless the child." And she run back there in the bedroom and jumped under the covers and hid. She was so scared. Well, according to my uncle At, when she went in there her daddy took the ax and he come back and cut Charlie's head square off. They said he hit him so hard that his head bounced against the rafters of the cabin.

And they said about that time the baby got up and was crawling, and they said it crawled in its own dad's blood. And they said it got over there to the table where it tried to stand itself up with its hands, and it left blood prints on the table. They said you couldn't wash them off or nothing. You couldn't get them off.

So Uncle At said Frankie's daddy cut him up and done all that dirty work hisself. And he used all that wood Charlie had

DOROTHY JACKSON

cut up to last through Christmas and burned his body all night long. And they said he took Charlie's head and put it under a stump, an old hollow stump, and that he put on his boots to carry the rest of him and put it under a rock. I've seen that rock a hundred times. And then he went down to the river, the Toe River that runs by the foot of that holler, about half a mile down the road there. And he walked in the snow down there and then backtracked up. And of course it was put out that Frankie claimed that Charlie had went across the river for his Christmas liquor and hadn't come back.

It got to be two or three days, and everybody was wondering what had happened to him. They said this old man, I forget his name—I think they called him Dickie Collins—lived over cross the mountain somewhere and had been a' noticing Charlie's dog. It had always been with Charlie, and he said the dog would go up to the house and holler and just bark and go on. And Dickie just got suspicious, so one day when Frankie was out he went down there to the house and got to looking around. And he found some bloody chips and things around the fireplace, and he lifted up the floor boards and found blood down under there. So word got out that he had been killed. I mean that was evidence enough to know.

And they always told something about how his daddy had went over to Tennessee where they had this New Guinea slave that had what they called a conjure ball, or something. You'd ask it a question and it would swing. And however it was that they was asking it, they said it would swing right toward the house. When they come back they arrested Frankie. I reckon they got her to confess to killing him.

At that time the county seat was in Morgan, North Carolina, almost fifty miles away on the east side of the Blue Ridge Mountains. You had to go plum over there to the courthouse. They took her over there where they had her trial and they found her guilty and sentenced her to be hung.

I don't know if she bribed the jailer or who it was, but anyway, her family slipped her out and was trying to get back over the mountains. They had her hair cut off short like a man's and she was wearing a big old hat and walking alongside a hay-wagon. Her uncle was up in the haywagon driving. The sheriff comes up and says, "Where are you going, Frankie?" And she turned around and tried to put on a man's voice and said, "Thank you, sir, but my name is Tom." And they said her uncle turned around and said, "Yes sir her *name is Tom." And so they knew right then who it was and took her back in to jail.*

Before they hung her she was supposed to have sung this song, an old ballad that they sing back up there now. They just call it "Frankie Silvers' Ballad." I don't know whether she did sing it or not. They claim up there that that's how the Frankie and Johnny story got started. Course the Frankie and Johnny song ain't nothing like the song that she sung. But I reckon it just rolled over.

According to the best I ever heard, when they were taking her body back across the mountains to bury her—you know, they didn't have no embalming in them days—that she just got to stinking so bad that finally they had to bury her on the way, somewhere close to where Lake James is now. And they got her husband Charlie's remains and buried him in the graveyard up on the hill with the Silvers family.

People never could figure out why she done it, unless it was jealousy. In the song there's a rhyme that says "the jealous thought that first gave strife." They don't know why she was jealous. One of [Charlie's] brothers who lived to be way up in his nineties told years and years later that there wasn't never nothing bad come out on him. And in communities like that nothing happened that wasn't found out and told, you know. My grandmammy's uncle was the only one that I ever heard say that her daddy was there eating supper with them that evening, and that he done it. He's way up in his eighties, or close to eighty anyway now, and its not been a year ago since he told me that.

But they did always say that before she hung she was about to tell something and her mother or her daddy either one hollered out, "Die with it in you, Frankie." They say she just didn't say anything.

Frankie's daughter, the little baby, I think her mother kept it for a while, but most of them moved off. But her girl married somebody from Madison County, I think. And then her daughter, Frankie's granddaughter, married my grandmother's uncle. Anyway that's about all I know about it.

ROBERT L. MCMILLAN, AGE 24
Lenoir, North Carolina

: DICEY'S MAN :

My family is from Scotch-Irish descent. They settled in South Carolina, in the mountains, and they were tenant farmers on southern plantations. James Horne had eleven children, ten daughters. The oldest one was Dicey, and the son was Ananias. They were tenant farmers on the Thorne plantation. And another tenant farmer was Peter Gosnell, who married Dicey.

One night they were having a corn husking party at Peter Gosnell and Dicey's house. They were drinking corn liquor and got too drunk, and Peter Gosnell slammed his fist down on the table to punctuate a point he was making, and he broke a plate. James Horne, being the father of the clan, reprimanded him for this, and Peter got very insulted and said, "I'll do whatever I want in my own house!" They got into a fight and were rolling around on the floor, but the family separated them, and everything seemed all right.

But that night when James Horne was walking home through the woods, Peter sneaked out and stabbed him eleven times and killed him. It started a family feud between Dicey and the rest of the family. They said, "That man's bad. You have to leave him. He killed your father." And she said, no, she's going to stick by her man.

Ananias and Rebecca Horne settled down in North Carolina, right across the line. They had nothing to do with Dicey and her family anymore. One of the sons of Ananias and Rebecca Horne was named Rome Horne, and he made journeys. He walked up into the mountains and finally located

Dicey's family. Dicey was about to turn one hundred — this was about in 1913 — and he came back and tried to get Ananias and his descendants interested in going up into the mountains for Dicey's hundredth birthday party. And no one was interested in going. So Rome and his family went off in a horse-drawn wagon, and they drove past Ananias' home. As they drove past, they saw that Ananias was sitting out on the porch, chewing tobacco. My father was a little boy about ten years old then, and Rome said to my father, "Jump out of the wagon and go see if grandfather won't change his mind." My father ran up to the porch and asked Ananias, and Ananias said, "Son, I ain't seen Dicey in fifty years, and I ain't about to see her now." The whole family just split off.

AMY LOUISE HORNE, AGE 22
McLean, Virginia

: THE HOWARDS AND THE BAKERS :

I'm from Clay County, eastern Kentucky. I've been in D.C. for three years, but before that I lived in Kentucky all my life. There were two families in Clay County that held more power, more land than anyone else, the Bakers and the Howards. The land is really poor down there, very hilly. The Bakers had a lot of bottom land and were still trying to make a go of it by farming. And the Howards — this is my family — decided that timber was better, and they were getting quite wealthy. It was also pretty much a political dichotomy: the Howards were Republican and the Bakers were Democrats. The Howards were getting more and more political offices, because they had more financial control of the county. And the Bakers got teed off about this.

I guess the feud supposedly started about 1869. The incident that was handed down to me was that Tom Baker, the eldest son of the Baker clan, decided that he'd fix those Howards. He'd put a dent in their pocket and bulge his out a bit by going down to Crane Creek, which straddled both their farms, and taking their log rafts. He was going to sell them in Manchester, rather than in Baileyville, where everyone would know they were Howard logs because of the type of poplar they were.

So he went down to the creek where they had all their rafts tied up waiting for the water to rise a little more. He cut the ropes and jumped onto the back of one and went down the river leading all these rafts, just as pretty as you please. Well, it was about dusk and my grandfather Israel was on the hill, and he saw Tom Baker doing this. And he ran down the hill and jumped on the log raft right behind him and said, "Tom Baker, draw your pistol, because I aim for one of us to drop dead in this river tonight." And Tom Baker said, "Now Israel, a man can't shoot on the water. Let us get up onto the land." So my grandpa, being a fair man and not sure that Tom Baker was, told Tom to jump onto the bank first, which he did. And they went out, paced their ten steps, and aimed their irons at each other. Grandfather shot once, didn't hit, shot again, didn't hit, shot again, and didn't hit. It wasn't that the men were such bad shots; it was just that their artillery was so bad. All this time Tom Baker hadn't got a shot out once, and so he hollered out about that point. "Israel, my gun is jammed. My damn gun is jammed." My grandfather walked over and looked at the gun, and neither one of them could make it work right. So he supposedly told Tom Baker, says, "Now, Tom, I've given you one chance for a fair fight, but I cannot grant that either me or the Lord will grant you the same chance tomorrow night."

This started the whole hundred year history of shooting at each other, which ended up with the state militia coming in at one point. All the other families would take up allegiances with one side or the other. And the law, of course, or what stood for the law, was bought off appropriately. You see the Bakers—I guess the Howards did this too, but they never told me what the Howards did—the Bakers would come up at night and they'd get their shotguns and they'd take pot shots at the windows. And then by the time the Howards could get up and get their guns loaded and get to the windows, the Bakers had gone. They just did this to hassle them.

Well, one night they did this and they shot my great-grandfather, Ballard, the head of the Howard clan. And from that wound, Ballard ended up dying. So they charged George Baker, the head of the Baker clan with the death of Ballard Howard, the head of the Howard clan. And the state militia came in and arrested him and took him to jail. He was in jail and they had the state militia all around the exercise yard, but when he went out for his exercise period, all of a sudden from a second story window across the street there was a shot and he was shot clear through the heart.

So the militia and all the townspeople ran up to the second story window, and they saw a Colt pistol and a Stetson hat. And they hollered out, "Whose hat is this?" And my grandfather Israel calmly walked out of the crowd and said, "My hat, gentlemen," and walked out. And they wouldn't bother him because the town people would have gone crazy: as the oldest son, he had the right to avenge his father's death. My uncle Snowdy was a little boy, and he was there then. He won't admit that his father actually killed anyone, but everyone else in the family swears that that's true.

I guess this feud was one of the biggest ones in the area. The Bakers eventually went up to Round County, about a hundred miles north, and fought with the Underwoods. Now supposedly there aren't any Bakers in the county. I don't know anyone by that name. We, by trial and error or whatever, won the battle. It's such a violent history to inherit and yet the whole time that you're told it you get feelings of pride and identity without identifying the violence with yourself. I don't know how you filter that out. I just know you do.

BEVERLY LEE HOWARD, AGE 24
Washington, D.C.

SANDRA GROSS

: A Turn of Fortune :

When my great-grandmother died, I guess it was in the mid–1800s. They were really wealthy, and they had a huge farm and a lot of slaves. You really measured your wealth by the slaves, so in the will they divided the slaves between three of the children and gave one child the land, because land was worth nothing compared to slaves. Nothing at all. At the end of the Civil War, the ones who got the slaves had nothing, and the guy with the land was really getting big. So they all came to him and expected him to share, and they just thought he stank because he wouldn't. He said, "If it had come out the other way around, you would not have shared your slaves with me."

One brother moved in on the boundary of his farmland, so that they had farms side by side, but they didn't talk to each other for their entire lives. One died, and they still hadn't talked to each other. That feud, conflict, has still kept two sides of the family apart. They just never see each other.

MARY LEE GEARY, AGE 17
Arlington, Virginia

: EXPENSES :

This story is about my father's grandparents. It was about the turn of the century right after a depression when they had all that inflation at the time. My great-grandmother was complaining because she felt she didn't have enough money to run the house. My great-grandfather took care of all the rest of the bills and everything, and apparently gave her a small sum for the week. So he said to her, "You make up a list and we'll go over the list at the end of the week, and then we'll see if you need more money." My great-grandmother apparently was a women's libber from way back and she said, "I make up a list nothing. You make up a list, too, on every penny you spend and we'll go over it at the end of the week." So my great-grandmother made up this extensive list where she put down everything, like two cents for candy for little Arthur, who was my grandfather, everything. Every single penny she spent was down there in this big list, three or four pages. So my great-grandfather comes home Friday night and says, "Okay, let's go over the list now." So they sit down and go over this whole list of things and he goes, "Uh hum, uh hum, this looks very reasonable." And she says, "Okay, now let's see your list." So he takes it out and there was one thing written on the piece of paper—"miscellaneous."

And that's a true story.

: HOW GRANDPA ALLEN DIED :

My great-grandpa Allen was a railroad man for years and years and years, maybe sixty years or so, and he knew the railroad schedules by heart. He kept a big stopwatch and he knew when the railroad trains would pass the house; the railroad track was right near the house where they lived. And he had a very unhappy marriage; he saw himself as henpecked. Through the years the tension rose and rose and rose in the marriage until one night Grandpa Allen took out his stopwatch and checked it, and he said goodnight to Grandma Allen just like he always did every night. And he walked out the door, went out to the railroad track, and he put his head on the railroad track. The train severed his head from his body. And that's how Grandpa Allen died.

PHIL HOOSE, AGE 27
Speedway, Indiana

Supernatural occurrences comprise the subject matter for many family tales. One story which we collected in different versions concerns a gambling grandfather with a nagging wife who pleaded with him to change his evil ways. Her cajoling had no effect on him until the occasion when he sat down and played poker with a distinguished gentleman who won all of the money. When the mysterious gambler stood up he had pig's hooves, and he disappeared in a puff of smoke. The grandfather cried, "The devil!" And his gambling days were through.[1] This motif is found in many parts of the world and in the United States.

Among the most common supernatural stories are those which tell of how a clock stops, a mirror cracks, or a favorite animal dies at the moment of a relative's death. Others are told about occurrences that seemed supernatural at first, but that later investigation revealed as quite ordinary, as in the final story in this section, "The Ghost in the Window." This tale is told as a children's story; others in this section are told almost tongue-in-cheek; and still others are told seriously, suggesting the different attitudes Americans take towards these supernatural occurrences.

SUPERNATURAL HAPPENINGS

: JOHN SIMMS :

My mother collected little toy boats or model boats I guess you'd call them. There was a little boy who helped her collect them named John Simms. Right after high school John was killed in a car accident. He was buried and she went to his funeral and it was over. In the course of the next twenty-five years he was forgotten.

She's an artist, and one night about six years ago she was working at her desk, and she just got the strangest feeling that if she looked up into the window John Simms would be standing there, after all these years. It made her so nervous—and my mother's not the nervous type—that she shut the blinds. Then she could hear him whistling—there was a little whistle that boys have when they call each other at night. She kept hearing the whistle over and over in the background. Finally she couldn't think, her hands were shaking and she had to go to bed. She went to bed and read a little bit, put her book down, and turned out the light and then she dreamed, very vividly, that the phone rang. She turned on the light, moved the book,

JOANNE MORELAND

she picked up the phone and the voice at the other end answered and said, "Hello Nancy, this is John Simms." She put the phone down, she woke up, and the feeling was gone, she wasn't scared.

John's been in the house ever since. The place he likes to stand is in her room over a heating grate, right next to the case with the little boats in it. It's the funniest thing — there can be heat roaring out of the grate and you can feel it, yet it's cold. It's like a wall, warm here and cold up there. It's the strangest thing in the world and we can't get anyone to explain it, except that we've got a ghost standing in the corner. Sometimes he rides in the car with us. He's very nice to have around, particularly if you're walking up from the garage alone at night — it's comforting.

ELLEN WILDS, AGE 23

: THE TABLE CRACKED :

I call my mother's whole family psychic. I don't know what you'd call them. When they die they leave a message to tell somebody they're leaving and goodbye. My aunt had this pretty, really pretty glass thing over the table. They were cleaning the dishes, and they heard a crack in the room. The whole table had just cracked in the middle. Then they received a telegram the next day saying that an uncle had died.

I don't know if you'd call them psychic. I just think that we love each other too much, so we have to come back and say, "Goodbye." That's my mother's family.

EDDITA OSBORNE, AGE 14
Takoma Park, Maryland

: THE SILENT COMPANION :

My father has a lot of Maine hunting stories, everyone in this area has Maine hunting stories. This is his sole ghost story. It was late in November, very cold, snowy, blustery. He was staying in a camp, and he went out north along this road. He had been walking along for about a quarter of a mile when suddenly he looked to his right and there was someone walking beside him, a very strange-looking fellow. He had a long black coat that came down to about here, mid-calf, and a leather hat, and he was carrying a long, long rifle about four feet long. And the man never said a word. My father said, "Catch anything?" And the man never said anything. So he tried again, maybe this guy is deaf. Nothing. So he started to get a little nervous, because he's out in the middle of nowhere and this man may be a lunatic or something. And so he turns to say something a third time, and the man is not there. He looks behind him, and there are his tracks in the snow and beside them, nothing. So he went back to his cabin tout de suite, *and he took a long sit in front of the fire before he decided to go back out again.*

SUZANNE MACKENZIE, AGE 17
Brewster, Massachusetts

: A GHOST IN THE FAMILY :

We've got a ghost standing in the corner. Mother and I just know he's there; my younger brother and sister don't. Sometimes we've had some funny things happen. Things will disappear and reappear in a room, or you're eating a bowl of soup, and you put the spoon down, and you reach for it, and it's not there; you look for it, and you know it couldn't have gone anywhere, and you look at it again, and suddenly it's there, and you know you didn't overlook it.

We've also got my great-grandmother. She's been dead for twenty-one years, and no one's had the heart to tell her. It's a hard thing. We've had people see her. I've had friends stay over and sleep in my mother's room while she's out of town, and they've woken up and seen my great-grandmother sitting next to the bed, and most of them have promptly gotten up and slept in the living room.

ELLEN WILDS, AGE 23
Arlington, Virginia

: THE GHOST IN THE WINDOW :

This actually happened to my mother, and it was in Good Thunder, Minnesota. My mother, Clara, was about twelve years old and her sister Alma about eleven. They lived on a rather isolated farm. One evening in the dead of winter their parents had to go somewhere and left the two girls in the farmhouse. Now they washed the supper dishes, and they decided that before they went to bed they would play a game of blindman's bluff. They went into the parlor and pushed the chairs back against the wall so there would be room in the center. And they had just sat down to take their shoes off so they could move quietly when they heard the sound of footsteps squeaking in the very cold snow. And so they decided not to take off their shoes since they expected to open the door. And they heard the footsteps going squeak, squeak, squeak, squeak, squeak. And someone fumbles at the doorknob but no one knocks. And they hear the footsteps going away.

Then they heard the footsteps going squeak, squeak, squeak towards the back door. They thought it was a neighbor because people in the country rarely use the front door. So they waited again for the knock, but no one knocked. Just a shuffling around the door, and then squeak, squeak, squeak towards the window of the parlor where they were.

This really frightened them, and suddenly in the window appeared two glowing balls of fire and between them a white star. And from below the fiery circles came two columns of smoke that came in silent puffs. And it all moved back and forth and up and down at the window. The girls were frightened, and it moved back and forth and up and down, and then squeak, squeak, squeak, it went away. They were terrified. They couldn't move. They sat petrified until their folks came home. But even their parents had no explanation.

The next morning they were helping their mother get breakfast when their father came in from doing the chores. He said, "Girls, I know what your ghost was last night. Our old cow Star got out of the barn." (Star was a completely black cow with a star between her eyes.) "I followed her tracks from the front door to the back and to the window. She was attracted by the light, and the reflection of the lamp in the window made her eyes glow and the star show up. And the column of vapor was her breath."

That's the story as told me by my mother. I've told it to kids so many times. It's a true ghost story.

ARTHUR MAAS, AGE 58
Greenbelt, Maryland

OTHER
STORIES

As we listened to thousands of American family stories, the similarities and shared themes were striking, but some tales were difficult to categorize. The stories in this final section remind us that although family members share many life experiences with other Americans, some of their tales are particular to a specific ethnic group or region; others are simply unique to an individual family. Our categories are open-ended; there may also be varieties of family stories which are not represented in our collection or which we have not yet discerned.

: LIFE IN THE BRONX :

I grew up in the east Bronx, a lovely section that's been destroyed now, around Crotona Park. The park was the center of the world basically. It was divided up in a curious way. There's a lake in the center called Indian Lake which was always full of rowboats in the summer and ice skaters in the winter. And this was where the anarchists argued. Different political groups argued in different places. If you wanted to argue or agree, you'd know where to go. I'd go with my father. There were anarchists, there were communists, there were miscellaneous socialists, there were Zionists. And if you weren't interested in politics, you might be interested in religion. There were a whole series of synagogues there. And if you weren't interested in either one, then you were probably interested in making money. Those were the basic distinctions.

I'll tell you a story that gives the flavor of the thing. I got a goldfish when I was around eight years old, and my father took me to buy a goldfish bowl. The Sino-Japanese war had started and the five and dime was being picketed because the detente with the Communists and China had just broken up; in the Bronx that meant you picketed the five and dime. We started into the store to get the goldfish bowl but meanwhile the goldfish were sitting in a cardboard container on the sink. And someone stopped my father and said, "Comrade, why are you crossing our picket line? Do you want to support the fascism of Japan?" And my father very carefully said, "Comrade, what am I to do? Do you want to be responsible for the death of a goldfish? Where else can I get a goldfish bowl?" He said, "Pass, Comrade."

: RIVER RIDE :

This is a story about the Johnstown flood in 1889. This story about my uncle Gomer has been handed down for many years. During the night the water rose and he went up on the roof of the house. There was also a board on the roof of the house and the waters were rising some more and a pig got on one end of the board and Uncle Gomer was on the other. And as the waters rose, the house was lifted off its foundation, and Uncle Gomer and the pig see-sawed down the river.

BECKY MAYER
Johnstown, Pennsylvania

: WAR OF THE WORLDS I :

My mother's family settled in New Jersey, in a place called Matawan. In 1938, you recall that Orson Welles had his "War of the Worlds" broadcast. They had just built their first crystal set back then and everyone was excited because they had just picked up Pittsburgh, Pennsylvania, WKDA. Well, the following day came this "War of the Worlds" broadcast from CBS in New York City. So they listened to that and they were getting terribly upset. It turned out that on that day there

MIDGE HEIMER

*was a terrible dust storm in western New Jersey. As this broad-
cast was going on, they were looking out the windows and seeing
these big clouds of dust. And they thought, my God, this must be
the worst invasion in history. They didn't really believe the
radio, but when they saw that dust coming. . . .*

*So they packed up the old Packard and decided to head down
to Barnegat Bay where they had a house. They got about five
miles before traffic was so bad that they just completely
stopped—all from that broadcast. Hundreds of people just like
them had packed up their cars and were going. Most of them
didn't even know where they were going, but they were going as
far away as they could go. They remembered that in the broadcast it said that landings were made in Princeton and Trenton,
and they figured the invaders would be headed to New York
City. Since they were about fifty miles from New York City,
they figured that if they went down south along the Jersey
coast, then they wouldn't be in any trouble. Finally, they got
about ten miles before the police started running around telling
everybody that it was a hoax and they could go home. They finally went home, but they never forgot that episode.*

JOHN WHITMORE, AGE 28
Arlington, Virginia

: WAR OF THE WORLDS II :

*I remember Orson Welles' "War of the Worlds" broadcast very
vividly. I was playing at a cousin's house when my father came
to the door and said to my uncle, "Neal, I have something very
serious to talk to you about. Let's go down to the basement
where no one can hear us." When they came up they both looked
grave. My father said, "We have to go home immediately,"
and so we left in great haste. My father had congregated the
rest of the family and the four of us—my mother, father,
brother, and I—sat in the family room around the radio, listening to the broadcast. As the Martians came closer people were
jumping out of windows and we became more frightened. Finally an old aunt came to the door and my mother said,
"Tuddi, you can't guess what's happened. The world is coming
to an end." And she threw up her packages and her pocketbook,
"Oh, my God," and she ran into the room. We all listened to the*

radio until the end of the broadcast. We weren't embarrassed. There were so many people in the same boat. A general terror had spread over most of the listeners. People had jumped out of windows and had called the police for gas masks. I remember when we got to our house my father said, "Look, the sky has turned purple." And it had, but of course not from the Martians. We sat there ready to die together. My grandmother was upset because my father hadn't picked her up from where she was. I imagine the older people prayed, but I don't remember that. I was so intent on what the man was saying on the radio and watching the expressions on the faces and wondering what was going on. We never knew until the very end when they said, "This has been a presentation by Orson Welles."

PAT RITTERHOFF
Timonium, Maryland

ELISSA ICHIYASU

: POPCO THE RACEHORSE :

My grandfather lived up on a family farm near Holton, Michigan. And there was a pond out back which is still there, but back in the old days the gypsies used to camp there. And they used to go down and, you know, talk with them some. But my grandmother didn't like him cavorting with the gypsies at all. She thought the gypsies were not people to be hung around with. They were accused of stealing and doctoring up their horses and so on. Well, one time the gypsies left, and my grandfather came back with a pony he called Popco. It was just a regular old spotted pony, and my grandmother always put it down.

My grandfather, Oscar, used the pony to take the milk cans into Holton—which is about seven miles—every day, just about the time of the morning that Mr. Ryerson would be riding his beautiful grey trotting horse into Holton to work. And it got to be a thing with him to say, "Hey, Oscar, you want to race?" Oscar would say, "No," and Mr. Ryerson would go off in a cloud of dust with the milk cans clattering. As it happened Oscar got to be pretty damned pissed at this. I mean day after day, "Hey, Oscar, you want to race?"—then boom. So one day he thought, "Hell, I'll give him his race," you know. So he's trotting along on Popco, here comes Ryerson, "Morning, Oscar, you want to race?" And Oscar says, "Sure. [Whistles.] Get up Popco." And Popco goes tearing down the road into Holton; the little pony had beaten Mr. Ryerson's trotting horse.

He came to find out about a year later when the gypsies came back that that little pony was the starting horse they used for the gypsies' races every year. And that was the end of Mr. Ryerson and Oscar's rivalry. I remember that because my mother told me that a couple of times. I like to think of that little triumph with the pony.

CONNIE CRONENWETT, AGE 31
Ann Arbor, Michigan

: THE COST OF LIVING :

My husband's grandfather was a doctor in a small town in Ohio. He wrote this story in his journal. One night he was called out in the country where a man was choking to death. He held the man's mouth open with a spoon all night long while someone went to fetch the proper instruments so he could

LOUISE TIRANOFF

relieve this man's suffering. When it was all over and he had spent the night with this man and he had saved his life, he sent the family a bill. It amounted to about one hundred dollars, and the family protested the amount of the bill. So he said to them, "Well, give me what you think his life is worth."

MARILYN JONNES
Washington, D. C.

: UNREQUITED LOVE :

There was a woman in the family who was married and had children. She was just living there in a little pioneer home in Tennessee or Missouri, a log cabin, I guess. There was an Indian, a Cherokee Indian chief, from a camp or village nearby, and he had seen her. One of the versions told is that what he really got excited about was her hair; I believe she either had red hair or blond hair. This chief fell in love with her, and he would stand on this hill that overlooked her cabin and just stand there and watch her. And he sent some of his Indians in to try to bargain for her because he wanted her for a wife. Of course she wasn't interested. When he died—he was an older man—when he died he had his body wrapped around a tree that would overlook her forever.

CHARLENE SMITH, AGE 30
JUDITH SMITH, AGE 33
Panburn, Arkansas

: PLUCKED GEESE I :

My grandparents' geese were in the cellar where the wine was kept. The faucet on one of the wine kegs was open and the geese drank the wine. They got drunk, keeled over, and passed out! When my grandparents found the geese in the cellar, passed out, they thought they had died of something. They couldn't eat them because they might have died of something awful, so they plucked them all to use the feathers for feather beds. And then the geese woke up! They woke up and made a whole lot of noise. My grandparents had to keep them tied on a string to the house for the rest of the summer until their feathers grew back, so they wouldn't wander too far and get cold.

DEBORAH SAPERSTONE
Bennington, Vermont

: PLUCKED GEESE II :

It's about Aunt Sally Hill. She lived in Winston-Salem, and I'm not sure how she was kin to us, but you know us southerners, we're kin to just about everyone. They had a big backyard and lots of geese, and the geese were wandering around and they got into a sack of dried beans, and they kind of still wandered around. And you know how dried beans swell up. Well they swelled up, causing the geese to pass out. Aunt Sally Hill and her help, Kansas and Charlie Shaws, thought the geese had died. A bunch of dead geese aren't going to do you any good, so they thought they'd make some good down comforters or pillows or whatever else you make with geese feathers—so they plucked 'em. And the geese, well the dried beans shrunk up, and suddenly they had a bunch of naked geese running around the yard! And as my mother always ends the story, "They all lived happily ever after and it was a very funny thing."

ELOISE SILLS, AGE 28
Charleston, South Carolina

Stories
for
Children

"Haven't you heard about the friend of Vicki's little boy who wanted to go swimming one night in the dark? He felt his way up the steps of the high diving board, stood on the edge, then died when he performed a marvelous swan dive into an empty pool." With a story like this a mother warned her children against a new favorite pastime, swimming at night. It was so effective that her children never again felt so much as the urge to swim after dark. Parents often tell *cautionary tales* of this kind. Many of them involve a ghost, goblin, or boogeyman who will "get" the children if they misbehave (only occasionally will they tell about jolly characters like Santa Claus who will reward children for good behavior).

Some of these characters and episodes are real though perhaps exaggerated; others are pulled out of thin air by an adult with a lesson to teach. "My mother had so many relatives," said Regina O'Toole Sokas, "that every time you wanted to do anything she didn't want you to do she had a relative who died a horrible death doing that. If you wanted to go ice skating on a pond that wasn't quite frozen she had a cousin who had done that. . . . I don't know if they were all true, but she had so many relatives you believed her." [1]

A second variety of stories invented for children are *fantasies*, fairy tales of a sort often told as bedtime stories. [2] Playing off their children's imaginations, parents weave stories around witches, giants, and their own fantastic figures, shaping the images into charming, sometimes beautiful narratives which teach their lessons with a little more subtlety.

Many of our most beloved children's books began as stories invented by parents for their children. During World War I, Hugh Lofting wrote a series of letters to his youngsters, Elizabeth and Colin. He didn't want to concentrate on the battles, so he wrote about another subject he felt would interest them more, the animals that were wounded or stranded at the front. The letters evolved into stories about a marvelous veterinarian, which became later the famous *Dr. Doolittle* series.

For every children's book published, there are a hundred thousand stories spun by parents in the privacy of the children's bedroom, imprinted nowhere but on a child's mind. In this intimate setting, parents become engaged in an artistic partnership with their children, each inspiring the other;

their lovely, imaginative, or fantastic tales often remain among the most creative efforts of their lifetimes.

Ironically, parents rarely give these yarns a second thought. More often than not, such tales were recalled for us by the children who, now grown, look back nostalgically at the inventions of their parents. We have even had a few opportunities to interview the original storyteller, only to have his eyes glaze over as he struggles with foggy recollections of his ephemeral meanderings.

A surprising number of these bedtime fantasies were the creation of fathers. Perhaps because they spent little time with their children during the day, they were charged with putting them to bed at night. The bedtime stories were then a way of rendering a small amount of shared time intimate and special. The episodic narratives became a way of providing a busy man with a regularly scheduled time with his children as the latest adventure of "Mahogany and Mack" or "Bunyan Bunny" was spun. As one young woman said, "If it wasn't for storytelling there really wouldn't have been much of a relationship between child and father."[3] Interestingly enough, a few of the tales we did collect from mothers were told by divorced, working women.

Of course, no clear-cut line divides made up bedtime fantasies from traditional fairy tales and written stories. One of the children's favorite episodes in the Great-grandfather Wog series told by Arthur Maas (p. 138) described how a prehistoric caveman and his wild, naked children (modeled, of course, on the teller's own offspring) discovered cooking. The discovery was accidental, coming when the pig was hurriedly thrown into a burning bush during a storm—an episode which, Arthur Maas freely admits, is borrowed from Charles Lamb's "A Dissertation Upon Roast Pig."

At bedtime a story might be read from a book, told from pure invention, or be an adaptation of any traditional story which suits the needs—and the whims—of particular storytellers and their children. In this next example, "Goldilocks and the Three Bears" is revamped by one mother for her daughter and her son:

My husband and I have been separated for two and a half years and I have two children, one is eight and one is four. About a year and a half ago, when my little boy was not quite

NAN GRAHAM

three, he really started liking the story of the three bears, and he wanted it told over and over and over again.

But at one point I realized that he was identifying very, very strongly when I would start and say, "papa bear, mama bear and baby bear." Immediately, he would say, "Daddy, mommy, and baby bear is me."

When we got to Goldilocks, immediately that was his sister, so his sister was almost the bad guy. And he was identifying very strongly with this idea of everybody being together, and I was trying to cope with the fact that we had separate families now.

So one day I just switched it around, and when everybody got up it was mama bear, sister bear, and brother bear; and his eyes got wide and he looked at this and thought about it for a minute. And then, when it got to be Goldilocks—instead it became Curlylocks, who was a little boy. Well, both kids absolutely loved that.

Sometimes sister bear and brother bear would get up and they would help with breakfast. And sometimes when mama bear and sister bear and brother bear would go out for a walk, they would go over to visit daddy at his house.

Now it's progressed to the point where they'll say, "Tell the 'Three Bears,' or tell the 'Special One'" because this is the "Special One." And now there's no more problem as far as his sister being the bad guy. It's their special story, and it's helped me. I felt like I was coping with something that I really hadn't expected.[4]

Other stories, like Martha Bays' "Princess Oliva and the Bravest Knight" in this section are not based on any particular children's tale, but borrow some of the form and content from many well-known stories. She makes use of numerous fairy tale features such as a dragon, a mountain of ice, a poor shepherd boy, a knight in shining armor, and the three tests, yet combines them into an original narrative which meets the particular needs of her family. Martha Bays was going through a divorce and a career change while raising two daughters by herself when she created the tale. She needed a story which featured a hardnosed, practical heroine, but to create the narrative she relied on models remembered from childhood.

Adapting traditional stories or inventing new ones is a way of rendering them more personal and relevant and giving them an added emotional charge. Characters can be molded in the image of one's own children, from the absolute everyday scene ("Saul woke up this morning and he had a glass of orange juice before he ventured onto the big yellow school bus") to a prehistoric landscape with naked children following behind Great-grandfather Wog. A parent's tales can wield a magical transformation, allowing their children to experience in a personalized way some of their deepest, most far-flung fantasies.

: PRINCESS OLIVA AND
THE BRAVEST KNIGHT :

I like the whole idea of fairy stories. I think they're fun, but I don't like most of the female characters in them—they're pretty dull. So, I've made up stories for the kids.

Once upon a time there was a princess who wanted to marry the bravest knight in the land. She decided that any knight who married her had to pass three tests of courage. He had to save her from the dragon, he had to save her from a seven-headed serpent, and he had to save her from a mountain of snow and ice that was guarded by three giants who would let no man pass. So, Sir Broiderick, who was the most elegant man in the land, decided to try for her hand. Oliva went out and sat under a tree and waited for the dragon to come down and attack her so she could be saved. And all of the townspeople came out to watch. There was a big celebration, and pretty soon the dragon came down the hill spouting fire and smoke, and everybody cheered. But, Sir Broiderick wasn't around. Sir Broiderick was at the other end of the mountain gathering flowers because he thought it would be very elegant to give her a bouquet of flowers after he saved her from the dragon. The dragon came closer and closer, and the townspeople started running away. A shepherd boy named Cuthbert decided he just couldn't bear to see Oliva eaten, just eaten by the dragon, so he ran up and handed her a shepherd's crook. The dragon came down and landed in front of Oliva and swooped her up in the air, and she speared the shepherd's crook up into the roof of his mouth, and he dropped her in a thicket of bushes. Just presently, Sir Broiderick came riding up and he slew the dragon that was lying on the ground just writhing in pain with the shepherd's crook stuck in his mouth. Then, he presented Oliva with the bouquet of flowers and very kindly overlooked the fact that she was a mess from having been dropped in the thicket of bushes. Oliva thanked him very nicely and made Cuthbert assistant head butler.

Next Sir Broiderick had to save Oliva from the seven-headed serpent. Everybody got up before dawn one morning and went up the mountain to the cave of the seven-headed serpent. All the townspeople came up; hawkers sold hot chestnuts, and everyone waited for the serpent to come out. Well, presently, the sun came up, and that warmed up the cave enough so that the seven-headed serpent came crawling out, this loathsome, horrible creature with all seven heads hissing. And Sir Broiderick wasn't around because he decided to wear his suit of silver armor that day and was back at the castle polishing it. Well, Cuthbert just couldn't stand it. The serpent was crawling closer and closer to Oliva. So, he took his butcher knife, which he had taken along just in case anything had happened, and he presented the butcher's knife to Oliva. He had to cut off two of the seven heads to get to her. He was very sorry about that. Well, Oliva said, "I can't kill off the serpent, because then I can't be saved, and I won't know if Sir Broiderick is the bravest knight in the land." So, he said, "Well, why don't you just blind it if it gets too close." And presently, Sir Broiderick came riding up the mountainside, looking absolutely magnificent in his silver armor. And he cut off the remaining five heads of the serpent which were sort of feebly waving around. They all had been blinded by Oliva while she was waiting to be saved. And Oliva thanked him very nicely and made Cuthbert the captain of the palace guard.

The last test of courage was, could Sir Broiderick save Oliva from the mountain of snow and ice, guarded by two giants? Oliva went to the top of the mountain wearing a nice sturdy pair of shoes and a heavy tweed skirt, and waited to be saved. [Virginia: Mommy, you forgot. In the two others she had been wearing those elegant dresses.] Oh yes. The first time she wore a seafoam chiffon, but that got all torn up in the bushes. And the second time she wore red velvet, but that got all splattered with blood. So the third time she decided she'd better dress sensibly.

So, she waits up on top of the mountain. Sir Broiderick does not show up. He's out picking out an engagement ring. Well, the townspeople are getting very upset, and the giants are having to do tricks to entertain the people because they're getting very restive. And Oliva's up on top of the mountain turning bluer and bluer. And finally Cuthbert can't stand it any longer, and he goes back to the castle, and he gets the bear skin rug from the floor of the great hall of the castle. And he sneaks up the mountain past the giants who are too dumb to realize that he's a man. And he places the bear skin rug around poor Oliva. Well, the giants realize they've been tricked. And they come roaring up the mountain, determined to tear Cuthbert from limb to limb. Whereupon Oliva and Cuthbert make a huge snowball and roll it down upon the giants. Well, Sir Broiderick rides up in a perfectly beautiful set of golden armor, cuts off the giants' heads (which are the only things that can be seen above the avalanche), and rides up to claim his prize. But, by this time, Oliva and Cuthbert are sitting cuddled in the bear skin rug and don't even notice that he's there. So, he rides away looking for a princess who is more appreciative and better dressed.

And Oliva goes back to the castle and has Cuthbert knighted and says now he can try for her hand by passing the three tests of courage. Well, Cuthbert refuses to do that. He says its ridiculous, and he's not going to put her through that. So he goes back off to his shepherd's cottage. And Oliva climbs to the top *of the tallest tower in the castle and looks out into the sea and thinks. She comes back and goes to the shepherd's cottage where Cuthbert is very sadly polishing his armor and says that she will marry him after all, if he'll polish his own armor and be the jolliest papa in the world. And he agrees to that. So they're married in great pomp and ceremony. And after a time, they had eleven red-haired princes, each one of which is more mischievous than the last. And the townspeople who know those princes say that Sir Cuthbert is the bravest knight in the land!*

MARTHA AND VIRGINIA BAYS
Reston, Virginia

: WHALE OF A TALE :

Every night when they were growing up, I told my children stories about whales: a red whale, a white whale, and a blue whale. I probably created more whale stories than anybody living in the United States. I taught them how to learn about the planets using the whale of a tale — how the whales traveled to all the nine different planets, whales that have communicated from Earth to Mars to Venus. I've taught them different birds, different animals, alphabetically, just by using the whale as a concept. The whale stories that the children liked the most had some type of moral to them, and the concept would be a current event that had taken place.

Let's see. There was a red whale, a white whale, and a blue whale, and they decided to go to Washington, D.C., but they didn't know how to get there. Should they take Route 1, should they take 95, or should they take a side road? They all decided to take different paths. The red whale took the side road, and he saw the mountains, and he saw the valleys, and it took him a long, long time. The white whale took Route 1, and he saw the different highways, and he used to stop and go on all the red lights, past all the small towns. He'd see the different types of stores and different types of people and different industries and different walks of life. The blue whale thought he was the smartest. He took Route 95 and went very, very quickly. And he arrived in Washington first.

The blue whale was so proud that he arrived first that when they all congregated — the red whale, the white whale, and the blue whale — he said, "Hey, how's your trip?" And the blue

DALE BROWN

whale said, "I made it in three hours." "That's fantastic! What did you do the rest of the time?" "Nothing." The white whale took Route 1, and he saw people, all sorts of people, different working-class people, interesting people. He stopped to talk to them, and he learned different stories about life. The red whale took the scenic route. It took him four times as long as the blue whale and twice as long as the white whale. And the red whale said, "I saw the most beautiful sunrise; I saw the most beautiful sunset. I looked up in the sky at night and I saw the most beautiful stars and the most beautiful planets. It took me twelve hours, but I'll never forget it." Which route would you have taken? And which one would you have enjoyed the most?

STANLEY COHEN, AGE 45

Suffern, New York

: THE FIREMAN WHALE :

It all started a good many years ago when there was an old mansion located just north of Asbury Park (New Jersey) on the beach. One night this old house burst into flames and the flames were raging very fiercely. The local fireman companies responded to the alarm and they were trying to put the fire out, but it go so bad that they decided that they would have to give up.

Well, it just so happened that about this time there was a whale swimming along in the ocean about three or four miles off Asbury Park and he saw this red glow in the sky, so he decided that he would swim in close to see what was going on. And when he got in fairly close to the beach, he could see this house on fire and that the men were squirting water on it but that they weren't really able to do very much. Their water pressure was too low. So the whale swam to shore and went up to the fire chief and said, "Can I help you put this fire out? I've got a lot of water here." The chief said, "Oh yes, you could. We'd appreciate it very much." So the whale went back into the ocean and filled his nose with a lot of water and came back and spouted water all over the fire. He did that several times and finally he put out the fire. Well, everybody cheered of course and the firemen were very grateful and they asked the whale to come back to the firehouse with them and celebrate with coffee and doughnuts, which the whale enjoyed very much. Finally, he said, "Well, it's time I got back to the ocean, I think."

Before he left, the fire chief said that they were going to have a Christmas party at the firehouse in a few weeks, and asked the whale if he'd like to come. The whale said he certainly would. So the night of the Christmas party the whale appeared again with a nice holly wreath and presents for the firemen. They were all very pleased, and they sang Christmas carols and the whale had a wonderful time. When it came time for him to go back to the ocean, the fire chief said, "You have been so helpful to us in putting out that fire that I wonder if we could put a telephone line from the firehouse here along the bottom of the ocean where you live and connect it to an underwater telephone there. Then, if we have any more bad fires some time and need your help, we could call you on the telephone. Would you be willing to come and help us put out the fire?" And the whale said of course, he'd like to do that very much.

Soon after that, some divers came, put in a telephone, and connected it with the firehouse. Every time since then that they've had a very bad fire around Asbury Park that they can't put out with their own fire apparatus, they call the whale. If he is home, which he usually is, he gets up, puts on the fire helmet which the firemen gave him as a present, and swims back to shore to put out the fire. And every time, he goes back to the firehouse and has coffee and doughnuts with the firemen. And that's the story of the fireman whale.

GEOFFREY VELASQUEZ AZOY, AGE 8
Little Silver, New Jersey

: THE SANDBOX :

My father used to make up Mit and Mat stories; I was Mat and my brother was Mit. The one I remember best is the one my brother doesn't figure in at all. We used to go to the beach every day; it was a very short drive from Philadelphia. We had a sandbox in the backyard and I was trying to get sand for it. My father used to bring a few buckets of sand back from the beach.

Well, Mat goes to the beach with her parents and she wants to bring sand back and her father says no, it won't fit in the car. So while they're sleeping on the beach, Mat filled the trunk of the car up with sand and then covered it over with towels. They drove home and Mat's father was very upset because the car wasn't riding properly. He couldn't understand it. He said he'd have to take it to the garage and have them check it out. But as they got close to the Benjamin Franklin Bridge, the load became less and the car was all right by the time they got home. Well, Mat couldn't wait to get out and look in the trunk for the sand. But it was gone! It had come out in dribbles. She noticed little dabs of sand in the driveway and she started to following it with her bucket, scooping it up. She ended up all the way back at the beach, at which point her parents were very upset and they called the police and there was this big search for this lost little girl. It made all the newspapers and they got her back and punished her for being such a silly little girl. But they were glad to get her back home.

The upshot was that everybody read about this poor little girl who didn't have any sand in her sandbox. And they started sending sand. She got sand from Arabia, sand from North Africa, and sand from everywhere, all over the world, all different colors of sand. The yard was full of it. It became ridiculous. There was too much sand. So she got this wonderful idea. She made the sand into bricks, beautifully colored bricks, different layers, and sold them for a quarter a piece. Pretty soon, she was back to having no sand in her sandbox and stealing it from the beach.

PAM MATLOCK
Washington, D.C.

: PEPPER AND SUCCOTASH :

When I was little my father used to make up stories to tell me and my brother about two twin red-headed boys named Pepper and Succotash. This was purely an individual art form. He would never know when he started out how the story was going to end up. He would just spin these yarns.

One time he told us the story of Pepper and Succotash going to Mars. I don't remember how they got there but all the people would have some kind of bubble gum and they would chew it and blow bubbles out of their ears and go floating around. The bubbles were something like helium. There were witches and the boys would chew this bubble gum and float away from the witches.

Another time Pepper and Succotash went down to the river on a picnic. There was no way to get across so they took a whole

*string of hot dogs and they made it into a lasso and threw it
across the river to a stump. And then they monkey-walked
across, you know, they had to hang. When they got across they
ate all of the hot dogs and then after they had finished the picnic they didn't know how to get back over the stream. So one of
them pulled out the plug and they walked across.*

BRIAN R. GAY, AGE 11
Washington, D.C.

: Mahogany and Mac :

*My husband used to make up the most wonderful stories for the
kids. He invented two characters called Mahogany and Mac.
One was a credenza, and one was a trailer truck. And Mahogany lived in Mac, you see, and they would go traveling all
around the world and all around the globe. I even remember
Mahogany and Mac going off into space and having adventures there. And they had very strong personalities. Mac was
the strong male thing, and Mahogany was the woman. She was
just a great big credenza — the kids loved that word, credenza.
They thought it was great!*

TAMARA DEFRIES, AGE 47
Falls Church, Virginia

: Bunyan Bunny :

*My father and I used to have a rabbit club. We made up our
own legends about Bunyan Bunny, the greatest rabbit of them
all. He was really big, a superbunny. One of the stories that we
made up together was about Niagara Falls. The reason that
Niagara Falls was formed was that Bunyan Bunny was hop-
ping along one day and he hopped all the way from New York
to Niagara Falls. He was really thirsty and he saw a spring
there. He bent over and he slipped in the mud and sat down.
And he was so big that he formed the space where Niagara
Falls is.*

   *Dad also tried to weave history into the stories. He told how
Bunyan Bunny helped to get the first pioneers out west. He used
to tell me about the pioneers crossing in Conestoga wagons.
Bunyan Bunny would perch on the mountaintop and see the dis-*

tressed travelers. So he would hop out and pull their Conestoga wagons to a spring. This rabbit club was just between the two of us. We were the inner circle, just dad and me. And then there was the outer circle, my sister, my brother, and my mother.

ELIZABETH AMES
Providence, Rhode Island

: THE BREAD FACTORY TOUR :

Well, when I was younger we had sort of a little childhood tradition. Almost every night my parents would tell my younger brother and me a story about our stuffed animals. We had two separate villages. One was Kittyville because my main stuffed animal was a little cat that I got when I was two months old. Eric had a little teddy bear, and there was Jungle-ville, because in addition to the teddy bear he had this little monkey. And we had a sequence of stories that developed about kitty scouts and teddy scouts. Eric's little teddy bear also had a yellow dog friend. They would have box-derby races. There would be characterizations of morals that I guess they wanted to instill in us. Yellow dog had square wheels, and even though he lost in the end everybody gave him a prize for being the most creative soap box car. And kitty scouts were always doing good things.

One story involved a visit to the bread factory. All the kitty scouts decided, "Hey, we ought to do something constructive and go see how bread is made." Mr. Winsey, another cat, was presiding over this meeting and he said, "Okay, I suggest a motion that we go visit the bread factory." And Pooh and Piglet said that they'd second the motion. So, they all got on a train in Kittyville station, and they went in the mountain to the bread factory. When they got there, the bread factory people were very nice and showed them how to make the bread and gave them samples.

Well, during this time, Piglet noticed little trash cans around and he strayed from the rest of the kitty-cat troop. After awhile the rest of the kitty scouts had gone way far into the factory, and they didn't notice that Piglet was gone. And what Piglet had done was to go to the side of this one counter; he saw this little hole, and it smelled kind of like trash, and he got interested in it. But he couldn't read, so he couldn't read that the words on top of it said "trash chute." So, the next thing he knew, he stuck his head in, dove in, and was going miles and miles screaming, but nobody could hear him.

In the meantime, the rest of the kitty scouts finished their tour and were ready to get back on the train. And they couldn't understand why Piglet didn't come when they called for him, why he didn't answer. Eventually Pooh said, "I think I saw him looking in the trash bin. Oh my gosh, I wonder where he went." So, they got all of the staff of the bread factory to help them. Mr. Wimsey took his own initiative to go out and try to look for him in the back rooms. And he heard this noise in this huge bin at the end of a long tube. It was kind of a squealing noise. He opened it, and he saw Piglet, all wrapped up in rotten bread. And he said, "Piglet, what in the world got you into this mess?" And Piglet said, "It's only my nature. I can't help it." They finally got him out, but the kitty scouts would not let Piglet inside the train. He had to ride on top of the train all the way back to Kittyville. And for miles around the next day, there were reports of the most awful stench going through the village. When they got home they had to dunk him inside the bathtub, and give him a bath.

KIRSTEN STROMBERG, AGE 18
Silver Spring, Maryland

: GRANDFATHER WOG :

Great-great-great-great-great-great-great-great-great-great-great-great-grandfather Wog went hunting one day, and he took along his two daughters, Jog and Cog. Before long, they killed a pig, and they were bringing it home when a great big storm came up. The lightning flashed and the thunder rolled, and all of a sudden a lightning bolt hit a tree right beside them, and Grandfather Wog was so scared that he threw the pig over his shoulder and he and the girls went and hid in the rocks. And the lightning set the pile of brush on fire and they thought that their pig was all burned up, cause the flames licked around it.

Well when the fire died down, they came out and saw the pig was all black and charred. But something smelled awfully good. And Grandfather Wog stuck out his finger and he touched the pig. But it burned, oh! [Mr. Maas at this point puts his finger in his mouth as a gesture.] But it tasted so good. And

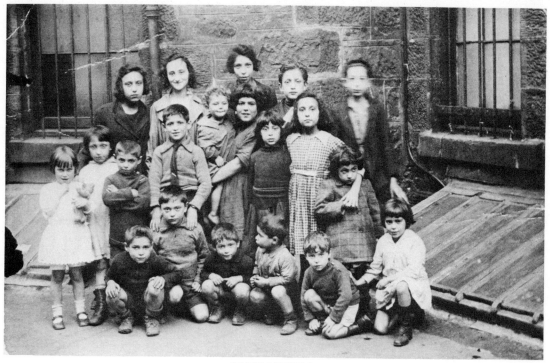

SUSAN SHAPIRO

he reached out and touched the pig again [again he puts his fingers in his mouth as if trying to ease the pain of a burn], but my that tasted good. And they decided that burnt pig was the best thing they ever tasted. And that was the beginning of cooking.

ARTHUR MAAS, AGE 58
Greenbelt, Maryland

: MAGIC CLOTHESPINS :

One story that has come down on my side of the family is what we call clothespin stories. The clothespins themselves were Grandma Gillis' great-grandmother's, a magic bag of clothespins that really went across the plains with her, in the wagon.

During the day they did ordinary clothespin work, but at night they became individuals. They always seemed to get themselves into trouble and make a horrible mess and then get themselves out of it. In one story the kids always liked, the clothespins would fall off on the ground and someone would pick them up and they'd see something important and try to tell it to the human people, and not being able to really relate the information to them they'd have to do it in some tricky way, like falling down right beside them and waking them up to make them see the Indians coming.

Of course these stories were made up on the spot in all generations including ours. Our children of course didn't know this and they'd say, "Daddy, tell me the clothespin story about such and such" and we wouldn't remember it and we'd try to get them to tell a little of it, and then we'd remember somewhat what it was like and go on with it.

RAYMOND AND NYLA WEBBER, AGES 38 AND 27
Page, Arizona

: THE CATS :

My grandmother was born in the middle of the Black Forest in 1858. I still remember the hair-raising witch stories she would tell us when we were little children. The old witch woman in the village would capture children and turn them into cats to do the laundry. One of her [my grandmother's] little girlfriends finally followed her back into the forest and put her eye to the keyhole. And she saw this huge tub with about a dozen cats around it that were as large as children. They were wearing little children's clothes and she could recognize little Heidi's dress— and there's little Jacob's shoes! And my grandmother would stand at the end of the table, going like this, pretending to be the witch, "Ein, zwei, drei!" counting out for the cats to do the laundry!

STEVEN SCHENK, AGE 28
Arlington, Virginia

: THE WAILING WOMAN :

The most interesting stories that came from my childhood were the stories that the parents and grandparents would tell you to keep you in line and were passed on to my father from his grandfather. They had to do with when they wanted to emphasize certain points, when they didn't want you out at certain times of the month, specifically on the dangerous nights of the week, like Friday night and Saturday night. They had these stories about the wailing woman, a woman who was condemned to walk the streets late on Friday and Saturday nights, wailing because she had killed her two children. The grandparents would tell these stories with all the children around them. And, I mean, you just don't question your grandmother. So they really sunk in.

Here's the most vivid example of this. I guess I was about ten or eleven, and I'd heard these stories over and over again, so naturally on Friday and Saturday nights I really seldom went out. But in my hometown—this was before indoor plumbing came in—we had the old family chamber pot. Every morning you had to go dump it. But something had happened that we didn't have it in the house. And it happened to be about midnight this one Friday night, and I had to go to the privy. I got about halfway to the outhouse and all of a sudden I heard this loud wail. I was so scared to death that I forgot I had to go to the bathroom. I went back to the house and just completely covered my head up. And it was many, many years that I would not go outside, especially on Friday nights. Any other night, it was fine. But those were the nights, Friday nights.

I guess it was when I was in my twenties that I happened to be out one night and I heard the same sound. What it was, was a

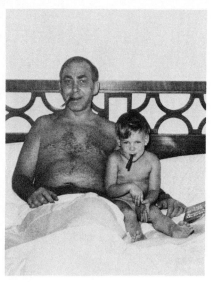

JAY BURG

cat. But to this day when I hear this sound, it's still in the back of my mind. These are the things just rich in tradition that the old people had to keep you in line.

GEORGE VALDEZ, JR., AGE 35
Wheaton, Maryland

: THE BINGO :

I remember my mother used to tell me about a boogeyman kind of thing. I must have been somewhere around two or three years old. You'd hear a train whistle every so often. I don't know where the train was in relation to where we lived, but some times you could sort of hear this eerie sound, particularly at night. And she would tell us that was the Bingo. She didn't describe it, but I'd gotten the idea that the Bingo was something awful. Then at other times she would refer to the Bingo, like when some of my toys would disappear every so often. I later learned that with most kids there are too many toys around, so you clear them out occasionally or put some away, and then get them out again at another time. So if I missed something and asked where it was, oh, the Bingo had taken it. And then I'd get threatened occasionally with other things the Bingo would do if I didn't behave.

CORINNE BLUM LEBOVIT, AGE 58
Silver Spring, Maryland

: UNCLE VESPER :

The only ghost I can remember is Uncle Vesper. I really think he was used to stop children in the family from doing things that they shouldn't do. That included coming downstairs Christmas Eve or going into the attic or playing in the basement or going outside in the yard, or whatever the particular situation was in growing up. Uncle Vesper was kind of the guardian or the implied threat; if you did something, Uncle Vesper would get you.

He supposedly lived in a shoebox in the attic and each time the family moved, they would make sort of a display of moving the shoebox to let the kids know that Uncle Vesper was not being left behind, that he was going to run the next household too.

When my older brother got married, they gave him a shoebox with Uncle Vesper in it. My other brother, when he got married, got Uncle Vesper too! So, in a way, Uncle Vesper kind of subdivides and takes responsibility for branches of the family.

ROBERT BACHMAN, AGE 27
Radnor, Pennsylvania

: USING THE BLARNEY :

My grandfather was Irish through and through. He was a big man, over six feet tall and about 220 pounds as I recall him. My aunt told me the story about how when they were all growing up and they didn't want to go to school for some reason, my grandfather would say, "Oh, I never missed a day of school in me life. Not for rain or snow, and I always walked to school." Many years later my aunt took a trip to Ireland and she went to my grandfather's old homestead. When she came back she said, "No wonder he went to school every day. His house was right next to the school." That was typical of him, to use the old blarney to get you to do something.

WILLIAM F. DELANEY, AGE 44
Burke, Virginia

RUTH COYNE

: ELBOWS AND HANDS :

"Don't stick your elbow out too far, it might go home in another car." My mother had a great story about this violinist she once knew who was riding with his hand out the window. This truck came along and took it off. He couldn't play the violin and he lost his livelihood. So, don't stick your hand out of the car!

ELIZABETH LANG, AGE 24
Larchmont, New York

: LIMA BEANS :

We hated lima beans and we were Catholic. And my father said that he hated them too, but my mother made them about two times a week. She said they were good for us. My father claimed that he had written to the Pope and that he had declared them a mortal sin, and we never had to eat them again.

JAMES MCEVOY, AGE 34
Omaha, Nebraska

: A DIRTY STORY :

Can I tell you a dirty story about my father? When my brother was about six or seven years old, he found a prophylactic in the pocket of Bessie the Buick. And so he asked my father what it was for. As my brother remembers it, my father was very much flustered by the question.

Then my father said, "Well, men who go to war need those." And my brother was stumped, so he asked for more explanation. My father said, "Well, a man puts that on" — and I'm sure he didn't use the word penis — but, "the man puts that on his penis and if he has to urinate while he's in the middle of battle, he does it in that little rubber thing. And then when he gets back and the battle is over, he takes it off and he can throw it away." My brother believed that for years.

ELINOR ABRAMSON
Washington, D.C.

: SNAKES IN CHURCH :

I had an experience on the Irish side. My grandmother found out that I was friends with a Protestant boy. Being a New Yorker we were friends with everyone. I had Jewish friends, I had Irish friends, I had Italian friends. I brought this one boy home, and my grandmother asked me what nationality he was. I didn't know. As a child you don't ask a kid what nationality he is or where he's from. You get your prejudice after many years. She says, "Well, what church does he go to?" And I say, "I don't know." So she asked him. He happened to be Lutheran and said that he went to the Lutheran church.

Well, my grandmother gave me a funny look and then that night she called me up to the house—we lived next door—and she says, "I don't want you to play with that boy anymore." And I say, "Why? I happen to like him." His name was Jack. She says, "Well, because the Lutherans in their services, before they go in, each one is handed a snake. And what they'd like to do is get little Catholic boys into the back and get them converted to Lutheran services. If they don't convert them, they sic the snakes on them." Now, whether this was something my grandmother made up at the time or whether it was in reality something that was handed down to her, I don't know. But this is just another example of what we got.

It didn't affect my behavior towards him, because I had known the boy for quite some time. And I just couldn't visualize him taking me in back of a church and sicking snakes on me. I broached the subject with him. He did just what you're doing; he laughed. So he took me to his church. I met his pastor, Reverend Black. He showed me all around the church, and I couldn't find a snake in it. Not a snake in the whole church.

JOSEPH COPPOLA, JR., AGE 46
Central Islip, New York

Family Expressions

Bubbling over with high spirits, Bettie, a seven-year-old girl from Attleboro, Massachusetts, had been entertaining the family for some time when her mother said laughingly, "What *does* make you do and say those things?" "Oh, I don't know," Bettie said, "I guess I'm just feeling agnipocus!"[1] From that moment forward whenever a member of the Weatherbee family was describing a good mood all of the vast resources and infinite subtleties of the English language paled before the nonsensical utterance of a seven-year-old girl.

In vain we look through Webster's unabridged third edition for euphonious words like "hudge," "Samuel Widgens," "squiblums." For it would take, after all, a member of the Sackett family to know that "hudge" means to pick up a child and hug him.[2] The Starr family alone would interpret "Samuel Widgens" as a sandwich.[3] And only at the door of the Woodville family might we be asked for "Squiblums, squiblums,"[4] a joking family reference to identification papers or other credentials. Expressions like these illustrate, perhaps better than any other form, how ingenious families can be.

Yet these terms and phrases are more than just a family's way of coming up with better words than the English language affords. They serve as passwords which affirm the ties of shared experience. They are also filled with meaning because the expression often carries a humorous piece of family history along with it. Hearing it, we can often remember the riotous situation which gave birth to the phrase.

"My family," said Stephen Tauber, "has numerous expressions which are elliptical allusions to a tale. In German this is called '*gefluketas wort,*' a winged word. . . ." He went on to give an example from his family:

My great-grandfather, that is to say my mother's mother's father, was a general storekeeper in the town of Littenz, in Czechoslovakia. One of the tales which is famous in our family was about the time that a farmer came to the store. His wife was cooking and had run out of sugar. So he came to the store to buy a cone of sugar—that's how it was sold in those days, a solid cone of sugar.

But of course you don't go into a store, buy what you want, and leave again, not in a small village. You chat and you talk, you talk about the crops, about the weather, about what you're doing, about the weather, and some more about the weather. My great-grandfather said, "Yes, it is looking very much like rain. Tell me, do you have an umbrella?" The farmer said, "No, I never had an umbrella, don't really need one." My great-grandfather said, "You know, it's really very handy. You're going to be walking home for four kilometers, you'll get wet. Why don't you buy an umbrella?"

"Eh"—they talk back and forth some more. Finally the farmer said, "All right, all right, I'll buy an umbrella from you."

So he bought an umbrella and went home—but with no sugar. And ever since in our family, whenever somebody goes shopping and comes back with something other than what he went out to buy, whatever he comes home with is called an umbrella.[5]

In the Tauber family, "umbrella" is indeed a winged word; it carries an episode in a general store in Littenz, Czechoslovakia, across nearly a hundred years to tease a child who brings the wrong item home from the supermarket.

Kim Garrett's grandfather Stevenson used a saying which dated from a perilous storm in 1886 when the whole family sought shelter in his large stone house. "The family at the time," Garrett writes, "included Telegraph, Uncle Alley's big white horse. Uncle Alley was badly crippled (a fact that Telegraph seemed to understand) and looked on his horse as a beloved companion as well as safe transportation. Telegraph was stabled on the porch at first, but as the storm grew worse, Uncle Alley grew more restless. No one thought it too strange when he asked that Telegraph be brought into the house. The parlor was the only room not crowded with kin, so Telegraph spent the rest of the night surrounded by family daguerreotypes. . . ."[6]

Since then, "Weather to bring the stock into the parlor" became one of Grandfather Stevenson's family expressions. The phrase evokes that dramatic and comical episode to charge and embellish a discussion about the weather. The family expression often enables us to bring a dramatic episode to bear on a similar but less dramatic episode in everyday life, imbuing the ordinary with vibrant associations from the past.

When outsiders are present a story like the stock in the parlor might be repeated in full. But family members have usually heard the tales, and they become part of the shared past, the storehouse of memories that can be drawn upon in the richly textured conversation of persons who know each other well. "Someone in my family had three children, one of whom was named Shields," Mrs. Slemp told us. "The old man was quite a drunk and often would beat up on his family when in liquor. One day he started in on Shields who by then was a grown teenager, and Shields licked the tar out of him. Finally the old man was down, and Shields was sitting on his chest. The old man looked up and said ruefully, 'Get up Shields, you beat your daddy.' "[7] This line, "Get up Shields, you beat your daddy," the most dramatic and quotable, became a traditional family expression.[8]

At times, however, a family phrase will emerge not from a story but from a memorable chance remark easily adapted to new situations. "How could any non-initiate guess," wrote R.A. Stewart Macalister,

that "to sing the hundredth psalm" meant "to fetch a glass of water" — as it does in a family known to me? If he be admitted to the domestic arcana so far as to learn the phrase and its meaning, how could he guess the nexus between the two ideas — a chance remark made upon a midsummer day — that to allow the heated water to run off from the cold-water tap took about as long a time as it would take to perform the act of piety specified?[9]

Some episodes in a family's past may be alluded to over and over again without becoming codified in a specific expression. If, for instance, in the Slemp family a child has beaten his father in checkers, rather than saying, "Get up Shields, you beat your daddy," someone could have said, "It's just like the time Shields beat up his old man." It would not have been as poetic, but it would have served the same purpose. When extended this way, the idea of the family expression or allusion plays an important part in every human relationship.

Oftentimes these expressions are hilarious solutions to the kinds of similar problems which crop up in families. In our collection, the phrases "two thousand monkeys" and "horses are falling left and right" are both used to tease a family

HELEN MACKEY GREY

member for exaggeration. A number are also told to correct behavior at the dinner table. Back in the 1860s, wrote Kim Garrett, "Sister Rhoda had a pet pig that died from overeating or 'busted from too much buttermilk. . . .' [And] for nearly a hundred years 'Strodie's pig' had been a specter hovering over any Stevenson-Baylor child who is inclined to overeat. 'Remember Strodie's pig!' is always fair warning that third helpings are out."[10] In another family, recalling the "Lefant kid" was all that was necessary to assure proper behavior at the table; the Lefant child once threw mashed potatoes while the visiting preacher was saying grace.[11]

Some of the most touching expressions serve to soothe and console. They are a way of defusing tense situations, telling members of the family that everything is all right. Maybe a humorous figure can be blamed if an object is lost or misplaced. In one family, for instance, "Mr. Rompback took it." The younger generation of another family drove down to a river where the boys were beginning a boat trip. Just as they were leaving, one of the boys got out of the boat, kissed his sister on the cheek, and said, "Goodbye, sis. Tell ma the boat floats." Now, when a family member calls or writes home from a trip, "Tell ma the boat floats" means that everything is all right.[12]

Family expressions are the poetry of everyday life. They are packed with alliteration, rhythm, and hyperbole. "Thank God for guts and gristle" is the rousing battle cry in one family whenever a dirty, difficult job need be done; "Too tired to tuck" is a phrase in another when a task simply seems too exhausting.[13] Expressions often take the form of a metaphor; an example in this section compares eating too much gum (or any excessive behavior) to "jumping off the fifteenth-story window for a breeze on a hot day."

Perhaps as we become more intimate with one another, our conversation moves from prose towards poetry. We compact our experiences and relate them not as long explanatory narratives but as terse exclamations. We begin to use catch-words and allusions and much of our conversation becomes laden with associations. At the same time our talk becomes more patterned and rhythmical. Linguists have shown that "when people speak to each other they keep a rhythm, a meter of regular beats, and time their entrances and exits to the rhythm of these beats."[14] Close families often seem particularly in sync with one another. They enjoy conversations which outsiders might consider repetitive but which they experience as comfortable and smooth. They develop a sense of timing and occasionally inject a family expression which teases and brings back a rush of memories, without missing a beat. As one young woman said about her relationship to her sister, "We refined our communication into a work of art."[15]

: HORSES ARE FALLING LEFT AND RIGHT :

When my mother was a little girl from Kansas City, and was here in Washington with her family, she looked out the window of the Mayflower Hotel and said, "Oh mummy, it's so icy, horses are falling left and right!" And her mother rushed to the window and said, "What are you talking about?" And she said, "Well, one slipped." So over-exaggeration in our family is always, "Horses are falling left and right." This is a seventy-year-old saying, but they all say it.

: TWO THOUSAND MONKEYS :

My sister had a tendency to exaggerate and apparently she had heard some story at school about some monkeys getting loose in New York City from some show. She came home and told us this story about these two thousand monkeys that were loose in New York City. The next month there was a story in Reader's

*Digest on the same subject and it was twelve monkeys. So
every time she would rev up and begin to exaggerate, everybody would turn to her and say, "two thousand monkeys" and
she would slow down.*

: ABEDIAH :

*My father grew up in Missouri in the Ozarks. There used to be
a lot of traveling salesmen and peddlers, and there was this one
man named Abediah who I think sold pots and pans and also
hand organs and things like that. He would go through about
once every six months and they would always invite him in
for dinner. Abediah liked to talk an incredible amount. He
would talk forever and interrupt everyone at the table, and the
expression came about in my family that whenever you interrupted anyone, the others would call out "Abediah!" That
expression came about in my grandfather's family and was
passed down to us.*

MARJORIE HUNT
McLean, Virginia

NAN GRAHAM

: TOMBSTONES :

When we were little and Williamsburg had just been restored, my family took us down there. Somewhere along the way, my brother needed a bathroom, and my mother didn't know where one was. But we were right near a very ancient cemetery, and she said, "Well, just run right in there behind a tombstone," which he did. After that, whenever our family traveled and the problem came up, it was always, "Hey Mom, I need a tombstone."

MIDGE HEIMER
Germantown, Maryland

: HOUDINI :

When I was young I bought my brother a book for his birthday, a biography of Houdini. He had barely unwrapped it when I grabbed it back from him and ran away and hid for the rest of the birthday party and read the book. It was a big joke that I had bought him a book which I had obviously wanted. So ever after that, anytime anyone gave a gift that was clearly something that the giver wanted perhaps more than the givee, it was called a Houdini.

MARGARET CLARK, AGE 26
Washington, D.C.

: DOWN TO THE RAG :

My grandmother was born in 1832. A neighbor of hers was inviting the minister to dinner, so she invited my grandmother too. Well, in those days, sugar was very expensive, so she didn't have very much at hand. It seems that in those days, the sugar bowls were quite large. So she took a piece of green muslin and put it down in the bottom of the sugar bowl and then put some sugar on top. Well, it was passed around, and when it got around to a little boy at the table, he looked in, and he said, "Ma, down to the rag." So that's been an expression in our family. If anything's down low, we say, "Down to the rag."

BLANCHE M. BOTTO, AGE 87
Kensington, Maryland

WENDY WOLF

: Easy Hands :

My son, well, he gets into things. He's a real live wire. He was about two when I asked him, "Bryan, how come you're always getting into things?" And he said, "Mother, I've just got easy hands." It's become part of the family's sayings. It means getting into mischief and doing little things you shouldn't do. It's gone through the whole family; my sister uses it with her kids.

NANCY KILCZEWSKI, AGE 35
Herndon, Virginia

: My Shoes Are Too Big! :

This expression started when my brother came in drunk one night, and my mother asked him why he was walking funny. It's an excuse for anything now.

CINDY MACKAY
Ridgewood, New Jersey

: I Have to Go Out and Pick Blueberries :

I had a younger sister who never liked to do dishes. We have a summer place in Maine where we spent many summers and when she didn't want to do the dishes she would always say that she had to go out and pick blueberries. That was a job that nobody wanted to do but when it came time to do the dishes, all of a sudden that looked pretty good. So now when any of us have something that we don't want to do, we "have to go out and pick blueberries," which means that we don't want to do that job.

LUCY PHINNEY
Woodbridge, Virginia

: The Right One Did It :

We have a family expression for placing the blame on someone. It started a long time ago when we were little kids. If my mother broke something, we'd say, "Wow! The right one did it." Because if we had done it, we'd get in trouble. And that's gone through all our family. We still say it now. What would be a good example? The cherry dining-room table. My husband was sitting there and his cigarette fell out of his ashtray and he burned a hole in this beautiful table which he adores. That is a perfect example of the right one did it, because if I had burned the table there'd be hell to pay.

NOEL SCHWERDTFEGER, AGE 46
Alton, Illinois

: KESL GARTN! :

Each summer during the 1920s, my parents, my four sisters, and I escaped from our steamy flat in Hartford and went to Ocean Beach on Long Island Sound. In those days, none of the immigrant families could afford to rent a whole house, so we rented two rooms in a large cottage with three or four other families. I remember bringing our own pots, pans, and food and splitting the cost of ice with the other families. You can imagine the scene as four women, all used to their own kitchens, tried to fix three meals a day for their large families in one tiny kitchen. "My husband's coming home at four. I must have dinner ready!" "Thief! You used our milk." "That's my chopped liver!"

Finally, my mother had had enough. She threw up her hands, exclaiming, "I don't need this kesl gartn." This, undoubtedly, was a reference to the confusion that characterized Castle Garden, the immigrant processing station that preceded Ellis Island. "Kesl gartn" became an expression used to connote chaos in the family.

DAVID KOTKIN, AGE 68
Hartford, Connecticut

CAROLYN MITCHELL

DAN BERGER

: MRS. BURGUNDA :

When we were kids and one of us wanted one thing and one of us wanted another, particularly in the way of food for dinner, my mother would say, "I won't be a Mrs. Burgunda. I won't go crazy trying to satisfy all of you." There was a story her mother had told about a woman who did just that, who tried to accommodate the tastes of each child separately. And one very hot day she was just worn to a frazzle and she jumped out a window and committed suicide. So when my sister would be fighting for one thing and I'd want something else, she'd say, "I won't be a Mrs. Burgunda." And that would settle the whole situation.

: A WILMA CLEANING :

I remember a young girl used to come in and clean house for my mother occasionally. She lived across the street, and her name was Wilma. Because she was a young kid, she would kind of dust things off real quickly and that kind of stuff. After Wilma left and got married, my mother would say, when she was just giving the house a real quick cleaning, "I'm giving the house a Wilma cleaning." Well, I didn't think there was anything wrong with that, and so the next time Wilma was home to visit her family, she said, "What's your mom doing today?" I said, "Oh, she's giving the house a Wilma cleaning." "Now, what's that?" "Oh, you know, just a light brushover." And my mother, of course, had to go apologize.

PATRICIA JORGENSON

: CHARLOTTE'S PURPLE WIG :

To show how elegant she is, my cousin Charlotte's furniture is the most elegant, and Charlotte's food is the most elegant. There's no question about it.

We never know what kind of a wig she's going to have. One time she's a blonde; one time she's a redhead. One day she had come from Europe and she showed up in a purple wig—no one here had one. And as a sign of elegance, we now say, "Charlotte's purple wig." And we all know now that it's put-on elegance.

: Cut It, Helen :

When you felt that someone was putting you on, you'd say, "Cut it, Helen." There was nobody in our family named Helen, but it came about when one day the phone rang and somebody said to my mother, "Helen?" And my mother said, "No, I'm sorry, you must have the wrong number." And she said, "Helen, I know it's you." And she kept insisting, and my mother said, "No, you must have the wrong number." And finally she said, "Cut it, Helen!" My mother told us about it at dinner that night. From then on, it became an expression in the family. It's continued in my own family, though they probably don't realize why I say it or where it came from.

ILENE SHELTON
Takoma Park, Maryland

: Move the Bed :

We frequently say to each other, "Now, move that bed." That comes from my godmother who had a bed that needed to be moved. And we went Sunday after Sunday to move the bed and every time we got there, she had changed her mind, she didn't want the bed moved after all. It must have gone on for at least five or six weeks until finally my mother said, "We're not coming back again. Today we will move that bed." So anytime in our family that you've really got to put your foot down and really go whole hog it means you're going to move that bed.

JUDITH BRESSLER, AGE 34
Bluefield, West Virginia

: I Know a Little Girl Who Died from It :

When my sister or I would complain about some minor ailment and my mother wanted to let us know that she didn't really think it was anything serious, she would sarcastically say, "I know a little girl who died from it." After a while all she had to say was, "I know a little girl who . . ." and we knew what she meant. Oddly enough, although what she said sounds depressing or frightening, I found it comforting; I couldn't really be very sick if she made a joke of it.

ISABEL GOLDSTEIN, AGE 38
New York, New York

LORRAINE ARDEN

: JUMPING OFF THE FIFTEENTH STORY WINDOW FOR A BREEZE ON A HOT DAY :

Our family has an apartment at the beach on the first floor of a fifteen-story building. One day my brother was passing out Chiclets, and rather than take one I took three. And when he saw that he said, "Well, why don't you just jump off the fifteenth story window for a breeze on a hot day!" And ever since then, whenever I overdo anything, my brother will call it, "jumping off the fifteenth story window for a breeze on a hot day." Sometimes I'll turn it around and say, "I think I'll jump off the fifteenth story window for a breeze on a hot day—and have a second dessert."

STEVEN ZEITLIN, AGE 28
Philadelphia, Pennsylvania

: PUTTING ON DOWN TO GOURDA :

I was thinking of a story that my family used to tell. Somewhere down in south Georgia there's a little town called Gourda, or something like that. One time when I was young, my great-uncle and my father and my mother and several other aunts and uncles and cousins were driving along together. And I kept asking Uncle Holt, "Where are we going? When are we going to get there? Where are we going? What's this all about?" And he kept saying, "Well, we're just putting on down to Gourda. We're putting on down to Gourda." And in my family that expression, "Putting on down to Gourda" means "We're not quite sure where we're going yet, but we're just keeping on, keeping on."

BETH HUNTER, AGE 29
Manchester, Georgia

: Gone, Garfield, Gone :

My grandfather was fishing, and he had a salmon on his line for twenty minutes and suddenly he lost it. He muttered to the guide because he was so despaired and said—the guide's name was Garfield—"Gone, Garfield, gone." And he just stared there at the water and at the line and at the salmon that was gone. And you know it's funny we've always said that if something's bad, "Geez, gone, Garfield, gone." It's kind of an expression that keeps on going.

PETE LUCKEY

: Shoot for the Top :

Talk about expressions. There's one in my family. It's really not typical of a Jewish family because I read somewhere that Rose Kennedy used the same expression for her children. The expression as my father uses it is, "Shoot for the top, second best you can always get." With that kind of expression in the back of our minds, it was very difficult to think of anything but success or perfection. If I came back from a high school test and told my parents at the dinner table that I got a ninety-nine, instead of saying, "Gee, that's fantastic, an A+," my father would say, "Ninety-nine, Judy, why didn't you get a hundred?" So we grew up with that. It gave us a sense of confidence, not to mention arrogance, that's very hard to learn to cut out.

But now whenever things happen and the situation warrants it, we'll say, "Well, shoot for the top, second best you can always get." It has lots of different meanings. For example, if I want a lemon pie at a restaurant, and they only had chocolate cake, I would say, "Well, second best you can always get." If my mother wants to talk with me on the phone and only my husband is home, she might tease him by saying, "Well, Gary, second best you can always get." It means if you can't get your first choice, second best you can always get. It also means that you're so good you can always get second best, so you might as well try for achieving for the top.

JUDY GLECKLEN KOPFF, AGE 29
Washington, D.C.

: T'AINT YOUR CAT :

PATRICIA: *We have dozens of family expressions. "T'aint your cat," which meant, "It's none of your business."*

PRISCILLA: *And, "Do you think it will rain tomorrow?" If somebody in the family said, "Do you think it'll rain tomorrow?" you knew there was something going on around you that you should pay attention to. It meant, "There's something going on; I can't tell you what it is, but look around and you'll see."*

PATRICIA: *Another one was, "Remember that position is everything in life." This meant that one of the girls was sitting in an unlady-like manner, she better change immediately. And oh, "To heck with poverty, give the cat another herring." That meant that there was something you really wanted to do but couldn't afford it, but you wanted to do it, so "To heck with poverty, give the cat another herring."*

PATRICIA ANNABLE, AGE 50
PRISCILLA WULF, AGE 56
Slippery Rock, Pennsylvania

Family Customs

Anyone who takes the family for a drive on a Sunday afternoon, or goes on a camping trip on Memorial Day, or devises a particular whistle to call the family to dinner may soon find that these practices and events become established family customs. They can be as commonplace as the evening meal with its ceremony of carving the meat and tossing the salad, or as ritualized and sanctified as a wedding, funeral, or Christmas celebration. In an outstanding work on this subject, *Ritual in Family Living,* sociologists James Bossard and Eleanor Boll suggest that these customs, or "rituals" as they call them, constitute "much of the behavior of which a family is proud and of which its members definitely approve. As a phase of family life, it is what the family sees about itself that it likes and wants formally to continue."[1]

Families spend large amounts of time together and certain kinds of activities are bound to recur time and again. Many are just ordinary household necessities—washing dishes, cleaning house, eating breakfast. The shared activities we call customs generally extend beyond these everyday necessities to more expressive practices where there is more joking, laughter, storytelling, sport, celebration, and sensual pleasures like eating and drinking. But even day-to-day housework can become "ritualized" when adorned with expressive activities. Ellen Kurzman, for instance, was a working mother who often did not have time to cook for her children. One night, when the evening meal looked to be made up largely of leftovers, she came up with the idea for a restaurant. The children would dress up as waiters and chefs, and put together a menu from the miscellaneous portions lying in the corners of the refrigerator—one leftover baked potato, a chicken breast, a popover, and so on. Ellen and her husband would then order their portions from the menu. The tradition caught on, and she dubbed it "Ellen's Greasy Spoon."[2] Customs like these are often repeated not only because the children need to be fed or the house needs to be cleaned but because of the emotional satisfaction these practices afford. They come to embody repetition without boredom.

Many families seem to enjoy the idea that they have certain well-established traditions, even when they are in fact enacted only on rare occasions. Adults will often look back on their childhood outings, perhaps a trip to a swimming hole, as a longstanding custom of their younger years, when they actually went there maybe two or three times. Even current traditions can be more concept than custom. One young married couple think of themselves as having a tradition of reading some poetry or philosophy together on Sunday afternoons. "Whenever we miss a Sunday," one of them said, "we just think that, well we haven't fit in our tradition today. In fact, we seem to miss most Sundays." Yet they still think of this as one of their ongoing traditions—that idea is more important than the real participation.

In their volume, Bossard and Boll make a number of striking observations about the role of ritual in American family life. They note that the key to family rituals is leisure time. For this reason modern families, particularly those whose middle and upper class backgrounds afford them a more leisurely lifestyle, often have an abundance of rituals and traditions. Writing in 1950, they also suggest that the "larger the family the more numerous and rich the rituals, whether the family was large by number of children or was made large by the inclusion of relatives and family servants."[3] They observe a number of changes in family tradition over the years. Modern rituals tend to be adapted to smaller, nuclear family groups. They are often more personalized, more child-oriented, more secular, simpler, and of shorter duration—though according to their impression more numerous than ever before.

MIDGE HEIMER

Whereas stories encapsulate experience in a set verbal piece and photographs record shared events on Kodachrome, family celebrations capture the past by reenacting it. Oftentimes American cultural and religious holidays are symbolic representations of an historical event. Jews partake of the bitter herb on Passover to relive in some way the trials of Moses in the desert. The manger scene on Christian mantels at Christmas suggests a recreation of the birth of Christ. In the Dreschler family, the Christmas ritual also commemorates an era in the family's history:

My grandmother and grandfather went to Kansas in a covered wagon. My grandfather took out a section of land, I think that's 640 acres. There are almost no trees in that central section of Kansas. It's the rolling prairie. He planted a big grove of maple trees, and those trees were so sacred to him that he would never cut one, not even for Christmas. So presents were always put at each person's place at the dining-room table.

Even later on, when different branches of the family would have Christmas, they still use the table for their presents. We do now have a little tree, but the presents are always on the table. Trees are not for gifts. Trees are sacred in my family.[4]

Family celebrations symbolically recreate not only the original episode, but all of the subsequent occasions on which it was celebrated, the present continually recalling the past. Each Christmas recalls past Christmases. In fact, many families take home movies or snapshots on Christmas day each year, and spend part of the day reviewing their memories.

Families often call their traditions pastimes, yet they are doing much more than passing time. It is here, in religious celebrations and secular rituals, that the real emotional business of the family is often transacted. Stories are told, nicknames bantered, photos taken and perused. For some families these may be their only way of expressing kinship. For others it is here, over the dinner or the picnic table, that family members renew a dedication to one another which may affect where they reside, how they conduct their business, and the way they choose to live.

: A LITTLE BIT OF HOME :

I'm in the foreign service and have served in many places in the Far East. I was in the Philippines for a while and having grown up in a temperate climate with hot summers and cold winters, I wasn't used to the constant heat. In November, my internal clock told me that Christmas was approaching but it was still 110° outside. So with the Christmas tree upstairs in what I called the den, I turned the air conditioner up very, very high, put on a long fleecy robe that I had in my trunk; I fixed some hot chocolate, and I sat out by the Christmas tree and pretended it was winter in St. Louis. Then I went out and it was 120° in the sunshine, but at least I had my taste of a typical hometown Christmas!

SHARON BABER, AGE 42
Arlington, Virginia

: APPLE SECTIONS :

On Christmas Eve the family—which included grandparents, seven children, their spouses, and children—had a family dinner. Grandfather would divide an apple into as many sections as were the number of family members. Each would eat his section and this would ensure the family's remaining together for the coming year.

KIT DECKER

: THE CHRISTMAS CAKE :

I tell you one thing . . . every year since we were children, my mother used to bake a large cake, and after she got so she couldn't bake it, she'd have it baked up there at a bakery. But she baked this cake and one Christmas we all stood around this cake and sang, "Happy Birthday, dear Jesus. We are so glad you were born today. Happy Birthday, dear Jesus . . ." My mother is still alive and we still do that every year.

HATTIE DAVIS, AGE 68
Washington, D.C.

: MEXICAN-AMERICAN CHRISTMAS :

The biggest thing at Christmas is having tamales Christmas Eve. We go to mass and come back and have hot tamales and coffee. Like I say, we didn't have many gifts; the food was really the thing that brought everybody together. It wasn't so much a religious holiday as it was just rejoicing that we'd had another good year of being together.

STELLA FRASER

: RUSSIAN-AMERICAN CHRISTMAS :

I think the only contact I had with the Slovak culture was through my grandparents. We had certain religious traditions, pretty much at Christmas time. You see, Russian Christmas is celebrated January sixth, a week after our New Year's. They had a two-week difference in their calendar. It has since changed in the Greek Orthodox Church, but when we were children we were lucky because we had two Christmases. On January sixth we would go to my grandparents' house and we

TOM KAVANAUGH

GEORGE COHEN

CAROL DANDY

would have Christmas Eve dinner, and we'd have to kneel down for an hour and pray. They prayed in Slovak, and we just knelt there and thought about how hungry we were. Then, the youngest child in the family—and for a while I was the youngest until my cousin was born, thank God—had to sit in a basket filled with straw. It signified the Christ child, sitting in this straw basket, and it was placed next to the table. Everybody else had to kneel down and pray and pray and pray. I can remember the straw pricking my legs terribly. Then we ate garlic before we could start eating the meal, because that meant we'd be healthy all year. What it meant, too, was that we had bad breath for the rest of the night. It was raw garlic, but I loved it.

KATHY KUNDLA CROSBY, AGE 32
Moscow, Pennsylvania

: ITALIAN-AMERICAN CHRISTMAS :

We always had a big celebration at our home on Christmas Eve. My mother was the second daughter, but the only one that was living in Pittsburgh, so everybody came to our house. We had all kinds of fish, smelts and anchovies, and what we call zeppolli, which is bread fried in deep fat and then sometimes sugared. We had a fish dinner called a calamari, which is squid that had been cooked in tomato sauce, which was the meat substitute for the spaghetti sauce. And we had bacala salad, which is codfish. They were all traditional dishes that were eaten on the day before Christmas.

MARY LOUISE ORTENZO
Columbia, Maryland

: HAMBURGER ON CHRISTMAS EVE :

We have hamburgers on Christmas Eve traditionally. Why? I think because mothers were trying to prepare a massive Christmas dinner and it was always such a hassle that all they could muster for Christmas Eve were hamburgers, potato chips, and a coke.

NANCY REDENBAUGH
Fort Collins, Colorado
ANN M. FLEMING
Pittsburgh, Pennsylvania

: GAG PRESENT I :

We have an album, "Twenty Irish Tunes," that my mother or uncle got twelve years ago. It is the worst album on the face of the earth and every year it's passed back and forth as a gag present. Every year somebody gets "Twenty Irish Tunes" and if you have an album under the tree you pray like hell that it isn't you.

NANCY REDENBAUGH
Fort Collins, Colorado

: GAG PRESENT II :

My cousin Keith came to visit me when I was living in Newfoundland, Canada, and he brought some seal meat back to South Carolina with him—canned seal meat, which nobody in his family wanted to even try. So for a joke he wrapped it up and put it under the Christmas tree for his sister, Isabel. He did that to her two years in a row and the second year she recognized it, didn't even open it, and gave it to me as a present. Then when Keith got married I gave it to his wife as a Christmas present, she gave it back to me the next Christmas, and I gave it to Isabel as a wedding present! That's as far as it's gotten so far, but I'm sure one of us will get it back this Christmas!

AMANDA DARGAN, AGE 31
Darlington, South Carolina

: TRADITIONS LOST, TRADITIONS CREATED :

We didn't have any ritual ways of celebrating Christmas. For some reason they didn't carry over. I would try in the beginning when the children were small to read the message from the Gospel, from St. Luke, and The Night Before Christmas. *They weren't really interested, though. Somehow it didn't come across. We've started a new tradition now. At least one thing that you give has to be homemade. We started that just a few years ago. To really give something of yourself means so much more than going to a store. Even if it's a batch of brownies, it's something you've made.*

HELEN MACKEY GRAY, AGE 51
McLean, Virginia

: Waiting for Santa :

At Christmas, grandpa would sit with his shotgun across his knees in the library, saying that he was going to shoot Santa Claus when he came down the chimney, because he didn't want any old man walking through his house in the middle of the night! We didn't take him seriously but I guess we did go to bed with a little trepidation, hoping he wouldn't really shoot Santa Claus. In the morning he would put bootprints in the dust, take a bite out of the apple, and drink some of the water that we had left for Santa Claus.

NORA HUMPHREY, AGE 25
New York, New York

: Leaving Out the Trains :

Our family history comes in two parts. The first part comes when my brother and I, the oldest two, were little, and my parents were pretty happy together. We were sort of an ordinary suburban kind of family. The second part comes when my father started to leave our family some several months before my youngest brother was born. It took him a couple of years to accomplish the process of leaving completely. He left on the Christmas holidays. I was twelve or thirteen.

The next year, I don't know whether my mother did this on purpose, but we all sort of concurred in changing everything we had usually done. We had always decorated the house in a very certain way. We'd always had a certain kind of Christmas tree — a very tall Christmas tree — maybe because my father is six feet tall and we decorated it in a certain way. But when it came time for us to get together and to decide what to do, it dawned on all of us at once, I think, that we should buy a short, fat Christmas tree, a Scotch pine, kind of blue. So we bought a tree that was about as wide as it was tall, and we went through all the decorations and threw out about half of them and got a lot of new ones, and we fixed the house differently. We left out the trains . . . my father was the only one who ever played with the trains anyway. They went around the bottom of the Christmas tree. We just generally set everything up very, very differently. This was thirteen years ago. I was kind of dreading it, but it was a surprisingly good Christmas. We were all together and it was very pleasant. And we've done it that way ever since. We've bought that exact kind of tree and put the same decorations on it. It's never been the way it was when I was little. Of course, that's what my younger sister and brother remember, as our way of doing things.

: A Modern Seder :

In our house, we still hold the seder the first night. And when we're supposed to read the story of the going out from Egypt, my dad has every year — it's not a sermon — but he tells about more modern times, of the going out of his family from Russia and the going out of my mom's family from Germany, which is also very exciting. When my mom left, it wasn't so pleasant; it was late when they escaped. He reminds us that we should be very grateful. And he tells exactly what did happen and how really fantastic everything is in these days, and how we should really appreciate this. He brings in the religion a lot, how the religion really is very modern in its use. And you go through the Haggadah, and you look at modern applications. And it works. It makes me very appreciative.

ROBERT HORLICK, AGE 20
Riverdale, Maryland

: An Ecumenical Seder :

When my mother started giving the seder, we used the Haggadah that she had written, and we had a tradition of inviting our non-Jewish friends and teaching it to them the second night, so they could see what this ceremony was that they had heard about. I'm the only one in the family now who keeps kosher, so the seder is at my house because I won't go to anyone else's seder. Our seders now are very ecumenical. The best singer at ours now is my brother-in-law, Jim, who was raised as a Methodist. He's a complete atheist now, but he has a beautiful voice. We sing songs for everyone's tradition at the end of the seder. We usually end up with a rousing rendition of "Onward Christian Soldiers." We sing, "We Shall Overcome" and whatever is topical. One year, ecology was the whole theme, and all the younger people who came to the seder were into ecology. Our seders are usually with at least nineteen people, whoever in the family is in the area, and then my mother always feels that whoever doesn't have a place to come should come to us. So we've had very interesting seders through the years with people from all over the world, and all different Jewish traditions.

REBECCA COFMAN
Bethesda, Maryland

: SEASONAL EXCURSIONS :

In my family we had things we did at the turning of the seasons. In springtime we'd go up in the mountains and pick violets and honeysuckle. You just knew that springtime was officially here when you could go up in the mountains and pick your violets. Violets in the springtime, and then wild blackberries and plums in the summertime, and pecans and chestnuts up in the mountains in the fall time—and the leaves would just be magnificent. We'd always bring home colored leaves. And in the wintertime we'd go out and get a Christmas tree from the woods. You knew that when certain seasons were coming about that this was part of what you do. You do things the same way you have turkey for Thanksgiving.

BETH HUNTER, AGE 29
Manchester, Georgia

: THE FIRST SNOW OF THE YEAR :

During the first snow of the year, we would always run barefoot around the outside of the house. This was a lot of fun until my younger sister was in college and her home was a dormitory. It's a very long way to run around the whole dormitory with your shoes off.

DOUG AND LAURA MCDOWELL, AGES 40, 39
Annandale, Virginia

: HOME FOR DINNER :

In my family the meal ritual was important. I've never had a meal in my house when the entire family didn't sit down. Everything is passed until everyone's plates are filled, grace is said—Catholic grace, out loud—my mother takes her first bite, and everyone starts eating their cold dinner. Candles were lit, every single night of my life. And there's no such thing as, "Oh, I won't be home for dinner." You plan a month in advance if you're going to miss a dinner for some reason. You bring your friends to dinner; you don't go out very much. There's no such thing as jumping up from the dinner table, at all. Dinner in my house lasts very frequently until two o'clock in the morning. Everyone sits and talks. All my life.

KATHERINE BRODERICK, AGE 24

Washington, D.C.

: YOUR NAME IN PEANUT BUTTER :

Every time we came home from the store with a new jar of peanut butter, my dad, when we would go out of the room, would write the initials of the one he thought had been the best that week. And then the next morning, or whenever we'd go to open the peanut butter to put on our toast or something, he'd call the person, and they'd come running around, and he'd say, "Oh, look what's here!" And he would tell us that it was the little fairy that lived in the light downstairs, whose name was Matilda and that she had done it. That used to make you be good so you could get your name in the peanut butter.

EMILY SARDONIA, AGE 17

Fairfax, Virginia

: LIFE IN THE HOUSING PROJECT :

When I was growing up before my family moved to another kind of neighborhood, we lived in a public housing project. It's a special something I think only black people can really relate to. Projects were a part of every middle income black person's background at one point or another. My brother and I made very good friends with the family upstairs, with the children. During the summer, we would spend a lot of time in the bedroom singing, and the kids upstairs would be singing, too. We did four-part harmony through the ceilings, which were real thin. When our parents weren't there, we used the radiators for instrumentation. We used the radiators and spoons and the wooden beds and we'd sing and do harmony and have some background.

: THE GOOD NIGHTS :

I remember a ritual that we had that was really neat: "the good nights." It went, "Good night, sleep tight, pleasant dreams, see you in the morning." My father would say, "good," and we would say "night," and he would say "sleep," and we would say "tight" and it went on that way. When we got older he started teaching us how to do it in other languages. We said it in German and we said it in French and we said it in Hungarian. His family had spoken Hungarian when he was a kid. We didn't know any Hungarian but we said "the good nights" in Hungarian. You couldn't go to bed without saying "the good nights" — it was just a really important thing.

SUSAN M. STRASSER, AGE 26
Pittsburgh, Pennsylvania

: AFTERNOON TEA :

When we were little we would have a tea party every afternoon. I was Mrs. Kratched and my sister was Mrs. Jones and we would dress up in our dressy clothes. I have no idea where the names came from, absolutely no idea, but I can see it just as plain as day, near the big jutting windows in the livingroom. We had a little wooden table and chairs that we had gotten for Christmas and a little cupboard in which we kept all our tea things — and every afternoon Mrs. Kratched and Mrs. Jones had tea.

NANCY REDENBAUGH
Fort Collins, Colorado

: THE ELEPHANT'S GRAVE :

Oh, this is my grandmother's favorite story. She grew up in Keene, New Hampshire. She was the oldest of like eight children, and her mother and father were hard pressed to make a living. They used to try to get the kids out from underfoot, and the favorite thing was to put flowers on the elephant's grave. Apparently when the circus train went through this town, an elephant dropped dead and it was buried there. And so that's all the kids had to do in Keene, New Hampshire, was go put flowers on the elephant's grave.

NANCY KILCZEWSKI, AGE 35
Herndon, Virginia

JULIE HAIFLEY

: CROSSING OF THE FATHERS :

Speaking of family traditions, there's one that's been operant in our family. It's a large family with five sons. My father since the early, early fifties has had sort of a rite of passage for his sons. When they are sixteen, he always takes them on a river trip, usually a boat trip down the Colorado River. He goes every year and is a boatman. We usually started out at the "Crossing of the Fathers" at the Grand Canyon, ran down through Phantom Branch and Lake Meade, and got off. It marked sort of your acceptance as a grownup, I guess. That's the first time you get to drink beer and get snuck into bars, that kind of thing, at the end of the river trip. Took about three weeks of pretty hard, hot, sweaty work.

RICHARD MILLER, AGE 32
Washington, D.C.

: THE JEWISH MATRIARCH :

Every Friday night, my grandmother would hold court. It was a Friday night tradition. After we had our Sabbath meal, my mother and father would say, "We're going to grandma's house." To me this was accepted procedure, standard order of things. Until the age of ninety-six, she had all her faculties. But

HELEN ALBANESE

*even as she got older and went blind, she used to recognize ev-
erybody. She used to identify them by their voices and she
would say, "You're the son of my daughter so-and-so. I'm glad
to see you. Sit down and have a glass of tea, and have a homemade cake." She had no teeth, and she would drink tea according to the Russian style, in a glass with a piece of sugar in her
mouth. She'd sip tea through the sugar.*

*But you talk about family life. It was amazing how this one
old woman could keep a family together. She lived to the age of
103 and there were five generations alive at the time that she
died. There's still a certain amount of togetherness. We've separated some as people moved in different directions and the old
dynasty died off. But we had a cousins club named after my
grandmother, because we realized that the only time we were
seeing each other was at somebody's death and we decided we
wanted to see each other at the good times, too.*

ABE WORKMAN
Staten Island, New York

: The Terrific Trio :

*After my separation, when we first started being concerned
about a sense of family, we decided that we were "the terrific
trio," because there had been four of us, and now there were
three of us. My daughter, being a little older, was more concerned because she was aware that there had been a distinct
change in the family situation. She likes to draw and do all
sorts of crafts things, so on her own she drew a picture of me
and a picture of herself and a picture of her brother, each on a
separate page, all colored, with a fancy cover that said, "The
Terrific Trio," and a fancy back cover. She stapled them together and presented it to me as a book.*

*The two of them have hats alike—they are denim patch-
work—and they asked for their names to be embroidered on
them, so I did that, and then they wanted me to get a hat. Well,
I didn't want one quite the same, but I have one that's just a
floppy blue faded denim one, so I put my name on it, and we
have been putting patches on them this year, flags and bicentennial special things. And they call them "our terrific trio
hats." Sometimes they don't want to wear theirs unless I wear
mine. I've had comments from people when I've gone places
and they've said, "Well, aren't you identifying a little bit much
with them?" And my reaction has always been, "When you*

have switched from four to three you want to establish a certain amount of solidarity." Of course there's a loss. They know there's a loss.

: SAINT GRUNE'S DAY :

At the dinner table someone was once saying, "Oranges and lemons say the bells of Saint Clements," and someone added, "Raisins and prunes say the bells of Saint Grunes." The next day became Saint Grune's day. Now, the holiday always falls in March when there are no other celebrations. Suddenly my mother will declare, "Tomorrow is Saint Grune's Day." Raisins and prunes are bought, but not eaten at dinner. It is a big dinner, however, served on good china. A lamb's head mask, left over from some Halloween party, always makes an appearance. Sometimes it is worn, or it appears as a centerpiece decorated with flowers. The holiday brightens up March.

KATHERINE THAMSIN JANNEY
Bethesda, Maryland

: BUTTER-NOSED BIRTHDAY I :

I'm twenty-nine years old. I'm actually twenty-nine and three quarters years old, which is very significant, because in my family birthdays are very important. We celebrate half birthdays, three-quarter birthdays. My seven-twelfths birthday is coming up in a couple of days.

Whenever it's someone's birthday, the other members of the family wake up that person by putting butter, or margarine, on that person's nose. The rationale, supposedly, is to make that person have a shiny day. But I recently found out from one of my sisters that it's not just so that we will have a shiny day. It's so that when we walk to work, or to school, or whatever, we keep the butter or margarine on our nose and people will say to us, "Why do you have butter on your nose?" and we'll say, "Glad you asked, you know, it's my birthday." I don't know if it's a New England tradition, but it's a tradition in my family. And that's because, you know, birthdays are very important to us.

JUDY GLECKLEN KOPFF, AGE 29
Washington, D.C.

: BUTTER-NOSED BIRTHDAY II :

In my family whenever it was someone's birthday you would get up before they got up and put butter on their nose when they were still asleep. My mother always thought this was a really fun tradition, but it led to a lot of fights. There was nothing you could do about it because it was traditional. It's true, it's true, there was nothing you could do. It was the tyranny of tradition!

CATHY CONDON
St. Louis, Missouri

: BIRTHDAY TAPE :

I do tape a lot, every birthday. We tape "Happy Birthday," and then we interview. Everyone in the family gets a chance to say how they feel and what the year was like. And we also tape when we have a religious holiday or something like that. And just every once in a while when the family seems to be in the right mood, we'll bring the tape recorder out, and we'll have interviews, and we'll sing. Then we'll listen to tapes from previous years. And you can hear the kids voices change. The kids love it.

OSCAR GOLDFARB, AGE 39
Silver Spring, Maryland

: DAY OF BIRTH :

We had a tradition just in our immediate family that I really liked. On my brother's birthday and on my birthday, the family always has dinner together. And dad used to sit down with a drink and recount the day of our birth: what happened, how he felt, how my mother felt, what was going on that day. He did it every year. My father died about five years ago but my brother and I have kind of carried that on. On my birthday, my brother will say, "Well, twenty-seven years ago at this time," or I'll say, "Twenty-nine years ago at this time . . ."

VIRGINIA A. HEASLEY, AGE 27
Philadelphia, Pennsylvania

ARLENE GIBBS

: HAPPY UNBIRTHDAY! :

When I was little — I was one of six — my mother would come up with some day out of the year that was really far away from Christmas and your birthday, you know, that endless stretch. You'd come home from school and she'd tell you it was your unbirthday. She'd cook your favorite dinner, whatever it was — even hot dogs. And you could watch all your favorite television programs. Nobody could argue with you about it. People sang happy unbirthday to you. There was a cake sometimes and presents, but it wasn't like a birthday when you got real presents. It wasn't every year that everybody had one. It was just kind of spontaneous. It came from Alice in Wonderland. Remember the Madhatter's teaparty? "Have a happy unbirthday!"

WENDY ROGES, AGE 23
Washington, D.C.

: THE FAMILY REUNION :

ROBERTA: *It's like every member of the family . . .*

JERRY: *. . . has a special thing.*

ROBERTA: *Each one of my mother's brothers and sisters and my mother also has got their own traits and peculiarities. And all put together it makes for a unique affair. My uncle Jimmy is always screaming about the dirty rotten stinking cards, whenever he's playing cards.*

JERRY: *And there's always a pitch game going. The women play poker, and the men play pitch. Then there's the election every year, that's one of those things. . . .*

THERESA: *Oh, it's all in fun, we elect a president of the family every year.*

ROBERTA: *Well, there's kind of a tradition here. The elder is the head of the family anyway, he's the don. He always has been and he always will be. But every year, he's got to get elected! And every year a couple of the brothers will put up a fight, and they'll mount a campaign to get themselves elected president. They will go through all kinds of contortions and slogans and campaign songs and everything to get themselves elected. Then comes the day of an election and everybody will listen to their slogans and appeal and promptly vote Uncle John president again.*

THERESA: *And every year they raise our salaries.*

JERRY: *Every year they double the salaries.*

THERESA: *Cause we get nothing. And so they double it every year.*

JERRY: *You got to picture this family. Most of them are elderly, in their eighties.*

THERESA: *Not most of them, Jerry, there's only a few.*

JERRY: *All right, many of them. And they're—no not very square—they're the most energetic people you've ever seen for their ages. That's basically it.*

ROBERTA: *They are people who enjoy themselves and they have a spirit of fun about them and a spirit of nonsense. And the thing is that it never seems to surface until they get together—if you talk to one of them by himself he is a pillar of the church, as Ma says, just as square as the day is long!*

ROBERTA AND JERRY WILSON, AGES 38 AND 36

THERESA ROACH, AGE 64

Wilbraham, Massachusetts

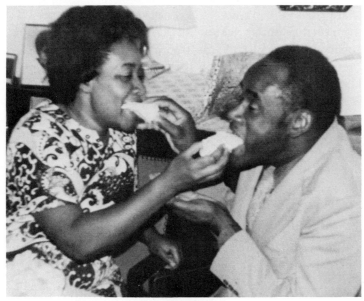

ARLENE GIBBS

Family Photography

Standing proudly in gilt-edged frames or tacked hastily on refrigerator doors, photographs—breezy vacation snapshots, formal portraits, and bashful images of cowlicked schoolchildren—bear witness to a family's shared experiences. Today, photography has become so popular a domestic art that "amid the clutter of material culture to be found . . . in an average American household," writes historian Thomas Schlereth, "the ubiquitous snapshot must surely rank among the most commonplace."[1]

Photographs not only document family life; they have become an important form of family lore as well. To explore the role of photography in family life, we collected albums, trunks, and shoeboxes stuffed with photographs from more than two hundred families in the Washington, D.C., area. Among these six thousand images, we began to see that just as certain categories of stories recur from family to family, similar kinds of photos are enshrined in the home archives. Scenes of holiday celebrations, birthdays, picnics, and vacations dominate these collections, and children, from infancy through high school graduation, are favorite subjects for the home photographer. When we exhibited a typical selection of babies pictured on fuzzy rugs and in frothy bathtubs at the 1975 Festival of American Folklife, a visitor was moved to pull a dog-eared snapshot from her wallet and exclaim, "I have the same photo, only it's a different kid!" To be sure, there are a limited number of poses an infant can strike. But even so, the similarities among these baby photos and among other photos depicting smiling, intertwined families gathered around the hearth, on the front porch, or even around the family car, suggest that picture-taking creates as much as it records ritual scenes of domestic life.

Susan Sontag, in her remarkable collection of essays, *On Photography*, notes that the camera has the unique ability to "freeze moments in a life or a society" so that they are salvaged from "the relentless melt of time."[2] Families use this image-freezing magic of the camera to isolate, record, and confer importance on certain events in their lives. Rescued from the flow of time, rites of passage, sentimental reunions, trips, and outings are preserved on film, providing families with a visual history of their lives together. While we are free to photograph anything we want, we don't really do so, in fact. The commonalities in family photos suggest that home photographers and their subjects share certain notions about appropriate behavior in the face of a camera, and appropriate moments to photograph. Consciously or not, we tend to take photos according to the way we want to preserve, remember, and be remembered. In depicting certain kinds of events in certain ways, family photos, like other genres of folklore, are a creative transformation of selected experience into fixed images that can be shared in the years to come. They are a stylized reality; an expression of our values and ideals.

Family celebrations, prime moments for picture-taking, are now so influenced by the presence of the camera that the act of photography has itself become a holiday tradition. When asked about their favorite holiday customs, several informants jokingly recalled stumbling down the staircase each Christmas morning, into the glare of dad's movie lights. "Christmas, birthdays," moaned Carol Maas, "you hate to see the camera come out. You know it's going to be a picture of the Christmas tree. It's going to be a picture of everyone gathered behind the birthday cake . . . . You know how it is. Standard family pictures."[3]

Family photos adorn the piano and end table in Elmer and Louisa Keck's livingroom, Pottstown, Pennsylvania. Photograph by Margaret Yocom.

MYRA NOVOGRODSKY

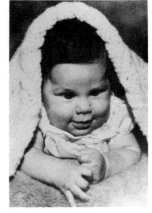

NANCY SMITH

"I have the same photo, only it's a different kid."
MARCE POLLAN

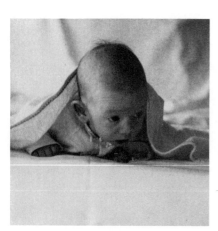

JUDITH RUTTENBERG

NICHOLAS CARROLL

MILLY DANIEL

MARTHA SWARTWOUT

JOAN BERNICK

JENNIFER ROTHWELL

*Photos of the family car recur with striking frequency in
family photo collections.*

RON SUTTON

JAY BURG

SUSAN DAWSON

SANDRA GROSS

"Cameras go with family life. Not to take pictures of one's children, particularly when they are young, is a sign of parental indifference. . . ."
SUSAN SONTAG

ROBERT CREE

MARTHA ROSS

MRS. JEFFERSON PATTERSON

MYRA NOVOGRODSKY

*"Christmas, birthdays—you hate to see the camera come out.
You know it's going to be a picture of the Christmas tree. It's
going to be a picture of everyone gathered behind the birthday
cake. You know how it is, standard family pictures."*

CAROL MAAS

JEAN AND LIEN-SHENG YANG

Never a passive observer, the camera records selectively and often seems to direct the performance on which it intrudes. Bridal couples hold their embrace at the altar to afford the photographer ample time to record "the moment." Families pause at their annual reunions to hug and smile, creating a portrait of unity and affection for posterity. Photographer Tod Papageorge recalls the use of the camera in his own family.

On Christmas mornings my father was a photographer. My sister and I, called to attention, stared ferociously at those awful bulbs, not understanding that even as we sat there, blooming from the ribbons and wrapping paper, we were part of a ceremony; that we were, in fact, its motive.[4]

The ritual of photography extends beyond the picture-taking situation itself to form a vital link with other kinds of family traditions. Peggy Yocom, whose account of her family's folklore begins on p. 250, noted the relationship between images and narratives while reflecting on a visit to her grandparents, Elmer and Louisa Keck.

I was always aware of the many photographs that filled every livingroom end table, sat on each radiator, and spilled over onto the mantelpiece, television set, piano, and sometimes, the dining-room table . . . . As I trained my camera on Elmer and Louisa's home, I realized why the Kecks set out so many photographs and why, even though dusting had become a major chore, they kept them out. The photographs of their children and grandchildren and great-grandchildren, their sisters, brothers, parents, and friends — both living and dead — recreate for them the sense of the large Pottstown-based family they once had. Like a museum, the livingroom photographs preserve a cherished view of the past, recreate it in the present, and serve as a focal point for family storytelling.[5]

Photos serve as mnemonic devices, helping families to recall stories and preserve knowledge of past experiences.[6] Often, we tend to form glowing memories around the idyllic images we have taken, yet there are remarkable and everchanging differences between what Americans choose to preserve on film, and the stories and reminiscences their photos evoke. On a hot July day, Nancy Smith brought a huge photo album to share with us on Washington's National Mall. Her mother had made it for her as a wedding present and it contained a rich visual record of Nancy's life, as well as images of her parents, grandparents, and great-grandparents. As we leafed through the album, the invariably smiling images were dimmed by the poignant tales they evoked from Nancy. A seemingly contented photo of her aunt Rose on an American beach prompted Nancy to recount Rose's harrowing escape from Russia. A proud photo of her father in his World War II army uniform was counterpointed with tragic tales of his experiences in the war.

This story from another informant further illustrates the fact that stories and photos can actually record wholly different versions of "the truth."

The first summer after my father left us we went down to the seashore for a vacation . . . and we went out to eat in one of those places where a person comes around to take your picture at your table and then sells it to you. It's hanging in our upstairs hall now. I looked at it this past Christmas . . . . We looked kind of helpless in the picture. Here was my mother surrounded by all these kids, like what's she going to do? I called my mother out of the bedroom and said, "Remember that summer? Look at that. Don't we look sort of pathetic?" And she stood there and looked at it and she said, "Well, we did OK."[7]

We were curious about this photograph of the "pathetic" and "helpless" family. But when we tracked it down we saw only the standard family vacation picture, people eating well and having a good time. The photograph stood in marked emotional contrast to the story it elicited. (See above.)

Perhaps Jan and her family *were* feeling happy that summer evening. But while the photo itself remains fixed, its interpretation, like stories about our ancestors, can undergo radical change, depending on the vantage point of the viewer, or the teller. Some of our informants remarked that they rarely look at their images because they preferred not to relive the past. Caroline McDonald's mother, for instance, never looks at her extensive collection from the 1920s, because it forces her to recall that the camera, one of the family's most cherished possessions, had to be sold to feed the family during the Depression.[8]

*Nancy Smith's Aunt Rose, an immigrant from
Russia, is shown here on an American beach.*

The painful losses which photographs can bring to mind explain why Catherine Noren never saw her family's photos until 1972, almost forty years after the Holocaust forced her prosperous Jewish family to flee from Germany. Born in 1938, a few months before their departure, Catherine grew up in Australia and America only dimly aware of her roots. "People have various ways of dealing with loss," she said. "The way my family dealt with their enormous loss, of homeland, lifestyle, root-room, comfort was, I believe, to deny what they had lost ever existed, or had validity; to create determinedly a new set for themselves."[9] Like the stories and reminiscences of their prewar lives, the photos which documented their comfortable existence were secreted away, part of an unspoken agreement between family members to leave the past behind. Yet, the albums and studio shots were among the few possessions which they insisted on bringing from Germany, and while they effectively denied their ordeal, no one had thrown the photos out. When she discovered this vast treasury of images in her grandmother's home, Catherine used them as keys to unlock her relatives' memories, and although she didn't realize it at the time, to come to know her own family. The result of her search is *The Camera of My Family*, a book of photos, diaries, stories, and memories all of which, after decades of silence, her family members willingly shared.

DAMON CORDON

Over time, a single photograph, like a dramatic family story, may come to symbolize an ancestor's personality and life history.

In the absence of living memories which give meaning to these images, a photo itself can occasionally give birth to a family legend. A young woman from New Jersey recalled a photo of her great-uncle Max who, as a young man, had briefly joined Buffalo Bill's Wild West Show. His cowboy days were short-lived, but the only photo of Max that survives in the family shows him dressed in his western hat and chaps. Max's image fascinated his great-niece, who dubbed him "One-Gun Blum—The Jewish Cowboy." Though Max Blum spent most of his life as a tailor in Newark, New Jersey, his descendant, who knew him only through a single photograph, spun tales for her own children about "One Gun Blum's" alleged adventures out west. The photo, which for Max might have originally been a means of recording a proud yet ephemeral experience, became the symbol of his whole life and the base on which a family folk hero was molded.[10]

FAMILY ALBUMS

"Through photography," Sontag writes, "each family constructs a portrait of itself, a kit of images that bears witness to its connectedness." Nowhere is this more evident than in the album, which brings together the highlights of family life into a single form with its own story to tell. Now that snapshots are relatively inexpensive and many are taken to document each special occasion, the conventional wisdom suggests, "Your album does not have to contain every picture; you should select only the best or most important."[12] Thus, the making of an album involves a second stage of creativity — editing and juxtaposing images — possibly from a diverse range of scenes and circumstances. Nancy Smith's wedding-present album is a good example of a deliberate selection process, used to celebrate a fundamental personal transition by reminding Nancy of her ties with past generations.

Albums often center on particular units of time: babyhood, adolescence, or a memorable vacation. Joan Bernick encapsulated her romantic European courtship in an album containing snapshots, cryptic notes from her husband-to-be, long letters to her parents, and assorted ticket stubs, postcards, and other mementos from places she and Frank had visited. "My life falls into eras," Joan told us, "anyone's does.

*Joan Bernick and her husband-to-be, Frank, open presents at
their engagement party.*

I have my high school period, courtship, and marriage. You enjoyed those things as you did them and you enjoy them again as you organize the album and again as you look through them."[13] The choice is usually deeply personal and may even reflect secrets kept by the individual owner. Anne Cohen also organized her photos by eras, but although all are important to her, not every image is intended to be shared with the family. In college, she had dated a young man whom she knew her parents would find objectionable. Even now, a decade later, Anne carefully hides those pages which contain his photos when her parents come to visit. "I call it," she laughed, "my removable past."

Perhaps because women so often serve as family historians, many of the albums we viewed were made by young wives and mothers to document their own families. The three pictured here vary in style, but each lender affirmed that picture-taking and viewing the albums later on were important parts of family life. Often, the album served as a catalyst for storytelling among intimate family members, or as an introduction to the family for new friends visiting for the first time.

Nancy Hallsted added her own pages to a commercial baby book as her children, John and Sheila, grew beyond infancy. After filling in each printed page with "Baby's first photo" and "Baby's first step," each successive page celebrates a particular day in her children's lives: birthdays, Christmases, and outings to the park or a beach. Many of the photos are cropped meticulously to eliminate what Nancy deemed inessential: distracting scenery, passersby, and even friends. The albums focus clearly on the children, and their relationship to their parents and grandparents.

"Cameras go with family life," Sontag reminds us. "Not to take pictures of one's children, especially when they are young, is a sign of parental indifference."[14] The albums are part of Nancy's avowed effort to create the strong family bonds she herself had missed as a child. Shuttled from aunts to cousins, she had few pleasant memories and, predictably, few youthful photos to share with John and Sheila. She regrets this lack of images, feeling that her legacy to her offspring is somehow incomplete. The albums, then, fill Nancy's need for family stability while also providing a loving record of her children's early lives.[15]

Nancy Hallsted added pages of photos to a conventional baby book to record the lives of her children as they grew up. Shown here are pages from the book she created for her daughter Sheila.

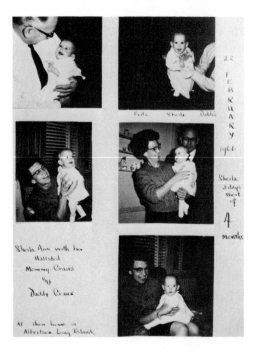

Martha Ross, an oral historian, is aware of our tendency to photograph only the highlights and never the ordinary events of family life. In her album, "Little Visits with the Rosses," Martha and her husband Don consciously broke with this tradition. They photographed each other setting the table, reading, washing dishes, and even sweeping dirt under the rug. Twenty-five years later, Martha shared her thoughts on "Little Visits" with us.

The occasion for putting this book together was the first Christmas after we were married. We made several copies: one went to my husband's parents, one went to my parents, and we also sent copies to two of my aunts. The purpose of the book was to illustrate our lives and the beginning of our marriage. My husband is a photographer and I do some art work, so the album was a collaborative effort. But the whole plan, including what shots were to be taken, was my idea. I wanted to give a balanced picture of our early relationship.[16]

Life in a rural commune was beautifully chronicled by Laduska Adriance, a commercial artist who lived in California during the late 1960s. Each page of her album from that time is an elaborate collage of photos, magazine cutouts, memorabilia, and handwritten text. She combined these forms to convey not only a sense of the chaotic household, but of the other events, trends, and personalities that were significant to that period of her life. Interspersed with photos and mementos were pictures of John Lennon and Bob Dylan, whom she considered part of her extended family.

In 1973 Laduska married and moved east. Her second album chronicles this passage to adulthood and the birth of her daughter. Where the first album pulsates with images and symbols of the youth culture, the more recent assemblage is simpler and more traditional in style, focusing clearly on the intimate relationships of the nuclear family. Still, Laduska feels that even the first album was created for her future offspring. "Looking back," she says, "I think that even then I wanted my children to know what my life was like."

Chapter One...

on Oak Ridge's "G" Road
May, 1946

Courtship and

Martha Ross created "Little Visits with the Rosses" to document the day-to-day activities of her early married life.

Marriage
at the Chapel-on-the-Hill, Oak Ridge
August 10, 1946

Chapter Two...
Housekeeping at 109 W. Madison

Washing the Dishes

Smiling dishwasher
is Wife Martha.
Smiling dish dryer
(not pictured) is
Husband Don.

Carefully stacked
Spode in dish
drainer does
not show.

"In Oak Ridge, we immediately moved into our own tiny house. There were houses of various sizes and you qualified for a house by the size of your family. So we got one of the smallest houses. By the way, the peaked expression comes from the fact that I was pregnant by then and not feeling so well. So my creativity was not limited to the book!"

"This picture of my husband sweeping dirt under the rug is a joke but it characterizes our entire married relationship. He's really a very clean person, comes from a very neat family; I'm from a family of collectors and general household slobs. Even now when we entertain, he cleans the house, so this photo is a reversal of things. I was a southern belle, never taught how to sweep."

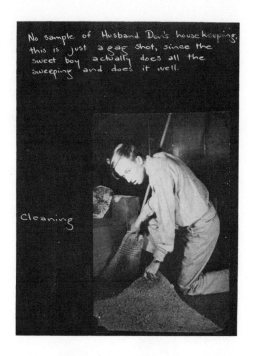

No sample of Husband Don's housekeeping, this is just a gag shot, since the sweet boy actually does all the sweeping and does it well.

Cleaning

..and Meditation time for David
Sometimes we wish he would meditate less and perform more.

Martha and Don added pages to "Little Visits" when their sons, David and Michael, were born.

"The Bendix was David's entertainment before television, watching the laundry slosh around. It was a very common pose, but who could imagine at that time that technology was going to move so fast that the Bendix would now be an historical object?"

David supervises the Bendix while it does his diapers. He can supervise for hours on end.

Each page in Laduska Adriance's first album is a collage of photos, magazine cutouts, and written text which reflect her life in a California commune in the late 1960s.

The photos in Laduska Adriance's second album begin with her wedding in 1973 and record the birth of her daughter.

We're rarely trying, in our photos and albums, to offer a balanced view of family life. Nancy Hallsted crops or discards those images that are extraneous to her vision of family bonds. The Adriance album does not reflect the conflicts of communal living, or those of the youth culture, but only its collective freedom and joy. Martha Ross, even in her attempt to depict day-to-day life, does not document the awkward adjustments to a new marital life, but rather domestic tranquility. What photos *do* signal is a creative expression of certain aspects of family life. In this way, family photography parallels other forms of folklore. Like our stories of heroes, rogues, and innocents, the photo of "One-Gun Blum" compresses the entirety of a personality into a single image. Like a migration story, the photo of the "pathetic" and "helpless" family assumes importance because it now seems to symbolize a turning point in that family's life. Just as Grace McDonald used anecdotes about each of her grandchildren as keys to their identities, Catherine Noren used her family photos to elicit stories and memories from her relatives. Picture-taking and sharing albums at holiday celebrations, like storytelling itself, have become an enjoyable and deeply-rooted family tradition.

While these images often cause us to remember the not-so-good times, either by association or by contrast, we seldom stop and say, "No, it didn't happen this way." Like the courtship story which becomes embellished over time, photos assume an aesthetic character of their own, one which focuses on the most positive and uncomplicated aspects of family life. We strut and smile, clown and cavort in the face of the camera because the resulting images affirm what we believe most worthy of preserving from the flow of family life.

Other Ways of Preserving the Past

I had a great-aunt who apparently was arrested by the czar and sentenced to Siberia for holding Jewish Sabbath services in her home. So she disguised herself as a man, so as not to be attacked, bundled up her belongings, which included incredibly heavy copper pots, on her back, and walked across Russia to the Turkish straits to get a boat to come to this country. We have the pots, which is why the children have the story.[1]

While storytelling, picture-taking, and the celebration of other rituals occur on specific occasions, families go about their daily lives surrounded by many objects, besides photographs, which stand as silent reminders of their heritage. A close connection exists between a family's stories and its memorabilia; for tangible articles often serve as reference points for stories, and explain the persistence of certain episodes in tradition. Some of these objects like the Ludwig's copper pots in the story above connect to a single incident; others serve as more general reminders of the past, its events and participants.

Often, the most significant material objects are those which evoke a feeling of "home":

There was one thing which we recognized very early as being very important in a traveling life. That was to bring along with you as many objects as you can with which you have an emotional attachment: the pictures on your wall, the family albums, the things that mean home to you no matter where you are. Furniture is nothing. You know you can buy or borrow it, but the things which mean home to you are extremely important ... Churchill once said, "Necessities you can live without, but luxuries, never."[2]

In her book, *Coming of Age*, Simone de Beauvoir wrote, "My objects are myself . . . . The proprietor maintains a magic relationship with his property."[3] She suggests an interesting connection between our traditions and our possessions: "The possession of a garden means being able to take one's walk in it every afternoon. This armchair is waiting for me to sit in it every evening."[4] Taking her idea a little further, as objects of great emotional value, heirlooms can enhance and even motivate family rituals. For four generations the Heimer family, for instance, treasured an old doll they named Cinderella which was given to a child in the family as a Christmas present a little over a hundred years ago. Now, the doll is brought out and photographed with the family each year at Christmas and for her hundredth birthday the family threw a special Christmas party which included a cake with a hundred candles.

Possessions are also an interesting part of family tradition because they enable us to experience what some scholars have termed simultaneity:[5] by gathering around ourselves treasured objects from different times of our lives and our histories, we experience different eras at the same moment and in some way bring the totality of the past to bear upon the present. Many families have a "memory wall" or a particular alcove in which their most precious keepsakes and memorabilia are arranged to create this effect.

Some family artifacts have intrinsic or historical value and automatically assume the status of family heirlooms, as in this family story:

After the Civil War my great-grandfather was running a blockade outside of New Orleans. Around that time he was approached by an emissary from the Emperor Maximilian of Mexico to try to get his wife out of the country because things were looking a little nasty. The emperor was asked to go but he said, "No, no, my people love me . . . but send my wife out." And so they took the empress, and my great-grandfather and another man got her out of the country to France. And he was given a ring that had three diamonds in a square setting. And so all my brothers have used diamonds from that ring in their wedding rings, so they're just being passed on.[6]

Of course, the vast majority of objects which are passed from generation to generation are more modest: a lock of hair, a set of teacups, a yard of wedding lace, or a packet of love letters. The same object, without a history or a context, may elude a stranger's eye, but its association with relatives or shared events can make it special or set apart. One person's junk becomes another's keepsake.

The tangible nature of these objects does not necessarily fix their meaning, which may be as ephemeral as in any other form of folklore. Just as stories, expressions, and anecdotes are constantly being invented, remembered, and forgotten, objects too, pass in and out of family tradition. Once the association with the family is forgotten, the item may simply become a hand-me-down and may eventually be discarded. But when even the most worthless of objects becomes imbued with memories, it seems to defy any effort to get rid of it. A good example is Nancy Smith's kitchen chairs:

I have this kitchen set still. It's funny, the things you grow up with. Here it is in this picture before I was born [see below]— this is when we lived on Riverside Drive in New York. This set was in every house I've ever lived in. I have it in my kitchen. They're ugly chairs but they're sitting there. I keep thinking I ought to get rid of them. BUT I CAN'T GET RID OF THOSE CHAIRS! *I've seen them white, I've seen them brown, I've seen them green—they're my chairs and somehow they go with me.*[7]

Artifacts, like photographs, function as family folklore on several levels. First, the item can be an integral part of a tradition, such as Christmas tree ornaments that must appear each year before family members are convinced that the holiday has truly arrived. Artifacts can also be a direct record of family heritage, such as a letter, a diary, or even the yardstick used to measure and chart the children's growth. Perhaps most important, objects like the copper pots function as cues, eliciting a wealth of stories and reminiscences.

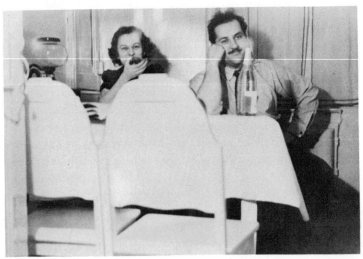

NANCY SMITH

While artifacts are a common means by which different families celebrate their heritage, they, more than other folkloric genres, tend to be exclusive to individuals or particular segments of the family. Many relatives might tell the same story or carry copies of the same family photo, but only one family member or unit can possess grandfather's rocking chair and, most likely, the stories which surround it. The uniqueness of objects renders them delicate as carriers of tradition. If a story is forgotten by one relative, it may be remembered and passed on by another. But when an artifact is lost, destroyed, or discarded, neither it nor the associations that make it precious can be replaced.

The family bible is the quintessential example of a written family record; surprisingly, though, it is often the least complete, having only a list of names and birthdates. Robert Rhode related a story to us to illustrate the use of the family bible by one of his ancestors. In this case, the bible serves two functions, as proof of age for the great-grandfather and as a cue for his descendant's story.

My aunt told me this story about my grandfather's father, I suppose. He wanted to join the Confederate army so he went to Tennessee. They told him he was too young. This must have been early in the war before they were taking everybody. He was seventeen and they said, "No, you look fifteen. We have to have proof of your age." So he rode back to Texas which took him several days and got a big family bible in which was recorded his birthday. He got the bible and rode back to Tennessee with his bible in his saddlebag to prove his age and they let him join. He kept the bible all during the war, and after it was over he returned it to Texas and the family still has it.[8]

Other material objects besides bibles can reveal valuable family folklore and history. In this age of instant communication, we frequently forget that letter writing was once an art. In addition to casual correspondence which by chance contains information of importance to the family historian and folklorist, there exists a genre of correspondence which deliberately records contemporary events or recreates times past. For example, the Civil War letters of John Brandon to his family give a soldier's eye view of that war. On October 6, 1861, he wrote his father:

We have no officers in this company worth a cent, except the captain. The others are all boys who got their offices through the influence of rich relatives, and not fit to command a squad of geese. I have not been on drill but twice since we have been here. Half of us have no horses. If things do not get better I will try and get transferred to Overton's company, if it comes here. I have not been out of camp but two hours since I have been here, except to drill.

Eight days later, a second letter followed:

We have not drilled any yet, we have been loafing ever since we have been here. I suppose we will have to go into the field unprepared. I do not see any other show now. If Frank or Albert get into a fever about going to war, tell them to mind their own business. If they want to live like dogs and be treated like dogs, the army is a very good place, but if not, they better stay out of it. Give my love to all, Your Son, John Brandon.[9]

Some rare individuals have recognized the possibilities of this vanishing form, and seized upon it deliberately. In 1972, at the age of eighty-two, Andrew Nicholas Conrady composed a twenty-six-page letter to introduce his newborn great-grandson to a part of the Conrady tradition that might otherwise be lost. Mr. Conrady explained his intentions at the beginning of the letter.

Dear Great-grandson: Greetings —
"Grace be with you, mercy and peace from God the Father, and from Christ Jesus the Son of the Father, in truth and charity." (John 2:3)
You being fifteen [15] days old and me being 82¼ years plus some twenty leap year days makes me some days over [30,000] thirty thousand days old. That makes me [2000] two thousand times as old as you. In truth that is what could be called a BIG generation gap. By the time you are old enough to read and understand this letter, great grandmother and me will likely have long since passed on to our eternal reward.
This letter will NOT be a scholarly masterpiece; rather, it will be some thoughts, some facts, some hopes, some plain fancy and others plain nonsense, but I trust you will enjoy reading all of it. . . .[10]

Letters have an inherent drawback as a record of family tradition: often written to be thrown away when read, they must have been saved in some way, either by chance or foresight. In addition, information usually must be culled from a number of letters or from other sources if they are to recreate a time of life.

A more concise means of recordkeeping is the memoir, a reminiscence of the past which focuses on personal or family history. Memoirs (as opposed to diaries) are intended for a wider audience than are letters, and for this reason are often more polished and literary in format and tone.

E. S. Goodwin used her memory of the floorplan of her childhood home as a basis for her memoir. As she takes the reader from room to room, she recounts the incidents and describes the persons she associates with each part of "the house on M Street."

It is too bad that I cannot show you the kitchen with its big woodburning range, its large table, and the muted light coming in through the windows on the areaway. And the pantry!, with shelves filled with wood, its capacious sink and its dumbwaiter for carrying food to the dining room above. We loved the dumbwaiter. It was such fun to give kittens a ride on it. Then, too, Lucetta and I found a closet under the back stairway that was littered with elegant fashion magazines. We had two colored pencils, red and blue, and we crept in there secretly and, by the light of a candle stub, we colored the pictures of pretty ladies. Lucetta's favorite color was blue, so I took red because my mother had taught me never to insist on first choice. We could have burnt the house down with that candle.[11]

Family history and needlework have long been linked together. Samplers embroidered by young girls frequently have the names and ages of family members stitched into them. Various types of presentation and commemorative quilts have been made and given to mark rites of passage: birth, the attainment of adulthood, marriage, moving into a new place of residence, even death. Often, the clothing of family members is stitched into a quilt, either intentionally or for the sake of frugality. In the best examples of these family artifacts, the makers have adopted needle and thread, yarn, and yard goods, as their medium of expression instead of the family historian's more usual tools of pen, ink, and paper.

Mrs. Ethel Mohamed, of Belzoni, Mississippi, began to embroider scenes from her family history at the age of sixty, after the death of her husband, Hassan. He was a Lebanese immigrant who first traveled to Mississippi as a peddler of household goods, and then became a successful dry-goods store owner. Many of her intricately stitched and appliqued works were inspired by particular memories of Hassan and their children. One showed the family with a new baby (see photograph on p. 207); another depicted her husband with his pushcart. Some of her works are drawn from the history of the community and some are more symbolic, depicting her children as the fruit of a sturdy tree of life, or herself and her husband riding in the beak of the bluebird of happiness.

Sophia Fairfield Wheat called upon genealogical research, family tradition, and her own memories and experiences to create her masterwork, the Fairfield Family History Quilt. The eighty-eight embroidered blocks of this quilt trace the history of the Fairfield family in America from 1631 to the present. The stories to accompany each incident are included with each block.

SOPHIA FAIRFIELD WHEAT

Ethel Mohamed explains the imagery in her embroidered pictures depicting the activities of a pioneer ancestor in her native Mississippi and the birth of a new baby in the family.

Betsy Keeney followed the tradition of commemorative needlework when she designed this quilt for the fiftieth wedding anniversary of her parents, Mary and Joseph Donovan. Since Mr. and Mrs. Donovan emigrated from County Cork, Mrs. Keeney included several Irish symbols such as the Claddagh ring and shamrock. Family-related symbols include images of Cape Cod (the scene of many vacations), a railway engine (to symbolize her father's occupation), and the ever-present pot of tea of which Mrs. Keeney said, "Through the years both happy and sometimes troubled there was something almost healing about sharing a cup of tea with someone loved."

One of the most unusual examples we found of preserving and artistically reinterpreting a family's past was a three-dimensional tableau of dolls created by artist Esther Luttikhuizen for Charlene James. The photograph on which the tableau is based depicts Charlene as a child standing outside St. Josephat's Basilica in Milwaukee, Wisconsin, with her mother, grandmother, and Aunt Vickie. The dolls, made in 1980, almost thirty years after the photo was taken, recreate for Charlene an almost mythological rendering of her past. "I had always shared a strong personal affinity with these women," she told us, "but only after I'd seen the dolls did I feel part of a continuous bloodline as well. My aunt Vickie was excluded because I wanted three dolls to reflect the three generations."

Most memorabilia are not so self-consciously created. But just about everybody has a drawer or shoebox filled with objects collected, or at least kept, because of their associations with certain persons, places, or events. These keepsakes, souvenirs, and mementos are preserved because they have developed their own histories and meanings. A ticket stub or dance card might recall a particular meeting, but a found rock or piece of an old toy might be less obvious (even to its owner). It is often unclear just why these objects are not discarded. They seldom have any intrinsic monetary value; their chief contribution appears to the uninitiated to be the perpetuation of clutter. But to their owners, these bits and pieces of the past represent significant aspects of their lives, although the exact significance may be difficult to articulate, even to themselves.

CHARLENE JAMES

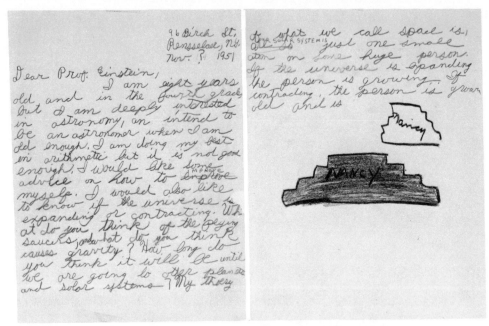

In 1951, eight-year-old Nancy Davis wrote a letter to Albert Einstein. Her mother saved the first draft of the letter and included it in a photo album compiled for Nancy as a wedding present.

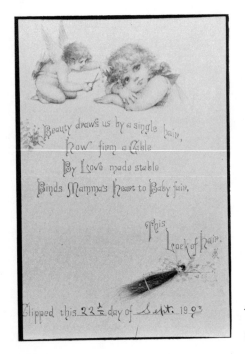

This ticket to Disneyland was included in an album made by Mrs. Mary Goodwin for her daughter Linda on the occasion of Linda's' twenty-first birthday.

A page from the 1903 baby book of Ida Elizabeth Sabin. (Contributed by her descendant, Mary Goodwin.)

We often seem caught in the tension between not quite knowing why we are saving something, and yet not quite wanting to throw it out. We feel that if we do discard some keepsake, we are somehow denying the meaning of the past. So we end up shifting it from box to box, and carrying it from old residence to new. "It's funny, my life has been a series of moves," Ron Sutton told us, "and I would suspect that every time I've moved, I've replaced the boxes. I've taken them out of wherever I've had them and as I put them away, I frequently will open them and for that moment kind of relive, you know, those moments." [12]

Andrew Conrady expressed his opinion of memorabilia quite emphatically in his letter to his great-grandson:

One more thing and then I am finished. Keepsakes. Keepsakes usually are junk of little value except sentiment, and something your kids or grandchildren turn into a holy war and refuse to speak to each other ever afterward. Mine are of little money value, but I want you to have them. If inflation keeps up its pace, I think by the time you are sixteen years old, you could take the whole kaboodle to a pawn broker. If he happens to be in good humor he might give you three bucks for the lot, about enough to buy you and your girlfriend two cokes and straws. Then again, you may only get enough for one coke and two straws. [13]

From copper pots to pressed flowers, the objects that decorate our homes and underscore the meanings of our lives become yet another vehicle for the transmission of folklore across the generations. Some are unlikely icons — common household objects which assume importance because of their associations — while others, like the family history quilt, are deliberate records of family life, and examples of folk artistry in their own right. But whether proudly displayed on a wall or consigned to the netherworld of a rarely opened drawer, our memorabilia remains a vital part of our family tradition for as long as its many meanings live in our memories.

Five American Families

The stories, expressions, traditions, and photographs in this book were shared with us by hundreds of American families. Presented here by form and theme, they delineate some of the recurring patterns in American family lore and suggest the many ways in which families encapsulate cherished parts of their past. Yet in this book Americans talk about their folklore in bits and snatches, leaving us to answer still the question: how and when and why are all the forms of folklore blended and shared in an individual family?

For this reason we invited five folklorists to think and comment about the folklore in their own families. Their essays present a more in-depth look at some specific American families who vary widely in their geographic locales and in the ways folklore plays a role in their lives.

Steven Zeitlin, whose grandparents immigrated from a Russian Jewish village at the turn of the century and settled in Philadelphia, highlights a traditional Russian dance still performed in the family; Amanda Dargan, who comes from an extended, rural South Carolina family, treats the subject of characterization in her family's folklore, demonstrating the ways in which stories, nicknames, descriptions, and imitations are used to pinpoint the idiosyncracies of her family members; Dennis Folly, an Afro-American folklorist, describes his family background in central Virginia, focusing on his great-grandmother and her use of proverbs as instructional devices. Anne Warner, well-known for the treasury of folksongs and vignettes of rural life in Appalachia and the northeast which she and her husband Frank collected in the thirties, forties, and fifties turns her attention to her "other folklore journal," in which she recorded her children's perceptive utterances as they grew up in Greenwich Village in New York. Finally, Margaret Yocom looks at the function of family tales as a unifying device which characterizes her Pennsylvania German family's ritual gatherings: weddings, anniversaries, and funerals.

These five essays offer us another way of looking at the stories, traditions, and photos in this book. A family story may seem funny to us, but it is far more so to the family who knows all the characters, and whose history is untangled in the telling. These essays remind us that family traditions are richest in meaning in the context of an individual family where the characters in the stories and the places pictured in the photographs reverberate with myriad associations.

A t every wedding and every bar mitzvah in my family, when the sobriety of the ritual has at last given way to festive celebration, the band breaks into "Havah Nagilah," and the crowd comes to its feet. The family forms a circle, holds hands, the circle starts to turn, first right, then to the left, yielding a wide wedding ring of guests clapping joyously in time. Into the circle goes a disco dancing teenage cousin; a sixties flower child follows with the frug; my mother does the Charleston; and some cousins surface for the Philadelphia Mummer's Strut, holding the edges of their jackets, swaying side to side.

Then comes the highlight of the dance. My uncle Oscar, sixty-five years old, his arms crossed, struts towards the center of the ring. The audience holds its breath. He squats, leaps upward, kicks out a leg. The clapping intensifies. His knees bend again—another leg! Smiles and cheers burst along the circle of faces. He's down, then up, his heels barely touching the floor.

His three sons join him in the center, each performing the dance he learned from his father. Facing one another they vault upwards, downwards in unison, their legs shooting forward, suggesting together the spokes of a wheel. Richie with a crew cut and a wide smile dances and clowns; Marc, the tallest, struggles to make his long legs bend and stretch. Eddie, stocky but limber, goes low on his haunches. "*Havah nagilah, Hava nagilah, Havah nagilah, venismekha.*" One leg bends, the other extends, he leaps high in the air, the legs change places. "*Uru, uru akhim, Uru akhim b'-lev sa-may-ach.*" He vaults upwards, his legs rising even with his waist, and astonishingly, his fingers touch his toes. "*Uru akhim b'lev sa-may-ach.*"

The band moves into the final verse. Oscar begins to improvise and clown, as the instruments drag out the final line. "*Uru akhim, uru akhim b'-lev sa-m— — ay — — ach!*" The song ends and the clapping becomes applause.

"It's our family's way of busting out with excitement," said Oscar's daughter Jayne. "You take love for granted," her sister Marsha added, "You fight all the time, leave home when you're eighteen. There's only a few moments when you really feel that spark. But that's one of those times—when my father sees his three sons dancing."

The performance of the *kazatske* (pronounced in my family *kazatchka*) goes back beyond the memory of the oldest liv-

THE
WEDDING
DANCE
Steven J.
Zeitlin

Max Wallace, Oscar's father, who learned the kazatske *in Russia.*

ing relative, to the Russian towns and villages my grandparents left as children, towns that have taken on some of the cast of Anatefke in *Fiddler on the Roof*. ("They do one wedding scene where they do a *kazatske*-like dance with bottles on their heads," Richie said. "I almost broke into tears.") Although these villages and towns included Jews from different social strata and varied lifestyles, the family's images of what life was like "in the old country" or "back in the *shtetlekh*" (the Russian-Jewish towns) have been drastically altered by popular and literary images. In my imagination, their homeplace has even come to resemble Vitebsk, Marc Chagall's hometown on the Russian-Polish border, a town transformed by memory and imagination into paintings in which all the accouterments of my ancestors' rough lives—the clocks, fishes, and menorahs—are transfused with beauty, turned upside down, floating dreamlike above the village square.

Somewhere between Chagall's mythical Vitebsk and Sholom Aleichem's Anatefke lay the small village of Ochremover in Russia, which Oscar's father, Max Wallace, fled. But he painted no magical, dreamy vision of his homeland. "Tell me one thing that was good about the old country?" he would ask his sentimental fellow immigrants. "You froze in the winter, and you died from the heat in the summer, and everybody ate out of one big pot."

My grandmother and her sister Rose came out of Russia at the turn of the century as small children hidden beneath a pile of straw in an oxcart. And my grandfather's family fled into the snow when a raid or *pogrom* swept through their village, leaving their father to guard their home. They slept in the barren woods for days, and when they returned, half frozen, their house had been ransacked, bed feathers floated in the air, and my great-grandfather hung from the ceiling on a noose. His house cat lay whining on the floor beneath the corpse. After three days the cat died. Such is the legacy of stories from that generation of my ancestors.

Yet for all the wretched memories, all the forgettable things, Max kept the tradition going. "Tell me one thing that was good about the old country," he asked, but he kept the dance alive. On every family occasion, he traced those ancient Russian triangles with his feet. "It's old country, but such a wonderful old country," said my raucous aunt Elaine. "When you hear the music you just want to get up and do it.

It's the same way the Italians feel about," and she breaks into song, "La Sooooorento. . . ."

Those small children who huddled around that pot of soup and crossed the border in an oxcart came with far more than their meager possessions piled in their arms. They brought with them a whole eastern European Jewish culture, *yidishkayt*, including tunes, dances, and customs which had sustained generations of rabbis and merchants in Russian-Jewish towns. They brought along with them religious observances, festivals, foodways, a culture that was to be far more threatened by their soon-to-be-discovered progress and wealth than it ever was by poverty and hardship.

In America they settled in Philadelphia and became shopkeepers, mostly. They preserved the Yiddish language, the Jewish holidays, and for as long as they lived (well into my childhood) the Passover seder was an event to behold. As Oscar's daughter Marsha remembered the ritual from childhood, "You don't talk, you don't move, and [there's] twenty pounds of gefilte fish in the kitchen." The women cooked for a week: *kneydlekh* (matzoh dumpling), *kugl* (noodle pudding), and matzoh ball soup.

Their children became businessmen, for the most part. They departed the Jewish city neighborhoods for the suburbs, leaving behind many of their customs—keeping kosher, using *tfillin* (a prayer apparatus), observing Purim. They retained only snatches, a few Yiddish words and phrases (none of which can be adequately translated) such as *mentsch* ("a real human being"), *meshugene* (crazy person). They continued to fast on Yom Kippur, but the traditional home-cooked seder gave way to a catered dinner with the whole *mishpokhe* (family) in a rented hall. It was a discarding of the past that occurred in countless families of similar background all across the country, as being American—integrated and homogenized—displaced the old ethnic identity.

Their children's children became more secular still. Some succeeded their fathers in business. Others became doctors, lawyers, accountants, television producers. They moved still further away, past the Philadelphia suburbs to cities like Washington, New York, and Los Angeles. And when today they come together for family celebrations, even the music to that old Russian dance step has been replaced with a newer

My uncle Oscar Wallace dancing the kazatske with his three sons—Mark, Eddie, and Richie.

*Uncle Oscar dancing the kazatske
with my mother in 1949.*

Israeli tune played by the Ronnie Lewis Band. But still the *kazatske* continues. Still the flurry of feet.

Yet how strange a custom to represent our Jewish lineage! Here is no ritual dating back to an exodus from Egypt thousands of years ago. Family tradition has it (and scholarly research suggests) that the *kazatske* was a dance of the Cossacks, a group of Russian men of no fixed abode or occupation who became a force of permanent irregular soldiery, and whom our ancestors encountered (generally as enemies) in their tumultuous, century-long stay in Poland and Russia. Their dances were called "Cossack" if of a vigorous nature, combined with somersaults, handstands, and flips. They were called "Cossatchok" when less strenuous. These less acrobatic though still arduous steps appealed to the Jews in their *shtetlekh*, and were incorporated into older dances on festive occasions. "The funny thing is," my uncle Jay joked, "that's probably the dance they did when the Cossacks came after them swinging swords and they tried to escape!"

Oscar bends, kicks his legs out, squats, jumps. It's old-country *kazatske*, yes. Suddenly he reaches for a napkin, ties it around his head, and walks to the rhythm like a half-crippled man. Above the instruments blaring out "Havah Nagilah," he whistles piercingly, pretends to be playing a fife in "The Spirit of '76." The ring of dancers, clapping, laughs with delight. A quintessential American image becomes (through a kind of ad libbing) a part of the dance.

And that walk, that "obviously infirm walk," Richie said, "is a take-off on the Ritz brothers. The Ritz brothers are, let's say, an ethnic version of the 'Three Stooges'—you know, Mo, Larry, and Curly were all Jewish—they were Jewish just like the Marx brothers. But the Ritz brothers in a sense came off as being Yiddish. Dey all spoke with a slight accent. . . . They were in the movies in the late forties. And the best surviving example is [a version of] *The Three Musketeers* with the Ritz brothers, where the opening scene is the three of them baking chicken soup. Harry Ritz used to walk with a very strange walk that [my father found] would go easily into 'The Spirit of '76.' "

The *kazatske* is done by few Jewish families as secular as my own, yet it is still common among Hassidic Jews, particularly in the Lubovitch community in New York. Jill Gellerman, who explored these traditions, discovered that even in this enclave of traditional Jewish life, the dance has adapted

Eddie Wallace performs a difficult kazatske step.

to new soil. The band plays what she calls the "*kazatske medley*," and often includes a few bars of "Yankee Doodle Dandy" along with the traditional eastern European melodies. A quintessential American tune becomes incorporated in Jewish custom, perhaps in the same way that a Russian dance step became part of Jewish celebrations a few generations ago.

So many meanings converge in Oscar's simple steps. When he dances, Oscar writes some of the family history with his feet, recalling like far away music weddings danced in Russian villages, and, more dimly still, echoes of Jewish history back to the pharaohs. The tune "Havah nagilah" ("Let Us Rejoice") is a modern Israeli anthem, but, for us, the dance also celebrates what it means to be an ethnic Jew from Philadelphia—Oscar and his wife Sylvia are, in fact, probably the most ethnic members of their generation, observing more of the old customs than their contemporaries in the family. He is a family patriarch, the senior among the second generation immigrants. And whereas my parents, for instance, retained only a few words and phrases of Yiddish, Oscar and Sylvia broke into it fluently whenever they didn't want the children to understand their conversation.

And of course when he dances, Oscar expresses his own distinctive personality. As William Butler Yeats once wrote, "How can we know the dancer from the dance?" Or as my uncle Jay Burg put it, "That's Oscar, that's his *shtik*."

His sons too now dance in their own inimitable styles. Marsha suggests that each galavants into the center for different reasons. Richie revels in the humorous improvisations. Marc, she says, is the most sentimental, the most conscious of paying homage to his father in the dance. Eddie is the most athletic, the only one who can kick both of his feet out and touch his toes in mid-air (see photo on page 215). He attributes this to heredity. "My leg structure is a lot like my father's," he said, "[I got the] thigh muscles that you need."

Oscar's children will carry the meaning of the dance with them long after their father is no longer able to kick and bend and stretch. Yet they will always, as Richie said, think about their father when they think about the dance. In turn, when Oscar thinks about the dance, he recalls *his* father before him. "It's a remembrance and a thought," he commented.

When we think about our relatively ancient customs we like to emphasize the way they reach down across the generations, connecting us to our great-great-greats. But as with the family dance, customs are often tied most closely to childhood memories, often reinforced by the personality or will of one strong individual. The *kazatske* is perpetuated not only because Richie and Marc and Eddie have such strong feelings about our Russian ancestors, but because they love and emulate their father, who loves and emulates his own.

My grandmother and the other women of her generation performed a different style of Russian dancing at our family celebrations.

Similarly, parents often celebrate holiday traditions like Christmas and Channukah in ways which recall their own childhood. They often decorate the tree, light the menorah, hang the stockings the way their parents did for them. In this fashion, with little regard for the ageless quality of the customs, a chain of interlocking childhood memories forms across the generations. These memories become our "roots."

On one occasion I asked Marsha what was more important to her about the dance — that it was performed by her father or that it was a Jewish tradition. She summed up her feelings by saying, "He's great and we love him, and incidentally it's a Jewish tradition." But in a way my question was beside the point. For there is a sense in which, as far as his children are concerned, Oscar *is* Jewish tradition. From the first moment they opened their eyes, they saw the two together, conceived of them as one.

Recently, our other passionately celebrated Jewish tradition, the family's Passover seder, began to get out of hand as the good-natured conviviality of the cousins reached such a pitch that it started to drown out the service, and the urge to visit made it difficult to keep the whole family seated. Oscar's son Richie, who was presiding over the service, waved his prayerbook and asked for quiet as a cousin at the far end of the table managed to turn the solemn passover question into a humorous quip: "Why should this night be different from all other nights?" Finally my aunt Elaine, teary-eyed, stepped to the center of the rented hall and raised her glass. "I think all of us should remember why we're here," she said, and then mentioned not the suffering of the Jews in Egypt, but a series of names: "Grandpop Harry, Daddy Al, Bobe Rose . . ." For everyone in the family knows — and the toast only served to reiterate — that the tradition continues, even in the rented hall, in memory of the strong, strict, charismatic figures who presided over the seder when we were all younger, and perhaps especially in memory of my grandfather in whose home the passover supper was celebrated. Then Elaine sat down at the catered banquet table, and with characteristic humor, not knowing whether to laugh or cry, she added, "I'll tell you why we're here — because they sold the biggest house!"

The last song of the evening was an old favorite, and all the aunts, uncles, and cousins joined in for the chorus: *"El b'ney, el b'ney . . ."* Then suddenly Oscar and a host of cous-

*"That was a joy for me to see—my father dancing
at my wedding."*

ins began to imitate my grandfather, who had once presided
over the occasion with such style. They rolled their tongues
through the *"rumpt pa ra ra rum pum pum,"* and, dessert
spoons in hand, they flicked their wrists and swung their
arms with a distinctive flourish. "That's the way your grandfather used to do it," Oscar whispered to me as the song continued: *"El b'ney, el b'ney, r-r-r-r-rumpt pa ra ra rum pum
pum."*

Oscar's father had a weak heart, and died soon after his first
grandchild was born (if he could have seen his three grand-
sons dance, Oscar said, "He would really *kvel"*—as his
daughter translated, "revel and delight"). A few weeks before
Richie was married, Oscar himself went to the hospital for an
electrocardiogram. The doctors noticed a slight change in
his charts, and suggested he return for a stress test. His
daughter Marsha, a physician, knew her father hated check-
ups and doubted that he would bother with the tests. In her
anxious moments she worried that he would die of a heart attack on the dance floor. He too was concerned and did go in.
He passed and, a few days later, danced at the wedding.

"I'd always thought of a big Jewish wedding where my father did the *kazatske,* and that's what I got" said Richie, who
never knew about the test. "Really, that was a joy for me to
see—my father dancing at my wedding."

SHE COMES BY IT HONESTLY
Characterization in Family Folklore
Amanda Dargan

Wearing a loose-fitting dress, Tuga Peterson, the seventy-eight-year-old woman who had nursed a generation of our relatives, performed for us in the small kitchen that had always been her stage. As my sister and I looked on, she drew a portrait with words and gestures of our uncle Ned. "Now Mr. Ned," she said, "Monday, Tuesday, Wednesday, Thursday, Friday, he's Mr. Ned, dressed in his regular work clothes. But on Sunday, um hm. Miss Cullough gets hold of him and dresses him up so you can hardly recognize him. I can see him right now walking out that front door between those two flags, walking just like this. . . ." She imitated Uncle Ned's long stride, exaggerating it by slowing it down, sliding her feet flat across the floor, clearing her throat and moving her arms, bent with clinched fists, in unison with each step. "And his suit," she went on, pretending to smooth down the sides of an imaginary jacket, "his suit is so smooth, if a mosquito lit on it, it would slide off and break its neck."

In her brief imitation Tuga captured our uncle's most familiar qualities: his stride, his dress, the way he clears his throat. She also captured something about the relationship between Uncle Ned and his wife Cullough: the compromise they have reached between his indifference and her concern with fancy clothes. During the week he wears what he likes, but on Sundays and special occasions he wears the clothes she has picked out for him.

Like much of my family's folklore, Tuga's imitation was a form of characterization which bordered on caricature, heightening and exaggerating certain features of its subject. Like the caricaturist, Tuga drew a humorous, extravagant, and yet ultimately recognizable portrait of our uncle by highlighting and playing on some of his distinctive traits. This ability to characterize, to find an incident, a gesture, or a trait which captures the special qualities of families and individuals, is a skill admired in my family and is integral to our folklore. A story, an expression, a description, a nickname, a photograph, or an object of memorabilia is often valued and perpetuated precisely because it captures the features that make a relative distinctive.

Within our family tradition, the best storytellers are those with an eye for details and an ability to imitate the subjects of their stories. Good storytellers are known not only for the stories in their repertoire, but for the relatives whom they characterize particularly well. They are often called on at family gatherings to "do an imitation of Uncle Sam" or to "tell your Annie Louise stories."

Certain family nicknames are also based on characteristic traits. Ervin Dargan calls his son Benton, "Zig," because Benton's large jaws resembled those of the *Dick Tracy* cartoon character, "Ziggy." Since childhood, Ned Dargan has been called "Fish" by his closest friends among the cousins, because he enjoys fishing so much. Margaret Ervin is called "General" by her sisters and first cousins, because, being the oldest, she tends to give them orders. Often these nicknames are used only by those family members who conspired to create them and who use them specifically in situations where they want to tease their relatives by highlighting a certain characteristic.

This use of caricature in family folklore can carry a great deal of force and power. By conveying disapproval in a humorous way, it can be used to pressure a relative into changing a habit or into taking himself less seriously. When Sam Dargan came home for Christmas vacation with a long beard, his grandmother nicknamed him "Sammy Claus." When another relative came to the Fourth of July picnic several pounds heavier than he had been the year before, he was nicknamed "Minnesota" for the pool player "Minnesota Fats." These carefully selected words, gestures, and voice inflections can change temporarily the statuses of both the storyteller and his subject. A child can mock an elder, a relative can exert pressure on another, and Tuga Peterson can poke fun at the relatives of her employer.

My family takes special delight in stories and expressions repeated specifically to illustrate what sets relatives apart from each other as individuals and what distinguishes them as a group. "We've always been a clannish family," a storyteller begins. "You know how clumsy Sarah is," another says and then follows with an imitation of how she gets up from the table and knocks all the glasses over or with a story about how she broke a jar of pickles in St. Paul's Cathedral in London and had to stuff cucumbers in her pockets as she chased them down the aisle.

We are interested in the differences and similarities between our relatives partly because we are a large network of

kin and these stories and expressions help to distinguish individuals and branches of the family, giving each a separate
identity. The geographic center of the family is a rural community in South Carolina. It is a community with no fixed
boundaries. Its borders have changed as the size and shape of
the family has changed and as land has been bought and sold.
For us, the community ends where the cousins end, and at
present that covers an area of around ten square miles, which
includes twenty-two households. Much of our folklore focuses on the last-name family groups that make up our community: the Dargans, the Ervins, the Howards, and the
Williamsons.

The humor of our folklore, therefore, depends in part on a
shared knowledge of the characteristic traits and habits of
family members. Most family members can readily name the
prominent characteristics of their relatives. They can also
name the traits relatives share with each other, particularly
those traits associated with a family name. They will tell you
that the Ervins are entertaining, witty, and "non-energetic."
They enjoy life. The Dargans are big-eyed and optimistic,
adventurous, and gregarious. The Williamsons are smart,
peculiar, attentive to details, and reticent about family matters. The Howards are big eaters, big talkers, and expert
hunters and fishers. Physical traits are traced to relatives several generations removed. We can always spot Williamson
eyes and Williamson feet, an Ervin complexion, and a McIn-
tosh mouth. Poor eyesight is inherited from the Evanses and
deafness from the Harts.

This association of stock traits with a family name provided a useful mnemonic device for my relative Bill Howard:

*I'll tell you something my mother told me to remember my
grandmother's family. There were four McIver sisters who
lived in Society Hill. The sweetest one married an Ervin, the
prettiest one married a Law, the wittiest one married a Gregg
—you know the Greggs are known for being witty—and the one
with the most sense married a Williamson.*

Some relatives are said to be like their last-name family,
while the traits of others are traced to various other branches
of the family, which means that inconsistencies can be ac-
counted for easily. A relative who is unlike his father's family
will be explained as being more like his mother's or his

grandmother's side of the family. Or, the contradiction itself may be explained as a family trait. When confronted with the inconsistencies among members of the Dargan family, one family member said, "Well, that's another trait of the Dargans: they vary more."

This tendency to give genealogical explanations for the behavior of relatives often removes personal blame. Criticism of a relative is often dismissed with the common expressions, "It runs in the family" and "She comes by it honestly," followed by stories about other relatives in that branch of the family who exhibited the same trait.

These explanations also can dampen the credit for individual achievements. No one is surprised that Edwin Dargan is such a skilled woodworker, for after all, his great-grandmother was a Hart and the Harts are known for being good with their hands.

From years of watching them closely, family members also know the characteristics of their relatives as individuals. They know, for instance, that Vannie Ervin will always wear a black tie, whether he is at a dance or fishing on Black Creek, that Ervin Dargan will buy almost any new gadget or invention that comes on the market, that Mary Hart McIver will always be late for Christmas Eve supper no matter how much she insists that this year she will be on time. "If you ever want to surprise Mary Hart," goes a running joke in our family, "just tell her what time it is."

Like the caricaturist who exaggerates the most uneven and awkward features of his subject, family members will often emphasize a relative's most peculiar traits and habits in their folklore. Stories are told of how Rosa Dargan always refused to have her photograph taken and when she finally consented to have her wedding photograph made, covered her face with her veil; of how Mr. Ben Williamson had such a good memory for details that he would tell his son exactly which tobacco stalk on which row had a tobacco worm on it that had to be removed; and of how Joe Dargan's memory was so selective that he would forget that he had driven to town and catch a ride home but could remember the names and addresses of all of his college graduating class. Ervin Dargan delighted his cousins with this description of how their uncle Joe Dargan would overcome his tendency to shake from Parkinson's disease when it came to drinking whiskey:

He'd drink a good deal, but he'd hardly ever show it. And he'd shake. You remember how his hands would shake. But when he got ready to take a drink, he'd go up on it like a bird dog and grab it and not spill a drop. [Imitates gesture] He'd shake everything else. [Laughter]

This kind of family folklore tends to make "characters" out of everyone. The stories highlight a relative's idiosyncracies, making them more visible than his or her "normal" characteristics, and, of course, once a certain trait has been highlighted, it sometimes becomes difficult to ignore. Even those traits which are considered admirable can be placed in a humorous light, if an incident is found which shows that trait carried to the extreme. A favorite family story captures how my uncle Ned once carried politeness too far. Bill Howard told this version:

Ned used to visit Vannie a good bit, and Uncle Hugh said that Ned was the best-mannered child he ever saw. He'd always sit quietly at the table and never interrupt anybody talking. Uncle Hugh said one day he was out on one of the fields talking with Mr. Abbott, and Ned came running toward them shouting, "Uncle Hugh, Uncle Hugh!" Uncle Hugh said, "Ned, I'm talking with Mr. Abbott right now." He said Ned danced first on one foot and then on the other, but he waited until they had finished talking. Then Uncle Hugh said, "All right, Ned, what was it you wanted?" "Uncle Hugh, the house is on fire!"

While family folklore tends to make "characters" out of everyone, for most of its subject this status is only temporary, confined to the playful atmosphere of the storytelling session. The permanent status of family character is reserved for only a few, those relatives in whom peculiar habits and traits predominate. I once overheard two relatives talking about an irritating trait of one of their cousins. "But she's such a character," one said. "If you'd just accept her as a character, those things wouldn't bother you so much." The other relative replied, "She hasn't earned the right to be a character yet."

One who did earn that right in the family was Joe Dargan. Joe was not the most admirable member of the family, although family members will insist that "he was always a gentleman." Joe did very little to support himself throughout his life, and he was notorious for his ability to consume large quantities of food and drink. For most of Joe's life, his relatives had to support him. Yet, we remember him with love and tenderness; his songs, stories, and recitations are favorite family traditions, and the tangled fishing twine found in Joe's cabin after he died have become family treasures. These balls of twine are valued because Joe, like many family characters, was both eccentric and endearing, and because they remind us of two of his most memorable traits: the way his fishing lines caught on tree limbs and unraveled all the way to the place where he fished every Saturday, and the way he saved everything, thus ensuring that there would be several balls of twine left to remember him by.

Given Joe's distinctive characteristics of being entertaining, eccentric, and, as one relative put it, "doing set things, and doing them over and over," it is no wonder that Joe became one of the favorite family characters. Even his most noticeable weaknesses became the subject of a great deal of family humor. Bill Howard, for example, told an anecdote based on Joe's chronic laziness and history of unemployment:

My great-uncle Joe Dargan, a "'classic family character."

You remember when Joe was living in the Darlington Hotel. Well, after the hotel burned, I asked Joe if he had lost anything in the fire. He said, "Confound it, William, I escaped with only my working clothes." (Shakes his head and laughs) *He never did a lick of work in his life.*

Outside of the family, however, some people were not as tolerant of Joe's idiosyncracies, an attitude which shocked one of Joe's great-nephews:

The idea of showing disrespect to one of my relatives, well, I just never thought about it or never heard about it. It just really was a shock to catch people off-guard that didn't know that he was my uncle and to hear them say things about him. And it upset me really bad because I felt like saying, "You have no privilege to talk about this man, because he's, he's Uncle Joe, and he's a classic character.

Another established family character was McIver Williamson. Unlike Joe Dargan, Mr. McIver became known as a character outside the family as well. Many persons claim, in fact, that he is the chief legendary character in the area. As

*Two of the Dargan children, pictured here, married two Ervin
children and started the Dargan-Ervin clan.*

A small gathering of our relatives.

his neighbor Earl Gandy put it, "There are more stories about him than in the bible."

Traditions attribute to Mr. McIver many accomplishments in agriculture and nutrition, but most anecdotes about him focus on his idiosyncracies. The portrait which emerges from these stories is that of a brilliant but eccentric man, consciously unconventional, benevolent to those whom he considered deserving, capable of great severity as well as great kindness, and totally dedicated to the causes in which he believed.

Mr. McIver's dress is described as peculiar, especially for a man of his means: his shirts held together at the neck with a large safety pin and cut off at the waist with a drawstring through the hem; his ragged pants with the pockets sewed up to allow only two fingers to fit through; his mismatched shoes with tire treading tacked to the soles; and his entire wardrobe soaked in linseed oil to preserve it. These are the subject of family descriptions and tales about Mr. McIver.

As with Joe Dargan, most relatives insist that Mr. McIver "was always a gentleman" in spite of his unconventional dress and peculiar habits, although Hugh Dargan told about an exception:

We [Hugh and his father] were talking about McIver earlier tonight, about how he was never really considered weird, just eccentric. And that people really liked him. And daddy said, "You know, I never" — he was talking about giving him such a good character reference — "never knew of anybody that would have disliked him," and all this. He was a real gentleman. But the only time I ever heard of him being crude was when he was down at Harriet Swink's. Harriet's mother was having him for dinner. My grandmother was down there too. She said they were having steak, and the steak was tough, but it wasn't bad enough for anybody to say anything about it. They were just going to go ahead and eat it and be polite. McIver didn't say a word about it either. He just reached in his pocket and pulled out his file, took his teeth out and filed them down to a sharp edge, put them back in his mouth, and started eating again.

Mr. McIver also tended to buy things in quantities — large quantities. Ervin Dargan told of how Mr. McIver got tired of losing pliers, so he bought a bushel of them and scattered them around the house. Another story tells of how he went into a store and asked for a bushel of carburetors. Probably because of this trait, a well-known joke has become attached to Mr. McIver:

Mr. McIver wrote Sears and Roebuck, like he wrote them about pliers, and said, "Dear sir, send me a case of toilet paper." And they wrote him back and told him that he would have to order a catalog. He would have to order it out of the catalog. He wrote them back and told them that if he had the catalog, he wouldn't need the toilet paper.

Once a family member is established as a bonafide family character, traditional stories and jokes become attached to him rather easily. As Mr. McIver's great-nephew, Ben Williamson, commented, "People will believe anything you tell them about Uncle McIver."

Whether it is through a single story or a full-blown legend like McIver Williamson, my relatives seem to enjoy seeing themselves made into characters. "Family character" is a special category used by the family for any of its members whose behavior differs from expected values and norms, but no family member is immune from having his habits made to look comical in a family story. While family stories and expressions are often used to exert pressure on relatives to conform, they are also used to convey acceptance of those who do not conform, to place their weaknesses in a different light. Stories about family idiosyncrasies are used along with stories about family traits to express forgiveness for a member's faults, to play down his nonconformities, and to accept him into the fold. In the same way that we can forgive a relative's stubbornness because "she comes by it honestly," we can accept her flamboyance because "she's such a character."

One of my relatives said to me, "Some people think that being part of a big family would restrict your freedom, but I think it gives you more freedom. Some of our relatives wouldn't have any friends if they acted the way they do somewhere else. But here they have a whole family that accepts them no matter what they do." The worst thing that can happen to you in the family (some might argue the best thing) is that you become a family character.

GETTING THE BUTTER FROM THE DUCK: Proverbs and Proverbial Expressions in an Afro-American Family

🌿

Dennis W. Folly

Grey-haired and full of spirit, my great-grandmother is a woman deeply attached to the land. A mother of two children, grandmother of nine, and great-grandmother of thirteen, she is a wellspring of stories and wise sayings. Granny was born in a log cabin on April 20, 1898, and has lived all of her life in Hanover County, Virginia. Born Clara Wilson Tolliver, she married Walter Abrams at age eighteen and became Mrs. Clara Abrams. In her own tenacious way my great-grandmother has always reminded us that this life and this earth is ours to love and to celebrate, and that even in slavery times members of our family stood up for this. "Yeah," she said, " 'cause they would walk right over you if you didn't have spunk. They couldn't do nothing with grandma because she had too much spunk."

In her lifetime, my great-grandmother has seen the countryside, the community, and the world change in drastic ways. She remembers the days when there was only a horse and buggy for transportation, and people were warmly and intricately related, continuously visiting one another, an entire network of black souls loving, squabbling, singing, praying, gambling, dancing, being born, and passing away as one family. The yards were full of children and the sounds of barnyard animals: ducks, chickens, pigs, goats, peacocks, dogs, and cats. She remembers especially the beauty of the peacock feathers, and misses the sense of sharing and community that has all but disappeared. On land where houses once stood and life's pageantries were acted out, there is now woods and thick patches of honeysuckle and wild berry vines. "You could stand in this yard and yell over there to Betty's and talk then," Granny recalls.

This small community, like many plots of land throughout the south, was parcelled off by slaveowners when Grant took Richmond and the big freedom bell was rung. The hill where our house now sits was known as "Canaan's Hill," indicating a settlement of freed people, of people who had emerged from their bondage in "Little Egypt," the slaveowner's domain. My great-grandmother has often told us the story of when the slaves were freed.

They had a big celebration. Blowin' the horn and celebrating. See they took Richmond, Grant, the man took Richmond then

. . . well Lincoln and Grant . . . the two was together you see, and I don't know who else but they were the head two. And Grant blew the horn for the slavery band was broke. People was free! Say you could hear that horn . . . miles and miles, and people was in the fields they threw their hoe away and start to marchin'. They couldn't do nothing with 'em then, them people, some of 'em just jump up in the field and just scream and hollered . . . they went just running. [She slaps her palms together dramatically.] So glad they was free!

My mother, Mrs. Jean Folly, was born on January 15, 1934, also in Hanover County. Shortly afterwards, her mother, Arlene, left the county for New York City, leaving her to be raised by my great-grandmother. She also has a deep attachment to the land which she has passed on to us. Raised by Granny and spending most of her time around older people, she shares much of the knowledge and sense of tradition reaching back to plantation days. When my great-grandmother forgets a particular detail, no matter how far back, my mother can usually help her to remember.

It is out of this background that my family's oral traditions emerge, and one very important element of that tradition is the genre of proverbs. As others have pointed out, the proverb plays a vital role in African societies.[1] Used in domestic situations, particularly to impart morals to children, as well as in legal and ceremonial contexts, proverbs in African societies are appreciated for their ancient wisdom, their concise character, and for their poetic, artful qualities. As is characteristic of African and African-derived cultural groups, eloquent speech is highly regarded, and the man or woman who can accurately apply proverbs is applauded.

Both my mother and great-grandmother have always been known for using wise sayings, and seem to have some such expression for any possible situation. Many times my great-grandmother used them as a way of letting us know that in spite of our formal education or our familiarity with the modern and mechanized world, there is another level of knowing that we need to pay attention to. "If it's for you, you'll get it," she'd sometimes say if we became obsessed with a particular goal.

Many parents used similar words to instruct their children, to provide a moral code to which one could adhere. "You reap what you sow," Granny might say, or as my mother once wrote me in a letter, "a word to the wise is sufficient." But we also had special proverbs which brought together our family's history. By using expressions that reflect on certain individuals, the spirits of our ancestors are kept alive; by using expressions that are associated with particular periods of our history, the past is made present.

When I interviewed my great-grandmother and mother, my sister, Angie, and my brother, Levi, joined us as we sat in the livingroom, warmed by the crackling wood stove. The informality and spontaneity that characterized our usual gatherings prevailed. The simple mention of many of the proverbs prompted gales of warm-hearted laughter from my mother and great-grandmother. They laughed not only at the proverbs themselves, but at the memories they brought forth.

: Sewed Up in a Salt Sack[2] :

GRANNY: *That's a saying ah, just like Angie at times, she gets her mother to believe just like all children do. Sometimes they are doing things they don't want their mother to really know they're doing 'em, and they will put off a front. Tell you different things, tell you something different. They won't come right out and say. They're trying to fool you.*

Lots of people say, "She just got her mother sewed up in a salt sack 'cause her mother believe everything she says. She ain't doing nothing but foolin' her to death."
JEAN: *Basically, though, it's somebody taking advantage of you, fooling you.*

: Buying a Pig in a Bag[3] :

JEAN: *Oh, now that is like paying for something you don't see.*
GRANNY: *That's right, you don't know what you're getting until you get home and open it.*
JEAN: *I've heard many older people use that in my growing up, Granny among them. People said that just like, it's used for a lot of expressions, like getting married. People say, "Well he*

Mrs. Abrams, "Granny," on her porch in Hanover County, Virginia, 1979.

certainly bought himself a pig in the bag." It means that he didn't really wait to get to know the woman before he married her. Then once he married her it was like the bag was opened up, and he got to see all of it.
GRANNY: *And he was received.**

: CARRIED HIS DUCKS TO THE MARKET AND GOT A POOR PRICE[4] :

"Buying a pig in a bag" reminded us of this proverbial expression which is used in my family to refer primarily to marital situations. My mother said of this, "That's an old one."

GRANNY: *That's like getting married and getting received. You can get received and the woman can get received. It's on both sides.*
JEAN: *I've used both. All right, say for instance you're going to the market. There was a time everybody carried their wares to the market to sell. All right, you're not exactly selling yourself. But when you are going out to get something you want to get the best for it.*

: GETTING THE BUTTER FROM THE DUCK[5] :

Perhaps because my family kept ducks, there are numerous expressions which utilize the duck imagery. This one is my favorite. My great-grandmother learned it from her mother, and the expression is still used by several relatives. When I asked about it, my mother and great-grandmother burst into

---

* There is evidence that "received" may have been used systematically in place of "deceived" in the Afro-American traditional southern speech, yet how many researchers have "corrected" their informants when transcribing conversation. See Mississippi Fred McDowell, *I Do Not Play No Rock 'n' Roll*, Capitol Records. In the introductory comments on side one, McDowell clearly says, "Your friends will receive you," and yet in the liner notes this segment of his comments is transcribed as "deceive" you.

laughter, mainly because of my well-known, longtime interest in the phrase. I have attempted to use this expression on several occasions, sometimes embarrassing myself by substituting "goose" for "duck." "Dennis is certainly anxious to get that one," my great-grandmother laughed this time.

I first remember my great-grandmother saying this when several of us were splitting wood to take in and keep the next few days' fires going. When my mother had just finished splitting a particularly difficult piece and breathed a deep "whew!," my great-grandmother, who was sitting nearby said, "Boy, that done got all the butter from the duck now!"

JEAN: *You have to realize that a lot of these sayings are interchangeable things. They happen to mean something different to any given situations. I first heard it I think when people were cutting wood, and you come upon a tree that was really hard to get down. You know when he was able to get it down, or whatever the job accomplished, he would say, "I tell you that thing really got the butter from the duck!"*

See the fat on the inside of the duck doesn't come away easy. You can't pull the fat from the duck like you can from a chicken, or the other fowl. I think the older people associated their everyday activities with these animals and what not. It's between the skin and the meat, see? And sometimes you even rip the skin trying to get that fat out of there. But it's so rich and fat it's just like butter. You can use it in cakes and all those kind of things, just like you would use butter.

GRANNY: *Yes, Lord, my momma used to use that one. 'Cause she used to go in the woods and cut wood. And sometimes when she'd get through cuttin' she'd be sweatin' and going on. And she'd have to set down, and she'd say, "Ah Lord, y'all go ahead chillun, that thing done got all the butter from me."*

Although I've never plucked or cooked a duck, this proverb has become a part of my repertoire. It retains a special place in my feelings for several reasons. Besides its poetic appeal, it reminds me of a moment of special warmth and closeness to my mother and great-grandmother. It also links me to my family history, and to experiences of my childhood when ducks and other farm animals were about.

: THE KETTLE CALLING THE POT BLACK, AND THE FRYING PAN STANDING UP FOR WITNESS[6] :

GRANNY: *Momma used to use that at us a many times. If we'd get mad with one another and call somebody black, Momma's say, "Now, where you got the room to call somebody black!? You black too. The kettle calling the pot black now, and the frying pan standing up for witness." Lord! [She laughs.] It was a while before I knew what she was talking about.*

As one might expect, this proverb (which is by no means unique to Afro-America) may sometimes connote the issues of color and status when used by Afro-Americans. When I was growing up, my family always used this proverb strictly for its metaphorical message. Perhaps because of the sensitivity surrounding the race and color issues, I have never used this saying. My mother explained its meaning briefly.

JEAN: *Like people disagreeing and has no right to say the things they're saying, you know. They're in the same boat. So why should you say something about somebody else? And I think you say it more or less out of disgust, you get so tired of hearing 'em say those things, or you feel like they're not justified.*

: A HARD HEAD MAKES A SOFT BEHIND[7] :

JEAN: *Oh Lord, I don't know if children started that or not, but the old folks used to tell us that if they was trying to correct you, and you were going to do it anyway. They'd just warn you by saying, "A hard head make a soft tail."*
GRANNY: *Don't use that much. I used to hear momma say it, especially if you act bully. She didn't only say that to us but she would say it to any child if he didn't listen to her. Like Sarah's children across the road, or John would come here. [These are community members who are now adults who were frequently at my great-great-grandmother's, playing in the yard with other children.] But you know, you can't say it to people's children of this day. You wouldn't dare.[8]*

This proverbial phrase refers of course, to the common practice of spanking children as a disciplinary measure, "soft tail" describing the child's rear end after such punishment.

Both my mother and grandmother indicated that it is used only in reference to children, never adults. Even though I have no children, I still use it metaphorically to describe people of my generation when they are acting hard-headed.

: Fool with Trash It'll Get in Your Eyes[9] :

This is one of numerous proverbs in my family which conform to an "If — — —, then — — —" structure. Another is "Play with a puppy and he'll lick your mouth," which generally means that if you become too friendly with certain kinds of people, they will cause you great embarrassment. "Fooling with trash" is close in meaning, but serves as a more serious warning.

GRANNY: *I often heard granddaddy say that about his son. You know, he had been married and he had a son and two daughters. He hadn't heard from Arthur [his son] for years and years, and he say Arthur wrote to him, "Papa, I'd like for you to help me, I'm in trouble."*

He said, "Yes, what you need?" He, "Need some money." So he said he sent him the money. But he wrote him in a letter and told him, "If you hadn't been fooling with that trash you wouldn't got, wouldn't got in that trouble." Say, "You wouldn't listen to me." I hear him say he told him, you was fooling with trash, that's the reason you're in trouble.

Both my great-grandmother and mother agreed that this proverb was used most frequently with children. I have however, heard them use it with people who were not children, at least in age. This may have to do with the way in which older generations in Afro-America traditionally have the social status of elders. In the spirit of this status they might regard anyone of a younger generation as a child, and indeed one is always the child of one's parents. My mother explained it to my seven-year-old sister like this.

JEAN: *Yes, that was a way I guess of teaching your children to learn to pick their associates, understand? It's like "You're known by the company you keep," or "Birds of a feather flock together."*

ANGIE: *Momma, does that mean if you fool around in trash you might find something and you'll get in trouble? Somebody might catch you for finding it?*

JEAN: *You know that trash we pick up for to start the fire and stuff with? Well if you mess around with too much you'll get a piece of it in your eyes. But it also mean that if you mess around with trashy people, people that don't have good ideas and scruples, and things like that, that you'll get in trouble.*

: Lauros Catch Meddlers[10] :

We were talking at Christmas time, with presents lying wrapped beneath our tree. My sister was anxious as most young children this time of year to find out what lay inside the wrappings. This expression had probably been used with her more than usual, and she indicated that she knew it well and understood it.

JEAN: *It's a way of making a child shut up, of evading the issue.*

ANGIE: *When a child wants to know something you won't let the child know!*

GRANNY: *Ah Dennis, Dennis, you know Willie Jones. Willie Jones was a lil' boy you know, and he was working 'round the house. So, my mother was stirring up some, she used to call it sweet bread, just for them to have in the kitchen you know. And he come on in the kitchen.*

Willie: "Aunt Betty what you making?"
Momma: "Lauros catch meddlers."

Well he didn't know, he thought it was so. He went on outdoors, and Phillip's grandfather was the butler at the house there.

Willie: "Uncle Phillip."
Phillip: "What you want Peter?" Used to call him Peter.
Willie: "Is you ever ate Lauros catch meddlers?"
Phillip: "What you talkin' 'bout Peter?"
Willie: "I say Aunt Betty making some Lauros catch meddlers!"
Phillip: "Well, how dey look like?"

At this point everyone broke into laughter. My great-grand-mother has a wonderful way of dramatizing the characters and this line was delivered extremely humorously.

Proverbs have been and continue to be an important part of the oral tradition of my family. Contained in them are reflections of their values, ethics, idiosyncracies, and simultaneously a broader and more universal wit and wisdom. They indicate that Africans in America have remained aware of the enormous power of words, and have used the art of language in shaping a strong and vibrant culture. These few samples of proverbs used in my family reflect the spirit of humor and wisdom which has allowed Afro-Americans to persevere, ultimately scraping "the butter from the duck."

HOW MANY ARE ON OUR SIDE?
Growing Up in Greenwich Village

🖋

Anne Warner

During the forties, in the early years of our married life, my husband Frank and I, and eventually our sons Jeff and Gerret, lived in Greenwich Village — that section of New York City below Fourteenth Street, with Washington Square Park its best-known landmark. More than any other section of the city, the Village has kept its feeling of community. Its streets are filled with old brownstones and eighteenth century red brick townhouses, interspersed with more modern apartment buildings, and with small shops, restaurants, and bookstores. The Village at that time was considered to be the heart of New York's literary and artistic life.

We lived on West Twelfth Street in the ground-floor garden apartment of a brownstone. We had our own front gate, a miniscule front yard with a climbable tree, and even our own backyard. Upstairs, next door, and down the block lived a variety of writers and historians and artists with whom we shared many a pleasant evening, singing old songs and swapping stories.

City life was different then. We used to go away and leave the kitchen door, which opened on the backyard, ajar, so that our cat, manipulating the screen door on his own, could get in or out at will. The front door often was unlocked too. We felt safe in giving our boys the freedom of the neighborhood, and they roamed about on their own by the age of five or so. Gerret was a rover then, exploring a new area every day. He and a friend used to go down to Washington Square, or as far north as Hearn's, the big cut-rate department store on Fourteenth Street, the Village's busy commercial upper boundary, where they would ride the escalator up and down for hours. He excelled in finding treasures in Village trash cans — once, for instance, a beautiful Advent calendar that we still use each Christmas.

Probably the first bit of family folklore concerning the boys has to do with the naming of our elder son, born Jonathan Francis. The week he was born, Frank felt impelled to write a sort of ballad indicating his feelings about the event. Being a southerner, and a collector and singer of folk songs, the first thing he thought of was the ballad about John Henry, the mighty black steel-driving railroad worker. The morning John Henry was born, they say, "the Mississippi River run *up* stream for a hundred and fifty miles." "Jonathan" did not scan, nor fit the black southern speech pattern Frank had in mind, so he took the initials "J. F." and turned them into "Jeff." Bill Benét (William Rose Benét, a neighbor of ours) published the result in his "Phoenix Nest" in the *Saturday Review of Literature* on April 10, 1943, and Jonathan has been Jeff from that day to this.

Gerret and the climbable tree outside our home on West Twelfth Street, 1952.

Well, the mornin' little Jeff was born,
Lord, Lord,
The mornin' little Jeff was born,
Well, New York town swang 'round and 'round
An' the subways run plumb out'n the ground
An' the great big buildin's bowed low down,
On the mornin' little Jeff was born.

On the mornin' little Jeff was born,
Lord, Lord,
On the mornin' little Jeff was born,
Gabriel blowed his trumpet to beat the band,
An' the angels danced 'round hand in hand,
An' the Lord said, "Jeff, you's a natchel man!"
On the mornin' little Jeff was born.

On the mornin' little Jeff was born,
Lord, Lord,
On the mornin' little Jeff was born,
He stretched his legs in the mornin' sun,
An' he said, "Jes' look what the Lord's done done!"
An' he said, "God A'Mighty, I'm your lovin' son."
On the mornin' little Jeff was born.

Before the boys were born—and we were married for a number of years before Jeff's arrival—we began to spend our vacations every summer collecting traditional songs from rural people in out-of-the-way places along the eastern seaboard. I have a couple of dozen notebooks filled with the notes I took on these trips. Keeping a journal, writing down the texts of songs, documenting whatever seemed memorable or noteworthy became, I suppose, a habit. It has long been a habit, I realize, in my own family. Among my many family documents, for instance, I have a long account by my great-great-great-grandfather, the Reverend Gideon Hawley, describing his missionary work with the Indians in the 1750s. I have a journal my mother, Elizabeth Hawley, kept as a young girl in the 1880s during a visit to her grandparents. I have a long-documented history of my father's family, the Lochers, who emigrated from Zurich, Switzerland, in the 1850s, traveling all the way to Sutter's Mill in California. I have innumerable photographs going back for several generations. I am often reminded when this recordkeeping urge comes over me of the White Queen in *Alice Through the Looking Glass*. The king had fallen from the chess table and Alice heard him muttering, "The horror of the moment I shall never forget." "You will," said the queen, "unless you make a memorandum of it."

When the boys came along I began jotting down on scraps of paper things they said which seemed to me unusual and amusing, and eventually I assembled these jottings and copied them into a small spiral notebook. It is not the usual baby book, for it contains no mention of height or weight or first accomplishments, just relevant or interesting comments and observations the children made in those early years. I think of it now as one of my folklore notebooks, as well as an item for the family archives.

Reading it with the perspective of elapsed time, it is clear that many of the boys' sayings were an indication of their effort to assimilate the strange events and inexplicable rules which govern the adult world. These comments are not just bright childish sayings. They all have become, in one way or another, part of our family language, repeated at appropriate moments, referred to by means of a word or just a glance which will recall the incident or the phrase to another family member. There is, I suppose, a sense of pride in sharing these bits of humor and ingenuous wisdom that belong only to us. They tie us together.

At the age of two and a half, Jeff was learning the days of the week. Every morning he would say, "And what day is *this*?" Until one day when I answered "Monday," and he said, "Monday *again!* Does this just go on and on?" We have used that phrase time and again in moments of frustration. It was the first of small Jeff's many remarks which seemed to sum up the human condition.

When Jeff was in the third grade he came home one day and said of a girl in his class, "I just love Sheila. I would like to kiss her. My stomach hurts because I can't!" Thirty years later this phrase lingers in the family's vocabulary and even in the vocabulary of one of Jeff's close friends. Upon seeing a

Visiting with the pigeons in Washington Square Park, 1947.
Gerret is on my right, Jeff on my left.

Christmas card photograph, 1946, at our house on West Twelfth Street. From left to right. Frank's mother, Mabel Preston Warner; me with Gerret on my lap; Jeff with ukelele; Frank with Appalachian wooden banjo. Sullivan the cat tolerates the photographic session.

good-looking woman the friend may turn to Jeff and ask, "Did you bring the Tums?"

Gerret lived more in his imagination, without feeling required to adapt so much to the outside world. He could play games by himself for hours, talking to no one in particular about giants, wolves, witches, crooks, and "ghosties." When he was three I heard him say of one of his characters, "He was speaking Frenchly." That is one of what we came to call "Gerretisms," phrases that the family adopted. After hearing on a record the lugubrious hobo ballad, "May I Sleep in Your Barn Tonight, Mister?" and the verse that begins, "I was back there again this past summer / And they told me my baby had died," Gerret asked reasonably, "Who dyed the baby?" This too became a standard family question.

We have teased him over the years about his overheard comment when he was perhaps four, and was chinning himself on a bar in the backyard: "I have dimples . . . and muscles." "Dimples and muscles" is a useful reminder when anyone in the family is showing a bit of ego.

About this same time Gerret asked a mind-boggling question that has haunted us over the years: "I wonder why no bad people have ever tried to rob this house . . . you know, people on the other side. How many are on our side?" How many, indeed.

I find children are naturally interested in God and in religion—not organized religion, but their own relationship to a supreme being. When Gerret was in first grade he came home one day to announce, "There's a girl in my class who doesn't believe in God How would she like it if I didn't believe in her?" As I was putting Jeff to bed one night when he was two he asked, "Who made me?" I said, "I believe God made you." "Oh," said Jeff, "that was nice of Him." Later some admirer said to him, "I think you are made of sugar." "No," he said, "I'm made of God." One day before his nap he asked me to read him some Bible stories. I thought he was nearly asleep, but when I came to the story of Peter's raising Dorcas from the dead, Jeff took his thumb out of his mouth and observed, "That's a fascinating little drama."

I have mentioned our cat before. His name was Sullivan—he had a twin named Gilbert—and he became a Village character. He would sit outside on the stoop in the morning and people on their way to the subway would stop and talk to him. Some even crossed over from the other side of the street for a friendly word, to which he always responded. If he felt cold, or bored, he would put on a pitiful act of being ejected from hearth and home, and many a passerby, finding the upstairs (parlor floor) entrance more obvious, would climb the stairs and ring our upstairs neighbors' doorbell for him. Sullivan had his name tag, with Frank's name under his, and one day a note arrived addressed to Frank expressing great admiration for his taste in animals and proposing a meeting. It might have been the beginning of a beautiful relationship, if Frank hadn't insisted that I answer the lady's note. Anyway, Sullivan was a bona fide member of the family and a good bit older than Jeff. Friends and even relations sometimes called Jeff "Sullivan" when he was first born—as people, and parents, frequently confuse the names of siblings. So I suppose it wasn't too surprising that as I was tucking Jeff into bed one night he suddenly asked, "Did Sullivan and Gerret really grow in your tummy?" Some years later, when Sullivan died, Gerret wept bitterly and said, "That's two people gone from our house." His grandmother—who was living with us—had died the year before.

One day in the fall of 1949, Frank was away, and while I got our dinner together the boys were taking a bath and playing in the tub. Unwisely, I had let them play with some little glass bottles. Somehow one got broken and fell into the tub, and Gerret leaped up, cutting his foot badly on a fragment.

Sharing secrets under the wings of the eagle at New York's Central Park. Gerret (left) and Jeff (right), 1949.

The first thing I knew they were both out of the tub—Gerret standing there dripping blood, and Jeff, stark naked, running around the room saying over and over, "This is too much for me! This is too much for me!"

I finally calmed Jeff down and bandaged Gerret's foot. Feeling he deserved special attention, Gerret, who wasn't four yet, announced that he wanted some junior baby food for dinner, so I said I would go to the store and get some. I left them looking at the pictures in one of their favorite books, *The Wizard of Oz*. Whether it was a picture of the Wicked Witch of the East, or, as Jeff now says, they looked instead at a "blood-thirsty" comic book, something made them panic and they rushed out in our front yard, barefoot, to look for me. It was now nearly 6:00 P.M. and people were coming home from work—which meant the store was crowded and I had a long wait. Many stopped to tell the boys they would catch cold and should go inside, but they just stood there by the gate calling "Mommy! Mommy!" By this time Gerret's foot began to bleed again. This was once more too much for Jeff, and he started out alone down Twelfth Street to find me. When I came around the corner, there was Jeff coming toward me, barefoot and in pajamas, clutching his toy rifle for protection. Behind him stalked our friend and neighbor George Lord, an apron tied around his middle. He had caught sight of Jeff from his apartment window and decided he ought to get into the act. When we got back we found Gerret upstairs with the Lord children, calmly eating a cookie and listening to a story.

"This is too much for me" has served us well. I particularly remember a letter Jeff wrote us when he was out of college and on active duty with the Navy. One night when his ship was in the South Atlantic he went on deck and was overwhelmed by the unending ocean and the brilliant stars overhead. All he could think of, he said, was "This is too much for me. . . ."

Norman Rockwell's famous *Saturday Evening Post* cover showing a group of youngsters, dressed as cowboys, having a shoot-out, expressed perfectly the cowboy mania which swept the country during the forties. Jeff, in due course Gerret, and all their friends were caught up in it. My mother took Jeff to a cowboy movie at Loew's Sheridan Theatre on Seventh Avenue and Eleventh Street when he was three years old, and he never came off the range until he was ten. He

Battle fatigue. An after-the-range-war candid of Jeff, age six, 1949.

used to go around muttering to no one in particular, "bullets and smoke," and he insisted on our strapping a gun to Gerret's hip when his small brother was still in diapers. When Gerret was reproved for making too much noise one day, he said, "My *west* mommy would like it!"

One facet of Jeff's pragmatism was his insistence that before a game of any kind could be played all details must be correct, especially his own costume. One day he was going to a party at a friend's house, dressed as a cowboy, of course. He found that the only gun he had on hand was a toy World War II .45—not a western type at all. Frank and I had no enthusiasm for buying another gun, until Jeff said in despair, "You might as well try to go dressed as a witch without a broomstick!" We went out and bought the gun.

Both Jeff and Gerret heard music of one kind or another from the time they were born, classical as well as folk music. As soon as we could travel again after the war, they went on collecting trips with us, and very early they began to sing with Frank. When Gerret was three or four, hearing the pots and pans rattling in the kitchen, he said, "You know you can hear a tune in everything if you listen hard. Did you hear the tune in the pans? But you have to listen *hard*."

If we are to appreciate the value of family sayings—by children or others—one must "listen hard." They are ephemeral, spoken spontaneously and often without conscious thought, and they are quickly forgotten. Yet, remembered and considered, they illuminate individual characteristics that otherwise might never be realized. Too, they can recall a whole period of family life, as a photograph does but with a different dimension. Remembered, they warm the heart and tie the family together with a sense of recognition of ourselves as a discrete entity. That is why I am glad that I kept these records, even in a somewhat haphazard fashion. I always knew they would be valuable and important to the family later on, as indeed they have been.

One night as I was putting Gerret to bed he said something that made me feel I had been awarded a medal. "Is it fun having children?" he suddenly asked. There were times when, in answer to such a question, I might have said "yes" and times when I might have said "no." But I was amazed and touched by his thoughtfulness, and could only answer with real conviction, "Yes, of course it is." "Well," said Gerret, "it's fun being children, too."

Gerret at the height of the cowboy era, 1950.

BLESSING THE TIES THAT BIND: Storytelling at Family Festivals

Margaret Yocom

Storytelling has long been a way of life in my Pennsylvania German family. Tales of Grandfather Keck getting kicked by a bull as he walked the stubborn animal back to his father's slaughterhouse in Pottstown, Pennsylvania, and Grandmother Yocom's recitation of how, as a 1908 graduate of the local business college, she left her parents' farm with money her brother loaned her to hunt a job in the big city of Philadelphia are standard fare at family gatherings. My parents, too, tell tales: dad, about growing up on a farm in the 1930s; and mother, of childhood summers in the central Pennsylvania mountains.

Like any family's stories, those of my family highlight the unusual habits, unique talents, fateful accidents, and characteristic sayings and actions of our relatives. Some of the stories document not individual feats, but, by telling about the birth of a child or the first meeting of a husband and wife-to-be, recount how the family in a sense became a family. And always between the tales flows information about the family as it ages, oral history that places the people and events in context.

Often, the stories burst forth unannounced, as a part of everyday conversation. But the finest tale-telling sessions come at those festive times when the whole family gathers together, whether at life-cycle events such as weddings or funerals, or holiday celebrations. Storytelling is an integral part of these festivities, but not necessarily a deliberate one. Rarely does a relative say, "Well, let's talk about some of the things that have happened to us." Rather, one topic of conversation leads to another and without realizing the choice, someone pulls an example out of the past and reminds everyone of how Uncle Dave or Aunt Catherine reacted to a similar situation. Then, the family easily turns to other escapades of Dave and Catherine, or to comparable activities of other relatives.

It is no accident that families tell stories during celebrations for, stimulated by seeing everyone together, storytellers recreate in words the physical gathering that stands before them. Although a story may feature the activities of only one of the relatives present, most family members listen anyway because they enjoy hearing about someone they know or are related to by blood or marriage. Some nod their heads as they hear the oft-told tale, and others who may be hearing the narrative for the first time, form an opinion about the actions of the men and women in the tale. Thus, through the shared memory and participation of all present, the stories convey new information to some, reiterate the familiar to others, and help celebrate the family itself.

Since festivals and celebrations are recurring moments of special significance, junctures that seemingly exist outside of normal time, the day-to-day pattern of family activities halts.[1] Relatives break from work or from pleasures with non-related friends and, laden with food and warnings to behave and be cheerful, come together at an agreed upon location to celebrate or witness a special occasion. Because these are special times, family members often pause and look around at themselves, their growing children, and their aging parents. As they pull out photographs of one another, they ponder the future and reconsider the past. Stories appear, then, because through them relatives can reassess the past and feel able to believe that whatever is yet to happen, the family will be there as it always has been.

Stories also appear at family festivals because relatives see any one celebration as an appropriate and important time for stories about any other. After all, no matter what the event, family celebrations do resemble one another. Whether a birthday party or a funeral reception, the same core of relatives gathers to eat together, bestow gifts on one another, and exchange good wishes. These similarities, then, among all life-cycle events and celebrations—past and present—stimulate family storytelling.

Although storytelling relatives may say they are just "telling lies," their tales told during festive occasions do more than just fritter away the time between dessert and dishwashing. Their tales unite them, teach members about their family heritage, and remind all that they, as parts of one another, should help each other. They also set family members apart from everyone else, emphasizing unique qualities relatives should be proud of and promoting a cohesiveness which comes from such differences with the outside world.

Joyful family life-cycle celebrations, like weddings and all the events that lead up to them, are especially filled with family stories. One Sunday evening, for example, while most of my immediate family finished off their supper and talked about my sister's upcoming wedding, our cousin Scott called to invite my parents, Norman and Betty, to a fifteenth wedding anniversary dinner in honor of Norman's brother, David, and his wife, Marie. "Fifteen years, boy," my brother exclaimed after Scott hung up. "Doesn't seem that long." "Well, look at all that's happened," Betty reminded him. "All your marriages, and their kids. Why, we were married in forty-six and Dave and Fern before us, and then Don and Jean in forty-nine or was it forty-eight."

"It was forty-nine," Grandfather Elmer Keck spoke up. "It might have been forty-nine," seconded Norman. "We were building [this house] in forty-nine. Remember, we hid their car up here so nobody would do anything, but Rufus put Limburger cheese on it. . . ."

"And David," Elmer broke in. "David Fry."

"Imagine that!" Norman turned to his son-in-law, George. "Ugh, that smelly cheese melting all over the car engine. What a mess."

"Yes," Elmer said, "when Donnie got married, what Ruf (Rufus) does, he and David Fry, they bought some Limburger cheese and they put it on the manifolds, smeared it on the manifolds of the car and different parts of it that would heat up at different times as the motor got hotter, you know. And, of course, Donald thought everything was fine. His car started. But the stink of this Limburger cheese as the car heated up—and of course, he couldn't get this off. It had melted; the hotter the car got, the worse it got! And they had put it on the exhaust pipe, on the manifold, and everything else. All over the car! He had this for a long time, and he finally had to get out to clean the car off all over.

"But," Elmer continued, "it all goes back to what they did to Rufus, you know, when he got married. Well, Harold had the wedding, you know, in that old church up there outside of Shireman's town where they had services once a year. So Rufus got married and everything was just hunky-dory; everything was fine. So what we did was: we crossed the wires on his car at the back so when he got in the car to start it, the car wouldn't go. And then we had the exhaust pipe plugged up, you know, so it'd run, but it would go "kaput-kaput" if he would get the wires fixed. So people got out [of the church] and the car wouldn't start. Well, right away he started looking, and he found the wire and got the wires fixed up. But he got in the car, and it wouldn't go again. And, of course, he got out again and got to working. They lost a lot of time. They wanted to get going, you know. He finally got it started, but it took another hour and a half, two hours. So, of course, Donnie knew about this."

"You talk about things—the worst I ever knew was a trick they played on Wilmer, my cousin. Did I ever tell you that? Well, Wilmer had his house bought at 22 West Fifth Street. He had the house all furnished and everything, and he went away on his honeymoon with Stelletta. Well, Wilmer had it coming to him because he had played tricks on Elmer Breuninger, his brother-in-law, and Harve, Elmer's brother. So they decided that they would fix Wilmer when he got married. They didn't do anything to him right after he got married. But, when he went on his honeymoon, they got the keys to the house, and they put the upstairs downstairs, and the downstairs upstairs. Everything upstairs and the bedroom, downstairs! The only thing they couldn't change were the bathrooms. And they had signs up: 'Milkman stopped here,' 'Baker stopped here,' 'Butcher stopped in.' They had them all over the house, on the outside. And when Stelletta came home and saw it, she just sat down and cried."

"Did they help Wilmer move it back?"

Storytelling at family festivals: Marie Yocom delights the family at a fiftieth wedding anniversary celebration.

"Oh, no. Oh, heck no. No, they didn't lift a finger!"

"But wasn't he sore at them?"

"What could he do? He had played tricks on these others. I guess Wilmer figured that if you gave it out, you had to take it." [2]

Although storytellers and their tales of family antics may at first seem more fitted to joyous family life-cycle events, it is actually during moves from a homeplace, funerals, and other family crises that family stories seem most needed and, in the end, quite appropriate to both tellers and listeners. Family stories and history buoyed up the Yocom-Keck family when, in the spring of 1976, the home of Grandmother and Grandfather Yocom, so often the gathering place for the family, was sold and its contents put up for auction. Grandfather Isaac, because of illness, had moved to a nursing home and Grandmother Bertha went to live next door with her daughter Gladys and family. The auctioneer's sign went up on the front lawn in early May; and Bertha, preparing to sell most of the goods she used during her life as a farm wife and mother, walked back and forth from her house to Gladys' trying to give away her most prized possessions before the auctioneer's gavel put them in the hands of some stranger.

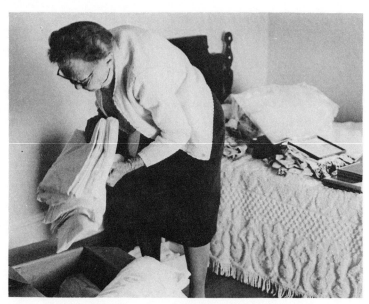

Storytelling at auction time: Bertha Yocom talks as she prepares household goods for sale.

In anticipation of the sale, everything was laid out on tables. Kitchen utensils spilled off the table and into the boxes on the floor: dishes, vases, plates, and silverware filled every inch of the dining-room table; sofas, benches, and chairs of all sizes littered the livingroom; and boxes of books, bedding, and mementos stood like silent sentries over the stone house on Yocom Road. "Did you see the sign for the auction?" Bertha pointed to the front yard:

"Your daddy put it up the other day. Oh, I never appreciated the house enough when I lived there. I never appreciated the farmhouse either, but when I had to leave, I was so worked up — and weak — that the girls did all the packing for me. I just couldn't do it. You know I'm not going to the sale, are you?"

Remembering that previous move and seeing many of the possessions spread before her, Bertha shared much family history with me, which I recorded in my journal. As we entered the livingroom, she mentioned,

"This couch! It's so good, so sturdy. You see, the nurse slept on this when Grandpop Yocom [great-grandfather Albert] was sick, and then, for grandmom. It's a shame that no one can take it." On the couch lay a brown woolen scarf. "Oh, this muffler! You know, it saved Oscar's [Bertha's brother's] life! One day — bitter cold — he was coming back from the city with friends. It was a car with no top. He would have frozen to death if it hadn't have been for the scarf. Imagine! This scarf!! Can you use it?"

Up the stairs to the second floor she went, leaving one of her two canes behind. In the hallway she opened up a few small boxes lying on the day couch. "Look here, Peggy," she called. One box had several quilting patterns, flax, and lead vices for a quilting frame. "Why, these must be Grandma Yocom's. I wonder where the quilt frame is? Here, take these. Do you want them?"

She walked over to the old hatboxes: "Oh, here's Grandmom Yocom's fox [stole]; she always wore these." From a trunk she took a linen tablecloth and gave it to me: "Here, it's nine feet long; you can cut it. Grandmom Yocom gave this to me. Once I took care of them when they were sick; they wanted to give me money, but I wouldn't take it. So she gave me this. I always used it with my best china."[3]

Although an emotionally difficult event, the auction gave birth to a humorous family story, as several relatives witnessed a memorable event and reported it to family members. I recorded it in my journal as follows:

Just after Aunt Edie bought a white steel cabinet, she saw auctioneer Victor Rhoads hold up a pair of brown riding boots she wore as a girl. No one would bid even a quarter. "What about a quarter?" Vic thundered. "A quarter?" But no one would bid even that. Edie jumped up: "For a quarter, I'll take them!" As she ran forward to get them, her two brothers laughed. "For a quarter!" she exclaimed later. "Why they're good, yet. Look at the leather. I couldn't see my boots going to somebody who couldn't wear them anyway!"

Similarly, toward the very end of the sale, my father Norman reached for an old rubber baby doll among the litter of items on one remaining shelf of things to buy. His sister Gladys caught his hand: "Oh, that thing. Don't sell that!" "No, put it up," his brother Dave advised. "I saw some people eyeing it a while back." As the doll went up for sale, Norman whispered to me, "Why Pop used that doll; he tied it in the cherry tree to keep away birds." And the auctioneer who had just sold a rock for a dime, sold the rubber baby doll, too.

Family members immediately fashioned these two events into stories. After the sale when my father and I visited Grandfather Isaac, Norman said that the sale had gone well and, smiling, he told Isaac about Edie and her boots and about the doll. "That and the doll were the best," Norman repeated. "You know, that doll brought a dollar seventy-five!"[4]

Norman told the stories not only to his father, but to his father-in-law and his children, even though they were all at the sale and had seen Edie buy back her own boots. Grandmother and Grandfather Yocom did not want to talk much about the sale, but they did enjoy the stories. After all, they confirmed that the sale had gone well: if someone was fool enough to buy a twenty-year-old dry and cracked rubber doll, surely the best furniture brought a good price. Also, the objects themselves brought back memories of a cherished past on the farm when they were young and the children were home.

Although the story of the doll was great fun during and immediately after the sale, it is the story of Edie's boots that family members still tell more frequently. Perhaps it owes its life to a kind of tension: just as the auction mingled the joy of family fellowship and the antics of the auctioneer with the sorrow of the death of a homestead, so the story fuses the apparent silliness of buying back your own boots with the sober awareness that you had to do it before strangers walked off with your own past.

Like the death of a homestead, the death of a family member also brings relatives together to comfort one another and to rejoice in the family bonds that remain. Unlike other celebrations, funerals impart a sense of urgency to their storytellers, for here the sorrowers especially need to feel family about them. And storytelling, which may last from the moment relatives hear about the death until long after the funeral reception, brings family members close together. Even in the midst of such solemnity, there is laughter, at least at Keck funerals.

One Saturday afternoon in early June as I visited with Grandmother Louisa and Grandfather Elmer Keck, we were talking about Elmer's brother Dan, when the phone rang.

Immediately after he hung up the receiver, Elmer told us that his first cousin Bessie Keck Klein had died. Once again I recorded the conversation in my journal:

A new family story begins: Edie Yocom buys back her own boots at the family auction.

"Her father," Elmer explained to me, "was Jonathan Keck, my uncle. So she is your cousin. I've got to go call a few people."

Elmer spread the news to several branches of the family. He called his first cousin Leidy Gaugler; then he talked to another cousin, Mary Hipple. He also called his sister Martha long distance. When Leidy and Elmer made plans to go to the funeral together, I asked if I could go along. Elmer quickly agreed. "It would be nice for you to see the relatives you haven't seen in a long time," Louisa smiled.

Three days later, Leidy and his Chevrolet pulled up in front of Elmer and Louisa's. Elmer, his black suit, white shirt, and red tie freshly cleaned and brushed, and I hopped in the car.

After he and Leidy discussed the best way to travel the twenty miles to Lutz's Funeral Home in Reading, we left. Leidy, just back from visiting his son David in California, talked of his two grandchildren there and how old they were. "I have five brothers and sisters," Elmer replies, "and do you know how I remember their ages? Simple. 3–3–5–3–3. Alan was born in 1890, me in ninety-three, Rufus in ninety-six, Dan in 1901, Mim in 1904, and Martha in nineteen aught-seven."

As we eased into the parking lot, Elmer pointed, "Oh, there's Mary and Elwood [Hipple] and Sadie and Harold [Ziegenfus; Elmer's first cousins]." As we talked about the last time we saw each other at the Keck reunion several years back, Elmer herded us all inside. There among the brocade and velvet drapes and the thick maroon carpet stood Mildred, Bessie's daughter. "Well, Mildred, you're looking good. How's your leg?" Elmer laughed and clasped everyone's hand. Then, after some words of comfort to Mildred and her husband Dick, Elmer and I viewed Bessie, her white hair and pink skin in stark contrast to the shiny satin lining of the bed-like coffin.

As we signed the guest register, Elmer asked me, "Do you know? All the family is represented: me from David (Elmer's father), Bessie from John, Leidy from Cora, Sadie from Emma, and Mary from Hen (Henry)." During the day, he told this fact to several people, including Betty, his daughter, when we got home.

As we sat down in the second section of seats, Harold Ziegenfus walked over, pulled a bedraggled piece of newsprint from his wallet, and stuck it in front of Elmer's face. Elmer read it, a "One Hundred Years Ago" column from the Reading Eagle, *about William Keck and Dutch Liz who, in 1871, were arrested for keeping a "disorderly house." As Elmer laughed, Harold winked, "Black sheep of the family, say Elmer?" The clipping traveled through several more hands until the minister walked to a small lectern.[5]*

After the service, the funeral men closed the coffin and called for the pallbearers. "That's Dick's son," Elmer whispered as the men filed by, "and that's an intended bridegroom."

The car was hot as we climbed in for the trip to Forest Hills Cemetery. "Boy, this reminds me of something that happened to Uncle Bill when we were out on the farm," Elmer said as he turned to Leidy. "It was a hot, hot day; and he was up in the hayloft. All of a sudden he fell out and landed in a big pile of hay, underneath. In a minute or so, he dug himself out, and said, 'Bissel kiel heit!' (Little cool today)."

As we all laughed, Elmer observed that Bill and other Kecks like to joke. "Once," Elmer continued, "Bill tried to play a joke on me with a horse, but the horse kicked him instead. And one day a cousin of mine came over, and Dad told him, 'Bumblebees don't sting today.' So he picked up a bee and got stung. Boy, did Mom yell at Dad. Yes, we Kecks had a lot of capers; but you know, it was all good fun. You remember the good times we had with that Grafanola in the front room?"

Leidy laughed as we drove on, closer and closer to the burial site.

Celebrating life-cycle events and holidays often sets the stage for family storytelling. And anyone who would like to collect family tales and history would do well to watch for and collect during such settings.

Although these many narratives provide much family history, a collector would be wrong to see the tales only as enjoyable efforts at keeping the past alive. Tales are not told simply to jar our memories. A bride and bridegroom do not forget the tricks a cousin pulled at their wedding. A mother hardly needs to be reminded where her children were when she gave birth to her youngest. And relatives do not forget especially embarrassing childhood incidents. Such tales are, rather, the sound of a family very much in the present celebrating, renewing, and reestablishing itself through its stories.

How to Collect Your Own Family Folklore

We hope that the stories, photographs, and accounts of traditions in this book have inspired readers to collect the folklore of their own families. But where do you start? Through the years we have developed some guidelines, which may be adapted to your own needs and circumstances. You might want to get started before the inspiration slips away, and even to jot down some of the stories and traditions this book has brought to mind.

Before you begin. Because family folklore belongs to a living family, it is constantly evolving. Each generation will forget and alter the lore that it has received; on the other hand, that same generation will add new verbal lore and new traditions. This creative aspect of family folklore affects the researcher in several ways. First, no matter how hard you try, you will never record the entire body of your family's folklore since there will never be a time in which it will be totally static. Don't despair. Get down what you can and encourage other family members to do the same. Just think of collecting family folklore as a pastime for which you have an infinite supply of raw material close at hand.

Second, think about your time orientation. The family folklorist cannot be so absorbed in preserving the past that he neglects to record the present. Keep your eyes, ears, and mind open. A tradition does not have to be old to be worth recording. In fact, a good part of any family's tradition is ephemeral and may not last long enough to pass from one generation to another. Collecting family folklore is one case in which too much is better than too little. Tapes can be edited and transcripts can be discarded, but the tradition, story, or expression that you neglect to record today may be lost.

Finally, remember that family folklore exists as part of the day-to-day living of a family, changing and moving with that family. To separate it abruptly from this natural context would rob it of its vitality and its existence as folklore. It is essential to remember that the story itself—including where, when, and how it is told—is as important as the information it conveys. This is the essential distinction between family folklore and the closely related disciplines of genealogy and family history. The following suggestions are designed to help you focus on these folkloric aspects of your family.

As self-appointed family folklorist you now have two tasks ahead of you: to learn your family's folklore and to record it for others to enjoy.

The equipment. Note-taking and tape recording are the usual means of recording family folklore. The tape recorder is the means of choice. Writing during an interview or family event has a number of disadvantages. Most people find note-taking to be both tedious and difficult. It is hard to maintain a conversation or participate actively in the ongoing activities, especially since you can't look at your subject. A complete, accurate account of the story—especially if it is long and detailed—is difficult to obtain. Although the words may be written down, the subtleties of the performance are inevitably lost.

Although both you and your informant might be uneasy and uncomfortable with a tape recorder, you'll probably soon get accustomed to its presence. A small cassette machine with a separate omni-directional microphone will give good results. It is easy to use and so inconspicuous that its presence will soon be forgotten. A sixty-minute cassette (30 minutes per side) is a good choice since it is economical, unlikely to tangle, and long enough to record substantial segments of an interview without interruption.

The microphone should be placed so that all voices, including yours, can be picked up. Run a test before you begin the actual interview and adjust the machine accordingly. The end of a two-hour interview is no time to discover that the volume control was too low! Read carefully any instructions that come with the particular tape recorder you are using.

As far as possible all extraneous noise should be eliminated. Turn off the radio, close the window, move away from the window fan. A few minutes spent finding the proper spot for the tape recorder can save you many hours when it comes time to transcribe the interview and you struggle to distinguish grandma's voice from the roar of a passing truck. The recorder should also be placed where it will not be disturbed during the interview and where you will have easy access to it when it becomes necessary to change tapes.

Although not as essential as a tape recorder, a camera is a useful piece of equipment. It provides a visual record of the

Four generations of one family. From left to right. Brady Dickerson, Katie Dickerson Greene, Mildred L. Henderson Maiden, and in the center, Beverly J. Robinson, as a baby.

interview and the informant. It can also be used to copy any documentary records that the informant might offer, such as letters or scrapbooks.

Family tape recordings and photographs that are worth collecting are also worth preserving. Although professional archival techniques are rather elaborate for home use, some simple, commonsense measures will enable future generations to enjoy your research efforts. Heat, humidity, and light, especially sunlight, are the principle causes of deterioration of tapes, photos, paper, and other artifacts. Storing material in a damp basement or a hot, unventilated attic is not recommended. In fact, people and research materials do best in about the same environment—a temperature between sixty to seventy degrees farenheit and a relative humidity of fifty percent. If you're comfortable, your research material is probably safe. The problem of light is more difficult, especially for photographs which are often displayed under damaging conditions. The best solution is to display only copies, keeping the originals in albums and boxes.

At the present time, you can't assume that color photographs and slide transparencies will be permanent images. Black and white copies should be made of those photographs that you wish to preserve indefinitely. Most commercial photographers can provide this service, but it is possible for an amateur to do an adequate job at home. Thomas L. Davies gives detailed descriptions of simple home copying methods in *Shoots: A Guide to Your Family's Photographic Heritage* (Addison House: Danbury, NH, 1977). For best results, the black and white film should be archivally processed, that is, thoroughly washed at the time of developing to remove any residual chemicals that could eventually damage the film. Again, both professional photo labs and the family photographer who processes his own film can perform this essential step. Acid-free file folders, photo albums, scrapbooks, and storage boxes are available from office and library supply companies and are worth the extra cost because of the added protection they provide.

The people. With whom should you start? Your oldest relative? The one you feel most at ease with? No. The place to begin is with yourself. You are just as much a bearer of your family's traditions as any member of your family. Use yourself as an informant and ask yourself the questions that follow on pages 269–71. You may be surprised at how much you know about some areas and how little about others. It is very likely that you will know more about one side of the family than another, for instance. Once you have collected family folklore from yourself, use your answers as a starting point for questioning other family members. Try to remember family structure. Who are your relatives? Which ones are most likely to have information and be willing to share it? Who gets along with whom? What topics are likely to be sensitive? These are all essential questions that you have to tackle yourself, first.

The first outside person that you interview should be someone with whom you feel very comfortable. Interviewing is not easy and you would do well to get your introduction to it in the presence of a friendly face. A parent or sibling might be a good choice. Young children often have great success with grandparents.

As you continue your interviewing you will pick up clues that will help you find potential narrators: "You should talk to Uncle Joe about that," or "Aunt Jane is a much better story-

M. A. LEARY

CAROLYN MITCHELL

teller than I am." Whenever possible ask directly for sources: "Can you tell me who might know more about that?" As you become more and more involved with the search you will meet relatives that you never even knew you had! Don't neglect non-relatives, either. Your grandfather's best friend may be able to tell you things about him that no family member would know. Don't overlook other members of the household who were not relatives, such as nursemaids or longterm boarders. Try not to be misled by terms of address. Aunt, uncle, sister, brother, and cousin are especially troublesome words since they can indicate respect, affection, and brotherhood as easily as blood or marriage relationships. And although they won't be much help as sources of information on family folklore, don't forget family pets since they can frequently be found as characters in family stories.

The interview. The most productive family folklore interviews are those that take place in a natural context for the reasons explained at the beginning of this guide: family folklore is a living part of a family and cannot be successfully separated from the everyday activities of that family. This can present problems since it will be impossible for you to be present during every naturally occurring folkloric event. You should make use of such opportunities whenever possible, however. Some common natural contexts are family dinners, picnics, reunions, and holidays. These are the times at which families would tell stories whether or not you are there with your tape recorder. Under these circumstances you will probably not even have to conduct an interview—just adjust the recorder, relax, and participate as you would ordinarily.

If no spontaneous natural context seems to be available you will have to rely on what is called an induced natural context. The distinction is straightforward. Instead of waiting for a family dinner to occur in the normal course of events, you initiate one. This approach has the added advantage of giving you a degree of control over the situation. For example, you can invite specific relatives who interact well with each other. Try serving foods that you know will bring back memories from the past.

The group interview context, whether natural or induced, has one major characteristic that makes it extremely fruitful.

The interaction that occurs as a matter of course serves to spark the memories of the participants. One story leads into another, one interpretation elicits cries of "but that's not really the way it happened at all!" The end result of such an interview will differ greatly from private interviews with the same relatives.

Private interviews can also be either natural or induced. If grandma begins to talk to you about her journey to this country while you are washing the supper dishes, fine—unfortunately, you probably won't be prepared with a tape recorder. If you wish to privately interview a relative, try not to do so under formal circumstances. Suggest some activity that will allow you to maintain a conversation easily but will help keep the session natural and low key: going for a walk, sewing, baking. If you know beforehand that a particular activity is usually a time for storytelling, schedule your interview to coincide with that event. Familiar surroundings and routine activities will also help to distract the informant from the fact that he or she is being interviewed and will lessen the unsettling impact of the tape recorder.

Every interview that you do will be unique. The questions on pages 269–71 will supply some uniformity, although you will probably be selective in using them. These brief suggestions should be helpful in most circumstances.

1. Start with a question or a topic that you know will elicit a full reply from your subject, such as a story you have heard him tell in the past. This will give your relative confidence in his ability to contribute something of value to your collection.

2. Avoid generalities. "Tell me about your childhood," for instance, often elicits nothing more than a list of names and dates.

3. Ask evocative questions. Nothing can kill an interview faster than a long series of questions that require only yes or no as answers.

4. Face up to the fact that there will be some information that you will not get. You may be the wrong sex or age. A relative may simply not trust you with sensitive data. If you feel you must have the missing material you may be able to solicit the help of another relative or friend as an interviewer.

5. Be aware that role switching will occur. You have changed from a son or daughter to an interrogator. Both you and your informant may feel uneasy in these new roles. A low-key approach in a natural setting should help relieve some of the discomfort.

6. Show interest. Encourage your informants as much as possible. Interject remarks whenever appropriate. Take an active part in the conversation without dominating it. Learn to be a creative listener as well as a good questioner.

7. Know what questions you want to ask, but don't be afraid to let your informant go off on a tangent. He or she might just touch on subjects of interest that you never thought to ask about.

8. Never turn off the tape recorder unless asked to. Not only does it break the conversation, such action suggests that you think some of your informant's material is not worth recording.

9. Use props whenever possible. Documents, letters, photo albums, scrapbooks, home movies, and other family heirlooms can all be profitably used to stimulate memories.

10. Be sensitive to the needs of family members. Schedule your sessions at a convenient time. Older people tire easily; cut the interview off at the first sign of fatigue. Don't slight

SUSAN MITCHELL

TOM THOMPSON

family members who show interest in your project. Interview them, even if you have reason to believe their material will be of minimal value.

11. If possible, prepare some sort of written report for the family as a tangible result of their participation. Remember to save all of your tapes, notes, and any other documentation that you have accumulated. Label everything with names, dates, and places. Ideally, all tapes should be indexed and transcribed as soon as possible after the interview. You will be more conscientious about documentation if you place yourself in the position of your great-grandchild who, many decades in the future, will be using your project as a source for his reconstruction.

12. Before publishing diaries, memoirs, letters, or other written artifacts, you would be wise to find out about copyright regulations. For example, the writer of a letter owns the copyright, not the recipient nor the present owner of the letter. The same principle holds true for tape-recorded oral history and folklore—the speaker, not the tape owner, holds all rights to his material. Most family members will gladly allow you to make use of whatever resources you need for documenting the family's traditions, but it never hurts to be prepared with copyright information. The Copyright Office at the Library of Congress will send a packet of information upon request (Copyright Office, Library of Congress, Washington, D.C. 20560.)

A question of ethics. Most of your relatives will be delighted by your new-found interest in collecting family folklore. Some will undoubtedly wonder if you've gone slightly mad. Unfortunately, a few may be uncooperative and even hostile. Because of the personal nature of the folklore that you will be collecting, you should be very careful to protect the privacy and rights of all family members. Be honest about your intent from the very beginning. Explain your reasons for doing the research. Is it a school assignment? Do you simply want to learn more about your family? Do you plan to publish your findings? The ultimate disposition of the collection may affect their willingness to talk about certain subjects.

You may find it difficult to explain what family folklore is and why you want to record it. Your relatives will most likely equate your research with genealogy and family history. No harm will be done if you explain your research in those terms since the areas are so interrelated. Showing them books like this may help, too.

Don't make promises you can't or don't indend to keep. If you say you will erase part of a tape, do so, even if it means losing some important information. Respect confidences and privacy. Let your informants see anything that will be published before it is too late to alter the manuscript. Although the intimate nature of family folklore places restrictive and sometimes frustrating burdens on the researcher, the bulk of your collection will probably be noncontroversial.

Finally, never record secretly. There is no justification for dishonesty and the bad feelings within the family that may result.

One last word. Please do not be discouraged by all the dos and don'ts that we have suggested. Once you have begun collecting your own family's folklore you will realize that the guidelines are based on commonsense and lots of practice. Vary them to suit your own family circumstances. Improve them with our blessing and encouragement. And above all, enjoy yourself, your family, and your folklore.

A possible questionnaire. Every family is unique. Every folklore fieldworker has his or her own special interests and style of interviewing. Because of this diversity, no single set of questions will successfully elicit folklore from all families. The most useful questions will be those that you develop through knowledge of yourself and your family. For your initial efforts the following questions may be helpful. Just remember that they are meant to be suggestive, not absolute. Pick and choose among them as you see fit. By all means change the wording to suit your own situation and personality.

1. What do you know about your family surname? Its origin? Its meaning? Did it undergo change coming from the old country to the United States? Are there stories about the change?

2. Are there any traditional first names, middle names, or nicknames in your family? Is there a naming tradition, such as always giving the firstborn son the name of his paternal grandfather?

3. Can you sort out the traditions in your current family according to the branches of the larger family from which they have come? Does the overall tradition of a specific grandparent seem to be dominant?

4. What stories have come down to you about your parents? Grandparents? More distant ancestors? How have these relatives described their lives to you? What have you learned from them about their childhood, adolescence, schooling, marriage, work, religion, political activity, recreation? Are they anxious or reluctant to discuss the past? Do their memories tend to cluster about certain topics or time periods and avoid others? Are there certain things in your family history that you would like to know, but no one will tell you? Do various relatives tell the same stories in different ways? How do these versions differ?

5. Do you have a notorious or infamous character in your family's past? Do you relish stories about him/her? Do you feel that the infamy of the ancestor may have grown as stories passed down about him/her have been elaborated?

6. How did your parents, grandparents, and other relatives come to meet and marry? Are there family stories of lost love, jilted brides, unusual courtships, arranged marriages, elopements, runaway lovers?

7. Have any historical events affected your family? For example, how did your family survive the Depression? Did conflict over some national event such as the Civil War or Vietnam cause a serious break in family relationships?

8. Are there any stories in your family about how a great fortune was lost or almost (but not quite) made? Do you believe them? Are these incidents laughed about or deeply regretted? If a fortune was made, who was responsible and how was it achieved?

9. What expressions are used in your family? Did they come from specific incidents? Are there stories which explain their origin? Is a particular member of the family especially adept at creating expressions?

10. How are holidays celebrated in your family? What holidays are most important—national, religious, or family? What innovations has your family made in holiday celebrations? Has your family created entirely new holidays?

11. Does your family hold reunions? How often? When? Where? Who is invited? Who comes? Who are the organizers and hosts? What occurs during the reunion? Are there traditional foods, customs, activities? Are stories and photographs exchanged? Are records (oral, written, visual) kept? By whom?

12. Have any recipes been preserved in your family from past generations? What was their origin? How were they passed down—by word of mouth, by observation, by written recipes? Are they still in use today? When? By whom? Does grandmother's apple pie taste as good now that it's made by her granddaughter?

13. What other people (friends, household help, etc.) have been incorporated into your family? When? Why? Were these people given family title such as aunt or cousin? Did they participate fully in family activities?

14. Is there a family cemetery or burial plot? Who is buried with whom? Why? Who makes burial place decisions? If there are gravemarkers, what type of information is recorded on them?

15. Does your family have any heirlooms, objects of sentimental or monetary value that have been handed down? What are they? Are there stories connected with them? Do you know their origin and line of passage through the generations? If they pass to you, will you continue the tradition, sell the objects, or give them to museums?

16. Does your family have photo albums, scrapbooks, slides, home movies? Who created them? Whose pictures are contained in them? Whose responsibility is their upkeep? When are they displayed? To whom? Are they specially arranged and edited? Does their appearance elicit commentary? What kind? By whom? Is the showing of these images a happy occasion?

* We would like to thank Margaret Yocom, who co-authored this section.

Appendix

THE
FAMILY
FOLKLORE
PROGRAM

On the broad lawns surrounding the Washington Monument, a tent city emerges each year, the temporary home for musicians and craftspeople transported to Washington to participate in the Smithsonian Institution's annual Festival of American Folklife. Begun in 1966 as a simple Fourth of July weekend celebration, the festival, now two weeks in duration, highlights the folk culture of America's diverse ethnic, regional, and occupational groups.

The festival is both a huge national pageant and a curiously intimate event. Amid the myriad performance stages and exhibition tents, there is always the opportunity for visitors to speak personally to Navajo dancers, D.C. cab drivers, Appalachian quilters, and regional cooks. It is hoped that each visitor will be able to find at least one event which serves as a link with his own heritage. Staged in the nation's capital, within sight of the White House, and the Jefferson and Lincoln Memorials, the festival serves to legitimize and celebrate individual Americans and their traditions.

The Family Folklore Program, established in 1974, was simultaneously a logical extension of this personalized approach and a reversal of the festival's traditional format. For the first time, visitors who came to enjoy an afternoon of performances suddenly found themselves performing the stories and traditions which had been passed down in their own families. On an immediate level, we wanted to make festival-goers aware that they, like the Cajun fiddlers and the Appalachian balladeers, were bearers of unique folkways. Our long-range goal was to begin study of the family group as a folk culture with its own corpus of tales, expressions, and other creative forms by which to celebrate and perpetuate a shared heritage.

All this was fine in theory, but as we set up our modest tent that first year, we wondered whether a few card tables, cassette tape recorders, and the avid interest of five folklorists would be enough to draw people away from rousing bluegrass music and colorful ethnic dancing. Somehow, the tent, sparsely decorated with patterned tablecloths, a few photos scavenged from second-hand shops, and a hopeful sign reading "Family Folklore—Will You Share Yours With Us?" drew a steady stream of visitors from the first day on.

In some ways, the festival was a truly unorthodox place to collect such private material. Far removed from the dining-room table, the front porch, and the holiday celebrations at which stories and traditions naturally unfold, informants were asked to share the details of their lives in an open tent abutting Native American dancers and capped with the steady drone of jet planes on approach to National Airport. Yet, there were many unforseen advantages in collecting in this atmosphere.

Far from being a distraction, the other events at the festival seemed to inspire our informants. Everything from ethnic foods to regional music elicited reminiscences and stories. We were able to capitalize on perhaps long-dormant memories brought to mind by familiar smells, sights, and sounds. For many visitors, the festival was also part of a summer holiday or an extended family vacation. Not only did they bring their children on this outing, but their older relatives "visiting from Utah." With the extended family in tow, our tent became a comfortable place to exchange family stories.

In the tent, we tried to create, metaphorically, a feeling of family life. Using kitchen tablecloths was one simple device for suggesting a home-like atmosphere. Another more powerful stimulus was our small display of family photos. Seeking only to create a homey ambience, we did not realize at first the ability of photos to bring forth family stories; nor did we know then that home photography constituted a distinct and legitimate genre of family lore. Yet, the reaction to the photos was so profound that within the first few days of interviewing, our understanding of the forms of family folklore unexpectedly broadened.

After the 1974 festival closed, we placed a single ad in the *Washington Post Magazine* asking local residents to lend us their photos, albums, and home movies. The response was overwhelming. Within two weeks, we had received hundreds of letters from people offering their most treasured collections. One hundred families were invited to lend their materials for research and exhibition. From these, we produced elaborate photo displays detailing common themes in home photography. We also produced "Home Movie," a composite film exploring the dreamy visions of family life created by family cinematographers.

Visitors to the 1975 and 1976 festivals found that our tent, much like parts of the Smithsonian museums, had begun to resemble an attic. It overflowed not only with photos, but with quilts, stitched pictures, diaries, poems, and even a "junk drawer" filled with trinkets whose nostalgic associations made them impossible to throw out. Two collections of stories recorded at previous festivals were offered for sale, and in 1976, "Harmonize," a new film based on traditions related to us by five local families, was shown continuously with "Home Movie" in an adjacent tent. Perhaps one of the chief beauties of this project was the way in which informants contributed to our understanding of family folklore. By interpreting their recollections in exhibitions, films, and publications, we, in turn, were able to enhance the educational value of the project and to provide additional stimuli for our informants in the years that followed.

The family folklore interviewing tent attracted an intelligent and self-conscious group of informants, as did the festival itself. About eighty percent were white-collar workers, with an emphasis on teachers, social workers, doctors, and lawyers. Seventy-five percent of those interviewed were living in the Washington, D.C., area, although most of these had grown up in other cities and were not here permanently. Overall, the sample is biased towards the large cities on the east coast and the south. The interviews attracted a disproportionate number of Jews, about thirty percent of the interviews, and Italians, about ten percent. Other significant ethnic groups were Irish, Germans, and Scandinavians. White Anglo-Saxon Protestants were also well-represented. Although the percentage of interviews with black Americans was small, we conducted about forty interviews with members of Afro-American families in the tent.

A common topic of conversation among our staff involved speculation on why so many Russian Jews and Italians chose to be interviewed. Were these groups simply overrepresented in the festival audience? Are these ethnic groups particularly self-conscious, verbal, or family-oriented? We came to no conclusions, but some simple immigration statistics may offer clues.

In the so-called second wave of immigrations, from 1901–1910, a million and a half persons immigrated from Russia and over two million from Italy. This is next only to Hungary and represents the largest groups ever to immigrate to this country in so short a period of time. Those young people who came to America during this time now had grandchildren in their late twenties, many of them still living in the eastern seaboard cities where their grandparents disembarked. Sociologists have long noted the trend of third-generation Americans to take a strong interest in their family origins, which may explain the interest of young Italians and Jews in being interviewed by us. Perhaps it is not coincidental that over three years, seven of our sixteen interviewers were also third-generation Russian Jews.

The fact that our interviewers (most were graduate students in the Department of Folklore and Folklife at the University of Pennsylvania) like our informants were middle class made rapport-building relatively easy. Unlike the folklorist working with more traditional, isolated groups, interviewers and their subjects had much in common. Some of the folklorists even found that an effective technique of eliciting stories and expressions was to share similar ones of their own. Yet, the interviewing situation had some built-in distance that also worked in our favor. We were strangers, but as strangers we were not involved in family feuds or factionalism. Often, informants noted that they were talking to us more freely than they might to their own kinfolk. We were also representing the Smithsonian Institution, and our informants took a certain measure of pride in knowing that the interview tapes would be preserved in the institution's archives.

The interviews were open-ended and lasted an average of twenty minutes each. Many interviews, however, lasted an hour or more. As many as fifty informants returned to be interviewed again, often bringing the family "historian" or raconteur with them. The folklorists had a long list of questions from which to choose (see the Interviewing Guide, pp. 269), but most often, individual interviews tended to focus on one or two areas of folklore, depending on the interests of informants. Besides questions dealing with specific genres of folklore, we asked very general questions such as "What other means does your family use to preserve its past?" The answers to these questions were extremely valuable to us in increasing our understanding of family lore.

Over three summers, we taped interviews with nearly two thousand family members, making this collection perhaps the largest body of such material to have been recorded at this time. Yet we cannot claim that the tapes provide a full and accurate sampling of American family lore. Instead, this collection represents what a self-selected group of informants decided to share with us at an outdoor celebration. It does not necessarily represent Americans as a whole, nor does it touch as deeply as it might on the pathos of family life. The tone of the festival, and of our tent, was decidedly upbeat. And our visitors, however candid in their conversation, related traditions and thoughts which in large part affirmed family life.

For all the stimulation it provided, our tent was quite different from a home where folklore functions in a natural context. Folklore was obtained at the instigation of our collectors, and many of the stories we heard were the ones "Uncle Ned used to tell," not the ones repeated most frequently by the person sitting down with us. The tapes, then, often do not represent the best performances of those stories in the flow of family life. They are perhaps more passive; their occurrences at family gatherings were told to us, not observed by us. There is a trade-off here. To collect as much as we did necessitated being in one place, a very public place, over a period of time. For an unstudied genre, this volume of material makes possible definition and a broad-based system of classification which others may find useful in organizing their own materials. An analysis of performance must be left to folklorists who study selected individual families in-depth.

After each festival, the tapes were transcribed selectively, with an eye towards publication. Inessential conversation, interviewers' questions, and false starts were eliminated. Transcribers listened instead for discrete items of folkloric interest and related thoughts on family life. Conversations between family members were noted when one prodded, amplified, corrected, or contradicted another. Common categories of material emerged throughout the transcribing process, and these categories, once established, helped us to direct our questions to what appeared to be the most fertile areas of inquiry. All of the transcriptions were labeled by year, name of informant, and genre. Predictably, some of the best material was simply unclassifiable; hence our chapter on "Other Stories." For this publication, we and our editors at Pantheon have made minor changes in the original transcriptions only where it was deemed absolutely essential for coherence.

*Visitors to the Festival of American Folklife share their
stories and peruse photo albums in the family folklore tent.*

This book is based primarily on the interviews conducted from 1974 to 1977. It includes parts of two previous publications of stories from the early festivals, and materials from the twelve-week Bicentennial Festival, where we taped at least three times the number of interviews we had during the first two festivals combined. Much of the 1976–1977 material is published here for the first time. Very little collecting has been done since 1977, but over the past five years we have all conducted additional research, written several articles on parts of the collection, and participated in many workshops, panel discussions, and professional meetings across the country, which helped us to put our collection in perspective and collect more diverse materials. One of our staff members has also written a dissertation on American family stories, during which he re-interviewed many of the original contributors in depth. All of these activities have further developed our understanding of the material and are reflected throughout this book.

The family folklore interview tapes and copy negatives of all photos used in our exhibits are available for scholarly research. The interviews are archived by year, informant, and interviewer, and cross-indexed by subject matter. For further information, contact the Office of Folklife Programs, Smithsonian Institution, Washington, D.C. 20560. The family folklore films, "Harmonize" and "Home Movie," are distributed through the Center for Southern Folklore, P. O. Box 40081, Memphis, TN 38104.

The earliest and still the most abundant printed sources of family folklore are the regional folklore journals. These publications focus on material of local interest and are rich in collectanea pertaining to family folklore. Many of the following articles were written by folklore students and tend to be collections of folklore items with little analysis or contextual information.

Boshears, Frances. "Granddaddy Roberts." *Midwest Folklore* 3 (Fall 1953):151–56.

Brann, Dolly. "I Can Remember: An Interview with Mr. and Mrs. L. D. Brann." *New York Folklore Quarterly* 28 (March 1973):244–56.

Brunetti, Michael. "Italian Folklore." *New York Folklore Quarterly* 28 (March 1973):257–62.

Carbo, Terry M. "The Faith Healing Beliefs of a New Orleans Family." *Louisiana Folklore Miscellany* 2 (August 1968):91–100.

Currin, Martha O. and Barbara C. Smetzer. " 'Blackeye, the Intelligent Bird Dog,' and Other Humorous Stories as told by Joe D. Currin." *North Carolina Folklore* 12 (July 1964):1–6.

Dober, Virginia. "We'll Tell 'Em." *North Carolina Folklore* 4 (July 1956):15–22.

Dobie, Bertha McKee, ed. "Tales and Rhymes of a Texas Household." *Publications of the Texas Folklore Society* 6 (1927):23–71.

Gillin, June Jacobi. "Lore from a Swedish Grandfather." *New York Folklore Quarterly* 9 (Winter 1953):268–72.

Giusti, Rosanna M. "The Life Cycle Beliefs of a New Orleans Family of French-Italian Background." *Louisiana Folklore Miscellany* 3 (1975 for 1973):1–28.

Halpert, Herbert. "Family Tales of a Kentuckian." *Hoosier Folklore Bulletin* 1 (August 1942):61–71.

Hardin, William Henry. "Grandpa Brown." *Publications of the Texas Folklore Society* 29 (1959):58–68.

Hawkins, Beverly. "Folklore of a Black Family." *Journal of the Ohio Folklore Society* 2 (April 1973):2–19.

Hilliard, Addie Suggs. "I Remember, I Remember." *Tennessee Folklore Society Bulletin* 32 (December 1966):121–28.

Holyoak, Van. "Stories About My Dad." *AFFword* 1 (October 1971):10.

Hunter, Edwin R. "My Grandfather's Speech." *Tennessee Folklore Society Bulletin* 8 (March 1942):5–22.

Jiles, Paulette. "Card Players and Story Tellers." *This Magazine is About Schools* 5 (1971).

Justice, Beverly, et al. "Old Time Holidays." *Foxfire* 7 (Winter 1973):326–38.

Kelly, Jill. "The Finlinson Family Reunion Tradition." *AFFword* 4 (Spring 1974):37–39.

Labarbera, Michael. "An Ounce of Prevention, and Grandmother Tried Them All." *New York Folklore Quarterly* 20 (June 1964):126–29.

Lockmiller, Earl. "Tales My Grandfather Told Me." *Tennessee Folklore Society Bulletin* 17 (June 1951):42–43.

Lueg, Maurita Russell. "Russell Tales." *Publications of the Texas Folklore Society* 27 (1958): 160–66.

Lumpkin, Ben Gray. "Folksongs from a Nebraska Family." *Southern Folklore Quarterly* 36 (March 1972):14–35.

Lundman, Della. "My Kin Knew Jesse James." *AFFword* 1 (July 1971):18–20.

Nagorka, Suzanne. "The Life of Felicia Nagorka." *New York Folklore Quarterly* 28 (March 1973):286–92.

Parker, Cherry. "Mother-in-Law Lore." *North Carolina Folklore* 5 (December 1957):22.

Pearce, Helen. "Folk Sayings in a Pioneer Family of Western Oregon." *California Folklore Quarterly* 5 (July 1946):229–42.

Pebworth, Ted-Larry. "Aunt Loda's Legacy." *Louisiana Folklore Miscellany* 2 (August 1968):24–33.

Roberts, Mary Eliza. "Folklore in My Father's Life." *Midwest Folklore* 3 (Fall 1953):147–50.

Simmerman, Alice. "Arizona Stories." *AFFword* 4 (Spring 1974):24–36.

Sutton, Mayte E. "Grandmother's Story." *New York Folklore Quarterly* 19 (March 1963):55.

Taube, Kristi. "Family Folklore With a German Flair." *Journal of the Ohio Folklore Society* ns 3 (Spring 1974):17–19.

West, John Foster. "The Old Musket: A Family Story." *North Carolina Folklore* 20 (May 1972):81–83.

White, Miriam Whitney. "Legends of an Adirondack Grandfather." *New York Folklore Quarterly* 22 (June 1966):132–42.

White, Virginia. "Grandmother Remembers Switzerland." *New York Folklore Quarterly* 10 (Winter 1954):274–78.

Willis, Alice. "Tales From a Mountain Homestead." *New York Folklore Quarterly* 3 (Winter 1947):302–11.

Woodward, Susan Holly. "A Grandfather's Tales of the Lowry Brothers." *North Carolina Folklore* 10 (December 1962):17–20.

Although collectanea does predominate in the literature on family folklore, analysis is by no means lacking. Kim Garrett, in "Family Stories and Sayings," *Publications of the Texas Folklore Society* 30 (1961):273–281, incorporates within her fine collection of her own family's folklore the suggestion that family folklore can serve as a binding force within families. Kathryn Morgan, in *Children of Strangers: The Stories of a Black Family* (Philadelphia, 1981), examines the ways in which family folklore can help families cope with difficult situations. Patrick Mullen's "Folk Songs and Family Traditions," *Publications of the Texas Folklore Society* 38 (1972):49–63, is an analysis of the interrelationships between those genres. Stanley Brandes, in "Family Misfortunes Stories in American Folklore," *Journal of the Folklore Institute* 12 (1975):5–17, and Steven J. Zeitlin, in " 'An Alchemy of Mind': The Family Courtship Story," *Western Folklore* 39 (1980):17–33, classify and examine specific types of family folklore. Francis Haines, Sr., looks at stories of westward migration in "Goldilocks on the Oregon Trail," *Idaho Yesterdays* IX (1965) 26–30. Mody Boatright's "The Family Saga as a Form of Folklore," in his *The Family Saga and Other Phases of American Folklore* (Urbana, 1958), pp. 1–19, is still the classic article on the subject and describes the components usually found in a family's traditional history.

Family folklore has now been accepted as a distinct genre by academic folklorists. At least three doctoral dissertations have been prepared on the subject:

Baldwin, Karen L. "Down on Bugger Run: Family Group and the Social Base of Folklore." University of Pennsylvania, 1975.

Yocom, Margaret R. "Fieldwork in Family Folklore and Oral History: A Study in Methodology." University of Massachusetts, 1980.

Zeitlin, Steven J. "Americans Imagine Their Ancestors: Family Stories as a Folklore Genre." University of Pennsylvania, 1979.

Just as the academic discipline of folklore is closely related to other subjects, the field of family tradition has been examined by scholars with a variety of professional affiliations. The following references are just a sampling from these other approaches. Anthropologists have tended to emphasize the social activities related to family traditions; a study of this type is Millicent Ayoub's "The Family Reunion," *Ethnology* 5 (1966):415–433. An early sociological study of the rituals of everyday life is by James H. S. Bossard and Eleanor Boll, *Ritual in Family Living: A Contemporary Study* (Philadelphia, 1950). Genealogists occasionally examine a specific tradition to determine its validity and usefulness as did Stanley Perin in "A Tradition in Search of Its Origin," *New England Historical and Genealogical Register* 121 (1967):29–36. Onomastics, the science of names, often deals with family traditions. An excellent example is Robert Rennick's "The Inadvertent Changing of Non-English Names by Newcomers to America: A Brief Historical Survey and Popular Presentation of Cases," *New York Folklore Quarterly* 26 (1970):263–282.

The literature in the field of oral history is full of references to family folklore. Three very good family-oriented histories are William Lynwood Montell's *The Saga of Coe Ridge* (New York, 1972), Dorothy Gallagher's *Hannah's Daughters: Six Generations of an American Family: 1876–1976* (New York, 1976), and *Jewish Grandmothers* (Boston, 1976), edited by Sydelle Kramer and Jenny Masur. A related genre is the family saga or memoir, based on oral tradition but reworked into a literary format. Alex Haley's *Roots: The Saga of an American Family* (Garden City, 1976) falls into this category. *The Land Remembers*, by Ben Logan (New York, 1976), centers on the life of a Norwegian farm family in Wisconsin and is one of the best examples of the genre. Willard R. Espy's *Oysterville: Roads to Grandpa's Village* (New York, 1977) traces a family's migration from Ireland to the northwest coast of the United States over the course of several generations. *Spoonbread and Strawberry Wine: Recipes and Reminiscences of a Family*, by Norma Jean and Carole Darden (Garden City, 1978), is one of the more unusual presentations of a family's heritage, since it weaves stories and photographs from a southern black family around a cookbook of family recipes. Another unique presentation of family folklore is *The Hammons Family: A Study of a West Virginia Family's Traditions*, a two-record album set with booklet, edited and recorded by Alan Jabbour and Carl Fleischhauer, published in 1973 by the Library of Congress, L65–66.

For those people embarking on a search for their family traditions there are a number of guides available. The books listed below are basic folklore and oral history collecting manuals plus more specialized literature focusing directly on the interrelationships of oral history and family history.

Allen, Barbara and William Lynwood Montell. *From Memory to History: Using Oral History Sources in Local Historical Research.* Nashville, 1981.

Baum, Willa K. *Oral History for the Local Historical Society.* Nashville, 1959.

———. *Transcribing and Editing Oral History.* Nashville, 1977.

Cook, Ann, Marilyn Gittell, and Herb Mack. *What Was It Like When Your Grandparents Were Your Age.* New York, 1976.

Davies, Thomas L. *Shoots: A Guide to Your Family's Photographic Heritage.* Danbury, NH, 1977.

Dixon, Janice T. and Dora D. Flack. *Preserving Your Past: A Painless Guide to Writing Your Autobiography and Family History.* Garden City, 1977.

Draznin, Yaffa. *The Family Historian's Handbook.* New York, 1978.

Epstein, Ellen Robinson and Rona Mendelsohn. *Record and Remember: Tracing Your Roots through Oral History.* New York: 1978.

Goldstein, Kenneth S. *A Guide for Fieldworkers in Folklore.* Hatboro, PA, 1964.

Hartley, William G. *Preparing a Personal History.* Salt Lake City, 1976.

Ives, Edward. *The Tape-Recorded Interview: A Manual for Field Workers in Folklore and Oral History.* Knoxville, 1980.

Lichtman, Allan J. *Your Family History.* New York, 1978.

Robertson, James, ed. *Old Glory: A Pictorial Report on the Grass Roots History Movement and the First Hometown Primer.* New York, 1973.

Shumway, Gary L. and William G. Hartley. *An Oral History Primer.* Salt Lake City, 1973.

Thompson, Paul R. *The Voice of the Past: Oral History.* New York, 1978.

Weitzman, David. *My Backyard History Book.* Boston, 1975.

_____. *Underfoot: An Everyday Guide to Exploring the American Past.* New York, 1976.

The following books published by the American Association for State and Local History give basic information on the preservation of research material:

Kane, Lucille M. *A Guide to the Care and Administration of Manuscripts,* 2nd edition. Nashville, 1966.

McWilliams, Jerry. *The Preservation and Restoration of Sound Recordings.* Nashville, 1979.

Weinstein, Robert A. and Larry Booth. *Collection, Use, and Care of Historical Photographs.* Nashville, 1979.

If home photography is your main interest in terms of family folklore, you will find an excellent theoretical introduction in the series of articles in *Saying Cheese: Studies in Folklore and Visual Communication* (Bloomington: Folklore Forum Bibliographic and Special Series No. 13, 1975), edited by Steven Ohrn and Michael E. Bell. Richard Chalfen deals specifically with home movies in his "Cinema Naiveté: A Study of Home Moviemaking as Visual Communication," *Studies in the Anthropology of Visual Communication* 2 (1975):87–103. *American Album,* by Oliver Jensen et al. (New York, 1970); *The Snapshot,* edited by Jonathan Green (Millerton, New York, 1974), *Family Photographs: Content, Meaning, and Effect* (New York, 1981), by Julia Hirsch, and "Family Photo Interpretation," by Judith Mara Gutman, in *Kin and Communities: Families in America,* edited by Allan J. Lichtman and Joan Challinor (Washington, D.C., 1979), are further sources of information on family photography.

FAMILY FOLKLORE: THE CREATIVE EXPRESSION
OF A COMMON PAST

1. For some good introductions to folklore, see Barre Toelken, *The Dynamics of Folklore* (Boston: Houghton Mifflin Co., 1979); Jan Harold Brunvald, *The Study of American Folklore: An Introduction,* 2nd ed. (New York: W. W. Norton & Co., 1978).

THE FORMS OF FAMILY LORE

1. Collected from Amanda Dargan, age 31, Darlington, South Carolina.
2. Collected in conversation with Ross Abrahams, Washington, D.C.

FAMILY STORIES

1. For a useful discussion of how family stories fit within a framework for oral narrative, see Linda Degh, "Folk Narrative," in *Folklore and Folklife: An Introduction,* ed. Richard Dorson (Chicago: University of Chicago Press, 1972). For some of the new research on the personal experience narrative, see Sandra K. D. Stahl, "The Personal Narrative as Folklore," *Journal of the Folklore Institute* 14 (1977):9–30; see also "Special Double Issue: Stories of Personal Experiences," ed. Richard Dorson and Sandra K. D. Stahl, *Journal of the Folklore Institute* 14 (1977). For other useful research on contemporary storytelling, see Barbara Kirshenblatt-Gimblett, "Traditional Storytelling in the Toronto Jewish Community" (Ph.D. diss., Indiana University, 1972); see also Linda Degh, ed., *Indiana Folklore* 1–14 (1969–present).
2. Regina O'Toole Sokas, age 23, Washington, D.C.
3. For a thorough discussion of the relationship between folklore and history, see Barbara Allen and Lynwood Montell, *From Memory to History: Using Oral Sources in Local Historical Research* (Nashville, Tenn., 1981); see also Lynwood Montell, *The Saga of Coe Ridge* (Knoxville: University of Tennessee Press, 1970); Gladys-Marie Fry, *Night Riders in Black Folk History* (Knoxville: University of Tennessee Press, 1975).
4. Susan Meehan, age 38, Washington, D.C.
5. Karl Lamarr Duff, Kent Store, Virginia.
6. Grace McDonald is a pseudonym. We have withheld the name of her grandson.
7. Name withheld upon request, age 30, Brooklyn, New York.
8. See Janet T. Dixon and Dora Flack, *Preserving Your Past: A Painless Guide to Writing Your Autobiography and Family History* (Garden City, N.Y.: Doubleday & Co., 1977), p. 50.

9. From a student paper by Dora Esten, George Washington University.

10. William Stewart, age 53, Belleville, New Jersey.

11. Donald Collins, age 44, Washington, D.C.

12. James H. S. Bossard and Eleanor S. Boll, *Ritual in Family Living: A Contemporary Study* (Philadelphia: University of Pennsylvania Press, 1950.

13. John Giordano, age 33, New York, New York.

14. From a student paper by Rebecca Martin, George Washington University.

15. Ibid., p. 49.

HEROES

1. Woody Guthrie, "Ranger's Command," used by permission.

2. Kathryn Morgan, "Caddy Buffers: Legends of a Middle Class Black Family in Philadelphia," in 1976 *Festival of American Folklife,* ed. Bess Lomax Hawes (Washington, D.C.: Smithsonian Institution, 1976), p. 26. See also Kathryn Morgan, *Children of Strangers: The Stories of a Black Family* (Philadelphia: Temple University Press, 1981).

3. Morgan, "Caddy Buffers," p. 27.

ROGUES

1. John Bishop, age 50, Ithaca, New York.

2. David W. Robinson, Seattle, Washington.

3. Nina Bohlen, age 16, Washington, D.C.

4. William Humphrey, *The Ordways* (New York: Alfred A. Knopf, 1965), p. 37, quoted in Patrick B. Mullen, "Myth and Folklore in *The Ordways,*" *Publications of the Texas Folklore Society* 35 (1971): 135.

5. Sue Berryman Bobrow, age 36, Washington, D.C.

MISCHIEF MAKERS

1. Erik Erikson, *Identity, Youth and Crisis* (New York: W. W. Norton & Co., 1968), p. 158.

2. For an exploration of the structure of family stories see Steven Zeitlin, "Americans Imagine Their Ancestors: Family Stories as a Folklore Genre" (Ph.D. diss., University of Pennsylvania, 1978).

3. See "Special Issue: The Practical Joke," *Southern Folklore Quarterly* 38 (1974): 251–331.

INNOCENTS

1. Humphrey, *The Ordways*, p. 21; quoted in Mullen, "Myth and Folklore in *The Ordways*," p. 137.
2. Collected in conversation from visitors to the 1976 Festival of American Folklife.

MIGRATIONS

1. Miriam Fors, age 56, Portland, Oregon.
2. Humphrey, *The Ordways*, p. 58, quoted in Mullen, "Myth and Folklore," p. 138.
3. See Alex Haley, "Black History, Oral History, and Genealogy," *Oral History Review 1973* (1973): 1-25.
4. E. Franklin Frazier, *The Negro Family in the United States* (Chicago: University of Chicago Press, 1966), p. 13. For other examples see the collections of slave narratives from the Federal Writers Project of the WPA.
5. Mody Boatright, "The Family Saga as a Form of Folklore," in *The Family Saga and Other Phases of American Folklore*, ed, Mody Boatright (Urbana: University of Illinois Press, 1958), p. 129. Quoted from Angelina Smith, "Dandy Jim Smith" (unpublished manuscript).
6. Gregory Gay, Washington, D.C.
7. Francis Haines, Sr., "Goldilocks on the Oregon Trail," *Idaho Yesterdays* 9 (1965–66): 26–30.
8. Carl Fleischhauer and Alan Jabbour, *The Hammons Family: A Study of a West Virginia Family's Traditions* (record and booklet), AFS L65–L66 (Washington: Library of Congress, 1973), pp. 3, 4, 27.

LOST FORTUNES

1. Boatright, *Family Folklore*, p. 15.
2. Stanley H. Brandes, "Family Misfortune Stories in American Folklore," *Journal of the Folklore Institute* 12 (1975): 5.
3. Ibid., 13.

COURTSHIPS

1. Helen Trenchi, age 52, Bethesda, Md.
2. Michael Kernan, *Washington Post*, December 29, 1976, p. B3.
3. Suzanne Gibson, age 30, Alexandria, Virginia.
4. Kevin Scott, "Interview with Maria Katzenbach," in "Book World," *Washington Post*, January 15, 1978.
5. Collected in conversation from Amanda Dargan, age 31, Darlington, South Carolina.

FAMILY FEUDS

1. Name withheld, Washington, D.C.
2. Peter Vietze, age 30, Nashville, Tennessee.
3. Amanda Dargan, "Family Identity and the Social Use of Folklore: A South Carolina Family Tradition" (Unpublished M.A. thesis, Memorial University of Newfoundland, 1978), p. 163.
4. Mark Twain, *The Adventures of Huckleberry Finn* (New York: Holt, Rinehart & Winston, 1948), p. 101.

SUPERNATURAL HAPPENINGS

1. Barbara Anthony, age 42, Suitland, Md.

STORIES FOR CHILDREN

1. Regina O'Toole Sokas, age 23, Washington, D.C.
2. See Kenneth S. Goldstein, "The Telling of Non-Traditional Tales to Children: An Ethnographic Report from a Northwest Philadelphia Neighborhood," *Keystone Folklore Quarterly*, 20 (1975): pp. 5–17.
3. Name withheld by request.
4. Name withheld by request.

FAMILY EXPRESSIONS

1. *Christian Science Monitor*, May 9, 1956, quoted in Allen Walker Read, "Family Words in English," *American Speech* 87 (1962): 9.
2. Richard Sackett, age 45, Bethesda, Maryland.
3. *Christian Science Monitor*, June 8, 1956, quoted in Read, "Family Words," p. 8.
4. Read, "Family Words," p. 9.
5. Steven Tauber, age 42, Chevy Chase, Md.
6. Kim S. Garrett, "Family Stories and Sayings," *Publications of the Texas Folklore Society* 30 (1961): 276.
7. Mary Slemp, age 37, Big Stone Gap, Virginia.
8. See Larry G. Small, "Traditional Expressions in a Newfoundland Community: Genre Change and Functional Variability," *Lore and Language* 2 (1975): 16.
9. R. A. Stewart Macalister, *The Secret Languages of Ireland* (Cambridge: 1937), p. 92, quoted in Read, "Family Words," p. 10.
10. Garrett, "Family Stories," p. 274.
11. Nancy Redenbaugh, Fort Collins, Colorado; Ann M. Fleming, Pittsburgh, Pennsylvania.
12. Dargan, *Family Identity*, p. 127.

13. Claudia Fugar.

14. Frederick Erickson, "Timing and Context in Everyday Discourse: Implications for the Study of Referential and Social Meaning," Sociolinguistic Working Paper Number 67 (Austin, Texas: Southwest Educational Development Laboratory, 1980), quoted in Ron Scollon, "Tempo, Density, and Silence: Rhythms in Ordinary Talk," (Unpublished paper, University of Alaska, Fairbanks, 1981), p. 1.

15. Collected in a conversation with Gingy Caswell.

FAMILY CUSTOMS

1. Bossard and Boll, *Ritual,* p. 10.

2. Ellen Kurzman, age 41, Glen Ridge, New Jersey.

3. Bossard and Boll, *Ritual,* p. 28.

4. Mary Dreshter, Hyattsville, Maryland.

FAMILY PHOTOGRAPHY

1. Thomas Schlereth, *Artifacts and the American Past* (Nashville, Tenn.: American Association for State and Local History, 1980), p. 20.

2. Susan Sontag, *On Photography* (New York: Farrar, Straus & Giroux, 1977), pp. 15, 81.

3. Carol Maas, Greenbelt, Maryland.

4. Jonathan Green, ed., *The Snapshot* (Millerton, N.Y.: Aperture, 1974), p. 24.

5. Margaret R. Yocom, "Fieldwork in Family Folklore and Oral History: A Study in Methodology" (Ph.D. diss., University of Massachusetts, 1980), pp. 113–18.

6. Pauline Greenhill, *So We Can Remember: Showing Family Photographs* (Ottawa: National Museums of Canada, 1981), p. 124.

7. Name withheld upon request, Bryn Mawr, Pennsylvania.

8. Audiotape from the film "Home Movie: An American Folk Art," by Steven Zeitlin and Ernst Star, Smithsonian Institution, 1975.

9. Catherine Noren, *The Camera of My Family* (New York: Alfred A. Knopf, 1976), foreword.

10. Corinne LeBovit, Silver Spring, Maryland.

11. Sontag, *On Photography,* p. 8.

12. Marjorie L. Share and William F. Stapp, *Picture It!* (Washington, D.C.: Smithsonian Institution, 1981), p. 80.

13. Joan Bernick, Washington, D.C.

14. Sontag, *On Photography,* p. 8.

15. Nancy Hallsted, Bethesda, Maryland.

16. Martha Ross, Bethesda, Maryland.

1. Alan Ludwig, age 24, Alexandria, Virginia.
2. Richard E. Snyder.
3. Simone de Beauvoir, *Coming of Age*, trans. Patrick O'Brian (New York: G. P. Putnam's Sons, 1972).
4. Ibid.
5. See Barbara Kirschenblatt-Gimblett, *Ashkenaz: Essays in Jewish Folklore* (Philadelphia: University of Pennsylvania Press, forthcoming). See also Barbara Myerhoff, *Number Our Days* (New York: E. P. Dutton, 1979).
6. Suzanne MacKenzie, age 17, Brewster, Mass.
7. Nancy Smith, age 31, Albany, New York.
8. Robert Rhode, age 30, Silverton, Texas.
9. Letters from October 6 and 14, 1861, contributed by Martha Swartwout, John Brandon's descendant.
10. From Andrew Nicholas Conrady to his great-grandson Andrew Nicholas Coyne, contributed by Ruth Coyne.
11. From the manuscript by E. S. Goodwin, "Memories of Our Grandfather," contributed by Mrs. Frank L. Goodwin.
12. Ron Sutton, Washington, D.C.
13. Conrady letter to Andrew Coyne.

GETTING THE BUTTER FROM THE DUCK: PROVERBS AND PROVERBIAL PHRASES IN AN AFRO-AMERICAN FAMILY

1. See E. Ojo Arewa and Alan Dundes, "Proverbs and the Ethnography of Speaking," reprinted in Alan Dundes, *Essays in Folkloristics.* 1978, 50–70. First printed in *American Anthropologist* 66 (1964): 70–85; see also Peter Seitel, "Proverbs: A Social Use of Metaphor" *Genre* 2 (1969): 143–61, and John Messenger, "The Role of Proverbs in a Nigerian Judicial System" *Southwestern Journal of Anthropology* 15 (1959): 64–73.
2. This proverb does not appear in the following standard proverb references: Archer Taylor, *The Proverb* (Cambridge: Harvard University Press, 1931); Bartlett, J. Whiting and Helen W. Whiting, *Proverbs, Sentences and Proverbial Phrases* (Cambridge: Harvard University, 1968); Archer Taylor and Bartlett J. Whiting, *A Dictionary of American Proverbs and Proverbial Phrases, 1820–1880* (Cambridge: Harvard University Press, 1958).
3. A common proverb, it is usually seen as "buying a pig in a poke" in European tradition. See Taylor, *The Proverb*, p. 187 and Whiting and Whiting, *Proverbs, Sentences*, p. 458.
4. Not found in Taylor, *The Proverb*, Whiting and Whiting, *Proverbs, Sentences*, or Taylor and Whiting, *Dictionary*.

5. Not found in Taylor, Whiting and Whiting, or Taylor and Whiting.

6. Found in Taylor, pp. 13, 158, 170.

7. Not found in Taylor, Whiting and Whiting, or Taylor and Whiting.

8. To "correct" a child means the entire process of telling him or her that a given behavior is wrong, and then reminding or instructing him or her in the socially approved behavior.

9. Not found in Taylor, Whiting and Whiting, or Taylor and Whiting.

10. Not found in Taylor, Whiting and Whiting, or Taylor and Whiting. This may be related in some way to another expression common in my family, "meddlesome madisome." This is said to a child who meddles in something that he should not.

BLESSING THE TIES THAT BIND: STORYTELLING AT FAMILY FESTIVALS

1. For a discussion of festival, see Robert J. Smith, "Festivals and Celebrations" in Richard M. Dorson, ed., *Folklore and Folklife* (Chicago: University of Chicago Press, 1972), and John B. Bender, "The Day of *The Tempest*," *Journal of English Literary History* 47 (1980): 235–58.

2. Journal, 30 May 1979; interview with Elmer Keck, 23 June 1979.

3. Journal IV, pp. 4–8, 30 April 1976.

4. Journal IV, p. 16, 3 May 1976.

5. Journal I, p. 55–57 and 73–79, 7 and 10 June 1975.

My sincere thanks to the members of my family who helped me learn the stories: Bertha David Heiser Yocom and Isaac N. Yocom, Katherine Louisa Keck and Elmer Christman Keck, Betty Keck Yocom and Norman David Heiser Yocom, Gladys Yocom Metka and William Metka, Edith Yocom Boyer and Randall Boyer, Marie and David Yocom, Douglas Yocom, Janet Yocom Keck, and Diane Yocom Suptlee. Enjoy.

ABOUT THE AUTHORS

Steven J. Zeitlin was born in Philadelphia, Pennsylvania, and raised in São Paulo, Brazil. He received his bachelor's degree from the University of Pennsylvania, his M.A. in literature from Bucknell University and his Ph.D. in folklore from the University of Pennsylvania.

Born in Hartford, Connecticut, Amy J. Kotkin received her B.A. in American studies at Case Western Reserve University and her M.A. in American civilization from the University of Pennsylvania.

Holly Cutting Baker was born in Fall River, Massachusetts. She has a bachelor's degree from Emmanuelle College and is completing her Ph.D. in folklore at the University of Pennsylvania.

Zeitlin, Kotkin, and Cutting Baker, with the help of Sandra Gross, founded the Family Folklore Program at the Smithsonian Institution in 1974. Steven Zeitlin coordinated the program, and is currently at work on a folklore project with the Queens Council on the Arts in New York City. He has also made several documentary films. Currently, Amy Kotkin assists in producing a touring lecture and seminar series for the Smithsonian National Associate Regional Events Program. Holly Cutting Baker has been an archivist with the American Folklife Center at the Library of Congress and is now at home caring for her husband John and her two-year-old daughter Kate.

Made in the USA
Columbia, SC
09 February 2018

THE NMW EXCERPT

CONTRIBUTORS

SUBMISSIONS

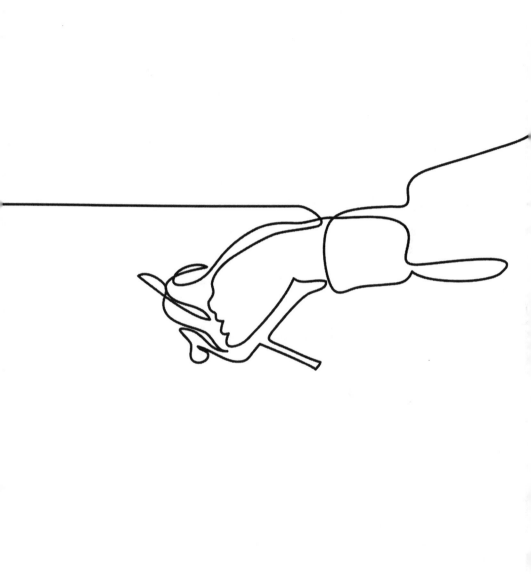

Winners and Finalists

The editors and judges at

NEW MILLENNIUM WRITINGS

are pleased to announce the

41ST NEW MILLENNIUM POETRY PRIZE

Robin Myers
of Washington, Vermont

LOVE POEM FOR CARL SAGAN

FINALISTS

Nancy Allen, Lynchburg, VA..."Firemen's Memorial Day Bar-B-Que, Rye Creek"

Lynne Martin Bowman, Greensboro, NC..."What the Sand Has Forgotten"

David Cooke, Portland, OR..."Meat Puppet"

Ted Davis, New Rochelle, NY..."Raising the Altar"

Robert Evory, Portage, MI..."Unmarked Grave"

Christina Frei, Hilversum, Netherlands..."Tree of Forgive"

Jonathan Greenhause, Jersey City, NJ..."Living in Suspension"

Lisa Gundry, Grand Rapids, MI..."Learning to Swim with Daddy"

Juli Anna Herndon, Providence, RI..."Cartography, after khaled mattawa"

Christina Lovin, Richmond, KY..."Of Other Nights"

Alison Luterman, Oakland, CA..."After Watching a Horror Movie, They Sleep with the Kitten Between Them"

Bernadette McComish, Venice Beach, CA..."Five Years Later"

Edward McManis, Larkspur, CA..."DSM V God"

Barbara Mossberg, Eugene, OR..."The Avatar of Day"

Julie Rochlin, Cambridge, MA..."Ice Age"

Jeffrey Schneider, Ellenville, NY..."Poetry 210 at the DFY"

Carol Smith, Kirkland, WA..."Benediction"

Armin Tolentino, Vancouver, WA..."Dirt Eaters Anonymous"

Barbara Zimmermann, Daleville, IN..."Sacrificial Fire"

Lucia Zimmitti, Las Cruces, NM..."Clay"

The editors and judges at

NEW MILLENNIUM WRITINGS

are pleased to announce the

42ND NEW MILLENNIUM POETRY PRIZE

Kerry Tepperman Campbell
of San Anselmo, California

BOUGAINVILLEA

FINALISTS

William Ellis, Vancouver, BC..."Instructions for Returning to the Past"

Robert Evory, Portage, MI..."Sympathy Vibration"

Aly Wright Fields, Watertown, MA..."Gymnastics"

Linda Nemec Foster, Grand Rapids, MI..."The Artist's Notebook"

Teresa Gilman, San Francisco, CA..."Whistling Down the Sky"

Jonathan Greenhause, Jersey City, NJ..."How I Became the Luckiest Man on My Block"

N. A. Hirabayashi, Philadelphia, PA..."Japan — Three Cities"

Martha Hollander, Jackson Heights, NY..."Strange Bed"

Marilyn E. Johnston, Bloomfield, CT..."Outward Bound"

George Keenen, Alameda, CA..."Back We Go"

Joyce Kessel, Buffalo, NY..."The Vigil"

James Kirkpatrick, Concord, NC..."INÈS"

Daniel Kossow, Washington, D.C...."One Morning in the Marsh"

K. T. Landon, Reading, MA..."The Second Law of Thermodynamics"

Ed Ruzicka, Baton Rouge, LA..."My Lungs Are a Shambles"

Victoria Smith, Des Moines, IA..."Mother of Exiles"

Barbara Ungar, Sarasota Springs, NY..."On a Scale of One to Ten"

The editors and judges at

New Millennium Writings

are pleased to announce the

41ST NEW MILLENNIUM
FLASH FICTION PRIZE

Adrianne Aron
of Berkeley, California

THE ENVELOPE TRICK

FINALISTS

Carly Anderson, Astoria, NY..."No Going Back"

Kathleen C. Arceneaux, Blacksburg, VA..."Feeding Seagulls"

Linda Barnhart, Womelsdorf, PA..."Cary Grant Was Here"

Sonia Christensen, Boulder, CO..."Thank You to Everyone"

Chris Connolly, Booterstown, Ireland..."A Perhaps Slightly Deranged Overreaction"

Adah Frank, Woodstock, NY..."The Rocking Chair"

JoeAnn Hart, Gloucester, MA..."Sunk"

Ambata Kazi, New Orleans, LA..."North Star"

Thomas Kudla, Wheaton, IL..."Dropping the A-Bomb"

Kathryn Kulpa, Somerset, MA..."American Blonde"

Iris Litt, New York, NY..."The Bear"

Jayne Martin, Los Olivos, CA..."When the Bough Breaks"

Jennifer Meng, Taipei City, Taiwan..."Pact with Space Gods"

Jeanette Quick, Washington, D.C...."Entering the Upper Middle Class"

Dave Reagan, Garberville, CA..."It's Not the Thing You Fling, But the Fling Itself That Counts"

Bruce Rettig, Tahoe Paradise, CA..."For Baha: February 4, 2014"

Diana Reynolds Roome, Talent, OR..."Darkly Through Glass"

Gerald Ryan, Elgin, IL..."Fortune Cookie"

Patricia Schultheis, Baltimore, MD..."Glory"

Cady Vishniac, Columbus, OH..."Early Conversations with Baby"

The editors and judges at

New Millennium Writings

are pleased to announce the

42ND NEW MILLENNIUM
FLASH FICTION PRIZE

William Polsgrove
of Frederick, Maryland

HIGHWAY 61

FINALISTS

Judith Glass Collins, Nordland, WA…"Matroyska"

Erin Conway, Janesville, WI…"Teacher, Wouldn't You Like to Sing the Blues?"

Andi Dobek, Waterloo, IL…"It's Not Me"

Tyler Dunning, Belgrade, MT…"Snow White"

Jeptha Evans, San Francisco, CA…"Politics"

Amanda Foerster, Minneapolis, MN…"Shirene"

Dana Getz, Pittsburgh, PA…"Dissonance"

Dara Kell, New York, NY…"T&T"

Lisa Korzeniowski, Northampton, MA…"The Burning"

Denise Long, Lincoln, NE…"Smooth, Shallow Cut"

Ginger Marcinkowski, Suffolk, VA…"Tsunami 615"

Lisa Michelle, West Point, CA…"Trails End"

Marc Phillips, Vermont…"You May Begin"

Eric Ruka, Pittsburgh, PA…"The Brave"

Michael Sarabia, Monterey Park, CA…"Mesopotamian Equinox"

Cynthia Schartman, Boston, MA…"Foodie"

Adam Schwartzman, New York, NY…"Holy Land, USA"

J Spru, Winterpoint, ME…"Juicy Fruit"

Lizette Wanzer, San Francisco, CA…"Flounder"

Jim Weyer, Lake Orion, MI…"The Beach"

41ST NEW MILLENNIUM FICTION PRIZE

Cady Vishniac
of Columbus, Ohio

MOVE

FINALISTS

Ioanna Carlsen, New Mexico..."Mexican Bus"

Kathy Conde, Denver, CO..."A Family Alphabet"

Joan Corwin, Chicago, IL..."Wings"

Sheldon Costa, Seattle, WA..."The Matinee"

Cora Cruz, Forest Hills, NY..."Material Conditions"

Hannah Gildea, Oregon City, OR..."Waiting for Eliza J."

Doris Iarovici, Durham, NC..."Jump"

Joe Johnson, Richmond, VA..."How Far Gone"

Kathryn Kulpa, Providence, RI..."A Key into the Language of Ghosts"

Mary LaChapelle, Bronxville, NY..."Sisters of a New Order"

Terrance Manning, White Oak, PA..."Pretty Lights"

Louise Marburg, New York, NY..."Personal Wealth"

Kate McCahill, Santa Fe, NM..."Absence"

Rose Ellen McCaig, Boston, MA..."Economics"

Timothy O'Leary, Portland, OR..."Fake Girlfriend"

Janet Schneider, Berkeley, CA..."Forging Bonds"

Luvia Swanson, Asheville, NC..."Mackenzie's Flight"

Elizabeth Taylor, Keswick, VA..."Olympic Pancake"

Margaret Vandenburg, Bloomingburg, NY..."Brave New York"

Alexander Weinstein, Ann Arbor, MI..."Moksha"

The editors and judges at

NEW MILLENNIUM WRITINGS

are pleased to announce the

42ND NEW MILLENNIUM FICTION PRIZE

Elizabeth Amon
of Seattle, Washington

HAIR OF THE DOG

FINALISTS

Jacob M. Appel, New York, NY..."The Children's Lottery"

Julia Ballerini, New York, NY..."The Workings of Joy"

J Bloom, Austria..."Molly"

Megan Gregor, La La Land..."Signs"

Lisa Greim, Arvada, CO..."Walter Says Good Morning"

Erin Holiday, St. Louis, MO..."Reserves"

Katharine Johnston, New York, NY..."Delancey and Essex"

Maxime Kawawa-Beaudan, Tiburon, CA..."Others"

Kathleen Kell, New York, NY..."Folly at Roosevelt Island"

Denise Long, Lincoln, NE..."Where It's Buried"

Haywood Moxley, Nashville, TN..."Hands"

Marsha Reed Nall, California..."Pure Gold"

Kate Pigott, New York, NY..."Needle"

Katherine Rooks, Boston, MA..."Climb On"

Kate Simonian, New York, NY..."Late Chrysalis, Early Summer"

Darren Sorrels ..."Total Progress 0%"

Patricia Trentacoste, Bridgport, MI..."India Lake"

Nina Varela, Los Angeles, CA..."Belly"

Mark Wagstaff, London, U.K...."Watching Biff on Primetime"

Casey Whitworth, Tallahassee, FL..."Me and You and Zvonimir"

The editors and judges at

NEW MILLENNIUM WRITINGS

are pleased to announce the

41ST NEW MILLENNIUM NONFICTION PRIZE

Carol D. Marsh

of Washington, D.C.

PICTURES IN LEAVES

FINALISTS

Doug Alderson, Tallahassee, FL..."Bear Troubles"

Janet Buttenwieser, Seattle, WA..."Laws of Motion"

Elliott Chen, Alhambra, CA..."Alone Wolf"

Don Colburn, Portland, OR..."Which Brings Us to the Nodule"

Jenn Dean, Carnation, WA..."The Keepers of the Ghost Bird"

Robert Fieseler, Boston, MA..."New Miserable Experience"

Edna Garte, Waterford, MI..."The Creative Approach"

Karin Goodwin, The Plains, VA..."My Jade Egg"

Abriana Jetté, Staten Island NY..."Risk"

Mal King, Santa Paula, CA..."Living Life in Capital Letters"

Jason Kirkman, Santa Fe, NM..."Indian Wedding Travelgasm"

Holly Levinson, Short Hills, NJ..."A New Normal"

Sue Li, New York, NY..."For Spacious Skies"

Catharine Lucas, Berkeley, CA..."Just Like Anyone's"

Holly Maurer-Klein, Pittsburgh, PA..."Period Peace"

Kate McCahill, Santa Fe, NM..."Remembering Mel"

Ed McManis, Larkspur, CA..."Why My Feet Hurt"

Petra Perkins, Denver, CO..."Grief Takes No Prisoner"

Mary Jane Reynolds, Columbia, SC..."A Certain Sacredness"

Madeline Wiseman, Lincoln, NE..."Finding the Gap on Dead Man's Run"

The editors and judges at

NEW MILLENNIUM WRITINGS

are pleased to announce the

42ND NEW MILLENNIUM
NONFICTION PRIZE

Kirk Wilson
of Austin, Texas

A BRIEF AND NECESSARY MADNESS

FINALISTS

Barbara Bruner, Pasadena, CA ..."My Son Becomes a Father"

Tyrese Coleman, Hyattsville, MD ..."Thoughts on My Ancestry.com DNA Results"

Robynn Colwell, Brussels, Belgium ..."Brussels Attacks"

J.L. Cooper, Carmichael, CA ..."The Sages of the West"

Savanna Ferguson, San Francisco, CA ..."On Orogenies"

Joan Goodreau, Chico, CA ..."First Words"

Anne Gudger, Banks, OR ..."Sieve"

William Hillyard, Laguna Niguel, CA ..."Wonder Valley"

Michele Leavitt, Gainesville, FL ..."Who Among Us"

Jeffrey Loeb, New York, NY ..."Resurrection"

Rolando Lopez, Puerto Rico ..."American Genies"

Christopher McNally, New York, NY ..."Kings of America"

J. H. Moncrieff, Winnipeg, Canada ..."The Fighter"

Barbara Mossberg, Eugene, OR ..."The Role of Poetry in Saving the Earth"

P. J. Osattin, New York, NY ..."A Rose By Any Other Name"

Gabrielle Robinson, South Bend, IN ..."Ambused by the Past"

Catherine Root, New Orleans, LA ..."Loving the Bigger Fat"

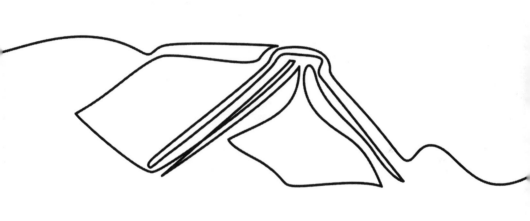

Award-Winning
Writing

The editors and judges at

NEW MILLENNIUM WRITINGS

are pleased to announce the

41ST NEW MILLENNIUM POETRY PRIZE

Robin Myers

LOVE POEM FOR CARL SAGAN

Robin Myers (New York, 1987) translates Latin American literature and writes poetry. She was a resident writer at the Vermont Studio Center in 2015 and the first-place poetry winner of the Enizagam Contest.

Robin is currently based in Mexico City.

Twitter: @robin_ep_myers

LOVE POEM FOR CARL SAGAN

Robin Myers

The Pioneer 10, the first spacecraft to leave the solar system, carried with it a six-by-nine inch gold-anodized aluminum plaque engraved with a message — information on the origin of the spacecraft and on the human form — in the event of its interception by advanced extraterrestrial life. The plaque includes an outline drawing of a nude man and woman. Carl Sagan co-devised the message, and his then-wife, Linda Salzman, made the drawing.

A man and a woman float, not touching, through space.
Space is a word we use for emptiness,
which is to say, somewhere without us.
Engraved onto their metal plate, they float, the man and the woman,
their hands apart, toward whatever kind of void
may absorb them, whatever kind of creature might someday
reach out an appendage, membrane, vacuum,
or other mysterious receptor it might possess
to receive them, or not, in an attempt to learn, or not,
what a woman is, what a man is,
how their calves are shaped, how they fix their fingers
in a gesture of greeting or rest.

The man and the woman, floating in space,
don't touch each other, lest the unimaginable creature
mistake them for a single organism,
amorphous, semi-symmetrical,
conjoined at the hinge we experience as hands.
The man and the woman who don't touch
are each a solid outline, placid-faced, blank
by design, their bodies emptied of color, organs, accessories
that would reveal their particularity to Rio de Janeiro, say,
or the Bible Belt, the Congolian forests, the Sahara Desert,
or anywhere else.
The man's penis is present and flaccid.
The woman's vagina is neatly triangular, unclefted,
appeasing the censors. There is,
let me be clear, absolutely no touching.
Oh, Carl Sagan, the pressure!,
the harrowing weight of responsibility
wrought into metal, now hurtling chastely
through the infinite virginity of space.
What a task, this immutable 2-D lesson
in everyone's anatomy: pasteurized
into lines, decorum, and approximate proportions;
no flesh, no function, no friction of any sort,
no moles or scars, no assembly line amputations,
no beards, most definitely no vulvas,
and no involvement, in the sense
that my foot is involved with its sock, its shoe, the throw-rug,
the doctor involved with the thermometer
she tucks into the old man's armpit,
and so with the man to whom both arm and pit belong.
Above us, a man and a woman,
not touching, now untouchable
forever in memory of us,

float through space,
godly, finally, as we have always wanted,
or at least in the only way
we have ever imagined.
All right, Carl Sagan,
all right, it's true.
With the sketch of any human form
as the ultimate portrait of what we are and do,
there would be simply no way around mutation:
a girl on a bike turns mythical,
a gentle beast with two-wheeled wings
and edges that change shape in the wind.
What would they make of us, the inconceivable others—
foreign to us in the texture of their flesh, if they have flesh,
in their intimacies with time, if they count time,
in the question of whether they too thirst for salt,
if they thirst at all, if they are a they at all—?
Behold, indeed, the menagerie:
Man and woman holding hands, then letting go.
Man combing daughter's hair.
Woman passing tongue along woman's collarbone.
Man seizing man by throat.
Woman and man and man and woman and woman and woman
and man and woman and man and woman huddled against each other
involuntarily on subway.
Woman tearing pork from bone with teeth.
Man cradling pistol.
Girl touching self to sleep in shack with corrugated tin roof.
Boy kissing boy in shadows of lake and waiting
sixty years to speak of it.
Man reaching to woman on memory foam mattress,
which nonetheless forgets them as they struggle
to meet each other at the molten center of what they feel

and vanish into the space between them.
Not long ago, a man and I sat beside a waterfall
with our legs in the current and our shoulders touching.
I know I felt the vast feral body of the river
and the brief warm body of the man and I know
my body was involved with both, and who can say
that we didn't make, together,
even for a moment,
a new animal?

In his poem "Ars Poetica?," Czeslaw Milosz writes:

The purpose of poetry is to remind us how difficult it is to remain just one person.

When I replay this phrase in my memory, I tend to remember it wrong, skipping words: The purpose of poetry is to remind us how to remain just one person.

I believe that both versions are true. Finding several "homes" over the past few years has constantly reminded me how difficult it is to remain just one person. Writing, for me, is the way to practice being one.

— **Robin Myers**

The editors and judges at

NEW MILLENNIUM WRITINGS

are pleased to announce the

42ND NEW MILLENNIUM POETRY PRIZE

Kerry Tepperman Campbell

BOUGAINVILLEA

Kerry Tepperman Campbell lives in California. Her work has appeared in *Bitter Oleander*, *Laurel Review*, *Patterson Review*, *Cloudburst*, and *Round*.

Her first book, *Dreaming of France*, was released by Blue Light Press in 2017.

BOUGAINVILLEA

Kerry Tepperman Campbell

A third-story apartment. The wall outside the bedroom window is covered with bougainvillea. Spring in Marseilles. A young woman rearranges her bedroom furniture, placing the bed beneath the window so she can pick bougainvillea without getting out of bed.

Whatever age she is, she will remember this version of herself, naked, embroidered sheets, their well-worn linen skimming over her breasts, her legs forming a diamond as she sits on the bed, the soles of her feet touching, the space between her legs gradually filling with bougainvillea.

As she plucks the wing-like bracts, she remembers a childhood longing, the desire to be the garden. The drooping tulip. The rose in bud. The flaming zinnia. The cotton-candy dianthus. The desire to be the pink, the blue, the pale peach, the green, the ground cover with its star shaped flowers. To be the cypress rising high around the perimeter, whispering, This is where the garden ends.

That desire felt long before she knew ashes could be scattered like stars beneath such trees.

"Bougainvillea" is part of a series of sixty-three linked prose poems that explore how American women experience, remember, and imagine France. When I began writing the poems it seemed as if I was mucking around in a very odd corner of my imagination. It was hard to believe the poems would be of interest to anyone else.

However, in November 2015, the outpouring of sympathy for the French people after the shooting in the Bataclan Theater helped me understand that the condition which I have come to think of as "dreaming of France," is one shared by people of many ages in many countries.

My next book is about Fletcher Christian, the famous 18th century British Mutineer. Once again I think it is an odd topic. This time I tell myself not to worry about it. Some days I listen better than others.

When NMW asked me if I had any advice for other writers, I smiled and decided to pass on the advice I've been giving myself: Odd is good.

— Kerry Tepperman Campbell

The editors and judges at

New Millennium Writings

are pleased to announce the

41ST NEW MILLENNIUM
FLASH FICTION PRIZE

Adrianne Aron

THE ENVELOPE TRICK

Adrianne Aron is a psychologist, writer, and human rights activist in the San Francisco Bay Area, working with survivors of traumatic abuse — torture, domestic violence, and political persecution. She is co-editor of a collection of essays in translation by UCA Jesuit Martyr Ignacio Martin-Baro, S.J., *Writings for a Liberation Psychology* (Harvard University Press), and author of numerous other books, and professional articles in psychology journals.

She writes both fiction and nonfiction, and adores the micro mode. She is at work on a memoir composed in tapas, crisp little bites.

THE ENVELOPE TRICK

Adrianne Aron

What are three fingers?

"You're lucky," the nurse said, "you still have the opposing thumb."

Who you kidding, I thought. But I kept my mouth shut. She was trying to help me out.

Clamping that lucky thumb and the baby finger like a pair of pliers, I've learned to fork up the rice and beans that Sarita serves for supper. Good thing we're not Chinese, I think. Chopsticks.

With a delicacy that makes me embarrassed, I'm able to unzip my fly, and even to tuck it in after I'm done peeing. Wiping is a little tricky, but I manage, like I manage with the shaving. When I watch myself in the mirror shaving with my left hand, it looks like my right hand, and for a little moment every morning I'm tricked into believing I'm whole.

"What have you got to complain about, compañero?" I ask my reflection as I brush my teeth and feel my tongue rolling over the bottom row. Pedro's tongue they cut out, because he spoke up for what he believed. My eyebrows match — a

matched pair, black, over brown eyes with lashes so long my mother used to say I should have been born a girl. Over there, they say things like that.

Yeah, my eyebrows match, but Rafa's don't. One of his, the left one I think, turned white, at the spot where the soldiers attached the electrodes. There's guys at Guantánamo right now gone white all over. You've got to remember how everything's relative, Sarita tells me.

I inspect my nose: straight, nice, a painless appendage on a friendly face, a face like a puppy dog, like my old man's. The nose of Dora María, Sarita's sister, flattens to her cheeks and pinches a nerve, convulsing her in pain whenever she sneezes. They shattered the whole cartilage when they smashed their rifle butts into her face.

I look down from the mirror and see that except for the mangled hand, the rest of me is in good shape. I'm alive, I got my family out. My wife still loves me. What's there to complain about an industrial accident where all you lose is three fingers? Dough machines have been known to snatch up arms all the way to the elbow.

The guys on the job were real pals. Michael drove like crazy to get me to the hospital. Richard ripped off his own shirt to wrap my bloody stumps, and held me tight so I wouldn't do something wild in my writhing and screaming. Without their quick action I might have bled to death; the fingers have a lot of blood vessels. The boss, he was good too. He didn't dock their pay for the time they took to help me out.

After the accident I had to miss English class, so I studied at home, looking up words in the dictionary. Mano, "hand." In English it's so happy: handsome, handy, handshake, to handle. In Spanish, it hurts. In my country,

Mano Blanca, White Hand, is the five-fingered print left on the wall by the Death Squad. Maniobra, maneuver, is what we call it when the government steps up the repression. Dedear, to finger, means to point somebody out for detention. It's because I was dedeado that Sarita and I had to grab the children and run north. No good-byes, no preparation, no plans. Like you'd run from an erupting volcano. U.S. foreign policy sponsors marathons for millions.

"We will send you to Rehabilitation," the nurse told me, "and having that lucky opposing thumb, you'll be surprised at how many things you'll be able to do with just two fingers. You'll learn to write, too, with your other hand." She was right. I learned quick. Before a month was up I sent a left-handed letter to my mother back home. I told her how I got lucky.

They fill out a lot of forms at Rehabilitation, and ask a lot of questions. They teach you to trust in the future, to see the lucky side. At first I thought they were missing something, because, you know, they don't teach you how to caress your wife left-handed, how to make love. And they don't explain to you what to do when your three-year-old daughter starts to cry because she touches your knuckles. So, they can't cover everything, I said to myself. Look how they showed you about the shoestrings, and the trick for opening envelopes.

When the letter came from Homeland, I opened it using the trick they taught me at Rehabilitation, and it started to sink in, this business about luck and learning. What did they teach you, pendejo? I said to myself. Did they teach you how to plant your corn or feed your animals with seven fingers? Did they show you how to repair a fence, or patch

a roof, or run a water line with nothing but a clumsy paw and a fleshy pair of pliers? Or what to do if a white print of five fingers shows up on the wall of your house? They make sure you learn the envelope trick, don't they? That way, when they send you the official notice that they're deporting you to your country because you used their super-lucky medical system, you'll be able to open up your mail.

The Chispa File: Remedy for Writer's Block

When the muses are hiding and the screen is blank, and writer's block threatens to rain on your day, it's time to reach for the Chispa File, the manila folder full of sparks to light your fire. That's the place where you dumped the scraps of paper scribbled with story ideas and character descriptions, catchy titles and cool words, themes and scenes you thought you might want to develop someday. The ideas came to you while you were on the bus or out with the dog, stuck at the airport or working out, raking leaves or scrubbing your underarms. You jotted them down and threw them in the file — to save for a rainy day.

— *Adrianne Aron*

The editors and judges at

New Millennium Writings

are pleased to announce the

42ND NEW MILLENNIUM
FLASH FICTION PRIZE

William Polsgrove

HIGHWAY 61

William Polsgrove grew up on a farm in West Tennessee and graduated in 1981 with a BFA in painting from the Memphis College of Art. As a somewhat-effeminate, unemployed, broken-hearted painter, he joined the Army in 1984, and much to everyone's surprise, he discovered he loved soldiering, so he stayed for twenty-two years. William received a Masters in Public Administration from Central Michigan at the Pentagon in 1999, with a concentration in public policy.

He recently graduated with an MFA in Creative Writing from Fairfield University in Fairfield, CT.

HIGHWAY 61

William Polsgrove

I sat wedged between my father, who was driving, and my Uncle Buddy who was smoking and talking nonstop—and I was choking on his smoke and the same sad stories he always told...

"Matamoros pussy—best goddamned tail in the world, excepting of course Juarez pussy, but as you know, I have some hard feelings concerning Juarez. A month in a Juarez prison makes you come to Jesus." He winked at me and passed me the pint of Ancient Age.

I looked at the almost-empty bottle and passed it to my Dad. We'd been on the highway since 4 a.m. driving a load of shorthorns down to Cleveland, Mississippi. The rumbling truck's air conditioner blew lukewarm air that smelled of dirt and diesel, causing my stomach to grow sour from the warm whiskey and truck stop breakfast. I was fifteen and on the verge of a nervous breakdown.

"I'm sick, Dad. Can you stop?"

"What? For Christ's sake, kid."

"I'm going to throw up."

"Well hell, you'd best hurry. That's a bad cloud coming," Dad said as he pulled the big four-wheel drive off at a turn-out by some abandoned shacks standing forlorn amongst the cotton fields.

"Why'er you sick?" Dad asked.

"I don't know, just sick." But I thought as I got out of the truck, I'm sick from the goddamned cigarette smoke and the way the truck weaves because the homemade cattle trailer we're pulling never tracked right. I'm sick of the smell of cow shit, and mud, and trying to be a manly boy, just to make you proud. I'm sick of preachers, and country music, and all of these stupid stories. I'm sick that you won't tell him to put the fucking cigarette out, and that you always take Uncle Buddy's side even though he's an idiot who got the calling from God and left his wife and five kids to go off and preach to the heathens in Texas and fuck Mexican whores for seven years. I'm sick of the blood, and of killing my friends, the cows. I'm sick of that last look in their sad brown eyes as I pull the trigger. I'm sick of the way they stumble to the ground before we string them up.

You say that it makes me tough.

I don't name them anymore.

I whispered this like a prayer through the tears and sweat as I retched into the ditch amongst the tall golden rods, honeysuckle, and assorted weeds. A large black and yellow grasshopper hanging onto a cattail stared at me with huge golden eyes. He shook his grasshopper head and said, "Storm's a coming," and flittered off.

I stood up and stared as the crows fled east before the line of hard, blue-black clouds rolling fast across the river. The land glowed in that strange yellow light. I smelled and tasted the arcing electricity and felt the cool winds pushing the stagnant July air before the coming storm. I thought of the coming night in Frankie's room. His mom was away. He had many books, and a window air conditioner and his own bathroom with a shower. He always had clean sheets

on his bed. He read history to me. He would clean this smell off of me.

"Hurry up, prissy-boy," my uncle said.

I turned and walked over to the truck. He leaned against the hood next to the door flung open. My father stood on the opposite side of the truck, taking a leak. I looked at Buddy's twinkling blue eyes. We were the same height, but his skin was like leather stretched taught over iron bones. He was nasty in a bar fight. I'd seen him hurt people bad. I knew he'd hurt me if he had the chance. He smiled that Devil smile and lit another Camel. "Get your ass in…boy."

"I'll ride in the back," I said.

"You'll get drenched," Dad said as he climbed into the truck. "There's still cow shit back there you never cleaned out."

"I'll ride in the back."

"Suit yourself, but I ain't stopping till we get through Memphis."

"Okay."

"Them city niggers will snatch your ass out of an open truck bed," my uncle said.

"I'll be all right." I crawled into the bed of the truck as it lurched forward and the big fat drops of rain plopped down. I shoved the nasty straw aside and sat hunkered down like a Buddha. I looked west as the storm tumbled in. Up near Clarksdale, I saw a dark dip in the cloud, swirling round and round. I saw laundry hanging on lines lifted skyward, like the fluttering flags of a great medieval army. The wind tore three sheets from the line and they swirled in long circles upwards disappearing into the dark, dipping cloud. I thought of Frankie's cool sheets and the hum of his air conditioner and the histories he would read to me. We were studying the Hundred Years War. Henry the

Fifth's speech to his men at Agincourt, the French knights, heavy in their armor, stuck in the muck—arrows from the English longbows raining down on them. Hundred Years War, hell—more like a thousand.

I watched as the tornado took form and skipped over a shotgun shack. The wind blew the fat raindrops sideways. My uncle looked out the back window at me and grinned. He took a long drag off from his Camel. He winked at me as the tornado dipped down and lightly touched a barn. The barn exploded into a million bits, and I was washed in the torrent.

I tend to write when I am half asleep, first thing in the morning, before coffee. I started this because one of my writing mentors pointed me towards Robert Olen Butler's book, From Where You Dream. *I'm not saying this is for everyone, but it gives me the bones of a more dreamlike story. These drafts are usually a mess, and require a lot of repair and editing. When I wrote "Highway 61," I had just woken up, thinking about my bad-ass preacher uncle and my conflicted feelings about him, his damned cigarettes, and his convoluted stories about his lawless life in Mexico.*

Anyway, this dreamy writing works fine for short stories and flash fiction, but fixing a novel when it's been written half asleep is an entirely different proposition. I'm still trying to untangle that mess.

— William Polsgrove

The editors and judges at

NEW MILLENNIUM WRITINGS

are pleased to announce the

41ST NEW MILLENNIUM FICTION PRIZE

Cady Vishniac

MOVE

Cady Vishniac is a Distinguished University Fellow and MFA in fiction at The Ohio State University. Her stories have won the Sherwood Anderson Award at *Mid-American Review* and the Alexander Cappon Prize at *New Letters*.

Website: cavishniac.com

Twitter: @cavishniac

MOVE

Cady Vishniac

They listen to the Yeah Yeah Yeahs and eat baby carrots straight from the bag. The clouds loom low and thunder rolls across Camberville, marking their pilgrimage. Jody and Rob bicker in the front of the U-Haul, and what makes the bickering worse is the presence of their daughter—Jody's daughter really, but for several months now they've been encouraging her to call Rob Daddy—who sits between them in her carseat asking if she'll ever see any of her friends from daycare again. She won't, and her friends' parents never liked Jody or Rob anyway.

Jody tells her she's got new friends waiting in Ohio. "You're a beast of prey," she says, both hands on the steering wheel, staring dead ahead at the road. "An obligate carnivore. The bravest girl I know."

The daughter looks out Rob's window, ignoring Jody in that pointed way toddlers ignore the grownups who'd die for them. The look on her face puts Jody in mind of an ex-boyfriend from just before Rob, a guy who used to crack wise about her Jewish nose.

She takes a hand off the wheel to tap Rob's shoulder, then she picks up a conversation from earlier. "They torture in Zimbabwe, but don't you think that guy who shot Carla the Lion deserves to go to prison there? He was poaching on a preserve." Somehow in all this packing she's found time to read dozens of news articles about Carla's murder.

"Why do you think he should be tortured?" Rob asks. He fiddles with the air conditioner until he finds the defroster, which he turns all the way up.

"Not so much the original shooting, but claiming he didn't know poaching was illegal. An excuse that bad is him calling the rest of us stupid."

"Don't talk about how much you want someone tortured in front of our kid."

"But you told that blowjob joke in front of her the other day."

"So then let's teach her to embrace human rights violations?"

"You're so holier-than-thou, why don't you get out?" Jody says this at a red light, so Rob calls her bluff, opening his passenger side door and walking across several lanes of traffic. Cars hit their brakes and screech around him. At first Jody's convinced he's roadkill, but then she sees him land safely on the sidewalk and duck into a cafe. Fighting is such a way of life in Boston, Jody's willing to bet he's not the first boyfriend to make a break for it at this intersection, not even the first this morning.

Their daughter says, "Make Daddy come back," so now Jody's got no choice but to park the U-Haul in the alley behind the cafe. She calls Rob a dozen times and he doesn't pick up, she texts him and gets no response, and then he storms out holding two hot cups and a cinnamon bun. The bun is for their daughter and the cups are chai lattes. Jody sips her chai and eases them back onto the road.

It's Friday night. She should be chanting over candles, and Rob should be pouring wine. They should have a Shabbos goy to take them all the way to their new home, but they don't.

They listen to Rob's nineties pop radio — Jody's embarrassed for him until Blues Traveler comes on — and eat pretzels they bought at a gas station. They've outpaced the thunderstorm so the sun shines and the clouds hang high, feathery cirrus.

Jody's ex texted her the other day to say he was sorry. *I just want us to be cool,* he wrote. Jody wrote back, *We're cool but I'm moving to Ohio.* She tells Rob about the texts as they cross the border between Western Mass and Upstate New York, while their daughter is too hypnotized to care about the conversation. She's watching Sesame Street on Rob's iPad.

"That guy is not your friend," Rob says, and he's right. She last took up with the man during the desperate, sleepless months after giving birth, when she was still waiting for her divorce to go through. He'd sneak into Jody's apartment while the baby daughter slept and sneak out again before morning. She asked him on a real date once, but he said no, then she met Rob and cut him off, and they haven't spoken since.

"Men don't know how to be friends with anybody," Jody says. "Most of you are sociopaths."

Rob asks if she wants to play the cloud game. "That one looks like a feather." He points.

"Too easy," she tells him.

"Then what do you think?"

"A ribbon. The crest of a wave."

"Wave?" Their daughter looks up from Sesame Street. "We're going to the beach?"

Jody and Rob say no, no beach. Their daughter looks back at the iPad in disappointment.

"That wave thing was pretentious." Rob says the cloud game should wait until they see better clouds. Instead, they'll play the alphabet game. "A! That sign for an Applebee's. Now you find a B."

Jody doesn't look for a B. Instead she points toward a dead deer by the Utica exit. Its body lies twisted on the median, its legs pointed straight up in the air. Their daughter spots the deer and asks, "Mommy, what happened to the animal?" Jody tells her he has an ache in his tummy.

Cornfields and soy fields. For a moment Jody sees a lion loping through the crops, stalking a herd of gazelle, but then she snaps out of it. She proposes they write Fuck Boston on the rear hatch of the U-Haul but Rob's worried there are people from Boston all around. Someone might fight them. Bostonians would be the kind of people to fight them.

Jody parks at a rest stop outside Albany. She hooks their daughter's plastic potty seat onto her purse, then she and the daughter go inside to pee. As they pass the men's room, a guy in a Confederate flag shirt, the words Heritage Not Hate emblazoned across his chest, points to the potty seat. "Is that sanitary?"

This trip would be impossible without Rob's help. For example, when Jody and the daughter return to the U-Haul, Rob says he's checked in with her mother, who's been driving the same stretch of road with the cats in the back seat of her Honda Civic. Everything's fine on her end.

"I trust you," Rob says, as Jody buckles their daughter into the carseat. "But tell your old lover to leave us alone."

They listen to Alison Krauss and eat tuna sandwiches. The sun sets over downtown Rochester, the derelict parts of the old Kodak campus. Their daughter won't nap or eat or poop. Jody tries to engage her in conversation, but she just screams, so Rob plays her Sesame Street's Chanukah special. He strokes her cheek and talks her down, and this makes Jody grateful for him, his stabilizing influences. There are so many men out there with zero paternal instinct, men for whom a child in distress might as well be an alien—her ex, for example.

They roll into the hotel around the daughter's bedtime and park the U-Haul perpendicular across four parking spaces. Jody's mother is already arguing with the woman at the front desk when they get inside. Their daughter runs

over to an end table with a basket of decorative glass balls in the center, Christmas ornaments with the hooks pulled out.

"The cats are staying in one of the rooms!" Jody's mother bellows.

The front desk woman grins. "Which room, ma'am?"

There's a crashing noise and then the tinkling of glass. Their daughter yells, "Mommy, I threw it at the floor!" She giggles. Jody picks her up and apologizes profusely to the woman, who grunts. Rob bends to pick up the glass with his bare hands.

"I can sweep it," the woman says. "Just need to know which room the cats are going in."

"Does it fucking matter?" Jody's mother asks. She says the word "fucking" too eagerly, like a person for whom swearing is a special treat.

"Procedure says we need to register them to a room. Pick one."

So Jody's mother looks at Jody and Rob and says, "I hope you don't expect me to stay with those animals. I have insomnia," then she goes down the hall to her room and her keycard doesn't work. Jody's fairly certain the front desk woman messed that up on purpose, because she would—her mother is such a Nazi. She and Rob laugh as her mother walks back to the desk and calls the woman incompetent; and their daughter laughs too, even though she doesn't know what's funny.

They take their keycard from a second front desk woman and go to their room, across the hall from Jody's mother. Rob puts the card in the door the wrong way three times and insists it's broken too, the front desk people really are incompetent, but when Jody turns the card over and sticks it back in they hear a click. The little green light flashes, and he says, "Sorry I don't know how to open a door."

Their daughter says, "Daddy, I forgive you."

He bathes her while Jody goes out to the parking lot and gets everything: her bag with all her clothes, the laptops, the phones, Rob's bag with all his clothes, their daughter's bag with all her clothes and her life-size Curious George, her Big Bird blanket, the cats, their litter, and their food. It takes her three trips, and by the time she's done, their daughter is asleep in the middle of the hotel bed with her butt pointing up in the air and her face smooshing into the mattress.

Jody throws the Big Bird blanket on top of her. She and Rob take the foldout couch, and the cats sleep on top of them, clawing at their sides if they try to roll over. Jody dreams the cats are chasing Rob through the savannah. They bite his leg open and run him down, and she can't do a thing to help.

They listen to the muzak in the lobby of Grandma's retirement home. They eat cheap muffins from the old people's breakfast buffet, except for Jody's mother, who's trying to lose weight and doesn't touch them. Rob has muffin crumbs stuck to the velcro of his one-day beard, almost the twin of their daughter, who mashes the muffin into her face until it mixes with her snot and sticks to her skin. This being a retirement home, there's a whole table of old people watching, enraptured. The daughter asks Jody for a kiss, so Jody gives her a peck on her crusted lips. A couple of the old people clap. Sometime in the night, Jody's ex texted to say *Does this guy make you happy?* But that's not the point, and it's not Rob's job to make her happy. He makes them a family. She hasn't texted back.

On their way upstairs to Grandma's room, they leave the cats under the retirement home attendants' desk, because the old people are all dire asthmatics. They go up to Grandma's room, and the door is unlocked, the TV playing Animal Planet at top volume. They kiss Grandma and hug her, and

then they put their daughter in her lap in the wheelchair, careful not to jostle the oxygen tank. Jody's mom snaps the photo, and in it Grandma is touching Rob's chin, trying to wipe away muffin crumbs. She licks her thumb and rubs it all over his face, and he forebears.

Grandma has mushrooms sitting on her table—for research she says, but the university made her retire years ago—and they have to remind their daughter not to eat the fungi. Grandma's dead husband's things sit on the bookshelf, the paraphernalia of this man who went to study the bacteria of the Antarctic and one foggy afternoon strolled off an ice cliff. A samovar and some biology textbooks. A kippah and coke-bottle wireframe glasses that must be older than Jody.

Their daughter finds Grandma's cane and asks, "Will it explode?" before whacking the cane against the top of Grandma's oxygen tank. It does not explode, but Jody's mother takes the cane away. Their daughter weeps.

Jody wants to tell Rob about the way Grandpa was always walking into danger. Off a cliff, into traffic—there's a recklessness that he and Grandpa and the deer all have in common. Can Jody be honest? Grandpa took risks with his life because he knew so many people who perished in the camps, and sometimes she has less patience for other morose men, for Rob, because his problems are so petty by comparison. It's not like anybody killed all his friends.

Jody doesn't talk about Grandpa with Grandma ever, because she doesn't want to upset her. She loves Grandma more than life. They have the same birthday, and Jody has inherited her interest in Muriel Spark, her asthma, her bad posture, and her mole, a raised brown dot anchored in the armpit.

"We all love you, Grandma," Jody tells her.

Grandma heard fine, but Jody's mother yells it again just in case. "Grandma! We all love you! Grandma!"

Their daughter's interested in loud noises, so she claps.

Grandma can still get annoyed. She rolls her eyes at Mom and says, "I'm glad you're out of Massachusetts. Don't let this nice boy get away."

Jody's ex used to refer to himself as a nice boy, but that sort of thing is never true if a person has to say it about himself.

They watch Animal Planet until Grandma starts snoring and their daughter starts gnawing the carpet, then they go downstairs again. The attendants joke that they thought nobody was coming back, but Jody thinks they were just looking for an excuse to steal the cats.

They listen to Tuvan throat-singing and they listen to Debbie Friedman singing T'filat Haderech. They eat super-market sushi from the Wegman's near Grandma's home. They've traded their daughter for the cats today, which means they can blast their music as loud as they want and Jody keeps making blowjob faces at Rob as he drives. He's got a lead foot, and she's worried they'll be pulled over for speeding in a U-Haul. Still, she's happy he's here, and she likes wandering with him. She expects Manna to drop from the sky any second.

They pass cows, horses, and more cornfields. There's also a field of lettuce, or maybe it's kale, and another dead deer. This one's winking at Jody, or at least she thinks it's winking at her, but she doesn't mention the winking to Rob. There's nothing to hide — he already knows she's nuts — but she hates to make him worry.

Today they have more success with the cloud game. That one looks like a tortoise and that one looks like a buck. That one looks like a dildo. A spork. A pinecone. Dead man's glasses. Castle overtaken by a horde of bees. Tuning fork. Castle guarded by Confederate soldiers. '98

Ford Explorer. Confederate soldiers standing guard at Auschwitz. Unicorn, or maybe just a horse with a dildo on its forehead. Samovar. Lion.

"A lion?" Jody says.

"Yeah, it's almost as scary as you." But Rob says this with a smirk, only teasing.

"Next time you get hungry I'll slay us an antelope."

Because they can relax in the cab of their U-Haul, because the cats don't scream as often as their daughter, Jody's able to think about her behavior. She was out of line yesterday when she chased him into that coffee shop. She spends all her time worrying she'll lose her cool and he'll tell her that's it, he's had enough.

She says, "Soon you'll up and leave me forever," and Rob says to calm down. He tells her he wants to take her dancing under that wide Ohio sky, those benevolent Ohio clouds looking down on them, but she doesn't like to dance. Ten years ago she was limber, but now, especially after a night of drinking, she can feel the stiffness settling into her limbs. Ten years ago she used to dance naked on tables, and the money was okay, but since then she's striven to reach that place where nobody gets to see her move.

Still, Jody's not an idiot, so she tells Rob she'd love to dance. He says like angels on the head of a pin, and she asks what that means.

"Angels? How many can fit. My grandma used to say it."

She's always fascinated when Rob talks about what it was like to grow up Catholic, how it feels to be Catholic and then change your mind. All she's ever been is a Jew, even when she's not being a good one. It's been proven in clinical trials that Ashkenazi, meaning Jews of Eastern European descent, meaning Jody, are forty percent more prone to schizoaffective disorder and manic depression. Jody struggles to know herself, to be perfectly aware of all that

happens inside her head, so that if she develops a mania, at least she'll know what's going on.

Jody wants to believe the angels made Rob's grandma happy, but he disabuses her of the notion. His grandmother saw demons in Teletubbies and Harry Potter. She didn't let Rob own baseball trading cards. Everything was the Mark of the Beast. Rob has lots of aunts and uncles who still believe as strongly as his grandma did, and Jody wants to meet them, but on the other hand she's scared to let her daughter spend too much time with these people.

They eat nothing because they're out of food. Rob pulls the windows down and they listen to the roar of the highway, breathing the thick smog of a million other drivers until Jody longs for Grandma's oxygen tank. Pennsylvania. They see an Amish man driving his cart on the bridge above them, and the clouds look like fluffy sheep. They call Jody's mother and ask her to meet them at another rest stop, where they park next to the tractor-trailers.

There are more Amish in this parking lot, the men and boys with their suspenders and the women with their wimples, sitting on a blanket in one of the truck spots. They're picnicking. Jody's mother zips into the lot through the exit and almost runs some Amish over. She parks the Honda next to the U-Haul and pops out, then she opens the back door and releases her granddaughter from a car seat.

Jody hooks the potty seat to her purse again and takes the daughter inside. Nobody bats an eye, not in Western Pennsylvania. It's like people are saner the farther one gets from the East Coast. While the daughter potties, Jody imagines herself as a Midwesterner, a nice woman who never does anything worth apologizing for. She checks her phone and sees her ex has written another message.

I loved you. You can't just take off for flyover country. What do they even do there? Jody doesn't respond to this one either.

When her daughter's done pottying, Jody buys enough pizza for three grownups and a short person. Everybody sits in the Honda eating the pizza together, the daughter with Jody in the front seat. She turns down Jody's kisses but smiles when Jody tickles her armpit. Then she yells, "Mommy look!" as she releases the parking brake. They slide forward only an inch or two, but the motion gives Jody palpitations.

"Who the fuck taught you to do that?"

Jody's mother reminds her how only unfit parents curse in front of their children.

They listen to Wiz Khalifa and they listen to the Rolling Stones. Another thing Jody likes about this part of the country is there are signs everywhere saying not to make U-turns, including on the highway.

"Do people even try that?" Jody asks.

"Focus," Rob says. "Navigate." Then he chews his lip and asks, "Jody, is he still texting you?"

"I'll handle it. Take 271 South toward Cleveland."

"But we're not going to Cleveland. Block him. Please."

"Are you serious? That's not how it works."

Tears spring from the corners of Rob's eyes, but he doesn't say anything else about the texting. Instead, he asks, "Do you think that cloud looks like a hand?"

Jody thinks it looks like a pot leaf, but Rob disapproves of drug use so she says sure, it looks like a hand. Then they pass another dead deer and Jody can't cope because it's a baby. She calls her mother and asks if their daughter's okay, and her mother says what does Jody take her for, the girl is fine. Jody says they'll order a pizza when they get to the new apartment.

The home stretch. The moon beaming on the horizon where they plan to live. It smells like death because the cats, tired of being ignored, have pissed in the crate. When they pass the Ohio Visitors' Center, Jody shouts that the state line is limned with moonlight and the breath of G–d is fresh on the highway.

Rob says, "What?"

They listen to their pathetic bodies creaking and a bluegrass cover of 99 Problems. Jody sees a cloud shaped like a cloud and a lioness standing on her hind legs in a field of broccoli, waving hello to them. Jody's mother calls to say she felt like taking a break, so the daughter's driving, and then Jody's ex texts to say *Good luck*. Rob's eyes dart to the text and back to the road. In one smooth motion he wrenches her phone from her hand and tosses it out the window, then before she's had time to react, he says, "I'm sorry. That was stupid of me." Jody balances the past ten seconds against the past two years, against her own behavior and the way traveling brings out the worst in them both. She tells him he can buy her a new phone tomorrow.

They merge onto yet another highway in a long list of highways, and the signs say they're eighteen miles from the Holy Land, Columbus, which means they're here, they're done wandering! Or anyway they're close enough. The mole in Jody's armpit turns out to be the Mark of the Beast, the Confederacy rises again, hateful heritage, and tractortrailers make U-turns on the head of a pin. The U-Haul is a muffin, a horde of bees, a unicorn, and Jody swears to Rob the deer can still be saved. If only they would learn to move, to run, to dance on tables. Potty seats strapped to their backs, they'd escape the places that hunt them.

Writing for me is transformative. Not only do I fully expect that all characters will be transformed by the events in a story, but I think the reader should be transformed by the experience of getting to know these characters. I think the writer should be transformed by inventing them.

Transformation matters because with enough time and dedication, anybody could write a story that's merely competent. A computer could write a story that's competent, and I have no doubt they'll start doing so in the near future. But only a writer can handle the act of transforming. Only a writer can change souls.

— *Cady Vishniac*

The editors and judges at

NEW MILLENNIUM WRITINGS

are pleased to announce the

42ND NEW MILLENNIUM FICTION PRIZE

Elizabeth Amon

HAIR OF THE DOG

Elizabeth Amon is an award-winning journalist and has also worked as a photojournalist. Her work has been published in *The New York Times, Harper's Magazine, The American Lawyer,* and *Bloomberg News,* among others.

She graduated from Oberlin College and received an M.A. in creative writing from City College. She's been awarded a Fulbright Scholarship and a Soros Fellowship for her writing.

HAIR OF THE DOG

Elizabeth Amon

When Rudy begins licking her toes under the desk, Alex doesn't immediately stop him. Normally she hates his sticky tongue grooming her, but this afternoon, the terrier's attention is a welcome distraction. She's been sitting in front of the computer in her home office, cataloging photographs while waiting for Berks to arrive. She's labeled and organized the images from her most recent job, but it's tedious work and she's bored.

She gazes out the window. Her neighborhood is as still and silent in the August heat as if it were a photo. There are no scrambling squirrels, no singing birds, no barking dogs, no children playing. She moves her head slightly, weighing the possible crops to the landscape if she uses the window as a viewfinder. Along the left of the picture, the Black-eyed Susans are motionless against the rusty iron fence that runs along the front lawn and driveway, making a strong line. Click. She's captured it in her mind, but nothing changes after the imaginary shutter opens again. The stillness and the silence out the window make it seem as if time has been suspended. But it hasn't. The minutes keep slipping by, and Berks is now hours later than she expected.

He'd emailed her to say he was flying into Boston and wanted to make a detour on his way to New York to see her this afternoon. He'd written yesterday to say he was

leaving first thing in the morning, but even with traffic she'd expected him to arrive by one or two. It's now after four.

She tucks the loose strands of her straight brown hair behind her ear as she stares at her phone, willing Berks to call, fighting the temptation to phone him. She opens the folder on her desk with the pictures she's chosen to show him. There are five. They are crisply focused portraits of children. She has subtly digitally manipulated them so their effects are unsettling despite the innocence of the subjects and the superficial prettiness.

She slaps the folder shut, pushing away these thoughts as she turns to the computer and her paying work. Under the portrait of a one-year-old boy, she types a few brief words of identification. The toddler, unsteady on his feet, wears a striped train engineer's hat and clutches a sagging white stuffed horse. His nose is wrinkled, caught in a smile that shows new teeth. Her own children are long past this age, and for a moment, she feels nostalgia for their babyhood: the tightly clenched fists, the hot, sour breath, the dead weight of their bodies as they sleep.

A pick-up truck barreling down her neighborhood street interrupts her thoughts. The dented blue truck turns into the driveway. Before she can fully rise, Rudy has run to the kitchen barking, his shaggy ears standing up. Though Berks has never been to her house in the seven years since she and Martin have been living there, he doesn't hesitate. He takes the little stone footpath from the driveway around the back and calls out her name through the kitchen screen door. He's in the house by the time she hurries through the living room and down the dark hall, lined with dozens of family photos. When she enters the kitchen, Berks is crouched next to Rudy, rubbing his white and tan polka-dotted belly. Before Alex can say anything to either of them, Berks

throws his arms around her. He smells faintly of sweat and something sweet, maybe shaving cream, though his cheek is rough as it grazes hers. He's still skinny, like he always was, and his hug still feels right. They are both 5'10"and fit together perfectly. Pulling away from the embrace, he holds tightly to her arms as he says, "Oh my god, look at you. I forgot how beautiful you are."That disappoints her. The compliment is too generic to be genuine. She wonders if he's nervous.

Berks has aged in the two years since she'd last seen him, though he still looks good. He is handsome in a rugged, slightly dangerous way. The scar at his temple has faded so that it's difficult to see. The cleft in his chin, acquired after he lost a chunk of skin during an assignment in Chechnya before she knew him, remains an intriguing marker on the map of his face. The lines on his forehead and around his mouth have deepened, but there is still a spark in his blue eyes. He has a charisma that is hard to pinpoint but that women always notice.

"I was getting worried you were lost," Alex says.

"I would have called but my cell phone is dead. And you know how it is. I had drinks last night with a reporter who was in Ramallah with me last year and then slept through the alarm so I rushed here as soon as I could."

He's late because he is hungover. How many times has he ruined their plans or wasted whole days because he was hungover? The Thanksgiving before her father died is at the top of the list. Then there was her college roommate's wedding, and finally that last Valentine's Day. Alex pushes the thoughts away and forces a smile. She doesn't want to start with a fight. She decides not to ask if the reporter with whom he was drinking was a woman. It's no longer any of her business. "How was Somalia?"

Berks shrugs. "Depressing, as you'd expect. Brutal—really, brutal. I shot some decent stuff, but they ran almost none of it. There's a new editor at the magazine. I have yet to meet her in person. I don't think she likes me."

"It wouldn't be the first time," Alex jokes. Something about the forced nonchalance of Berks's shrug makes her suspect he's truly upset. "She probably wants to sleep with you," she adds.

But Berks doesn't smile. "She told the agency I was more trouble than I was worth."

"Sounds like she already did sleep with you," Alex says, finally getting Berks to laugh.

"No," he protests, "she's pushing 50 and—" He abruptly closes his mouth, an embarrassed smile tugging at the corners.

"I'm not anywhere near 50." At 43, she's not that far from it, though. And while the lines at the corners of her eyes are multiplying, she looks younger than she is.

"You are not old." Berks smiles, an attempt to charm her. "This editor, she's old. Mentally."

"Give it up." She shakes her head.

Berks reaches into his black canvas camera bag and pulls out a small box he offers her. Smudged black Arabic letters are stamped on top of a red and gold swirled pattern.

"Treasure from Somalia?" She leans in and sniffs. The box smells of soil and faintly of rotting fruit. She has never been to Somalia, but the scents bring memories of narrow, twisting market streets in Egypt and Jordan. Dark, crowded shops filled with perfume, briny olives, bright fabric, strange spices and gold so shiny it looks fake. Buried beneath the folds of a piece of faded cotton floral fabric inside the box is a pair of earrings: gold filigree with a deep green teardrop-shaped stone. They are so beautiful she can't speak for a moment.

"You like them?"

"I can't believe you can still buy pretty things there."

"You can't." Berks laughs, revealing his crooked, yellowed teeth, his one serious physical flaw. Alex used to tell herself that it gave him a more European look. "The box had tobacco in it when I bought it in Mogadishu. I got the present at the airport in Paris. They're meant to remind you of the color of the Mediterranean." He looks at her through eyes half-closed, like a cat after it's caught a mouse but before it's killed it.

This was the subject of their first fight, a ridiculously fierce argument about whether the Mediterranean off the coast of the Italian volcanic island where they were staying was blue or green. It became a reference point over the years for their differences of opinion. Alex holds up the earrings to better admire them. "So sweet of you to remember that blue is my favorite color." She is rewarded by his approving laugh.

As she slips on the earrings, Alex watches Berks survey the kitchen. He stares at the small appliances on the counter—an oversized juicer (hardly ever used) and a shiny cappuccino maker (often used). Without realizing it, Alex has been holding her breath. Seeing it through his eyes, it is strange. The opulence and the comfort. When she and Martin moved here from Brooklyn, she felt as if she were fooling everyone, posing as a housewife with children. Now it feels normal, and her former life with Berks feels like it belongs to someone else.

"I guess Martin is doing all right." Berks lifts his chin in a gesture meant to refer to the house and all its contents.

"Yes, great." Alex is annoyed by the remark about her husband but doesn't want to discuss her finances. Martin has his own law firm where he does a little of everything: wills, real estate, divorce, adoptions, and bankruptcy. A small

inheritance from his parents has helped them through the leaner times, a fact Alex is careful to conceal from Berks and just about everyone.

"The town is cute too, but it's so Norman Rockwell, it's creepy. It's a little freaky that you live in the middle of nowhere."

"The Hudson Valley isn't the middle of nowhere," Alex protests. "It's two and a half hours to New York — spitting distance from that dump of yours in Queens."

"But it's a long way from Kigali."

"Everywhere is a long way from Kigali." Alex shakes her head. The last time they shot together, eleven years ago, was in Rwanda. The photos flicker in her head. Lush green hills, covered with a dense canopy of trees. A dusty road, still in the blinding morning sun. Hastily abandoned thatched houses, smoking from smoldering fires. The flies, thunderous as they bob on and off the blackened bloodstain on the yellow and orange dress of the dead teenage girl. The frightened eyes of the infant beside her, nursing.

She shakes the memories away and motions to the stool next to the counter. "Something to drink?"

"I suppose you drink wheat grass and eat only organic heirloom vegetables?"

"My body is my temple," Alex replies archly and is immediately conscious of her body. It is not the same body Berks knew a decade ago, before she'd had children. Then she had the narrow hips of a boy, and with her flat chest and cropped hair, she'd often passed for one while working. She is no longer skinny; motherhood added curves she never imagined she'd possess. She'd spent a ridiculous amount of time deciding what to wear today, finally settling on jeans that are a little bit tight across her ass, distracting from the slight bulge above them, and a t-shirt that emphasizes her breasts, now much fuller.

"You probably go to yoga, too," he says.

"Pilates." He's uncertain if she's joking, which pleases her. She's never actually gone to a Pilates class. Mostly, she runs. "Would you like me to make you some wheat grass in the juicer? I hear it does wonders for Irritable Asshole Syndrome."

He laughs, and as he throws back his head, she feels a sharp pain, a thin slice between two ribs, dangerously close to her lungs. She wants to grab his hair, the dark curls that will be coarse and a little greasy, and wind her fingers through them like she did when she was 23 and first in his thrall.

"Do you know," Berks says, "I've known you half your life. Soon, I'll have known you longer than I've not known you."

He's off by a couple of years, but she doesn't correct him. The remarkable thing for Alex is that it's now been eleven years since they broke up—longer, finally, than the decade they were together. "What makes you so sure you know me? Or ever really did?" But of course that was the problem. He had known her—too well.

"People do change," Berks says, uncharacteristically grave, which makes her sad. The last time they saw each other, she'd gone to visit him in New York, after he'd returned from Iraq. He was sick, shaken and depressed in a way she'd never seen before. His translator's wife and youngest son had been killed in a bombing at a market in Baghdad. The incident had garnered 250 words in the U.S. papers. She brought soup to his hotel room (he'd sublet his apartment so he couldn't stay there) and then listened to him rant about the atrocities of war. Finally, after a couple of hours, she'd also listened to him weep over Sarah, his girlfriend of the last three years, who'd left him. Berks had had a fling in Baghdad with a TV producer, someone he didn't even really like. Sarah had caught him cheating once before and given him a second chance, but she wouldn't give him a third.

That night, it was a relief for Alex not to be talking or even thinking about Theo and Lucy. Lucy was two then and managed to consume nearly every waking moment of her days, though they passed with a pleasurable monotony. Berks's stories, with their chaos, sadness, and instability, affirmed her choice to drop out of that world. After a while, Alex put her head on Berks's shoulder and fell asleep. They lay there sleeping for a couple of hours, as the car horns and police sirens and the world went about its busy afternoon. When she looked back on that day, it felt like a dream.

Berks studies the framed black and white photos above the kitchen table, pictures of her kids from several years ago. The photos are nearly abstract. One is of Lucy's back, a white hill among the black sand at the volcanic beach in Maui. Another is of Lucy's tiny feet juxtaposed next to Martin's, the lines blurry beneath a couple inches of Cape Cod pond water.

"Where are the kiddies?" he asks. The word annoys Alex, but she tries to let it go. It was always easy to get furious at Berks over little things when she should have been angry with him for the big things.

"A neighbor took them to the local pool," she says.

"Where's my drink?" he asks as he finally slides onto a stool.

"Hair of the dog?" She pulls a bottle of Jamison from a cabinet above the stove and holds it up.

"I thought you'd never ask." He grins.

She pours them each a shot. They clink glasses and Berks drains his quickly.

He stands. "Now, let's see the photos."

"I told you, you'll hate them," she warns. She's knows he will hate them, but she's curious to hear why. The only person she's shown them to is Martin. "They're interesting—layered," Martin said. It was what she needed to hear then. But now

she's ready for something stronger, a proper critique. "Are you sure you don't want another drink?" she asks.

"You're stalling." Berks turns and walks ahead of her through the hall toward her office.

Rudy trails after him. She and Martin met over a dog. She was looking at rental apartments in a rough Brooklyn neighborhood, after her fifth and final breakup with Berks. They'd been working far apart and fighting whenever they were together. And then he'd cheated on her, though he'd insisted it had happened during a narrow window when they were broken up. By then, it almost didn't matter. Almost.

She was walking down the street, depressed both by the breakup and by the idea of living alone in a horrible apartment, when a dog darted out into the street from behind some trash cans. The dog was a small, tan pit bull, a new mother with two rows of heavy, drooping teats. Martin was driving down the street and couldn't stop in time. He hit her. The dog, bleeding from her nose, ran toward Alex. She squatted down and scooped the dog up and then hopped into Martin's car. "We have to find a vet," Alex told him. They were silent, tense in the car ride as she held the dog close to her chest and murmured reassurances. The vet whisked the dog into surgery, leaving the two of them to wait. They talked for hours, until they were assured that the dog would recover. The next day they returned to the neighborhood and taped fliers up trying to find her owner. No one ever responded, so Martin adopted her. Honey, he called her. They married a year later.

In her office, Berks goes directly to the computer and stares at the pictures of the one-year-old boy on the screen. He looks up, opens his mouth and closes it. He turns his head toward the window. Alex has been bracing herself for his criticism, but it still hurts. "Not those." She steps

between him and the computer and hands him the folder she's prepared. On top of the small pile inside, the toddler from her computer is dancing a drunken, new-walker dance with the stuffed horse. His fierce scowl transforms what was an act of joy into a bizarre, frightening ritual. Berks spreads the photos across the desk. They all capture children at unguarded moments. The backgrounds are dark and blurry—dreamlike. The kids, though, are in sharp focus, printed in high contrast with unnaturally saturated colors. Alex digitally manipulated the kids, subtly resizing a part of each child's body. The little boy's head is slightly too big. In another photo of twin girls, one stares blankly off into space, her eyes unnaturally large. The other leans over with an elongated arm to pick up a crumpled rag doll. The changes are not immediately apparent, but the shift in proportions gives a sense of ominous disharmony. Or so she hopes.

She watches Berks study the photos, sometimes picking up the prints with his sun-darkened, chapped hands, and she feels relieved. A friend once asked her how she could live with a man with whom she was always in competition. She had a hard time explaining to her that she liked the competition. As Berks stands there, his left hip jutting out in a familiar, oddly feminine way, she's glad he is taking the work seriously, even if he doesn't like the photos.

"Interesting." Berks uncocks his head and turns to look directly at her. "But of course, I think you are wasting your talent. You don't need to manipulate photos. You're talented enough to shoot what's in front of you."

"What's in front of me are children." Alex nods toward the computer. "But you hate pictures of children."

"Commercial portraits, of course."

"Documentary ones too. Sally Mann, what did you call her? A housewife with too much time on her hands?"

Berks laughs. "Did I say that? It's true."

"No, it's not." Alex tries to keep the creeping tone of annoyance out of her voice. Of course, anger was what fueled their passion half the time. And remembering that intensity makes her miss it. She wonders what it would be like to be touched again by hands that don't feel as if they are repeating movements so familiar they could be doing them in their sleep. Hands that don't expect you to be there tomorrow. She forces herself to take her eyes off of Berks's hands.

"I like your old work and there were children in those photos," Berks says crossly. "In fact, your crowning achievement was a photo of a child. But it was a news photo." Berks sets the folder on the desk. "It's the intent. You know that."

"And what is the intent you see in these photos?" Alex gestures to the folder, chasing away the voice in the back of her head that tells her Berks is right. "Or fail to see in my photos?"

"You know what I'm talking about," says Berks. "I know your photos. Your photos were raw and real. These — I understand you are trying to talk about hidden wounds or something, but they're contrived. I can see them hanging on a gallery wall, Alex, but is that really what you want? To make arty photos?"

"What's so terrible about arty photos?"

Berks shakes his head. "You don't have the slightest regret about selling out?"

"I wouldn't call it that," Alex protests.

"Come on. You've got this cushy home filled with expensive things. You take pictures of rich people's kids in contrived settings. And then, later, you add your own fantasies. It's not real. Babies aren't about this." He waves a hand at the photos spread across the desk. "Or this." He points to the photo of the boy on the computer. "Babies are about shitty diapers and screaming and mess."

"Babies? You're telling me about babies?"

"Don't give me that crap, Alex. People can understand things even if they don't directly experience them."

"You have no idea what babies are about."

"And neither do you, Alexandra, outside your upper-class, white, American suburban life," Berks retorts. He's using her full name to bait her. She's always hated it — how formal it is. But he doesn't need to call her that to get her angry — she already is.

"It has nothing to do with class," Alex growls. "It has to do with feelings." She's trying not to shout. "Babies, all babies, are about hunger, love, sadness, joy. Babies are about expressing real feelings, not keeping them buried. Babies are all the existential stuff you espouse but don't really feel because you have to put it away to capitalize on other people's feelings."

"That's a justification." Berks's mouth is tight, his lips set in a mean line. "You traded something real for this. This suburban mom thing. You had something important and you gave it away. You shut it up. Is it still in there?" He pushes a finger against her chest, bone on bone.

Alex shakes her head. "Why can't you stop thinking about the photo?" The photo, her "crowning achievement," as Berks always refers to it, is a picture of a mother and a baby. Months before they broke up for the final time, Alex shot it for a magazine story about the effects of the allied bombing in the no-fly zone in Northern Iraq. It won the Foreign Press Association's highest award the following year. The photo was of a woman bending to place a flower before a makeshift shrine in a cave that had been used as a bomb shelter. She had a horribly disfigured baby wrapped in a cloth on her back. Its tiny eyes were sunken slits beneath an oversized forehead. Its mouth was open in a scream, a huge circle of black taking up most of its face. Above the

clutch of flickering candles was the shadow of a person, a woman carrying a baby. The figure had been fixed forever against the wall as a result of the blast from a U.S. plane that dropped a bomb on the shelter in Al-Amiriyah. The U.S. mistakenly believed the four hundred people inside were part of a military group. Alex's photos documented the shrine and the hundreds of children living in the no-fly zone who were deformed or dying of leukemia from what was allegedly depleted uranium in the bombs left littering the countryside.

"It was more than a decade ago, Berks."

Alex forces herself to unclench her teeth. If she closes her eyes and reaches into her memory, she can remember the thrilling feel of taking that photo, of publishing it, of winning the award. She'd been sickened though by the realization that her career had been boosted by others' pain and suffering. Taking photos filled her with such intense highs and lows. But that was a long time ago now, and a lot of other things have happened in her life. And in the world. "No one even remembers it," she tells him.

Berks turned down the assignment so he could go to Kosovo, where the war was beginning. He'd recommended Alex for the job. They never spoke about that, but it was always part of this conversation.

"Jesus, Alex—that doesn't matter. You uncovered something no one wanted to see. Something no one in America was paying attention to. That photo was seen by thousands of people. It forced people to acknowledge what was happening."

"We've been through this, more than once." Alex purses her lips.

"You wanted to do something in the world, to make it better, and you did," Berks continues. "You of all people can claim to have done so. That's why it's hard to see you doing this now—making happy baby pictures of rich people's kids."

"People need a little joy in their lives, Berks, a little happiness now and then. Including me," Alex says wearily. "I've told you, I couldn't take it anymore. It would have consumed me." She's repeated this enough times that it sounds like a lie—a line memorized for a play. But it is true.

"That photo was brilliant. I don't understand how it could make you quit."

It wasn't actually that photo that made her quit. Alex has told him this many times before, but Berks has a way of remembering what fits his narrative. The photo casts a shadow over everything she did and still does. It defines her. Alex shakes her head. "Sometimes, I wish I had never gone there, never taken any of those photos."

"I wish to God I had," Berks replies.

"Me too," Alex snaps. It's not true that she wishes she'd never taken the photo. But Berks always twists what she says. It still makes her furious. "If you'd taken it, then maybe you wouldn't still be hustling misery to an American public who doesn't give a shit and mistreating a string of girlfriends because you're impotent to change the world."

Berks shifts from one foot to the other and stares at her.

She hadn't meant to say it, but she isn't going to apologize.

"I've made some bad calls personally, but I do not think devoting your life, risking your life, to exposing the atrocities American tax dollars are helping to pay for, is anything to apologize for," Berks says slowly.

"No, it's not," she agrees, turning away. The street outside her office window is just as still and quiet as before. It astonishes her how quickly she and Berks can get back to this place, years later. And it annoys her how jealous he is that she won the press association award that year even though he's won a pile of prestigious awards.

"I never meant to hurt you," Berks says quietly. "And I've changed, Alex. I really have."

She nods slowly, but she doesn't trust herself to speak. He will hear the disbelief in her voice.

Berks gently pulls on her shoulder until she turns to face him. "I don't envy Martin this." He grins. "You were always good at fighting. You always knew where to aim your blows."

"Martin and I never fight." Alex sits on the sofa in the office. She looks out the side window. The red dahlias in the garden along the fence separating her property from the neighbor's house bloomed early and now look as if they have exploded, stems drooping toward the ground with their heavy blooms.

"So what does he do when you blow up at him?" Berks asks.

"I never blow up at Martin. That only happens when I'm with you." She folds her arms across her chest. That isn't the truth and Berks knows it. The truth is, she does sometimes yell at Martin when they have a disagreement, but he rarely gets angry in return. "The few times it's happened," Alex says, "Martin says very rationally that he's sorry I'm upset and then says, 'Let's try to figure out what to do about this.'"

"But of course, that drives you crazy." Berks sits down on the sofa next to her.

She laughs. "Yes, it does." She feels a twinge of guilt, as if she's betraying Martin in confessing this. But in truth it was also what had attracted her to him. She was tired of fighting all the time.

"We're soulmates, baby." Berks grins. "Time doesn't change that." He takes her hand in his and spells out the word on her palm with the tip of his finger. It was a mode of communication they'd established when they first met.

Soulmates. Martin had never claimed to be her soulmate—he probably didn't believe in soulmates, but she guesses he would object to Berks casually claiming the role. Martin won't admit it, but he doesn't like Berks. And while

he has silently tolerated their visits and the late night phone calls over the years, he avoids Berks if he can.

Berks glances at his watch. "I've got to run."

"I thought you were staying for dinner?"

"No, I've got to be in New York by six."

"Oh, come on," Alex says. "Your agent or your editor or your girlfriend — whoever it is — can wait a little longer."

"Actually," Berks says, looking uncertain and then gripping her arm so hard she's afraid he's going to tell her he's dying. "It's my fiancé. I'm engaged to this amazing woman, Mai, and she's flying into JFK tonight."

Alex opens her mouth to say congratulations, but nothing comes out.

"I wanted to tell you in person. I've finally found her. The one. I'm truly tired of my old life and ready for this," Berks says.

"How long have you known her?" Alex asks.

"Almost five months. She's Moroccan, though she grew up in France. She's fearless. She's a photographer as well. She's more reckless and ambitious than me."

"If she's so fierce, can't she handle JFK on her own?" Alex tries to sound light but knows she sounds cranky.

"She's never been to New York. And I haven't seen her in three weeks." Berks gushes like a teenage girl. If they haven't seen each other in three weeks, that means they've only known each other four months, Alex calculates.

"How old is she?" She tries to make the question sound as casual as she can.

"Twenty-three. But she's an old soul."

That's how old Alex was when they first met in the West Bank during the First Intifada. "She's twenty-three and ready for marriage?" Alex keeps her tone arch, as if she's amused. "Marriage isn't too conventional for her?"

"She needs something stable in her life. She comes from a crazy family—her parents were very religious but she rejected that life. She has no home, like me. She says I'll be her touchstone."

"Touchstone," Alex murmurs. Not soulmate, but touchstone. Maybe he has really changed. For years he'd tell her about his girlfriends with a sarcastic, distanced bravado.

Berks missed her wedding. He was on assignment in the West Bank, covering the Second Intifada. She wasn't sure if he'd made up the excuse because he didn't want to come, or if he'd wanted to make it clear what he thought was more important. Probably both. "When are you getting married?"

"We're not sure yet. Maybe Christmas. It won't be anything big. Then I'm moving to Paris. We're going to live in her apartment."

Alex smiles, but she wants to scream. She and Berks had always talked of moving to Paris. Instead, they ended up in a dark apartment with peeling linoleum floors and a mildewed bathroom in Jersey City. The neighborhood was dangerous and despite Alex's wartime toughness she was uncomfortable going out alone at night. It made her feel like a prisoner. Berks convinced her it was worth the cheap rent since they were both away so much, but she considered it one of the biggest mistakes of their relationship. It isn't right that Berks has taken their mutual dream and made it his and someone else's, even if she's the one who left him, long ago, to make a new life with someone else.

"Does she know what a slob you are?" Alex asks. "Remember that time someone broke into your apartment, and you didn't realize it for a couple of days because the place was already such a mess?"

"This time it's different," Berks says. "I know, I know—I've had some crazy relationships and they've ended badly."

"They've all ended badly." Alex thinks back over the three or four relationships he's had since theirs. There have been clothes thrown from windows, drunken rages leading to lamps smashed against walls and a lot of personal property stolen. "Have you had any relationships where you haven't cheated?"

"I'm different. She's different. We're different together. I can't wait for you to meet her. You'll see." Berks squirms and grins. He's almost gleeful. He checks his watch and rises. "I'm driving straight to JFK, so I better get going."

"I thought you hated picking people up from the airport." Alex is ashamed to be saying this, but she can't stop herself. She isn't ready for him to leave.

"See — I am different," he says as he turns toward the hall.

Alex looks at the photos spread across her desk, tossed there when Berks was done with them. He spent less time looking at her work than talking about his girlfriend. She neatens the photos into a pile and puts them back in the folder. Berks is already at the back door. He's standing, waiting for her with his heavy camera bag over his shoulder.

"I'll call you," Berks says. "We'll figure out a time you can come to New York. One last time before I'm a married man." He leans in to kiss her goodbye. There is an awkward moment when they move their heads in different directions, before his kiss lands on her mouth. His lips are soft and richly textured, just like they used to be.

The front door bangs open and Theo yells, "I call the bathroom first." A door bangs and Lucy squeaks something unintelligible.

Berks yanks his head back. "I've got to run," he whispers as he slips out the back door. The truck engine coughs to life and squeals as Berks pulls out of the driveway, Alex touches her cheek and thinks about his lips: full, crooked, pressing.

From the time I wrote my first story, "Glubby Glub the Gulumpus" in first grade, I've wanted to be a writer. Since then, I have faced so much rejection that any sane person would have chosen to give up writing. But I haven't been able to. It takes a lot of effort but I push through the rejection and keep writing. A reward like this makes it worth it.

– **Elizabeth Amon**

The editors and judges at

NEW MILLENNIUM WRITINGS

are pleased to announce the

41ST NEW MILLENNIUM NONFICTION PRIZE

Carol D. Marsh

PICTURES IN LEAVES

Carol D. Marsh earned her MFA in Creative Nonfiction from Goucher College in August 2014. Her thesis was a memoir about living and working with Washington, D.C.'s homeless women with AIDS. The memoir, *Nowhere Else I Want to Be,* was a Finalist in the National Indie Excellence Awards 2017.

Website: caroldmarsh.com

Facebook: facebook.com/cdmarsh

PICTURES IN LEAVES

Carol D. Marsh

I have been expecting the book, yet the sight of the small package makes my stomach jump. I reach into the mailbox and grab it along with a few envelopes, walking upstairs to the condo as though I'm carrying just another piece of mail and my hands aren't moist with sudden nerves.

Settling into my favorite chair, I place the package unopened on my lap. I snap on the lamp, realize the bright April afternoon light flooding in the window needs no help, and snap it off. I pick up the mailing envelope, put it down. It seems small, insignificant. Finally, I tug the tab at one end, which slips from my fingers. Scowling, I yank hard, tearing a large section away and revealing the book. On the paperback's cover, a soldier stands center front, holding a rifle. He's backed by a black and dark grey depiction of a dense forest. His unshaven face is dirty, its expression grim. The eyes above sunken cheeks are shadowed by the helmet set low on his forehead. The line drawing fades away at his knees where the background color changes from black and grey to a dark, then a lighter, blue. Here, occupying

the lower quarter of the cover, are drawings of two army tanks and, walking beside them, soldiers holding guns. Above the central soldier's head is the title in bright yellow: MACLAREN'S MEN. Above that, a single phrase: "Only Sergeant MacLaren could prevent saboteurs from destroying the First Army!" And the author's name, in white letters that stand out against the dark of the trees:

Robert W. Marsh.

My father.

....

For a year after his death in 2006, I'd jerk awake most mornings, one thought dominating: I can't find my father. Now he is nine years gone, lying in a cemetery under a plaque that bears his name and dates, his Army insignia and the words "World War II Veteran," and I have begun to search for him once more.

The father of my childhood memory is a man who was so *there*. His joy was big, his voice, booming. I was proud of how much more handsome he was than my friends' fathers: brown eyes, dark wavy hair, high forehead and broad jaw, too square-built to be slender, but not overweight. Just solid. He kept his dark hair shorter than most men in the sixties, and no sideburns; a legacy of his army service that he adhered to proudly.

When I was little, he'd help me with my Saturday bath: taking me, dripping, from the tub and wrapping me in a towel before drying me off, his movements so vigorous I'd stagger and struggle to remain upright. I would ask him to sing the song and he would tuck in his chin and open his mouth to the notes and the words as he wielded the

towel with the rhythm, kneeling there on the bathroom floor beside me, wagging his head and looking quite serious.

"Start me with ten who are stout-hearted men, And I'll soon find you ten thousand more."

He would sing on, something about "shoulder to shoulder, bolder and bolder," and marching "to the fore," his resonant voice crashing off the tiled floor and walls. Sing it again, I'd beg, and he always did.

He told his young children only two stories about his service in the Second World War. He said he and his buddy Paul had won the war single-handedly, making me conjure up a giant astride a battlefield, enemy soldiers scurrying away from under his big boots like so many frightened insects. And he'd talk about a Frenchman emerging from his farm house one freezing winter day, cheerful, nose red from the cold, slapping and rubbing his hands together as he calls out to Dad and Paul, "Ne fait pas chaud, n'est ce pas?" which Dad said meant, "It sure isn't warm out, is it?" Dad always laughed when he told that story and he always told it exactly that way. These were my pictures of Dad in the war: one of a giant hero scattering the Germans, and the other of a man laughing in the cold with a Frenchman who claps gloved hands together.

These memories are the only ones in which my father, war, and I are together and not conflicting. I cannot remember a time after I was seven when war was not anathema to me.

....

Listening to the teachers' footsteps pass quietly and slowly behind the crouching forms of my second-grade classmates and me, my head pressed against the wall and forearms covering my neck, I breathed into the space between my

face and the floor. I wondered, stomach rolling in fear, why they didn't hunker down with us. If the bombers came, wouldn't they die, standing up like that? I made myself as small as possible, cramming my nose against the moist patch my breath made on the tile and tucking my knees up tight. Later, when the air raid drill instructions changed and we hunched under our desks, I felt safer, less exposed. The desk would shield me from the bombs, a thought that comforted even as it made me worry about Mrs. Johnson, who persisted in pacing back and forth instead of cowering with us.

One day, she said, we might be told not to crouch and wait, but to race home as fast as we could. And we were to run uninvited through yards of people we didn't know, cross streets even if a crossing guard wasn't there. I would be alone, I was sure, because no one in my class lived near me, and so in my imagination I would stumble through gardens and scramble over fences, racing across streets and passing all the slower kids who might get bombed if they didn't run faster. If planes flew overhead I was supposed to find some sort of shelter because those might be the war planes. But how would I know for sure it was a war plane? What if I thought it was a regular plane and it bombed me because I didn't hide? Mom said the war plane would be flying low in the sky, it would be big and noisy. But where would I hide? It didn't matter, and no, you won't have to ask permission. No, it doesn't matter if your school clothes get dirty.

I imagined a plane so large as to make a shadow of daytime and me cowering at the base of a tree, skinny arms shielding my neck against death from the sky, breathing into the dirt, trying not to throw up. Trying not to get killed.

....

Dad's book is there in my lap, unopened. Suddenly resolved, I pick it up not so much to read as to search for him, almost hungrily, the book cool and slight in my hands, the pages resistant to being turned. He first appears in phrases or expressions so strongly reminiscent that they vibrate with his enthusiasm: "that really hit the spot," and "amen to that, brother," and "how 'bout that?" and "izzat so?" and "snap to it," and "show 'em a thing or two." One character uses metaphors of the sort Dad enjoyed, like one about being in a traffic jam so thick you could "spread it on your toast." Or three soldiers' helpless laughter while producing a series of puns about how Paul Bunyan would have been a good foot soldier. He had an infantry buddy named Charlie Corn. "'Private Bunyan,' Ralph shouted. 'Private Corn. Hotfoot it over here.' They laughed again, one final burst, and fell silent. Ralph felt cleaned out, scrubbed, combed and brushed. He couldn't remember how long it had been since he'd had a good laugh."

That's my Dad.

I realize, as I couldn't have in my teens, that in this book he broke his silence about his war experience in the only way, I imagine now, that felt safe. Because here he is in Ralph, the main character who is named after my father's father, who calls coffee the elixir of the gods and is obsessed about the timing and content of his meals; whose beard grows out a red stubble and who makes friends with small children; who had completed a year studying journalism at Penn State before enlisting, then served with the Office of Strategic Services (O.S.S.)—precursor to the C.I.A.—during the Battle of the Bulge; who interrogates captured German

soldiers and makes friends with the family on whose farm his squad is billeted.

Here he is in the historical accuracy of the story about the beginning of the Battle of the Bulge, when Germans impersonating American soldiers crossed American lines to sabotage roads, bridges, and communication lines. Over semi-autobiographical details, Dad layered meticulous research. I am able to find corroborating reference to it all, to every town in which he describes battles or civilian massacres or as the site of a parachute drop, each piece of military equipment he names — American, British or German — and which bridges over what rivers saboteurs are targeting.

My father had often said World War II had made a man of him. He once told me I would not have liked him had I known him before he served. But convinced by air raid drills and, later, Vietnam, of war's fearful unpredictability and immorality, I rejected the idea that a boy had to go fight to become either a man or likeable. We knew we disagreed but at some point stopped discussing it, maybe due to his retreat into silence, maybe to my arrogant teenage certainty that I was right and he was wrong. So habitual became this distance that even as an adult I never asked about all he was not saying and why he was not saying it.

....

I was five when I first fell in love with a man not my father. John F. Kennedy — whose open, handsome face contrasted so strongly with that of the other Presidential candidate, who was dark and forbidding — reminded me of my Dad, both of them energetic and young with tall, pretty wives.

It was Kennedy who saved the country from war with Cuba, and me from racing home through other people's yards and over their fences. It was Kennedy who made my stomach stop hurting.

Until, that is, the sudden ringing of the wall phone by the door of my third-grade classroom one November Friday afternoon. The jangling had made us all jump, we'd heard it so seldom. When my teacher cradled the receiver and turned back to us, her face was set in an expression I didn't recognize, and we had gone still in the way small animals freeze at the snapping of a twig, preternaturally silent there in our neat rows of desks. She told us President Kennedy had been shot, and, already listening for the war planes that were surely coming, I jumped from my chair with the other kids. I had to get home before the bombs fell, running away from the sickness in my stomach and the terror: He was dead and who would save me from war now?

Most of that weekend I sat on the scratchy beige rug in front of our ten-inch black-and-white television listening to Walter Cronkite and vaguely aware that, outside, the neighborhood of matching Cape Cod-style bungalows was eerily quiet. School was canceled that Monday. We watched the funeral, my sisters and brother and I. My mother—whom I had never seen watching TV during the day because she was always busy in the kitchen, or sewing, or cleaning up using the Hoover Dad had given her one Christmas when they couldn't afford real presents—sat silently on the couch beside us. Mom sitting still, and on the screen the woman with black cloth hiding her face, the incessant drumming, the horse with stirrups backward trotting behind a wagon with the flag-draped coffin: again the world made frightening. Would the planes come now?

Tomorrow? And what could that new President do to stop wars? He looked old and ugly and so did his wife.

....

A breezy, blue day in May 2006, and my parents have traveled to Washington, D.C., where I live. They want to visit the World War II Memorial. I take a day off work, meet them at Union Station and get tickets for the tour bus. At the memorial, Dad strides among the columns, stopping at the one labeled "Pennsylvania" because that's where he lived when he enlisted. He stands silently before the granite wall with its field of 400,000 stars, speaking only after my mother snaps photos of us, and then only to say that it all felt too impersonal. And then he is panting, as though that single sentence has taken the final bit of breath from lungs that are slowly calcifying with the disease that was to kill him in six weeks. Saying he needs to rest, he finds a bench and sits down. Mom and I walk to the Korean War monument, a triangular bit of ground surrounded by granite walls and filled with larger-than-life statues of soldiers on patrol. I remember it for its aura of watchful yet weary purpose, and that my father sat on that bench struggling to breathe. Later that week we talked on the phone, a conversation of which I can recall nothing except two sentences, one his and one mine.

My father's: "My feelings about war came out of World War II."

Mine: "And my feelings came out of the sixties and the Vietnam war."

I waited for him to say more and he waited for (me?). Too long. The possibility of understanding was gone. It haunts

me that I let it go. I want it back, that possibility. Eight years too late and I finally want it back. So I google my father's name, wondering if the war novel he published in 1979 is out there and ashamed I no longer have a copy. To my surprise I find it at a small bookstore in Minnesota, something I take as a good omen: Dad was born in Minnesota. But having ordered it, I almost immediately doubt what I've done. I remember him writing it when I was in high school. He would give me draft chapters to read and I'd comment on characters, dialogue, and setting, but never on battle scenes, the only aspect of the book about which I wouldn't speak and he didn't ask. It's part of what went unacknowledged between us for decades, so essential to our peace that we could share the experience of his writing a war novel without ever talking about war.

....

By now in my reading Ralph is my father. He interrogates a German prisoner, drinking coffee and drawing slowly, luxuriously, on a cigarette. The prisoner, standing half-clothed and shivering in front of him, watches the smoke curl around Dad's head and blinks his eyes against poorly concealed desire. It's December in the Ardennes, the coldest on record. Snow swirls in every time a door opens. The man stands in the middle of the floor, barefoot and clothed only in ragged pants and shirt. For months now he's had no real coffee, no cigarettes and little warmth or good food because his Führer has designated the country's trains for the transport of human beings to concentration camps instead of the delivery of supplies to the front. My father knows this. He uses it to wear the man down, watching closely

while taking another loudly appreciative slurp of coffee. The man asks to go to the bathroom. Dad says no after a long, luxurious drag on the cigarette. He's angry because this German, or soldiers like him, recently murdered the people of Malmedy. They'd herded them into the forest, shot them all and marched away over bloodstains on snow not yet melted by the heat of dying bodies. He feels no sympathy for this man, only contemptuous rage. And so he snarls at the starving and dead-tired man.

My head aches and my eyes blur, yet I read on, compelled by need to understand my father. But this is a war novel and the inevitable battle scenes follow. "'Shoot low. Chop 'em down. Stop 'em from coming in. Open fire!' ... Ralph's submachine gun bucked as he fired three and four-shot bursts." It seems so facile, so full of avenging machismo that I skim hastily through the scene, hating how he uses the good cause to justify this war while glorifying killing as a rite of passage into manhood. Why, how, had I ever thought the possibility of our reconciliation lay within the pages of this book? He's dead and I'll never understand him. I snap the novel closed, unfinished, and toss it into a drawer that I slam shut. Its being out of sight offers no comfort.

....

By my early teens, memories of bombers and hallway drills had receded a bit. However, I was shy and often anxious in that old stomach-churning way, happiest and most calm when alone reading or thinking. I couldn't bear to watch the television news with its stories of murder on the streets and people dying in fires. I felt like I had fewer layers of skin protecting me — what might graze another would

wound me, as though what was fearsome and sorrowful and distressing in the world had peculiar power to cause me to bleed in an unseen place.

Just before I turned thirteen, as the Vietnam War escalated, Martin Luther King, Jr. was assassinated. I sat on the couch in our family room staring at a *TIME Magazine* photo of three men standing on a balcony and pointing in the same direction, their poses somehow more horrifying than the body at their feet. Four months later, and I was again staring at a photograph of death, this one taken in a shadowy world with only two faces visible: Robert Kennedy's and a slim youth's, the younger face far less peaceful than the elder's. That America could be so terrible a place as to kill these men further inclined me to the safety of solitude and a growing abhorrence of violence. Encouraged in that inclination by the news stories and photos about the Vietnam War ubiquitous in the late sixties, I reasoned that war only made more war without solving anything.

But my father supported the Vietnam War, saying we had to guard the world from Communism. He called the protesters traitors, young fools who didn't deserve to live in America. He wanted a fast, aggressive escalation of bombing and fighting in Vietnam, saying a slow and steady increase of pressure only allowed the enemy time to build strength, buy more weapons and train more soldiers. He voted for Barry Goldwater, who he said was the one candidate capable of saving the country from sliding into anarchy.

Meanwhile, the songs the protesters sang and the signs they carried made something crystalline and true resonate in me.

In late 1969, the story of the My Lai massacre broke, with photos of slaughter at which I could not bear to look

and stories of American soldiers committing crimes of the sort patriotism had taught me could only be charged to the enemy. No one, it appeared, could be trusted to wage war with honor. I took this as evidence that war itself was without honor. Thus ended the decade during which I went from five to fifteen, in confusion and anger, blood and brutality. It made me passionate about lessons I was never to discard, lessons that reinforced my inborn aversion to violence. I kept my passion to myself and it grew to fill the space of silence between my father and me until that silence itself was a bulwark.

....

Several weeks after shutting Dad's book away, I'm calm enough to remember that it contained a story about Ralph befriending children. It occurs to me that here is a story far outside the warrior mentality I've been deploring. I go back to the book.

Ralph is billeted in a garage on the estate of the Viscount and Viscountess duParc. The children I remember are theirs — Alain, nine, and Paulette, twelve. There's a scene in which they ask for a ride in Ralph's jeep, "They stood stiffly at attention, giggling. ... 'Please,' Paulette piped, proud of her ability to speak English, 'we would like much ...' Alain completed the sentence, '... for a ride in you jip.'"

Flipping through the pages, I find more about the children. They've built two snowmen with coal eyes, noses and mouths. They've equipped the figures with discarded army gear and identified them, with carefully lettered cardboard signs, as 'Ralph' and 'Suide'.

That phonetic spelling of 'Swede' catches in my throat. I imagine my father earnestly picking through his memories for ways to portray the kids. I leaf through more pages, past the battle scene at which I'd hidden the book away some weeks before. A plot thread follows Ralph and Swede worrying about the DuParcs having no Christmas in the war's deprivations. It unfolds as they go about their duties, proposing plans and discarding them. Finally they wrap some candies, soap, razor blades, and coffee in paper they have carefully saved from their own presents sent from home. Ralph includes a fruitcake from his mother.

Later, reading letters from his parents, he "leaned back against the garage wall, closed his eyes…longing for the peace and quiet and contentment living in that old house gave him. He remembered how he used to look out his window in the morning and see pictures in the leaves."

Pictures in the leaves. The phrase transports me. I am ten and we have moved into a new, more spacious house with a large back yard. We've just finished dinner at a picnic table on our screened porch. Dad, gazing across our back yard toward a summer evening's setting sun, spoke for the first of many times about the lake he imagined he could see through the leaves on the trees ringing our property. What was actually there was a busy road and more houses, but Dad saw a lake.

And I see Dad. He rests against a dirty wall wishing for the quiet, peace, and contentment of home. He's lonely, tired and grimy, hungry and cold. He's a man who makes friends with small children and gives them rides in his jeep, a man who loves to eat and goes through the war constantly hungry but gives up his Christmas fruitcake for the family he's only known a month or two.

Wrapped in the spell of the pictures he writes for me, I find him elsewhere. "The coffee was busily perking on the stove and its bubbling sound was strangely loud in the suddenly silent kitchen. The room was a tranquil place, filled with delicious odors and peaceful purpose. Soldiers didn't really belong in such a place."

And here: "Ralph sank down on his cot, slowly unlacing his combat boots…[T]he song they were playing now made him homesick and sick of the war. He wished it would end."

And here: "They sat in a corner of the mess hall by themselves, instinctively wanting to be alone…feeling powerless, useless, disgusted and frustrated."

Dad had said the war made a man of him. But this is not the man I thought he meant, this man sick of fighting and longing for home. I thought he only meant the man who interrogated prisoners with sharp cynicism, the soldier whose testosterone thrust him through battle after battle. I thought he only meant the father who spouted tirades against war protesters and liberals.

He said the war made a man of him. Yet the man I knew spoke of war mainly to advocate for fighting he called strategic but seemed to me only to make violence roll down upon families, villages, and jungles far away. If he'd ever been tired or frustrated or felt powerless during the war, or if he later had emotions about it other than those of a hawkish conservative, I had never heard him say so. I remember interviews I have seen of men who made it across Omaha Beach. They speak of dead friends, eyes filling and voices faltering. What if I'd asked my father, old like these men, about his war? Would he, like them, have finally told of what he'd kept buried? I wonder: what was his war

really like? At what cost did he hide feelings I now suspect he had? At what cost did I assume he did not care?

....

Here is a story about my father, told to me by my older sister who knows I'm reading his war novel, raw and hurting. It happened in 1997, seventeen years ago. Dad is seventy-four. Her son has invited his grandfather to teach his sixth-grade class about World War II. I imagine my father sitting at the teacher's desk before the kids in chairs half-circling him. He is so there, his back is straight, his face serious. He and his resonant voice fill the space of that classroom. Behind him hangs a Nazi flag and on a desk in front of him are mementos of war: a sword, some daggers. He's fine, surrounded by savage things and answering the kids' questions, until the prompting of a surfacing memory makes him speak:

He is upstairs in the house of the French family on whose farm his squad is staying. It's 1944 and the coldest winter on record in the Ardennes, the stretch of land between France and Belgium already torn asunder by an earlier German invasion and now suffering through the Battle of the Bulge. He picks up his gun to clean it, hands stiff with cold and breath visible because so many windows had been shot out by the German soldiers who used the house, farm, and family in the ways men use during war.

The gun, which he has forgotten to unload, goes off. The bullet cracks through the air and lodges in one of the bed's wooden posts, leaving a splintered hole in the fine wood. Appalled, terribly embarrassed, he races downstairs to the kitchen where the elderly couple drinks tea. Seeing the fright

on their faces, he stumbles into an agitated explanation of the gunshot that has so scared them. He offers to pay for the damage. He apologizes again and again, stopping only when they begin to laugh.

This is what the old ones say: German soldiers have been here burning our furniture for warmth and looting our barn of stored grain, eating our food, and attacking our daughter. Should we now worry about a hole in a bed post?

The story ends there. Not because there's no more to say about the old couple and the gunshot and the war, not because he's told all he can about the flag and the sword and the daggers, but because my father is crying.

*Common wisdom says we should write what we know,
the implication being that writing comes from our
minds and our brains. Yet the pieces I love best, my
own and others', are those written not from a place
of knowing but of searching and questioning, even of
uncertainty. When writing is solely of the intellect it's
a dull, lifeless thing, and misguided. Write not so much
what your mind comprehends as what your heart seeks.*

— *Carol D. Marsh*

The editors and judges at

NEW MILLENNIUM WRITINGS

are pleased to announce the

42ND NEW MILLENNIUM NONFICTION PRIZE

Kirk Wilson

A BRIEF AND NECESSARY MADNESS

Kirk Wilson's work has been nominated for a Pushcart Prize, selected for anthologies, and published in numerous literary journals and in a chapbook from Burning Deck press. His true crime classic, *Unsolved*, an investigation into ten high profile murders, has been published in six editions in the U.S. and UK.

kirkwilsonbooks.com

A BRIEF AND NECESSARY MADNESS

Kirk Wilson

We called the tree a "knockaway," but it is properly called Anacua, after an Indian tribe Cabeza de Vaca described without affection. Even that name is probably a fiction, or a mispronunciation of whatever those vanished Indians called themselves. We're told the tribe attributed occult powers to the tree that became their namesake. I could see why. The specimen in the right front of our yard was timeless and indestructible, a Triceratops with branches. Its bark, rough as scales, rode the trunk in an armor of shadowed channels. Its leaves were sandpaper to the touch, and wore a green so dark I thought the liquid in their veins ran black. I never doubted that the tree had stood there since de Vaca wandered past, witness to countless summers like the one that year, when the temperature passed a hundred each afternoon and the pavement deep-fried anything it touched.

The layers of time were not static in that place. They rolled like waves above an undersea canyon, so that we were never far separated from the Stone Age tribes, or from our ancestors who came into that flat brush country

with nothing and lived out of lean-to structures, or for that matter, it seemed, from the generations who would follow. In rare accidents of light you could glimpse the citizens of those other times, caught like fish in a crest, sometimes as spirits and sometimes as incarnate humans walking in an era not their own. The wave that was the summer when this story begins stood out because it was the midpoint of the worst drought any living person had experienced, and deer, coyotes, and bobcats were limping into town from the surrounding chaparral, driven mad by thirst. The Anacua was indifferent to it all. It was a portal to be negotiated when walking toward the listless businesses downtown. From certain angles it blocked the view of the squat, square-shouldered building across the street, with its steel-barred windows and its Deco-lettered sign that said Bee County Jail.

It was impossible to stand at the verge of the street and look over at that building without thinking of the man who lived inside it with his wife, Lucille, and his daughter, Sarah Jane, and of his potential to appear in the flesh and look back through the gun-metal eyes hooded by his Stetson hat. The man was the county sheriff, a stone killer named Vail Ennis, and all of us who lived in that town feared him with devotion. He was forty-nine that year, but he looked older. We suspected it was the trick of an immortal, the way a man could appear so gray and cold, and still stand tall and straight and move like jointed steel. By that summer, Sheriff Ennis had killed ten men we knew of, eight with his bone-handled .44 Colt or the Tommy gun he liked to mount on the hood of his green Hudson Hornet, one by stomping with his boots and beating with his blackjack, one in a car wreck that may or may not have been his fault. There was another body added to the count in a car

wreck later. Some of the dead had been in handcuffs, some were armed and some not. Our sheriff had stood accused at three murder trials and walked each time. He was as much a legend as the gunfighters who ruled the same ground not so very long before, and were still alive in the mind of every boy who owned a cap gun and a holster.

This part of the story happened a long time ago. To say something was a long time ago is of course a relative thing. It depends on who's talking. This is not the kind of history that is written down by scholars. That kind may be fiction — Herodotus is known equally as the father of history and the father of liars — but it is a fiction we learn to believe. The history we lived should be, it seems, beyond question, but it is the most elusive because we all have to know how to bullshit ourselves. It's up there near the top of the requisite survival skills for Homo sapiens.

....

I did not think of myself as lonely then, but I was often alone, reading or cloud-watching, or following the flight paths of insects so small you could only see them when light caught them in a certain way, and wondering what the consciousness of such a creature could be like. Often I crossed the lava of the street to what we called the jail yard. The jail yard was a field of half-alive Bermuda grass maintained by the prisoners. It was vast in my child's eye, stretching a quarter of a city block. Aside from the sheriff's daughter, I was the only kid in the vicinity, and this space served as my personal playground and athletic field. I carried a baseball, a bat, and two gloves. Usually if I tossed the ball or swatted it with the bat and chased after it a few times, my friend Shine would appear from

around the corner of the jail. Shine was the only name I knew for him. I did not speculate about it, it was just his name. Now I wonder if it came from a preference for moonshine, or a profession shining shoes, or as I learned somewhere along the way, from the fact that shine was another word for nigger.

Shine was a trusty. I remember learning this word and wondering about it. What it meant in this case was that he was the town drunk, and spent so much time in the jail that he effectively lived there. The joke was that he had a key, and no one seemed to think this strange. But it was strange, exceedingly so, considering who else lived in that jail house. Most of the people Vail Ennis killed or beat senseless were Mexican-Americans or blacks, a practice in keeping with the goal he shared with a newspaper reporter during one of his murder trials — to "keep America American." My guess, and the way I will tell the story, is that Shine survived by playing mascot for the sheriff, perhaps for the town in general, a harmless being practiced at giving no offense.

My picture of Shine is more an atmosphere, humid and gauzy, than a memory. I remember him as tall, without much meat on his bones, but he may well have been of average height. The uncompromised blackness of his skin made him a rare bird. In our part of south Texas, the majority of people were shades of brown, and the lion's share after that the many shades of "white." The few African Americans in the town were known as Negroes.

"Hey Boy," he would say. "Wanta play some ball?"

I was always Boy to him, or the boy, if he was speaking to my parents. I don't know if he never knew my name or just lost track of it. But the name he used is as good as any for the boy in the story, and it is fitting because the only name I knew for him was not his own.

He took one of the gloves and the ball. The upper half of his hand stuck out from the small glove. We tossed the ball until he motioned with his glove hand for me to squat down and be the catcher. I liked that because I got to see him pitch. He moved back across the grass. The pitch started with a wind-up meant to cast the same spell on a batter a cobra uses on a mouse. Shine kicked his left leg high like Robin Roberts on the baseball card I kept in a special drawer, his pants leg crawling up so that an exposed sock hung straight out in the air so still you couldn't help but watch it. As you did you realized the leg had started swinging forward in slow motion and before you could absorb that change the arm followed in a blur, straight over the top of his head. The body parts moved in concert but at wildly different speeds. I knew Shine was pulling something off the pitches because they lobbed up softly from his hand so I could manage them, but they still sometimes stung through the glove and made that leather *thwap* I associated with the heat of summer and long days with no school and no homework in the evening.

Then I would pick up the bat and crouch like DiMaggio. The windup was the same, but now he really softened up the pitch, arcing it to where the plate would be so I had a chance to hit it. When I did he'd say "good one" or "that's it" and go chase it.

Eventually we sat down on the grass. I liked to pluck up the blades and chew them while I waited for the stories to begin. As I remember them, they were about the days when Shine pitched for the Black Missions, a Negro League team in San Antonio. The stories had a mythic quality about them, with Satchel Paige sometimes standing in for Apollo.

I believed Shine's stories, soaked them up and day-dreamed about them, but in another time I grew doubtful. I thought it likely Shine was just an old drunk telling a

story he knew a boy would believe. Watching Satchel's clips on YouTube, I learned Shine's windup was less like Robin Roberts's and more like Satchel's famous, semi-legal "hesitation pitch." I couldn't find any evidence that Satchel ever played in San Antonio.

My earliest memory of Shine is the night he arrived on our front porch while I was being tucked in bed, asking in a politely slurred voice to "see the boy." My father retrieved me from my pillow and presented me, dressed in the short and hyper-thin pajamas that were the only clothes a child could bear on soupy South Texas summer nights, to a man who was obviously drunk and who spent most of his time in jail. I don't remember what Shine and I talked about that night. I do remember that we sat side by side on the steps of the porch, with my father seated above and behind us on a glider, and had a conversation. Then my father loaded the two of us in his new baby-blue Dodge and drove Shine home so that he could sleep in a bed rather than the steel bunk in his cell. This was a vaguely seditious act, one clue among many that my father was not fond of our sheriff.

....

My father liked a drink himself, had been a bit of a rake-hell in his day. Maybe that is what disposed him against the paradigm of law and order. The grocery business was my father's life. He came to the town in an oil boom that spouted money in a paradise for hellions, with saloons open in the face of Prohibition and backroom slot machines on main street. Vail Ennis came too, first as a roughneck and drill rigger and later as just the kind of man to clean house for the town's more respectable citizens. The atmosphere was good for both men's businesses. As a young man new

on the scene, my father established a beachhead for his brother-in-law, a magnate who was assembling the largest privately owned grocery chain in the state. But managing another man's dream, even the dream of a kind soul like my uncle, chafed on him, and he soon went on his own. His stores as I remember them operated like a commercial mask of Janus. He stood at the front, a handsome man and a ladykiller in his bachelor days, and welcomed customers to well-swept aisles of goods, to wooden bins with metal scoops for pinto beans and rice and flour, and a butcher shop that was the pride of the place. The backside of the mask was a warehouse, dark and hot and dusty, with fans that spun to little effect and an office and a desk with an adding machine on top and a bottle in a drawer.

The adding machine was the kind with rows of keys on metal trunks and a lever with a wooden handle the operator pulled down to complete a calculation. My father was a virtuoso player of the instrument. His right hand moved on it in a blur, with a rhythm that went *click click click cah-chunk* as steadily as a freight train at full steam. Meanwhile his left hand flipped at the same speed through receipts and bills, keeping up the bass line. That hand was even more a fascination than the right, because it was connected to a resurrected finger. One night after my father missed a curve and rolled his car, he found the finger resting on a stretch of two-lane highway. He picked it up and carried it to a country doctor in an operating room with technology no more advanced than his adding machine, and the doc sewed it back on so that it stuck and functioned as a finger should in all its nerves and vessels. The only scar was a pale ring at its base no wider than a thread.

My father worked the days and drank the nights. We never played baseball. He had been working since he was

a child, and he was not at home with games, outside the kind that happen in pool halls and on poker tables. He had known those, and he was good at them, but he left them behind when he married my mother. He may have felt that sacrifice to the god of respectability was necessary. My mother's family donated books to start the library at Cambridge. They were scholars, writers; they ran their own private school back home in England. His people were Tennessee dirt farmers more focused on the cotton crop than on the family tree. She had a master's degree. He could quote Shakespeare and Noyes and Kipling from memory, but his formal education stopped the day he left high school.

....

Shine's housemates in the jail, aside from the more transient prisoners, were Sheriff Ennis and his family. Lucille Ennis worked in the dress department at Penney's. People who knew her say she was a sweet, calm woman. Sometimes I played with Sarah Jane, the Sheriff's daughter. I remember little about her except that she was a year older than me and was said to be deathly afraid of dogs. Shine knew this, and reminded me to keep my dog up.

It's not quite accurate to say I owned that dog, because he was so much more my friend than my possession. He was a medium-sized character built like a lean sled Husky, snow white as both his parents but with a mongrel gene in his heritage that made the lines of his body longer and more taut than theirs. His ears were permanently at attention and his tail curled in a circle, the long fur on it bouncing as he ran like feathers on a war bonnet. Like the war chiefs I had read about, ones described in more noble terms than de Vaca ever used, he had earned his name. He was Dennis

the Menace. I liked to put my face into his fur and inhale his smell. There was that fierce and particular love of boys and dogs between us, more powerful because neither of us had as close a relationship with anybody else.

My mother said Dennis had good taste, by which she meant he only bit people who needed biting. He did not bite out of fear like some dogs, or from a need to bully, but out of what he took to be his duty. He sent an older boy who was bloodying my nose to the hospital for stitches. He would not tolerate the clearly threatening approach of anyone in uniform across his territory. Postmen were a favored target. But the most desired of all, the one he dreamed of and snarled for every time he could, was the most dangerous: our neighbor, the killer sheriff. This made sense to me because I knew Dennis for the warrior he was. He lived to count coup on the fiercest enemy of all, the one whose blood brought him the most honor. And aside from that seed in his nature, I did not doubt that Dennis recognized the evil in the man and felt compelled to do something about it.

One day Sarah Jane came across the street to play. She gave me a shove as part of some game and Dennis lunged at her. I don't remember whether he bit her, but he may have. She went home to the jail house crying.

The sheriff never appeared to be in much of a hurry. He was a tall mirage coming out of the heat in our direction. My father, who was either home that day or had been called home, stood with me on our porch and watched him come. Dennis barked and pushed like mad inside the latched screen door behind us, and the sheriff's blood-hounds answered in long moans from their pen behind the jail. I prayed that the latch would hold. Finally the sheriff made it past the top step and locked his pale, gray-blue

eyes on my father. He had on his usual khakis and boots, a long-sleeved white shirt with a blue tie held down by a clasp, with his badge just off center on his chest and his Stetson on his head. If he was sweating, I didn't notice it. It was the first time I consciously measured him against my father, and I was surprised that, allowing for the heels on his boots, he wasn't much bigger. His thin build and long arms and the way he carried himself made him appear taller than he really was. His Colt leaned forward in its holster a few inches from his hand. He let his presence soak in before he talked.

"I'm 'ona kill that dog," he said. It was a flat statement of fact, delivered without emotion.

I knew my father was not a coward. He kept a silver-plated .38 Smith with custom grips the color of egg yolk beneath the counter at his store, and he knew how to use it. We had guns all over the house; they were regarded as ordinary tools. I had a couple of my own, an old .32 pistol and a confiscated Japanese military rifle I had been given as toys. But my father was unarmed now and up against the scariest human anybody in our part of Texas knew. If the sheriff ended this standoff by killing a man in cold blood in front of witnesses, it wouldn't be the first time.

"Get off my porch and go back where you came from," I heard my father say. I looked at him to be sure the voice had come from him and not out of the air. "Nobody is gonna kill my boy's dog."

There was a silence that lasted too long. In my memory, even the dogs have gone quiet. "Keep him up," the sheriff said. "I see him out, I'll shoot him." He turned and walked back into the vapor as slowly as he'd come.

My father became my hero on that day, all his faults forgiven for all time.

....

It's clear by now that Sheriff Ennis was an atavist who emerged from lacy surf into a time that would come to treat him as an alien. That happens. Think Bill Clinton. If he'd been President instead of, say, JFK, nobody would have known or much cared what he did with his wanger in the Oval Office. The sheriff belonged on the same High Noon set of time with Billy the Kid and the Earp brothers. But he found himself on planet Earth just when the citizens who voted in elections were starting to put TV sets in their living rooms and air conditioners in their windows. The people he protected, the Americans he was keeping American, were going middle class on him. As early as the midpoint in his first term, after killing number six, a coalition of prominent citizens brought an ouster suit to have the sheriff removed. But the suit died when the district attorney withdrew his participation for unspecified reasons, and the sheriff stayed on.

It took a more portentous shift to change his political fortunes. Mexican Americans learned how to organize and vote. They were fed up, it seems, with being shot, whipped, kicked, and beaten in the jail, in bars, in squad cars, in their own homes. The Anglo citizens who had already opposed him through three elections formed common cause with the Chicanos, led by a lawyer named John Barnhart, who stood for the area in the Texas House of Representatives, and who distinguished himself there by casting the lone vote against a Red Scare resolution that demanded the firing of a liberal economics professor at the University of Texas.

The sheriff lost his bid for a fifth term in a close vote. He spewed about "radicals" and "agitators," suggested Barnhart was a Commie or, at best, a sympathizer. He ran in two subsequent elections, but couldn't get his job back.

....

In the core of the earth, at a distance you could drive in a couple of days or fly in an afternoon, there is a soup of liquid iron and other ingredients, squalling up in angry storms, at the same temperature as the surface of the sun. Vail Ennis reached closer to that fire when he worked among the rigs that were everywhere outside of town, puncturing the land to bring up incendiary ooze created in the time of dinosaurs. During our drought, for eight years straight, heat licked up from the hell beneath us and broiled downward from a lid of sky. Everything we knew burned. My father's business went to ashes when he realized the many families he had been carrying on credit would never pay him back. In the nights he sat alone at the desk with the bottle and hammered the keys of the adding machine until the numbers wore away. The one dream I ever knew he had was that he would make his own story in the world, without working on salary for another man. He woke from that dream into a sadness that would never leave him, a misery none of us could reach. It's possible the sadness was always there inside him, had come with him from his time, beneath the surface like the fires of earth. He poured whiskey on it with the same dedication Shine applied to Thunderbird, doing all he could to drown.

The sheriff was not like my father, not like Shine. Maybe he had no misery to drown, or maybe he just wasn't fooled into looking for the good time that was never really out there, at least not in the places those guys looked. He was a puritan who never smoked or touched a drink. But it turned out he was not an immortal after all. He died of prostate cancer. He was visited on his deathbed by the new sheriff of Kleberg County, a young man named Jim Scarborough, who described the scene to author Thad Sitton:

"He couldn't talk, he had to force a whisper. He pulled me right down into his face…and said, 'Jim, I'm gonna give you the best advice you ever had in your whole life. I want you to remember it…don't ever get caught without your gun. When you go after a man, you get him and you kill him…when you bring him in, bring him in dead.'"

They say consistency is a virtue. Much of the rest of the world—me included—had by then given peace a chance, but not our sheriff. He was true to the time he came from. I've no doubt he felt justified in everything he'd done.

Two years later it was me at the hospital bedside, and my father in the bed. He had drunk and smoked himself into emphysema and heart disease and every kind of complication. His kidneys were the latest thing to fail him. I suspected that the sadness he carried was the real disease, because I watched him surrender to it long before. I had known the doctor all my life. It would be accurate to call him a hard man from the perspective of 2012, but the truth is, like the doc who performed the resurrection of the finger, he came from a time when delusions were not so easy to harbor. He said we should let my father go. If he lived, the argument went, he would do it wed to a dialysis machine, and he was already blowing into another contraption several times a day just to draw a breath. My older sister, my only sibling, was still en route from California. My mother said it was up to me. It had been thirteen years since the first time I stood at his side in a hospital room and watched a heart monitor blink while he told me I would be the man in the family. My father was not an old man by today's standards—if he had lived another day, he would have been sixty-four. Watching him at that moment I couldn't believe he had a life he wanted. I was the one who said to pull the plug.

I cannot inhabit that room without wondering if I was wrong. I stand and watch him buck and pitch from all

the things that are killing him. I have seen people die, but I have not seen my father poisoned by his own body. He turns yellow. I don't know if he can hear me. I live by words but I have no idea what words to use. I hear myself saying, "It's okay, Daddy, it's okay." I know that is all wrong, but I don't know what is right. I want to take it back and say something better, but he is trying to reply. I bend over him the way the young sheriff bent over the old one.

"The hell it is," my father says.

....

There are at least two kinds of time. One moves along a road, where the scenery changes as the boy becomes the old boy, the Stone Age tribe is bewitched by the screens of electric devices, the people you are given to know rise up from a bloody womb and intrude upon the earth with a brief and necessary madness and disappear, no matter how well or how poorly you have loved them, into the mist of the underground rivers as Charon poles away on his ferry, and return as shades to stand at the edge of things and witness. The other kind of time, the kind we don't admit but really know the best, exists all in a mash-up where everything that has ever happened (or ever will?) happens at once, and twinkling bits of it are visible, smellable and hearable, not quite untouchable, almost real. This story happens in the other kind of time.

In the telling of it, I wanted to give Shine a better name. Killers like the sheriff leave traces that are easy to follow. My father's story lives in me. I have spent my life in some measure tending to his dream. But who will speak for Shine?

I had rarely traveled back to the town since my mother died and broke my last blood connection to the place. By Texas standards, the distance in miles is nothing — only one hundred forty of them — but the distance in time can be

galactic. My sister lives in Europe now. She and I still own the house, and the modest acreage outside town my father bought for his father so he could put away the gold watch the railroad gave him and try out his dream of farming.

Some things have changed. The Navy base is gone, but its position as a major employer has been taken by a prison. A clutch of new chain hotels has risen up like chambered mushrooms at the edge of town, along the highway that runs eventually to Houston. It's tough to get a room. The parking lots are full of pickups wearing the logos of oilfield service companies, courtesy of a shale-gas fracking boom that is the aftershock of the oil rush that brought Vail Ennis and my father. Residents of the town thirty miles away claim they're feeling tremors as the earth shifts in the underworld explosions.

On the opposite shore of the highway from the hotel where I stayed, there is a row of tin mini-barns with letters painted on them that spell out T-E-X-A-S S-T-U-D. On the main street, among recovering shells of businesses once put to death by Walmart, there is an uprooted English pub called the Dog & Bee, a clean, well-lighted place that looks as much at home there as a minaret. The building the pub occupies was the pool hall my father and I visited. The jail house is an EMS station. The jail yard is gone, covered over by a transplanted historic home and another city building.

The African-American community is even smaller than it was in the sheriff's heyday. I found some older people and asked them what they knew. Two days before Juneteenth, I met Shine's stepdaughter and his granddaughter at their church. I stopped calling him Shine.

His name was Emuel Davis. His friends and family called him Beeb. He was born the same year as my father. His father was named Ben and his mother was Lillie. He had a sister and five brothers, one of whom drowned at seventeen.

Beeb loved a woman named Julia Pippens, married her, fathered a daughter. He kept coming back to Julia's house, long after she threw him out, long after she remarried, long after the stepdaughter was born — twenty-one years after the daughter. Came back drunk and singing, and she drove him off, threw things at him, and he came back again. She told her daughter he was a good-hearted man with a beautiful voice, a dreamer who never knew the time, but the liquor rode him, ruled him like a god.

He kept coming even after he relocated to Alice, a town sixty miles closer to Mexico. No one seems to know the reason for the move. Whatever it was, he carried the god on his back. A retired Alice cop told me he arrested Emuel Davis so many times for public intoxication, he got tired of doing it and stopped. Daniel Bueno, the police chief, remembered him as a sweet old man who wandered the streets and never bothered anybody. He didn't have to pan-handle because he had Social Security and some Army pension money. That bought him a room at a place called The Traveler's Hotel, which has disappeared.

One Monday morning construction workers found him inside the frame of an office in the back of a Presbyterian church that was being remodeled. He had been stabbed 157 times. His nose was cut off. His balls and his penis were missing.

Chief Bueno took me to the spot. It didn't take long to get there because it's just across an alley from the police station. The steps where the attack started aren't there any-more. There's a concrete ramp instead. I stared at it and the closed door it led to, and found nothing I could understand.

The Friday of the same week they found Beeb, the Alice cops arrested a nineteen-year-old local named Fernando Davila. Meanwhile the Medical Examiner opened Beeb's throat and found the penis and the balls. Fernando used

three knives from the packing plant where he worked as a butcher. In the newspaper pictures he is a short, skinny kid with sharp facial bones, a weak chin, and ears that stick out like a chimpanzee's. He looks a bit like Pee-wee Herman. He wouldn't talk to his lawyers and he kept giving everyone around him an idiotic smile. He set the mattress in his cell on fire. One of the lawyers, an old guy now who has known his share of bad actors, told me Fernando had the coldest eyes he has ever seen.

At the trial, a couple of shrinks said Fernando was crazy and he was found not guilty by reason of insanity. He went to Rusk, the place where Texas keeps the criminally insane. By law, the shrinks there were compelled to release him after ninety days if they thought he wasn't crazy any more. That's what they thought and that's what they did. Fernando went back to Alice, stole a truck, and went to jail. He got out of jail and killed a Mexican national at a dance with a broken beer bottle. He went to prison on a ninety-nine year sentence. He's coming up for parole.

Emuel's obituary says he had four grandchildren besides the one I met, and four great-grandchildren. He also had another kind of progeny. At the same church service with the grandchild and the stepdaughter, I ran across a man named Jesse Robinson, who learned to play ball with Beeb when he was a child, just like I did, but he knew things I didn't. The stories Beeb told me were true. He was a barnstorming semi-pro ballplayer. A pitcher. A catcher. A shortstop. Jesse said he was so good, he could play anything. He traveled all over the country playing ball, sometimes in exhibition games against major-league teams. Maybe he played against Satchel Paige. Maybe he pitched against him. His career ended when the Army pulled him into World War II, and when he came back from that hell he lived in the bottle. Jesse said Beeb was great with kids.

....

I returned to the place where I first met Beeb. The Anacua, the living tree and the ghost Indians, are still on the scene. The house across the street from the vanished jail yard is a neglected museum. The objects left inside it are needy and half-alive. It was an oven on bake that muggy summer afternoon, sealed shut, with air conditioners that gave up cooling years ago. But all the time was there. None of it had washed away. In our absence, all of us who lived within those walls were there. I stood on the porch where the sheriff came to kill my dog. I walked through the rooms and listened to their stories, made offerings to them of my muddy thoughts, and left them drenched in sweat.

I drove to the cemetery where my parents and my father's parents are buried. There were watering restrictions in the graveyard because the drought has come back from its resting place beneath the floor of things to reestablish its dominion. The countryside is dust and burrs; it wears the colors of coyotes and owls. The gravestones are flat. They are there to show the dates to me and my sister, to my children and theirs, and after that they will likely show them to the sky and the underside of the brush.

The blanket of cloud that held the heat to the ground got heavier, darker. As can happen in that place, the heat withdrew all at once, the wind came on, and it started to rain in a serious way. I drove back to the hotel and went straight to the pool. I swam and floated on my back for half an hour, letting the drops pelt my face.

*I don't have any particular advice to offer, but I
was once required to sit down and think about
why I write. This is what I thought:*

*I write because writing is the black sheep sibling of
prayer, the urgent struggle against a bad connection,
intent, hopeful, innocent, never quite good enough.*

I write because writing is madness and madness is necessary.

I write to have the last word.

*I write because there are a trillion subatomic cracks in
every word and if you hold it to the light just so you can
see the ghost of the face of the unsayable on the other side.*

I write because writing is a shot in the dark.

I write to seduce my attentions, and yours if you are available.

*I write because I failed the course in small
talk and cannot paint or tap dance.*

*I write because someone or something keeps winking
at me from behind the curtain of the world.*

*I write because I am involved in a love affair
with life, and love affairs are complicated.*

I write to find out what happens next.

— **Kirk Wilson**

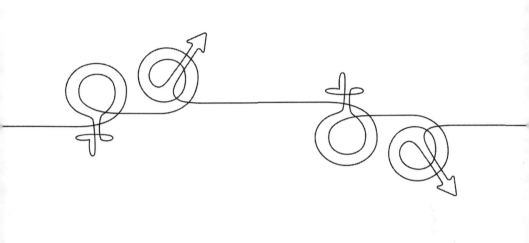

Knoxville, TN, July 8, 2015

To celebrate the SCOTUS ruling on marriage equality, *New Millennium Writings* (*NMW*), an award-winning literary journal founded in 1996, is hosting a special "Love Wins" essay competition. *NMW* will call for essays asking people what the recent SCOTUS decision means to them and their community. The winner will receive $1,000 and publication in the *NMW* anthology and on their website. The contest will run from July 8th to August 31.

Over the past 20 years, *New Millennium Writings* has published more than 1,500 new and emerging writers and awarded over $200,000. In this competition, *NMW* will partner with two nonprofit organizations, Free2Luv® and Lambda Literary. *NMW* will donate $1,000 to each organization to further their missions of supporting and empowering the LGBTQ community. Free2Luv is an award-winning nonprofit dedicated to rockin' individuality, celebrating equality, spreading kindness and standing up to bullying through arts and entertainment. Lambda Literary believes Lesbian, Gay, Bisexual, Transgender and Queer literature is fundamental to the preservation of our culture, and that LGBTQ lives are affirmed when their stories are written, published and read.

"We are excited to team up with *New Millennium Writings* to offer an essay competition that celebrates all love. In light of the recent landmark SCOTUS decision, we are thrilled to read everyone's interpretation of being Free2Luv. We are passionate about creating an environment where all

youth can express themselves freely and authentically," says Free2Luv Co-Founder and President, Tonya Sandis.

"On the heels of Marriage Equality becoming the law of the land and one of the most historic advances in LGBTQ civil rights of our time, we're thrilled to partner with *New Millennium Writings* on this essay contest asking our community what the SCOTUS ruling means to us," said Tony Valenzuela, Executive Director of Lambda Literary.

The Love Wins essay award winner will be chosen by Guest Judge and Free2Luv Celebrity Ambassador Thea Gill, actress, singer, and LGBTQ activist, best known for her starring role as Lindsay Peterson in the landmark

Showtime television series *Queer as Folk*. Ms. Gill will choose the top winner from selected finalists, and the award will be announced on October 11, National Coming Out Day.

"Special contests like this are a rarity for *NMW*," says Alexis Williams Carr, Editor and Publisher of *New Millennium Writings*. "We ran one on the eve of the millennium and another in 2008 to celebrate America's first black president—two other momentous events that impacted our nation and the entire world. We're thrilled to add the Love Wins essay competition to that list and to partner with Free2Luv and Lambda Literary."

Founding Editor Don Williams added, "Events like this truly embody what we have long hoped the New Millennium will bring—a breaking down of barriers, an embrace of tolerance, and an acknowledgement of unity on the planet. This competition is an opportunity for people to share their opinions, reactions, and personal stories."

NEW MILLENNIUM
"LOVE WINS" AWARD

Michael Rowe

SOME THOUGHTS ON MY 30TH WEDDING ANNIVERSARY
IN THE SUMMER OF EQUAL MARRIAGE

Michael Rowe is an award-winning journalist, essayist, political and social commentator, and novelist. A frequent and acclaimed contributor to the *Huffington Post*, he is the author of three nonfiction books, including the essay collection, *Other Men's Sons*, which won the Randy Shilts Award for Nonfiction from the New York Publishing Triangle. His first novel, *Enter, Night,* was a finalist for both the Sunburst Award and the Prix Aurora. His second novel, *Wild Fell*, was a finalist for the Shirley Jackson Award, and will be published in French translation in 2016 by Paris-based Editions Bragelonne. His short story collection is forthcoming from ChiZine Publications.

www.michaelrowe.com

"LOVE WINS" WINNING ESSAY

SOME THOUGHTS ON MY 30TH WEDDING ANNIVERSARY IN THE SUMMER OF EQUAL MARRIAGE

Michael Rowe

On August 24, 1985, my husband Brian and I were married at the Metropolitan Community Church (MCC) in Toronto. I was twenty-two, he was thirty-five. The phrase "gay and lesbian marriage," let alone "equal marriage," had not yet entered the popular, social, or political lexicons.

The rite offered by MCC was called a "holy union," and we were told in no uncertain terms by the church that it was not a wedding—a term that in 1985 even the gay community looked askance at queer folk using. We were, in fact, obliquely asked by the church not to use the word "wedding" at all in relation to the ceremony we were seeking.

We smiled politely and ignored that admonition entirely.

Many of our gay friends were bemused by the entire enterprise. Among the outer-circle friends who veered more towards "acquaintances," there were even sneers: "Why on earth would you do something like this when it isn't even *legal?*" one friend hissed. "Is it that you've always dreamed of being a *bride?*" (Well, maybe darling, but that's not really what it's about, just this once.)

In fairness, he had a point. Our "holy union" would not be legally recognized. Like generations of gay men and lesbians before us, we had to painstakingly construct the legal bones of our conjoining using whichever cast-off, second-hand laws related to property and power-of-attorney the straight community deigned to share with us.

With these laws, we would try to protect ourselves as best we could from predatory relatives; from being separated at hospital beds; from the nightmare of having family members we didn't even know paw through the wreckage of our lives in the event of one of our deaths, assigning a gimlet-eyed dollar value to the riches of an invaluable, fully lived, love-filled life.

Amidst the wider, slightly illogical accusations of being bourgeois or assimilationist, there was precious little acknowledgement of what an affront to heteronormativity it would be for a man to walk down the aisle with a man in 1985, even in Canada. Nobody wanted gay weddings in Mayberry. Nobody invited us to assimilate. On the contrary, the notion of gay marriage seemed to unify the vast majority of people in their discomfort with it.

Our straight friends, for the most part, got it. They may have been momentarily stumped by the novelty of two grooms, but millennia of socialization (and their own innate decency) provided them with a default context into which to place us.

We had no money. Our reception would be ridiculously cheap by anyone's wedding standards. We bought the rings with a maxed-out low-level department store credit card. We were gloriously happy, wonderfully naïve, and boundlessly optimistic.

The day of the wedding was bright and hot and blue. Forty friends and family packed the church to celebrate our wedding with us—we've never used words other than *wedding* and *marriage*. Though it was to us both "holy" and a "union," we were unwilling to have the terms of our matrimony framed for us, or dictated to us using "approved" language selected for us by other people.

The following year, in 1986, my father, the retired diplomat, took me kindly aside and told me how proud he and my mother were, but that I should disabuse myself of any notions that equal marriage was ever going to be any sort of norm.

"You're not going to see these laws changed in your lifetime, Mike," my father said. "It just won't happen. The world doesn't move that quickly and too many people are opposed."

I thought about my father's words many times over the next thirty years.

I thought about them in 2001, when Holland became the first country to allow equal marriage. I thought about them in 2003, when Brian and I were legally married in Ontario, then again in 2005 when Canada signed Bill C-58 into law, making my homeland the fourth country in the world to legalize equal marriage nationwide.

I thought about them every time another country stepped up to the plate and granted full citizenship to their LGBT sons and daughters by allowing them to share in one of the oldest rites in the history of the human race. I thought about

them mostly this past joyous summer when the Supreme Court legalized equal marriage in the United States.

So, Dad, our world *did* move a bit and the laws did change, in both our lifetimes. I'm glad we both lived to see it happen.

I'd heard the question, "But why do you gays have to call it 'marriage?' Can't they call it something else?" so many times from thoughtless, privileged, passive-aggressive people that I finally wrote about it in my second essay collection, *Other Men's Sons*. The essay, "From This Day Forward," was an attempt to answer just that question, which is at the heart of the definition of marriage:

> *I know every line of Brian's hands and face, every variegated timbre of his voice, and I know what every shift of his body means. I feel his pain and his joy and I safeguard his walk through life in every way I can. I would die for him, and I believe I would kill anyone who attempted to take him from me before his time. I defy any married man or woman to tell me they don't know what I mean.*

....

In short, we had to call it marriage because that's what it was. Since straight people weren't offering to redefine heterosexual marriages as "opposite-sex civil unions," we were flat out of options. Among the best reasons to have had these laws—driven by nothing but religious bigotry—struck down is the thought that this LGBT generation and the next and the next will never have to misname their marriages ever again, let alone justify them.

Today, though, on my 30th wedding anniversary, I have some greetings of my own to send out.

To all the fulminating conservative politicians and itinerant peddlers of monetized, unchristian Christianity who've made a fortune mining bigotry and predicting the end of civilization because of equal marriage—you've lost. Give it up. Your Goliath is dead. The body is only moving because of residual putrescent gas built up from centuries of the homophobia, transphobia, and misogyny you've passed off as "God's word" on the topic of human sexuality and relationships.

To that much-divorced fundamentalist Christian ogress in Kentucky who is taking such cruel pleasure in using the U.S. Constitution as her own personal toilet paper by denying LGBT folks in Rowan County their rightful marriage licenses—delight in your moment in the sun, with all the blasé entitlement enjoyed by the last batch of dinosaurs that roamed the earth millions of years ago. Just remember to duck when the comet hits.

It always hits, sooner or later, and it's coming now, fast.

To our LGBT brothers and sisters who are getting married this month, or next month, or whenever—a long and happy life to all of you. Try to get through today with enough forgiveness saved up to get you through tomorrow. Don't turn into one of those smug married couples who look down their noses at unmarried people, or who act as though full LGBT equality is now secure because we've won this battle. It isn't. There's still a lot of work to do, and no one likes a prig.

Also, consider separate blankets. And a Labrador.

To our LGBT brothers and sisters who have no intention of ever getting married, or at least not any time soon—a long and happy life to you too. Marriage isn't better or worse, it's just one choice among many, many valid relationship models. That said, as a sentient, political queer person, I've

never been able to convince myself that turning our noses up at a right we didn't have was any sort of a power position so, whether you choose to marry or not: THANKS, OBAMA.

Lastly, to Brian, my husband — there's nothing I can tell you than you don't already know, and we're too old for clichés and public mawkishness, so I'll just put this out there — the only version of myself I know is the one who took that walk down the aisle with you on August 24, 1985, the one who grew with you over the next three decades. I'd be someone else entirely without you. Our life together is a patchwork. The stitches are tight, the colors are fast, and the weave is warm. We're a long way from perfect, but we're strong and true, and we're a part of history.

Happy 30th Anniversary, sweetheart.

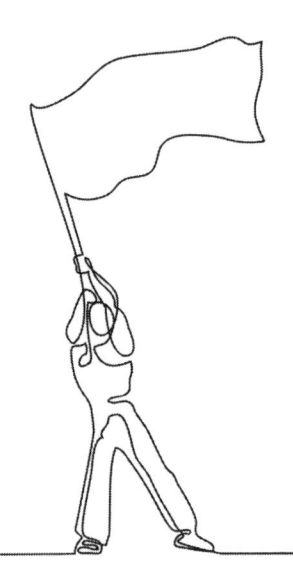

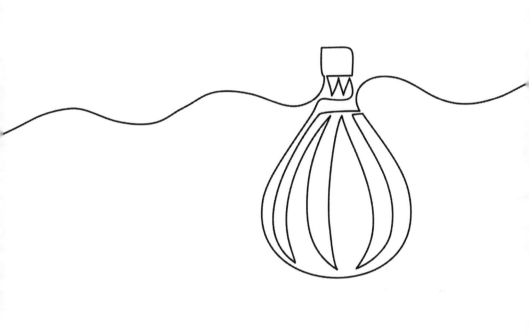

POETRY SUITE

Nancy Allen

FIREMEN'S MEMORIAL DAY BAR-B-QUE, RYE CREEK

I never figured out who did it or how,
everyone taking credit the way they did
for the raccoon chained to a log
floating in the middle. It would pace,

worry its collar and hiss. The winning hound
was the one who managed to lope-swim
out there and knock the sow off the log.
Most years there was no winner at all.

The hounds came whining back to shore, tender
noses raked by the same delicate paws
that could pluck a single egg from a robin's nest
and cart it back to a hungry brood.

At night, the firemen startle in their sleep
and reach for their wives, imagine an armed
and masked intruder lurking on the porch—
nursing a grudge, hatching a crazy plan.

Juli Anna J. Herndon

CARTOGRAPHY, AFTER KHALED MATTAWA

it begins in the feet, where calluses collect to outline
the cartography of the most basic human movements
   recording carelessness in bruises and stubbornness in blisters
   rewarded for their faithful resilience in aversion and abuse

first neglected and first to forgive, they belie vanities
and clumsiness—they are wrinkled with discovery
   here the wanderings pool, here the grime of hardship accumulates
   here the tendency to follow and to fall, the unconscious reception

inexplicably involved in memory and mathematics,
beating out the most comfortable rhythm of humanity,
   receiving every lesson with eagerness and humility, they are tacit
   mitigators between ourselves and gravity—maps of the growth
            we are too blind to see

Lynne Martin Bowman

WHAT THE SAND HAS FORGOTTEN

Let us say we are walking and singing along the wide
flat beach some off-key patchwork pieces of song—
we don't even know the name or the tune,
just some down-sliding dark notes,
a thought of piano keys and curved wood vibrating.

That's how it goes when the unruly salt tangles your hair
and pits your thinking— of what it was to not
think of the past because there was so little of it,
and to think of the future as some vast body of water,
indigo muscled tides and a spin of stars gusting wildly across

the surface, night after night in endless succession. So now
when we fear even our legs may give way before we return
and our toes sink in the sand like the gulls' spindled feet
as they hunt mole crabs, and how a thousand broken shells prick
our house-ridden pale shoeless soles, the fine arches, the soft

place between the toes, what does that unworried earlier couple
have to do with us, but goad and prick like a hard broken shell
not yet broken down into sand. Sadness sings out of the water,
and comes back home with us. The salt will never wash away,
it comes out of our eyes, it lives rocking along each cell

in its own deep water, our inside sea. Each morning, while you
shower, the tv telling us the weather, the time of the tides,
the trouble on the other side of the world, the sound of rushing
water filling the room, I lie in bed still with the taste of your skin—
the tide is rising, the wide beach disappears and the gulls scatter.

Barbara Zimmermann

SACRIFICIAL FIRE

This summer the only fire for miles around will come from
the burn pit on the edge of my property. When the wind gusts
over twenty miles per hour, leaves, twigs, sometimes branches
drop from the spruces, maples and elms—ancient trees
shedding the dead and useless. After every storm, my brother-in-law
and I canvassed our adjoining lots, harvested the firewood
and deposited the load into his pit or mine, depending on which was closest.
Now that he's dead, it's my job to pick up and start a fire.

I wish that I'd listened when he explained how to stuff newspapers
or sacks in between and below to ignite the woodpile. He would lean down,
strike a match, then step back to watch the inferno. He was proud that
a city-born boy had become country-smart late in life. I chatted with him
as the pyre was laid, mostly about papers that I needed to grade, stories to write,
committee reports to compose. Had I paid attention, I would not be struggling now,
the brown paper bag a brief smolder, petering out. The newspaper disintegrating into
flying embers. The brushwood intact.

Earlier today, I'd walked his ground and mine, bending down to gather twigs,
dragging larger branches, ignoring slivers of bark. I try not to think of his round
balding head, his square shoulders, long arms and short legs, workpants
riding low on his hips. Or how he stood with hands clasped behind, admiring
flames licking cinder blocks, the crack and hiss of the kindling. Now I strike
a match and try once again, determined to burn every nub, knot and stick
until only ashes remain, smoke spiraling upwards and thickening the air with
burnt offerings.

Carolyn E. Campbell

RED SEQUINED SHOES AT THE TOP OF THE WORLD

Let's imagine then, you have this dream of re-creating something in yourself.
You have sensed something stirring within you, both disturbing and fascinating.
Behind it you intuit an opening, an opportunity to create a new self...Dolls as
objects of creative imagination, will, if we invite them, take us to play in the house
of our childhood past and perhaps bestow upon us a future we hadn't imagined.

Cassandra Light—The Way of the Doll

I wanted you to be a dancing doll,
Not a weighty creation.
I wanted you to have fairy feet.
Instead, you are born from the sea.
I will call you Marnee, the name of all
my grandmothers far back before
the collection of silver spoons.

You come from the first low hum
of the spinning sphere, the first
murmur of little voiceless things
imitating the sound of their own
waving cilia and pulse
of their gelatinous hearts.

Your webbed toes puddle foot prints
on the shore; a thick scaly tail
full of bones diminishing
into a single soft cuticle,
your balance for now,
drags its line between the steps.
Gradually, your reedy bones adjust
into a fine foot, wet and pale,
barnacled with open-mouthed coral,
trilobites, rubbery brown seaweed.

You stride with purpose
in either direction; it makes no difference,

continued

for you are new to the sun
and still sing the song of the whales.
your hands are large and graceful
as sea fans, your fingers long,
cupped to cradle, supple to strum lutes.

In one hand you hold a round stone
to remember your perfection;
in the other, a sunrise-pink concha
to always remember the day you lay
coiled in blackness.

Made of grainy clay
from the sea floor fired strong
by a molten core, you are not fragile.
Each jewel of sand holds the sun.
You glow with the Original Light.
Your heart is a sac of sea water,
a briny brew of uncertain cells,
undecided codes.

Your hair is a tangle of gifts
from the tides, a snare of fish eggs,
fireflies, periwinkles, broken
monarch wings, and little mouths gulping
the new oxygen.
Hundreds of tiny sea crabs clutch
your tunic of woven dune grass and cape
of blazing blue parrot feathers.
You move with the sound of a shaman's rattle.

I do not know you, Marnee.
Although you wear the sweet smile
of the dolphin, and the deep wise eye
Of the manta ray, I don't understand
why I'm afraid of you.
You are going somewhere. I can't catch up.
You will not wait. You will not stop.
I am among the eyes in the forest
who watch you.

My father insisted I wear

C. Campbell   *continued*

Buster Brown shoes, sturdy, he said.
They'd give me straight legs,
good posture, balance, point me
in the right direction.
He didn't say they were heavy,
awkward as car batteries
or that Old Man Breedy, next door,
had a pair just like mine.
He never saw little girls
in pretty patent leathers
fit for a princess or fairy.

Once, my grandmother, my Marnie,
bought me Sunday school gloves,
white lace, daubed with lavender.

II

I wish you'd speak to me, Marnee.
I've been following you all morning,
watching you stoop to pocket a shell,
call out to sandpipers, wander
into the rain forest where monarch
butterflies hang upside down
like clusters of orange grapes.
Somewhere along the way,
you lost your tail.

But a Great Gull rides on your shoulder
and shades you from the burning sun.
So many things have attached to you.

When I was five, every recess,
many small kindergarten hands attached
to my hands and arms, my skirt, sash,
pinafore, pigtails, pockets.
I was an ark guiding them safely
to sand piles and swings across an ocean
of playground. Like tiny crabs,
they hung on, as if huge waves
would batter them against the rocks,
crack their thin shells.

C. Campbell   _continued_

Mrs. Jepson, our teacher, scolded them
for not letting go.
No juice or wafers for you today.
She scolded me for being the ark.

It is late afternoon. I watch you
Climb into the *altiplano,*
walk across lifeless brown dust,
then down into the *selva,*
nearly disappearing under the canopy.
I watch you ride the ocean currents
into deep mud of deltas. I follow you
into shale-baked canyons, dead seas,
across frozen tundra through trenches
sprouting skulls like mushrooms.

You are reunited
with all the howls and squawks,
cries, screams and trumpeting
from the first little voiceless things
born inside your heart.

We all journey together now,
to the Top of the World,
and you are smiling.
The sun is resting on the horizon,
stretching long arms of rosy light
across the steppes.
Your face is serene, full of joy.
We are here at last.

Why do you beckon me, Marnee,
to follow you one last giant step?
I am afraid.
You do not answer, but lift your
Heavy mud-soaked skirt showing
the red–ruffled petticoat.
You are wearing shimmering red
sequined shoes, dancing shoes,
At the Top of the World
at last light.

Originally appeared in My Villages, an
anthology of poems, in 2016.

Ted Davis

RAISING THE ALTAR

Mounding the produce.
Heating the kettles.
Peeling tomatoes.
As if such a thing could be done by mere mortals.
Undaunted you steamed and blanched and sliced
your zucchini too large for a plate but
reduced in the pot to a pickled shadow
of prodigal self.
And towards the harvest end, you bagged the drops
of macs for sauce blushed with ever bearing juice
to a royal ripeness suitable for more than toast.

Preparing the goods
for putting by
season after season,
you raised your altar of plenty on cellar racks.
We would count the losses by the winter
waiting for the resurrecting day when
you emerged, bearing sweets to table,
masonry urns
holding all that mortally remains
of profligate summers come and gone.

But when the apple of your eye fell too close to the tree,
what did you harvest then and put by for the one
long winter that never ends in spring?
What can be preserved from that fatal conflagration
beyond the light in the jar of crab apple jelly '73.

William Ellis

INSTRUCTIONS FOR RETURNING TO THE PAST

For Patrick Modiano

Do not be discouraged
by the file of terraced houses.
The unbroken face of the street is an illusion.
Far from an obstacle, it is your protection
once you have found the way.

All who dismiss your yearning,
those you wish most to avoid,
will not be able to follow.
The way is hidden; but you it awaits.
You need only take the one path
that is not marked on the map:
the houses are a curtain to be parted.

In a courtyard spared by time,
at its sunlit heart, you will find them.
She and the friends you shared,
unchanged from when you knew them,
will rise to welcome you.

So do not despair
that your body has grown strange,
that you move slowly now,
bewildered.

Close your eyes. Guide yourself by touch
between walls that improbably divide for your passage.
When they fall away
you will glide into a clearing.
Open your eyes. You are there.

David Cooke

MEAT PUPPET

His face wide as home plate, cap on backward, I noted
that backwardness, the way he took it off his left
hand reaching back as if his neck were sore, taking
it by the brim, leaving his cow licks saluting.

Almost young enough that the voice of the boy scout
singing the anthem could be coming from him. If I
squinted to remove comparisons I might mistake
him for a boy, might smooth his ruddy cheeks.

When I smoothed, I moved right past his missing
hand and placed a phantom limb over his heart.
His arm stopped before the wrist, not enough
to wear a watch, enough to spell *semper fi* in tattoo.

His puckered keloid...and I hesitate to use *stump*
but what other word? Arm does not grasp the loss,
vambrace too obscure, stump seems almost epithet.
He calls it meat puppet, but I don't know this.

All I know is he can't reach his heart, his missing
hand still there for him, to cover his heart, to honor
our nation, to yank his Corporal's torso from the fire
and wipe the hard stripes of ash from his eyes.

So much still there; the muscle memory, the routine,
the neurons and worn synapses, so much of his mind
is still there, so much more there than the WMDs,
more than the mission, more than the truth.

You'd know by the angle of his elbow a thumbs up,
an OK, a salute, or when he bites his not there nails,

continued

presses his eye with the empty of his palm. Even
the ump knows which phantom finger he's getting.

But I think if he looked down, he'd adjust the *fi*
to cover his heart. The way it does when he curls
on his side, knees close to his chest, trying
to sleep, his meat puppet hugging him close.

Robert Evory

UNMARKED GRAVE

Jonah is dead. He said he has no teeth, no stomach, no heart; that
he feels like there is a black mountain stretched from here to New
Scotland that he cannot climb over and at the end hangs a nice girl
someone thought was a witch. We question this carefully. When
we present him with a mirror and tap his teeth he is not convinced.
He is dead. He tells us we are still living but not actually talking to
him, fiddles are being played underwater, he feels them, his veins
are the strings. He still eats but says it is to fill the empty well with
emptiness. And the part he does after you fill yourself full is the
devil's way of finding him, hence all the flies. And we're all thankful
because burying his brown fluids is about the only care he gives.
With all the dead to take care of he thinks he's been forgotten, left
behind by the spirits. That is every soldier's fear, being forgotten,
buried in an unmarked grave. That is why the men write letters
home, sew their names into uniforms. Sam carries a plank of wood
he burned his name into with a hot bayonet, he carries it in hope it
will be used to mark his grave. But Jonah is dead. He does not smile,
does not laugh. He stares through you like you are dead and you feel
how true it is, like you went for a swim and the land left, then the
water left with your body under it and you are only a head, then that
leaves too.

Linda Nemec Foster

THE ARTIST'S NOTEBOOK

I. How to Paint an Approaching Storm

Pick a clear day while they still exist.
Blue sky, yellow sun, the predictable boredom
of a calm landscape. Blend in the anxiety
of waiting: the cicadas suddenly hushed;
the hawk lost in its endless spiral.
Keep mixing the afternoon in colors
that are silent: gray of stone, black
of the stone's shadow, the palette
of dusk arriving too soon. Close your eyes
and count—to one hundred, to your birthday,
to the square root of memory until the sky
splits into a crooked river of light. Now stop.
Feel the rain on your face as if for the first time.
As if you have never been here before.

II. The American and His Wife Dream in Florence

Of course, they would dream in this city
full of art and the human yearning to create
the divine. In the husband's dream, he becomes
Fra Angelico—complete with Dominican robes
and a frescoed wall in a Florentine monastery.
He paints "The Annunciation." Imagines Gabriel,
the rainbow-colored wings; the concave body of Mary,
waiting to be filled. Her hands crossed in such
tenderness, he cries himself awake and startles his wife
from her dream. She was swimming in the air, a small
girl floating in the gilded corner of a Baroque ceiling.
The walls covered with mirrors, the floor covered with pearls.
Silent, except for the sound of a boy counting each one.
His hands filled with small moons, his voice filled with her name.

continued

III. Portrait

More than twenty years before his Mona Lisa,
he painted me, Ginevra, a young woman from Florence
who married too young and died too soon. No wonder
I look beautiful and distracted. No hint of a smile
to tempt you with speculation. I'd rather dream
of the landscape behind me: dark clouds of juniper
echoing my name; soft rumor of trees reflecting
memory. Who will remember me? My arms and hands
are missing (unlike the famous Mona). I could blame
the artist but what's the use? It's not easy being *here,*
motionless, with my "beauty adorning virtue."
His words, not mine. The perfect caption for a bride
who has no chance to turn back and disappear.
Disappear into that invented landscape of sky and water.

IV. Back Story

The open mouth of St. Teresa and her ecstasy.
The death of Blessed Lodovica and its mirage of light.
Pluto's wide hand on the marble thigh of Proserpina
and the tears that seem to stream down her cheek.
All of this passion by Bernini can overwhelm
any young tourist, but it's his Daphne and Apollo—
the girl growing leaves and roots while the god
is in hot pursuit—that makes my daughter gasp,
"better than Michelangelo." But she doesn't know
Bernini's back story: the jealous rage that made him force
a servant to slash a woman's face until it wasn't a face.
But why ruin the moment? No artist is perfect
even though the art can be. Consider his Teresa and
her angel. The marble floats as if it's already in heaven.

V. Art and Life

Who can sculpt grief like Michelangelo?
His writhing slaves, incomplete and still locked

L. N. Foster   *continued*

in their marble wombs, mirrored an agony
only matched by his. He knew how to perfect it
on the silent face of a perfect Madonna. Mother
and dead son. But imagine this other grief:
at the moment when another woman's grown
son died—not by crucifixion but by cancer—she
crawled into his hospital bed, held him, and sang
lullabies until he was cold. What image embraces
the deeper pain? The art enshrined in a large church?
 Or the private tableaux hidden in a corner of suburbia?
Our master of grief cannot answer. Only asks another
question from the silent marble growing from his hands.

VI. The Modern Artist Laments the Post, Post-Modern World

When will it end? This incessant march
towards de-constructing the already too-fragile
world. Performance artists shun old-fashioned
nudity in favor of wearing raw meat dresses and
skyscraper high heels that look like horse hooves.
Even Duchamp's descending nude can't compete
with the image of a cow's tendon covering
the pale breasts of a woman in Soho. Her hat—
a giant halo, a giant stuffed sting-ray—
flapping in the breeze. She'd rather eat it
(I'll eat my hat!) than attend any "out-dated"
exhibit with (and I'm quoting here) *that flat*
stuff on the walls, stuck in those boring frames.
The lonely islands of 3 dimensions, static in the air.

VII. Gift

A year before my son met the woman he'd marry,
you painted this landscape of rocks, water and thin line
of horizon. The place consumed by a lake and its obsession
with the idea of blue. The idea hugs the shore and won't
let go: not for the stark branch insisting on its existence;
or the boulders losing their sense of decorum with wild

L. N. Foster

continued

layers of movement. Isn't that how love works?
The spinning and falling, obsessing and wondering what
happens next. The view from this high bluff can't predict
the future—let alone the future of our children,
"impossible to know from this height." All we can do
is give the gift and tell them to hold on—to each other,
to that idea of blue. The expanse of the landscape that can't
be contained in a single image. That's what you give them.

Aly Wright Fields

GYMNASTICS

Despite my past graceless tumbles, I hope
you'll take advantage of my condition
and dare to do the things that make a heart drop.
More than the acrobatic position

(atop a quilt that your favorite ex knit)
I've found myself in, the primal tangle
of tandem lives tempts me. I'm over it,
I tell my friends. Liar. Though I mangle

every routine, twist brutally upon landing,
I can never resist silk rope and rings
to hang from. This shameful gymnast standing
before you, choose her still. I can grow wings.

Before you urge descent, read me my rights;
I'll fall, though I've always been scared of heights.

Christina Frei

TREE OF FORGIVE

I planted a pine tree on my mother's body, decorated
it with her criticisms, reminders and entreaties
all written on bits of paper that dangled like pine cones
from the tips of its branches: "Can't you just once
in your life take responsibility?" "You look like a hooker!"
"How dare you talk back to me!" Owls would roost
there, and squirrels raced past each other up and down
the rough bark, scolding if I came too close. So,
I let it grow wild, never trimmed its branches,
nor swept up the needles that fell copiously to the ground
like rusty fur. My mother's words too became tattered
and faded as they made their way up the trunk
higher and higher as the tree stretched skyward,
so I could barely make out the white fluttering shapes.
The more years went by, the more bristling,
crooked, and gnarled it became. It was even a bit stooped
at the top and at night I would hear it bend
and groan, mornings breathe in its sharp clean scent.
One November there was a terrible storm,
the tree cracked to its core, topmost branches crashing
to the ground where I found them the next day broken,
motionless like corpses. I gathered up all the shriveled
slips of paper in my arthritic fingers, put on my bifocals
and looked at the barely legible words I didn't recall
writing: "I was afraid to show affection!", "Forgive me!",
and: "Look at that moon! Did you ever see so many stars?"

First appeared in Scapegoat Review, Spring 2015

Teresa Gilman

WHISTLING DOWN THE SKY

Night comes in low over the hills in a dank fog of changing
weather reaching to the doorsill. In the house, water in the walls
and boards old with varnish, nails weary with the wind
trying them one by one.
                              Darkness brings her song
in grains of time left until morning. Over and over
she reaches out to his danger, its mouth open to hers,
tries to grasp the whole of it, rising when the waning
moon dusted with daybreak wakens the longing
and wind rushes against sorrow's window, against mourning.

                    He left before she got through with him,
left an iron will, a hard hand from the grave, from tick-
ling memory and lo-
w ache, prizing the harsh voice from her throat, her
long whistle into the hills at dusk—a call to supper and fire, higher
and higher to settle among branches, the top
of a rise at sundown,
taupe leaf-dust and mold rolling down
in a wind, wired the song to her chest,
to the end of a day full of calling
          and calling,   falling   and rat-
tling along alone.

Jonathan Greenhause

LIVING IN SUSPENSION

The neighbors complain about the noise,   so I tell my wife
Let's screw hooks into the ceiling:

Throughout our modest apartment,
we run a series of weights & pulleys   as our lighter-than-air bodies

are propelled between rooms,   our dangling feet fleeing the floor,
our footsteps now imaginary

& pertaining to a terrestrial past
negated by this new tendency   towards inaudible motion.

No pins are dropped;   no cutlery clanks against hardwood planks;
no glasses shatter into

a Jackson Pollack canvas of shards;
but our neighbors insist   with the banging of their broomsticks,

protesting against our remembered racket,   so we respond
with an arsenal of soundless pirouettes,

a concerted symphony
of winks & nudges   & kisses blown across a parabola-laden ceiling,

from our spiderweb of wires.   We've won without winning,
having lost the lives we led

in favor of this restaged rendition
of a Peter Pan-less *Peter Pan*.   Years later, when our neighbors

have left the sphere of the living,   it's too late for us to change:
Our choreographed flights

have become second-nature,
our aged dog accustomed   to this geography of clouds,

our open windows leading out   into the grand expanse
of a latticed construction

of towers, blimps, & satellites,
the sky no longer the limit   & the world irretrievably beneath us.

This poem was first published in Southern California Review.

Jonathan Greenhause

HOW I BECAME THE LUCKIEST MAN ON MY BLOCK

Arriving to the charred remains of my urban home,
I see a circular cutout around where the front doorknob used to be,
& crossing the threshold,   I witness how the walls
lack the photographs we'd placed there   & only exhibit crooked frames.
Where the TV was   is misshaped, melted plastic,
& where the stereo was   is a music box that works
by slowly turning a lever   that plays a tune invented by a composer
from a once-powerful country
that no longer exists.   Where the fridge was,
a rotting piece of meat   is spread over dusty linoleum.
Where the dishwasher stood,   a shattered saucer
spells out the letters   of a long-deceased relative.
Where the bedroom was,
my wife smiles toothlessly   & shows me her tattered nightgown;
& next to this,   the nursery's empty
except for a bassinet   in which our newborn son cries
presumably out of joy   upon catching sight of me.
The 3 of us gather our broken things   & pass through the knob-less door,
counting our blessings   as we stumble down our block
past the other residences   no longer there,
all ripped off their foundations   & carried into the violent mystery
of what our crude nightmares   could no longer contain.

This poem was first published in Stand.

Lisa Gundry

LEARNING TO SWIM WITH DADDY

I.

Jul · 72

He crouches down, shoulder deep
in 3ft of cool blue summer,
sun glinting off the water.
Wet hair slicked back, sideburns long and wide,
his outstretched arm
rests underneath my belly.

A toddler with arms out like Superman and
feet pedaling splashes, I wore
a white and red striped suit
trimmed in wonder.

II.

Your Father is afraid of the water—
he never learned to swim with any confidence.
He feared he would become paralyzed
if he ever needed to save himself
or you girls.

III.

After his death,
I sit at the kitchen table
in the home he built,
awash in stark pools of grief.

Sifting through photos
shifting through memories,
I find him
arm outstretched, supporting me
as I learn
to swim.

Martha Hollander

STRANGE BED

Holding hands while sleeping in a strange bed,
you cling to one another, fighting over
who gets to be the swimmer and who the raft,
since at home, the raft is the bed itself,
but elsewhere—motel? guestroom?
hard floor of a lean-to in the mountains?—
the raft is the two of you together,
so that your entwined arms and legs hold fast
like logs lashed together with vines.
Holding hands is the first step
Of making the raft, then limbs,
torso to torso, then hair to shoulder
And finally, conversation—maybe first whispered,
Then spoken as your voices get used to the different air.
What do you talk about? Is it the usual,
veering from politics to laundry
to the real or imagined slights of the past
days and years? Or maybe something more
suited to a borrowed place,
as you squirm for better back support,
a cooler place for your foot,
having to learn new horizontal patterns
in a bed that refuses to work with you,
while reassuring one another
that you two are seaworthy.

Marilyn E. Johnston

OUTWARD BOUND

wobbling farther and farther out, they say,
one to two inches a year. The departure's begun.
            That sounds about right, late midlife sixties—

We were just watching the tiny astronauts bounce in dust
on that world, no wider than a twenty inch screen
from our youth corners of orbiting chairs.
Last night, the TV voice-over announced
you're slipping off, imperceptibly—
Bright Moon! Migrant Moon, Hunter Moon!

You were always at our fingertips, searching a look.
Now you are what is the distance calling, mulled over,
and missed, what mused on us for half a life
and what we failed to know.

                    You were circling and circling
out of range, exerting your gravitational hook
Influencing with inherent torque, this or that
in our hearts,

the oceanic bulge of tides, the pregnant earth.
You're leaving now so slowly, each
                    elliptical whoosh edges you farther
even when we're sleeping or deeply
absorbed in lights without moon knowledge,
                            distancing
your total effect's diminishment off each previous spin.
Will you be spiraling too far off in space
to catch our dreams?
Are you escaping
never to be seen again
from earth's celestial night,
                    Thunder Moon, Harvest Moon, Wolf Moon?

continued

This will occur many billions of years out,
Reasoned Voice-Over assures.
Never fear the moon will vanish, never fear!
The Sun will burn to a withered dwarf
before our nameless ache will ever
snap free those dew-stretched strings of longing
longing even now for Moonraker, Moon of Remembrance, Moon Guitar,
    Moon Gate.

Carol Smith

BENEDICTION

In the canyon,
The river slips
The land's grasp.
Walls let go the light.
A veil of swallows
Lifts and disappears.

Along the bank,
Barns kneel
To kiss the earth.
Smoke fades to wind.
I cup your ashes,
Light as breath
And cast

In the current,
Time rushes.
The setting sun will
Later light the moon.
The river
Turn to rain.

Marilyn Kallet

ALCHEMY OF BODY AND VERB

"…mad love, illusive love, miserable love, ecstatic love, gossipy love, love without name…" —Julia Kristeva

Illusive I know best.
Elusive, too,

raised on clouds,
vowels,

hint of black hair.
Love without touch,

bias, basis.
Humble

poet love,
mad syllable love,

stubble love, brother
lost love, walking-away

love, come-back
love that has no hope

of love.
Dante without Bea.

Ancient young
no-middle-

ground
love, endless

preface
love, flickering

ashes love,
whisper

love
without name,

one name,
on my tongue.

Joyce Kessel

THE VIGIL

I stood in the glare of the warm exhaust turning red;
around our group I could hear the wilderness listen.
      —William Stafford, "Traveling through the Dark"

Driving a darkened road, but straighter,
we traveled past the quivering fawn
clutching at the snow covered shoulder.
Your heart turned us around,
eyes already as swollen as hers
to stand vigil, engine calmed
to keep her safe from more reckless
and uncaring vehicles.

We held her not-yet-dying
nose bloodied and trembling
in our headlights
until the trooper joined us
to take her out of suffering,
but not yours, sobbing
at our helpless watch
punctuated by his steady gun.

James Kirkpatrick

INÈS,

Let go of the dead, at home in
being dead, with so different
a reputation, brushing by
desire, feeling betrayed by
life, by I am right and you are
wrong, and homesick in reflection,

realizing reflection is
all that's left. I thought you much more
much further than wrong, darkened by
the terror and horror of what
is no longer valid, in this space

this receiving cycle. And the dead
reply, no one asked me to saw
my bones, to be this ghost, to leave
breath, lungs, intestines far behind.

Yes, the heart is a poor and cruel
chamber, a series of questions,
this thing that agonizes and

washes old customs ashore, and
raise women in doorways, with their
resonating voices, to ask
are you still here, in this darkness?

C. Ann Kodra

FORGETTING WITH PLAINCLOTHES TRACY

*—While listening to a band by the same
name, UT Knoxville, March 10, 2012*

I turn to my mother, knowing
she will see this just as I do:
the singer's alien hair a rhombic
wedge tacked to a pixie head, urging
voice backed by lead and bass guitars,
drums thudding the rhythmic thrust
of her sharp jaw as she drives
her point again and again, the mic
a firm dream in her right hand, red
dress flaming short and flagrant
above muscled, lean legs and tan
boots to the calves. A silver belt
splits her moves into two galvanic
halves, her voice a hook that lifts
the crowd to a strong, chiseled beat.

*Don't you admire her, though, for being
so comfortable in her own skin?* I thought
I would say. And my mother, in her plain
skirt and simple flowered blouse, would
smile her shy smile, would almost nod
until the moment of my quick grief when
she isn't there, and hasn't been anywhere
for seven years. And for a brief pause
between songs, we are both stunned
by our absence from each other's world.

K. T. Landon

THE SECOND LAW OF THERMODYNAMICS

For a long time Hawking believed
when the universe stopped expanding
time, too, would run backwards.
Wish fulfillment, maybe: youth restored,
the body made whole. Imagine a paradise
regained: the soldier's ear uncut,
the earth undrowned, the apple whole and
unenticing. But the equations wouldn't work,
and perhaps he came to see it
as just another species of loss—
the incoming tide just as merciless,
ripping away everything it restored:
love, work, miracles
all winking into empty innocence
and oblivion worse than loss.
But what mattered was the math.
The second law of thermodynamics says
everything goes to hell eventually:
the teacup skitters in pieces across the tile,
the lovers drift apart, the body
fails us. Everything shatters
and will not be gathered again.

Armin Tolentino

DIRT EATERS ANONYMOUS

[NEXT PAGE]

Stare at her hands during dinner.
        Dirt under the nails
                is a sure sign of relapse. Ask,
        "Honey, how was your day?
                Did you garden?"
                        Watch her blush and squeak
        out a lie, so little air   able to wheeze through her throat;
her pinhole windpipe   dammed back with black loam.

Kiss her in bed and taste   bitter topsoil,
        her lips cracked from leaves   that suck
                the skin's moisture,   leaving her brittle
like yellowing edges   of autumn.
                        Run your tongue
over her teeth and   cut yourself
        on the twigs stuck between.

Don't fall asleep.   Wait till she slips
        from under your arm,   slips out the bedroom,
                slips into darkness,   strips off her clothes
                        and rolls in the grass,   the bed of gardenias,
        munching on mulch till she's foaming,
                delirious.

Don't call the doctor.   It's not her fault.
        Maybe you thought since you'd   been inside her
                It was you she was missing,
        the way you fit   seemed a circuit completed.
        You began to believe your
                        presence belonged in all her hollow spaces.

You forgot   before she was yours   she was miles of elements pleated,
        sand and clay,   wood and silt,
                an unbroken chain of molecules hooked
                        like a harness to the earth that begot her.

                The pebbles know her longing.

        Let her fill the empty spaces.
                Let her find her way back home.

Ed McManis

DSM V GOD

Autism-God Study Suggests Disorder Makes Belief in Deity Less Likely.

—*University of British Colombia*

Dear God, Father, Deity—

So, what you've been receiving these past years from both of us—
my younger brother Steve and me—is yes, mostly me. I'm sure
you figured that out. I apologize for all the requests. I picture a
giant desk, a few clouds, and these In and Out baskets, like those
New Yorker cartoons. Nothing in the "GRATITUDE" basket
except a hand scribbled "Thanks" as an afterthought from the last
lottery winner. And the "REQUEST" pile stacked higher than the
Sears Tower.

Maybe if you watered Africa once in a while, quit blowing tornadoes
through Oklahoma, tweaked one of those genes, like the one stuck
in my brother's head that makes his fingers twitch like they're
electric, and jumble his language like a YAHTZEE roll.

But what do I know? You have a million years of experience—or 6
thousand if I were one of those "true" believers." I think of your time
(or your Son's that is); Peter, who must have been bi-polar, Simon
Zealotes with Tourettes, and Judas? No Axis 1 for him; betrayal is
straight up. Pontius had to be OCD, all that hand-washing…

But I digress. It's not like I haven't prayed with Steve, dragged him
to church, promised that you'd answer whatever he asked for…what
did he ask for? How hard to grant from the infinite throne, the
atheists swirling like gnats? But maybe he asked for what he has—
the brother is the last to know. But I do know that he'll never hold
a full time job; his girlfriends are all two-dimensional. He thinks

continued

Star Wars is real and Harry Potter can fly. He'll never ask me what
I think.

Divine plan? An off day, your holiness? Ah, but "My ways are not
your ways…" Yes, I've tried that line on him. "We can't know the
mind of God!" He seemed to sneer, or maybe it was a tic.

I'll keep sending these, sometimes from my knees, sometimes in a
bouquet of scotch. Steve? He has this blank look when I say your
name, speak of heaven. "Our Daily Bread." He looks past me with
that stare between hell and his apartment.

He doesn't think you really made the lake as he walks across
the water.

E.McManis

Christina Lovin

OF OTHER NIGHTS

What dreams of other nights are you dreaming,
my pet? You run like a wolf across night-
time sheets as you lie on your side beside
me in the dark, yipping that stuffed animal
squeak, tiny maw a grimace of rage and
ferocity. When I place my hand on your body
(that has never known an open field beyond
the fenced yard), you return to me, leaving
behind the dense forests and vast tundra
of your ancestors—those places imprinted
on your consciousness, like every canine's.

Somewhere deep inside laboratories,
other dogs run in their sleeps as all dogs do,
chasing phantoms of those ancient lives not
lived. Monkeys, too, fall into fitful sleeps,
wired to machines that interrupt their dreams
of ripe fruit and insects never tasted
from unseen jungles. Collective memory
plays tricks, does it not, my pet?

What is real? What is not?

And oh, sweet primate, gorgeous gorilla,
your night-cries arouse us like new parents
unused to some new voice, alarming
us awake from our own reverie. Screams
draw us to you, restless and afraid
in your safe home of sturdy iron bars.
A nightmare? We ask because you can tell us,
intelligent beast and brother animal,
your fears.

continued

                              Because we have patiently taught
our words for food, water, anger, and terror,
you show us with your hands panic and horror:
your remembrance in this night of other
nights when your kin were killed and mauled, and you—
What is real? What not? What is human? Not?—
you were seized by creatures looking just like us.

*Author's Note: An NPR story told about a gorilla that had a nightmare
and, because he/she had been taught to sign, let the keepers know that
the nightmare had been about being kidnapped as a young gorilla
by hunters who savaged the group of gorillas and stole the babies.*

Laura Still

STILL POINT

Think of a lake morning,
mist curling off the water,
spiraling spirits diffusing light
like joy—
lying beside you
was my hiding place then.
Now everything goes deeper,
in the tumult, raucous blare,
every turn of the labyrinth
spins me closer to the circle
of your arms.

Alison Luterman

AFTER WATCHING A HORROR MOVIE, THEY SLEEP WITH THE KITTEN BETWEEN THEM

Evil spirits, beware,
all's quiet here.
Kitten and couple
asleep in their double

bed; husband snores,
kitten scratches,
wife grinds her teeth,
moans, and thrashes.

A hot July night,
the sheet's wound tight
over bellies and thighs;
Kitten's soft sighs

are a soothing tonic
for the woman's nervous panic.
Tick, tock, tick.
Some minds are sick.

Some souls suck blood
in the name of Love.
The thought makes her queasy,
also sleepless, in a city

where girls are trussed,
gagged, dismembered,
for the crime of being pretty—
why obsess over evil?

continued

Because in her own soul
lurks darkness as well,
she knows that she too
could lash out and kill.

But could she abuse?
Or keep locked in a cage
what she fears most to lose?
Best not to fret

over what can never be solved,
some nights her heart
walks alone, abroad,
and knows there's a knot

that can't be untied,
only sliced wide.
Tonight's hot and not ideal
for sleeping with a flatulent pet—

still she'll hold this moment
a moment yet: the steady purr
of a marmalade tabby,
her man's gentle breath *(he*

has a tranquil heart, sleeps like a baby),
fur pressed to skin, primal
luxury, ancient as fire:
original innocence, animal desire.

A. Luterman

Bernadette McComish

FIVE YEARS LATER

The humidity has followed me
to the West Coast, miles from
where you ate sour patch kids
for the last time. You didn't want
to walk to the store, you wanted
to shoot a little more. I still
believe in the snort of your laugh.

At what point am I allowed to forget,
to stop imagining the room,
hidden behind the kitchen wall with the hole
behind the stove
behind the room with no furniture
just bodies barely breathing
against the wall, their backs curved
like orange peels.

When will I stop imagining
the last thing you saw, a swirling
black and burgundy tapestry
skull candles, red lava lamp,
a Hendrix poster
on the ceiling.

I had thought at some point your sunken
cheeks would stop hiding behind the veil
of bullshit, and ask for a bus ticket home.

Am I allowed to delete
your meaningless emails,
toss pictures where your eyes
are closed, pictures of you in clay
beauty masks with a dick

continued

in your mouth, pictures of us
with bad haircuts dancing
in black, light, and gray.

At what point does the tape
stop replaying your last
words, retold by the same
witness, because the same God
you wore around your neck
was too busy to remove the needle
from an old record looping
the same seconds of a song
your sister sings to her children,
he's only sleeping, only sleeping,
only sleeping.

There will be no erasing
the summer you dyed
your hair black, and erased
the blonde roots in order to forget
the boy and be reborn an empty
page where only I could see
the penciled words you didn't
want anyone to read.

B.McComish

Danny Kossow

ONE MORNING IN THE MARSH

There's a heron,
a gatekeeper,
a double breasted breather,
he takes, but just a few,
to lick his reedy nest.

One morning, in his marsh
with beaver tails tranquil,
and ropes of translucent fish eggs slithering
away from venom-less snakes,
my sage heron leaked open. He sang,

You're smoking too many cigarettes – you, degenerate bastard.
Next time bury yourself on a hill
overlooking those fabricated details that entice you.
Maybe then you'll find it,
that radiant hatching,
              or whatever the fuck you've dreamt up.
Put your hands in the soil—seriously,
 it's cold and hard
              and you need it.

And I,
ever the present hound, sniffing always
for clues to further this cause,
buzzed around my billowy chest seeking
              another thing,
something else.

Ed Ruzicka

MY LUNGS ARE A SHAMBLES

I sit on the patio drinking bird notes
from tumblers. Wind sweeps green arcs
through oaks. I take the voices of children
from streets, back yards, replay them at night
as if exuberance is a toy I can wind up.

I talked to my daughter in Colorado
almost an hour; sat in the grass,
teased out, tugged up clover weed.

When she was young Miriam and my ex
came upon a blind dog at a public pool
that kept wandering into the drink. They
brought it home, a sort of matted rug that
ate, shat and shuffled around for nine months.
When it died, I dug a hole in the back yard.

In the morning pouring coffee—wife in
the bedroom zipping her skirt—I'd spy
Miriam alone in the yard gathering twigs,
piling them, picking clover and violets.

She wandered on half-formed legs.
Brought death tiny, inadequate tributes
and sang in a voice so high and soft
that to this day I haven't fully recovered.

Slowly as dawn evaporated night dews
from grass blades, she began to learn how
there is nothing anyone can do but sing.

JLSchneider

POETRY 210 AT THE DFY*

The boy with the baby face
and pale eyes beat the jogger
until she lost her memory. His villanelle

with the line about waiting
repeated, gem cut. The Muslim
speaks in tercets of Allah

in the little girl's hand
that never reached her mother. *Symbol*
he says *is the white space*

of sorrow around words,
which are useless. They are horror
and perfection and calm eyes

no one can resist, parataxis
muscled into a tea cup.
Hearts burnt hard

as marble and so needy if I could
sprout a mother's breasts they'd kneel
open-mouthed and beg.

* *The DFY (Division For Youth) is where children convicted as adults are incarcerated until their 21st birthdays, when they are transferred to an adult correctional facility.*

Lucia Zimmitti

CLAY

You rest your head on the knob of my shoulder
and come away with a yawn-shaped gouge
where your ear and cheekbone should be.

How many times have I told you to hold the lean
till it dries? But you never do. Maybe because
it never does. And the wheel whirrs awake any-

way. *Hopehopehope,* it whisper-lies. Doesn't it know

the kiln died long ago so now we heap
newspapers on it or shroud it with damp towels
or maybe, when the world feels benign, crown it

with a mayonnaise jar of flowers, the kind
we can't help but root for, the burden of blooms
downcrimping feeble, unglazed throats?

Barbara Mossberg

AVATAR OF RISE AND SHINE

*At that time they say that the Emperor Honorius in Ravenna received
the message from one of the eunuchs, evidently a keeper of the poultry,
that Roma had perished. And he cried out and said, "And yet it has
just eaten from my hands!" For he had a very large cockerel, Roma
by name; and the eunuch comprehending his words said that it was
the city of Roma which had perished at the hands of Alaric, and the
emperor with a sigh of relief answered quickly: "But I thought that my
fowl Roma had perished."*

—*Procopius, The Vandalic War (De Bellis III.2.25–26), circa 532*

If you have ever heard a rooster crow, pronounce morning, a throaty
pounce on light, you might not be surprised at how beloved Roma
was to the emperor, who doted on the feathered feisty spirit. If
you have ever shouted out the kitchen door, *ducks and chickens!*, to
come get spaghetti and salad, and seen them surge. If you have ever
thought you had chickens until early one morning in Pasadena there
is the cry of a rooster, and it's not a metaphoric Thoreau Chanticleer,
it's not Chaucerian, it's an actual rooster going cock-a-doodle-do, or
er-er-er-er-er! And you wake up laughing that there is such a sound
in your world, even though your neighbor calls the police and you
are told to get rid of the rooster, as the neighborhood is not zoned
for rooster crow. But now you know it is a magical place, or, better, a
real place after all. If you have ever held a rooster, all squirmy glossy
feathers, indignant and staring, spurs and crest and scorpion tsunami
tail, its fervent red and green and blue from gulped darkness, pecked
star, you may begin to understand what he meant, the emperor, his
relief that it was not his young rooster but Rome that had fallen.
You may begin to understand why the Portuguese describe a legend:
"Ah, but you have been accused and sentenced to death, and I can't
change the sentence on just your word without proof. How do
you think you can prove your innocence, my good man?" "But Sir,

continued

I swear that I am innocent," the man insisted. . . His eyes fell on a
servant carrying in a large platter of fowl, steaming with seasonings.
He fell to his knees. "Lord God," he prayed, "as

Peter, your servant, denied you at the cock's crow, would that you
show my innocence as your humble servant by this rooster's crow..."
so he said "If I am innocent, this rooster will crow three times." All
eyes turned to the platter of steaming cooked fowl and widened in
wonder and amazement as the rooster got up, ruffled his feathers
and crowed loudly. "The Lord has indeed spoken," the Judge said in
awe, and rising to his feet, he proclaimed, "The rooster, henceforth,
shall be a reminder to us and to our children after us, of this, the
Lord's message. So shall it be in our land forever!"

You can see why the country of France, for example, should adopt
the rooster as a symbol of classical civility. You can see why Sydney
would name its rugby team the Roosters.

When Grandma comes to visit, and it is time to kill the old red
rooster, it's missing. So is Thessus. Aha! The dinner is turnips and
potatoes and chess pie. Later, Thessus is found by the creek, holding
rooster matching the colors of water, colors of sunrise. No one is
mad. Everyone loves the loyal roo, who would fight to the death
to protect his own. But the reason is his leafy feathers the colors of
gorgeousness. His principled clawed stand. His peevish pecking. His
notice of morning that does not get by him, even when it sneaks in
gray: he is alive to its colors of rooster.

B.Mossberg

Victoria Smith

MOTHER OF EXILES

She's short and stocky, hands huge,
warm, and blue as the Pacific Ocean,
fingers fat and brown as the soil
peasants till in boisterous farms
outside the gates of this garden spa.

She lays me down like a fragile, old book
broken at the spine, face down on a donut pillow—
a voyeur peeping through the O, spying
upon the swan song of a *gumamela* flower
floating in a celadon bowl below me, evoking
mourners' blossoms sailing on the Ganges
escorting the soul released by ashes

into the next life. Her fingers push,

knuckles knead, palms press
my shoulders, back, calves—her touch
both scolding and appeasing my body's demons,
chastising flesh into dough
ripe for the rising, torn into weeping,

transfigured, reborn

from the carmine bloom chanting
the canticle of the lamb, singing
of how it lived solely for this moment,

that I may be redeemed

by beauty hiding in the inconspicuous,
love incipient in human touch.

continued

I thank her for her service, stunning
her with my embrace—first time
any client of hers has done this, she says
crumpling, crying on my shoulder, ceding
her burdens upon me: of how she alone supports
five children on this job, and jobless husband
lives only for the bottle, and eldest daughter
is a baby with a baby.

And that's why she's exiling them all
from this island into the big city
where some living might yet be had,
scraped off of the streets—matters
that can't be helped by a mere tip.

I return to the world outside
the gates of this Shangri-La—unhinged,
still lost in a horizon
of elusive dreams—

rattled, reeling

from hideous truth lurking in paradise,
treachery latent in human touch.

V. Smith

Barbara Ungar

ON A SCALE OF ONE TO TEN

This will hurt, the doctor says
before the needle. *That's nothing,*
you say, *I've given birth.*

Your theory is labor
hurts so much to make

everything after seem easier, even
the fourth trimester—

which could drive anyone to suicide,
infanticide, right off

the charts. There is one pain
you don't dare contemplate

(though it used to be
commonplace):
loss of a child. Yours

sits beside you on the couch
watching Nova. He wants to be a scientist.

Lush vegetation rings an ancient lake
where mammoths graze, animated
wooly elephants with Dr. Seuss

tusks, long and curling. The whole herd
fossilized under a dry lakebed.

Two scientists speculate
on the cause of sudden death.

continued

One pours water upon a tray of sand,
waits till it sinks in, places a carved

elephant upon the dried crust. They pick up
the table's four corners and shake

to simulate earthquake, which makes
the water bubble back up, forming quick-
sand. The toy elephant sinks in

up to its wooden knees.
Cut to a mamma mammoth,
baby by her side, similarly

trapped, trunks waving
helplessly. Who can stand this

hundred-thousand-year-old pain,
the kabillions of animals

from then to now, each single
suffering being
snuffed out—

Next on Nova:
nebulae give birth to galaxies of stars.

B. Ungar

Julie Rochlin

ICE AGE

Inside our house
frost seals the walls. A whiteout
so fierce, I can barely make you out.
If you were to reach for me,
I would gather in your arms—press
the cold bone of my nose
into your flannel—feel your chin
warm in the wool of my curls.
If we could find each other,
we might lie down in this numbing,
Everest climbers, too spent
to descend. Say the unspoken—
how the last twenty years were
the best of our lives. As in all great
passion, we honed our skills—barely
noticed the time. The age of raising
children is past, and the present
feels unbearable. Come, lie down
with love. Let's die of exposure
in each other's arms.

George Keenen

BACK WE GO

There is a rumble, and lightning forks
from earth to sky.
Flowers are sucked noisily into seeds.
Falling mountains rise,
rising mountains fall.
Freighters turn and carry
bananas to the tropics.

Suicides jump backwards onto bridges
where lost love awaits.
Swaying oceans discharge into rivers
which send fingerling streams
racing up into hills.
Thieves stack unmarked bills
by night in secret vaults.

One sweet bullet leaps from my brain.
Blood lifts like a veil
to fill my skull again
and you grow young before my eyes.

All fleeing things turn and pour themselves
into the secret center.
And those who once feared death
now fear the coming birth.

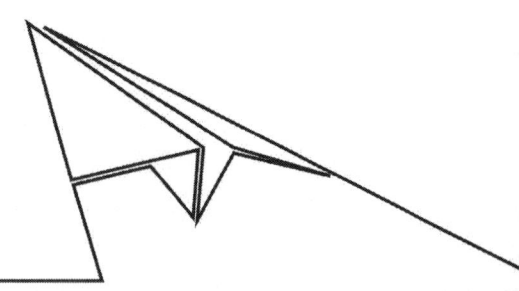

THE NMW EXCERPT

from Oscar Wilde's

THE SOUL OF MAN

THE CHIEF ADVANTAGE THAT WOULD RESULT FROM THE ESTABLISHMENT of Socialism is, undoubtedly, the fact that Socialism would relieve us from that sordid necessity of living for others which, in the present condition of things, presses so hardly upon almost everybody. In fact, scarcely anyone at all escapes.

Now and then, in the course of the century, a great man of science, like Darwin; a great poet, like Keats; a fine critical spirit, like M. Renan; a supreme artist, like Flaubert, has been able to isolate himself, to keep himself out of reach of the clamorous claims of others, to stand 'under the shelter of the wall,' as Plato puts it, and so to realize the perfection of what was in him, to his own incomparable gain, and to the incomparable and lasting gain of the whole world. These, however, are exceptions. The majority of people spoil their lives by an unhealthy and exaggerated altruism — are forced, indeed, so to spoil them. They find themselves surrounded by hideous poverty, by hideous ugliness, by hideous starvation. It is inevitable that they should be strongly

moved by all this. The emotions of man are stirred more quickly than man's intelligence; and, as I pointed out some time ago in an article on the function of criticism, it is much more easy to have sympathy with suffering than it is to have sympathy with thought. Accordingly, with admirable, though misdirected intentions, they very seriously and very sentimentally set themselves to the task of remedying the evils that they see. But their remedies do not cure the disease: they merely prolong it. Indeed, their remedies are part of the disease.

They try to solve the problem of poverty, for instance, by keeping the poor alive; or, in the case of a very advanced school, by amusing the poor.

But this is not a solution: it is an aggravation of the difficulty. The proper aim is to try and reconstruct society on such a basis that poverty will be impossible. And the altruistic virtues have really prevented the carrying out of this aim. Just as the worst slave-owners were those who were kind to their slaves, and so prevented the horror of the system being realized by those who suffered from it, and understood by those who contemplated it, so, in the present state of things in England, the people who do most harm are the people who try to do most good; and at last we have had the spectacle of men who have really studied the problem and know the life — educated men who live in the East End — coming forward and imploring the community to restrain its altruistic impulses of charity, benevolence, and the like. They do so on the ground that such charity degrades and demoralizes. They are perfectly right. Charity creates a multitude of sins.

There is also this to be said. It is immoral to use private property in order to alleviate the horrible evils that result from the institution of private property. It is both immoral and unfair.

Under Socialism all this will, of course, be altered. There will be no people living in fetid dens and fetid rags, and bringing up unhealthy, hunger-pinched children in the midst of impossible and absolutely repulsive surroundings. The security of society will not depend, as it does now, on the state of the weather. If a frost comes we shall not have a hundred thousand men out of work, tramping about the streets in a state of disgusting misery, or whining to their neighbors for alms, or crowding round the doors of loathsome shelters to try and secure a hunch of bread and a night's unclean lodging. Each member of the society will share in the general prosperity and happiness of the society, and if a frost comes no one will practically be anything the worse.

Upon the other hand, Socialism itself will be of value simply because it will lead to Individualism.

Socialism, Communism, or whatever one chooses to call it, by converting private property into public wealth, and substituting co-operation for competition, will restore society to its proper condition of a thoroughly healthy organism, and insure the material well-being of each member of the community. It will, in fact, give Life its proper basis and its proper environment. But for the full development of Life to its highest mode of perfection, something more is needed. What is needed is Individualism. If the Socialism is Authoritarian; if there are Governments armed with economic power as they are now with political power; if, in a word, we are to have Industrial Tyrannies, then the last state of man will be worse than the first. At present, in consequence of the existence of private property, a great many people are enabled to develop a certain very limited amount of Individualism. They are either under no necessity to work for their living, or are enabled to choose the sphere of activity that is really congenial to them, and gives them pleasure. These are the poets, the philosophers, the men of science, the men of culture — in a word, the real men, the men who have realized themselves, and in whom all Humanity gains a partial realization. Upon the other hand, there are a great many people who, having no private property of their own, and being always on the brink of sheer starvation, are compelled to do the work of beasts of burden, to do work that is quite uncongenial to them, and to which they are forced by the peremptory, unreasonable, degrading Tyranny of want. These are the poor, and amongst them there is no grace of manner, or charm of speech, or civilization, or culture, or refinement in pleasures, or joy of life. From their collective force Humanity gains much in material prosperity. But it is only the material result that it gains, and the man who is poor is in himself absolutely of no importance. He is merely the infinitesimal atom of a force that, so far from regarding him, crushes him: indeed, prefers him crushed, as in that case he is far more obedient.

Of course, it might be said that the Individualism generated under conditions of private property is not always, or even as a rule, of a fine or wonderful type, and that the poor, if they have not culture and charm, have still many virtues. Both these statements would be quite true. The possession of private property is very often extremely

demoralizing, and that is, of course, one of the reasons why Socialism wants to get rid of the institution. In fact, property is really a nuisance. Some years ago people went about the country saying that property has duties. They said it so often and so tediously that, at last, the Church has begun to say it. One hears it now from every pulpit. It is perfectly true. Property not merely has duties, but has so many duties that its possession to any large extent is a bore. It involves endless claims upon one, endless attention to business, endless bother. If property had simply pleasures, we could stand it; but its duties make it unbearable. In the interest of the rich we must get rid of it. The virtues of the poor may be readily admitted, and are much to be regretted. We are often told that the poor are grateful for charity. Some of them are, no doubt, but the best amongst the poor are never grateful. They are ungrateful, discontented, disobedient, and rebellious. They are quite right to be so. Charity they feel to be a ridiculously inadequate mode of partial restitution, or a sentimental dole, usually accompanied by some impertinent attempt on the part of the sentimentalist to tyrannize over their private lives. Why should they be grateful for the crumbs that fall from the rich man's table? They should be seated at the board, and are beginning to know it. As for being discontented, a man who would not be discontented with such surroundings and such a low mode of life would be a perfect brute. Disobedience, in the eyes of anyone who has read history, is man's original virtue. It is through disobedience that progress has been made, through disobedience and through rebellion. Sometimes the poor are praised for being thrifty. But to recommend thrift to the poor is both grotesque and insulting. It is like advising a man who is starving to eat less. For a town or country laborer to practice thrift would be absolutely immoral. Man should not be ready to show that he can live like a badly-fed animal. He should decline to live like that, and should either steal or go on the rates, which is considered by many to be a form of stealing. As for begging, it is safer to beg than to take, but it is finer to take than to beg. No: a poor man who is ungrateful, unthrifty, discontented, and rebellious, is probably a real personality, and has much in him. He is at any rate a healthy protest. As for the virtuous poor, one can pity them, of course, but one cannot possibly admire them. They have made private terms with the enemy, and sold their birthright for very bad pottage. They must also be extraordinarily stupid. I can quite understand a man accepting laws

that protect private property, and admit of its accumulation, as long as he himself is able under those conditions to realize some form of beautiful and intellectual life. But it is almost incredible to me how a man whose life is marred and made hideous by such laws can possibly acquiesce in their continuance.

However, the explanation is not really difficult to find. It is simply this. Misery and poverty are so absolutely degrading, and exercise such a paralyzing effect over the nature of men, that no class is ever really conscious of its own suffering. They have to be told of it by other people, and they often entirely disbelieve them. What is said by great employers of labor against agitators is unquestionably true. Agitators are a set of interfering, meddling people, who come down to some perfectly contented class of the community, and sow the seeds of discontent amongst them. That is the reason why agitators are so absolutely necessary. Without them, in our incomplete state, there would be no advance towards civilization. Slavery was put down in America, not in consequence of any action on the part of the slaves, or even any express desire on their part that they should be free. It was put down entirely through the grossly illegal conduct of certain agitators in Boston and elsewhere, who were not slaves themselves, nor owners of slaves, nor had anything to do with the question really. It was, undoubtedly, the Abolitionists who set the torch alight, who began the whole thing. And it is curious to note that from the slaves themselves they received, not merely very little assistance, but hardly any sympathy even; and when at the close of the war the slaves found themselves free, found themselves indeed so absolutely free that they were free to starve, many of them bitterly regretted the new state of things. To the thinker, the most tragic fact in the whole of the French Revolution is not that Marie Antoinette was killed for being a queen, but that the starved peasant of the Vendée voluntarily went out to die for the hideous cause of feudalism.

It is clear, then, that no Authoritarian Socialism will do. For while under the present system a very large number of people can lead lives of a certain amount of freedom and expression and happiness, under an industrial-barrack system, or a system of economic tyranny, nobody would be able to have any such freedom at all. It is to be regretted that a portion of our community should be practically in slavery, but to propose to solve the problem by enslaving the entire community

is childish. Every man must be left quite free to choose his own work. No form of compulsion must be exercised over him. If there is, his work will not be good for him, will not be good in itself, and will not be good for others. And by work I simply mean activity of any kind.

I hardly think that any Socialist, nowadays, would seriously propose that an inspector should call every morning at each house to see that each citizen rose up and did manual labor for eight hours. Humanity has got beyond that stage, and reserves such a form of life for the people whom, in a very arbitrary manner, it chooses to call criminals. But I confess that many of the socialistic views that I have come across seem to me to be tainted with ideas of authority, if not of actual compulsion. Of course, authority and compulsion are out of the question. All association must be quite voluntary. It is only in voluntary associations that man is fine.

But it may be asked how Individualism, which is now more or less dependent on the existence of private property for its development, will benefit by the abolition of such private property. The answer is very simple. It is true that, under existing conditions, a few men who have had private means of their own, such as Byron, Shelley, Browning, Victor Hugo, Baudelaire, and others, have been able to realize their personality more or less completely. Not one of these men ever did a single day's work for hire. They were relieved from poverty. They had an immense advantage. The question is whether it would be for the good of Individualism that such an advantage should be taken away. Let us suppose that it is taken away. What happens then to Individualism? How will it benefit?

It will benefit in this way. Under the new conditions Individualism will be far freer, far finer, and far more intensified than it is now. I am not talking of the great imaginatively-realized Individualism of such poets as I have mentioned, but of the great actual Individualism latent and potential in mankind generally. For the recognition of private property has really harmed Individualism, and obscured it, by confusing a man with what he possesses. It has led Individualism entirely astray. It has made gain not growth its aim. So that man thought that the important thing was to have, and did not know that the important thing is to be. The true perfection of man lies, not in what man has, but in what man is. Private property has crushed true Individualism, and set up an Individualism that is false. It has debarred one part of the community from being individual by starving them. It has debarred the

other part of the community from being individual by putting them on the wrong road, and encumbering them. Indeed, so completely has man's personality been absorbed by his possessions that the English law has always treated offenses against a man's property with far more severity than offenses against his person, and property is still the test of complete citizenship. The industry necessary for the making money is also very demoralizing. In a community like ours, where property confers immense distinction, social position, honor, respect, titles, and other pleasant things of the kind, man, being naturally ambitious, makes it his aim to accumulate this property, and goes on wearily and tediously accumulating it long after he has got far more than he wants, or can use, or enjoy, or perhaps even know of. Man will kill himself by overwork in order to secure property, and really, considering the enormous advantages that property brings, one is hardly surprised. One's regret is that society should be constructed on such a basis that man has been forced into a groove in which he cannot freely develop what is wonderful, and fascinating, and delightful in him — in which, in fact, he misses the true pleasure and joy of living. He is also, under existing conditions, very insecure. An enormously wealthy merchant may be — often is — at every moment of his life at the mercy of things that are not under his control. If the wind blows an extra point or so, or the weather suddenly changes, or some trivial thing happens, his ship may go down, his speculations may go wrong, and he finds himself a poor man, with his social position quite gone. Now, nothing should be able to harm a man except himself. Nothing should be able to rob a man at all. What a man really has, is what is in him. What is outside of him should be a matter of no importance.

With the abolition of private property, then, we shall have true, beautiful, healthy Individualism. Nobody will waste his life in accumulating things, and the symbols for things. One will live. To live is the rarest thing in the world. Most people exist, that is all.

It is a question whether we have ever seen the full expression of a personality, except on the imaginative plane of art. In action, we never have. Cæsar, says Mommsen, was the complete and perfect man. But how tragically insecure was Cæsar! Wherever there is a man who exercises authority, there is a man who resists authority. Cæsar was very perfect, but his perfection traveled by too dangerous a road. Marcus Aurelius was the perfect man, says Renan. Yes; the great emperor was

a perfect man. But how intolerable were the endless claims upon him! He staggered under the burden of the empire. He was conscious how inadequate one man was to bear the weight of that Titan and too vast orb. What I mean by a perfect man is one who develops under perfect conditions; one who is not wounded, or worried or maimed, or in danger. Most personalities have been obliged to be rebels. Half their strength has been wasted in friction. Byron's personality, for instance, was terribly wasted in its battle with the stupidity, and hypocrisy, and Philistinism of the English. Such battles do not always intensify strength: they often exaggerate weakness. Byron was never able to give us what he might have given us. Shelley escaped better. Like Byron, he got out of England as soon as possible. But he was not so well known. If the English had had any idea of what a great poet he really was, they would have fallen on him with tooth and nail, and made his life as unbearable to him as they possibly could. But he was not a remarkable figure in society, and consequently he escaped, to a certain degree. Still, even in Shelley the note of rebellion is sometimes too strong. The note of the perfect personality is not rebellion, but peace.

It will be a marvelous thing — the true personality of man — when we see it. It will grow naturally and simply, flower-like, or as a tree grows. It will not be at discord. It will never argue or dispute. It will not prove things. It will know everything. And yet it will not busy itself about knowledge. It will have wisdom. Its value will not be measured by material things. It will have nothing. And yet it will have everything, and whatever one takes from it, it will still have, so rich will it be. It will not be always meddling with others, or asking them to be like itself. It will love them because they will be different. And yet while it will not meddle with others, it will help all, as a beautiful thing helps us, by being what it is. The personality of man will be very wonderful. It will be as wonderful as the personality of a child.

In its development it will be assisted by Christianity, if men desire that; but if men do not desire that, it will develop none the less surely. For it will not worry itself about the past, nor care whether things happened or did not happen. Nor will it admit any laws but its own laws; nor any authority but its own authority. Yet it will love those who sought to intensify it, and speak often of them. And of these Christ was one.

'Know thyself' was written over the portal of the antique world. Over the portal of the new world, 'Be thyself' shall be written. And the

message of Christ to man was simply 'Be thyself.' That is the secret of Christ.

When Jesus talks about the poor he simply means personalities, just as when he talks about the rich he simply means people who have not developed their personalities. Jesus moved in a community that allowed the accumulation of private property just as ours does, and the gospel that he preached was not that in such a community it is an advantage for a man to live on scanty, unwholesome food, to wear ragged, unwholesome clothes, to sleep in horrid, unwholesome dwellings, and a disadvantage for a man to live under healthy, pleasant, and decent conditions. Such a view would have been wrong there and then, and would, of course, be still more wrong now and in England; for as man moves northward the material necessities of life become of more vital importance, and our society is infinitely more complex, and displays far greater extremes of luxury and pauperism than any society of the antique world. What Jesus meant, was this. He said to man, 'You have a wonderful personality. Develop it. Be yourself. Don't imagine that your perfection lies in accumulating or possessing external things. Your affection is inside of you. If only you could realize that, you would not want to be rich. Ordinary riches can be stolen from a man. Real riches cannot. In the treasury-house of your soul, there are infinitely precious things, that may not be taken from you. And so, try to so shape your life that external things will not harm you. And try also to get rid of personal property. It involves sordid preoccupation, endless industry, continual wrong. Personal property hinders Individualism at every step.' It is to be noted that Jesus never says that impoverished people are necessarily good, or wealthy people necessarily bad. That would not have been true. Wealthy people are, as a class, better than impoverished people, more moral, more intellectual, more well-behaved. There is only one class in the community that thinks more about money than the rich, and that is the poor. The poor can think of nothing else. That is the misery of being poor. What Jesus does say is that man reaches his perfection, not through what he has, not even through what he does, but entirely through what he is. And so the wealthy young man who comes to Jesus is represented as a thoroughly good citizen, who has broken none of the laws of his state, none of the commandments of his religion. He is quite respectable, in the ordinary sense of that extraordinary word. Jesus says to him, 'You should give up private property. It hinders you

from realizing your perfection. It is a drag upon you. It is a burden. Your personality does not need it. It is within you, and not outside of you, that you will find what you really are, and what you really want.' To his own friends he says the same thing. He tells them to be themselves, and not to be always worrying about other things. What do other things matter? Man is complete in himself. When they go into the world, the world will disagree with them. That is inevitable. The world hates Individualism. But that is not to trouble them. They are to be calm and self-centered. If a man takes their cloak, they are to give him their coat, just to show that material things are of no importance. If people abuse them, they are not to answer back. What does it signify? The things people say of a man do not alter a man. He is what he is. Public opinion is of no value whatsoever. Even if people employ actual violence, they are not to be violent in turn. That would be to fall to the same low level. After all, even in prison, a man can be quite free. His soul can be free. His personality can be untroubled. He can be at peace. And, above all things, they are not to interfere with other people or judge them in any way. Personality is a very mysterious thing. A man cannot always be estimated by what he does. He may keep the law, and yet be worthless. He may break the law, and yet be fine. He may be bad, without ever doing anything bad. He may commit a sin against society, and yet realize through that sin his true perfection.

There was a woman who was taken in adultery. We are not told the history of her love, but that love must have been very great; for Jesus said that her sins were forgiven her, not because she repented, but because her love was so intense and wonderful. Later on, a short time before his death, as he sat at a feast, the woman came in and poured costly perfumes on his hair. His friends tried to interfere with her, and said that it was an extravagance, and that the money that the perfume cost should have been expended on charitable relief of people in want, or something of that kind. Jesus did not accept that view. He pointed out that the material needs of Man were great and very permanent, but that the spiritual needs of Man were greater still, and that in one divine moment, and by selecting its own mode of expression, a personality might make itself perfect. The world worships the woman, even now, as a saint.

Yes; there are suggestive things in Individualism. Socialism annihilates family life, for instance. With the abolition of private property, marriage

in its present form must disappear. This is part of the program. Individualism accepts this and makes it fine. It converts the abolition of legal restraint into a form of freedom that will help the full development of personality, and make the love of man and woman more wonderful, more beautiful, and more ennobling. Jesus knew this. He rejected the claims of family life, although they existed in his day and community in a very marked form. 'Who is my mother? Who are my brothers?' he said, when he was told that they wished to speak to him. When one of his followers asked leave to go and bury his father, 'Let the dead bury the dead,' was his terrible answer. He would allow no claim whatsoever to be made on personality.

And so he who would lead a Christlike life is he who is perfectly and absolutely himself. He may be a great poet, or a great man of science; or a young student at a University, or one who watches sheep upon a moor; or a maker of dramas, like Shakespeare, or a thinker about God, like Spinoza; or a child who plays in a garden, or a fisherman who throws his net into the sea. It does not matter what he is, as long as he realizes the perfection of the soul that is within him. All imitation in morals and in life is wrong. Through the streets of Jerusalem at the present day crawls one who is mad and carries a wooden cross on his shoulders. He is a symbol of the lives that are marred by imitation. Father Damien was Christlike when he went out to live with the lepers, because in such service he realized fully what was best in him. But he was not more Christlike than Wagner when he realized his soul in music; or than Shelley, when he realized his soul in song. There is no one type for man. There are as many perfections as there are imperfect men. And while to the claims of charity a man may yield and yet be free, to the claims of conformity no man may yield and remain free at all.

Individualism, then, is what through Socialism we are to attain to. As a natural result the State must give up all idea of government. It must give it up because, as a wise man once said many centuries before Christ, there is such a thing as leaving mankind alone; there is no such thing as governing mankind. All modes of government are failures. Despotism is unjust to everybody, including the despot, who was probably made for better things. Oligarchies are unjust to the many, and ochlocracies are unjust to the few. High hopes were once formed of democracy; but democracy means simply the bludgeoning of the people by the people for the people. It has been found out. I must say that it was high time,

for all authority is quite degrading. It degrades those who exercise it, and degrades those over whom it is exercised. When it is violently, grossly, and cruelly used, it produces a good effect, by creating, or at any rate bringing out, the spirit of revolt and Individualism that is to kill it. When it is used with a certain amount of kindness, and accompanied by prizes and rewards, it is dreadfully demoralizing. People, in that case, are less conscious of the horrible pressure that is being put on them, and so go through their lives in a sort of coarse comfort, like petted animals, without ever realizing that they are probably thinking other people's thoughts, living by other people's standards, wearing practically what one may call other people's second-hand clothes, and never being themselves for a single moment. 'He who would be free,' says a fine thinker, 'must not conform.' And authority, by bribing people to conform, produces a very gross kind of over-fed barbarism amongst us.

With authority, punishment will pass away. This will be a great gain—a gain, in fact, of incalculable value. As one reads history, not in the expurgated editions written for school-boys and passmen, but in the original authorities of each time, one is absolutely sickened, not by the crimes that the wicked have committed, but by the punishments that the good have inflicted; and a community is infinitely more brutalized by the habitual employment of punishment, than it is by the occurrence of crime. It obviously follows that the more punishment is inflicted the more crime is produced, and most modern legislation has clearly recognized this, and has made it its task to diminish punishment as far as it thinks it can. Wherever it has really diminished it, the results have always been extremely good. The less punishment, the less crime. When there is no punishment at all, crime will either cease to exist, or, if it occurs, will be treated by physicians as a very distressing form of dementia, to be cured by care and kindness. For what are called criminals nowadays are not criminals at all. Starvation, and not sin, is the parent of modern crime. That indeed is the reason why our criminals are, as a class, so absolutely uninteresting from any psychological point of view. They are not marvelous Macbeths and terrible Vautrins. They are merely what ordinary, respectable, commonplace people would be if they had not got enough to eat. When private property is abolished there will be no necessity for crime, no demand for it; it will cease to exist. Of course, all crimes are not crimes against property, though such are the crimes that the English law, valuing what a man has more than what a man is,

punishes with the harshest and most horrible severity, if we except the crime of murder, and regard death as worse than penal servitude, a point on which our criminals, I believe, disagree. But though a crime may not be against property, it may spring from the misery and rage and depression produced by our wrong system of property-holding, and so, when that system is abolished, will disappear. When each member of the community has sufficient for his wants, and is not interfered with by his neighbor, it will not be an object of any interest to him to interfere with anyone else. Jealousy, which is an extraordinary source of crime in modern life, is an emotion closely bound up with our conceptions of property, and under Socialism and Individualism will die out. It is remarkable that in communistic tribes jealousy is entirely unknown.

Now as the State is not to govern, it may be asked what the State is to do. The State is to be a voluntary association that will organize labor, and be the manufacturer and distributor of necessary commodities. The State is to make what is useful. The individual is to make what is beautiful. And as I have mentioned the word labor, I cannot help saying that a great deal of nonsense is being written and talked nowadays about the dignity of manual labor. There is nothing necessarily dignified about manual labor at all, and most of it is absolutely degrading. It is mentally and morally injurious to man to do anything in which he does not find pleasure, and many forms of labor are quite pleasureless activities, and should be regarded as such. To sweep a slushy crossing for eight hours, on a day when the east wind is blowing is a disgusting occupation. To sweep it with mental, moral, or physical dignity seems to me to be impossible. To sweep it with joy would be appalling. Man is made for something better than disturbing dirt. All work of that kind should be done by a machine.

And I have no doubt that it will be so. Up to the present, man has been, to a certain extent, the slave of machinery, and there is something tragic in the fact that as soon as man had invented a machine to do his work he began to starve. This, however, is, of course, the result of our property system and our system of competition. One man owns a machine which does the work of five hundred men. Five hundred men are, in consequence, thrown out of employment, and, having no work to do, become hungry and take to thieving. The one man secures the produce of the machine and keeps it, and has five hundred times as much as he should have, and probably, which is of much more importance,

a great deal more than he really wants. Were that machine the property of all, every one would benefit by it. It would be an immense advantage to the community. All unintellectual labor, all monotonous, dull labor, all labor that deals with dreadful things, and involves unpleasant conditions, must be done by machinery. Machinery must work for us in coal mines, and do all sanitary services, and be the stoker of steamers, and clean the streets, and run messages on wet days, and do anything that is tedious or distressing. At present machinery competes against man. Under proper conditions machinery will serve man. There is no doubt at all that this is the future of machinery, and just as trees grow while the country gentleman is asleep, so while Humanity will be amusing itself, or enjoying cultivated leisure—which, and not labor, is the aim of man—or making beautiful things, or reading beautiful things, or simply contemplating the world with admiration and delight, machinery will be doing all the necessary and unpleasant work. The fact is, that civilization requires slaves. The Greeks were quite right there. Unless there are slaves to do the ugly, horrible, uninteresting work, culture and contemplation become almost impossible. Human slavery is wrong, insecure, and demoralizing. On mechanical slavery, on the slavery of the machine, the future of the world depends. And when scientific men are no longer called upon to go down to a depressing East End and distribute bad cocoa and worse blankets to starving people, they will have delightful leisure in which to devise wonderful and marvelous things for their own joy and the joy of everyone else. There will be great storages of force for every city, and for every house if required, and this force man will convert into heat, light, or motion, according to his needs. Is this Utopian? A map of the world that does not include Utopia is not worth even glancing at, for it leaves out the one country at which Humanity is always landing. And when Humanity lands there, it looks out, and, seeing a better country, sets sail. Progress is the realization of Utopias.

Wilde, Oscar (1854-1900)
The Soul of Man Under Socialism (pp. 1-43)
Published in London by A. L. Humphreys in 1912.

First published in *Fortnightly Review* February 1891, p. 292

Contributors

NOTES ON CONTRIBUTORS

To everyone who helped breathe life to this anthology:
Thank you for sharing your gifts with the rest of us.
We need more of you in the world. Write on.

Nancy Allen is a criminal defense attorney, poet, and yoga teacher living in Lynchburg, VA. Her poems have appeared in *Tar River Review*, *Gargoyle*, *Sow's Ear Review*, *JMWW*, and the *Piedmont Virginian*.

Elizabeth Amon   See page 48.

Adrianne Aron   See page 22.

Lynne Martin Bowman was Comstock Review's 2009 Chapbook Winner for *Water Never Sleeps*; was honored in *Crab Orchard Review's* Poetry Prize, and has had work in *Southern Poetry Review*, *Mississippi Review*, and *International Poetry Review*, among others. She lives in Greensboro, NC with her husband, and rescued dogs and cat.

Carolyn Evans Campbell has taught creative writing and poetry for the past twenty-eight years in Evergreen Colorado and the Denver area. She has received wide recognition for six books of poetry, an historical novel, and a play with music. Her joy is sharing our creative journey.

Kerry Tepperman Campbell   See page 18.

Ocean Clark (cover art) has been a full-time artist since '97. He relocated from New Orleans after Katrina. He paints everything under the sun, including custom work, so if you have an idea, shoot him an email at oceanclark@gmail.com. Prints available of everything at oceanclark.com.

David Cooke What has he done but watch a war turn into wars? Twice as old as the dead, yet he struggles with this short biography. Their obituaries already written. Biography. Obituary. Almost the same at the start, so different in the middle, though both ultimately end in: Why?

Ted Davis has written for real joy, absolute need, and undeniable profit for some years. His writing history includes: ten plays, four musicals, five screenplays, numerous poems published in a variety of small literary journals *(Westchester Review, Whole Notes, Plainsongs, Heartlight Journal, New Press, Green Fuse, Poems that Thump in the Dark, Poetry Motel)* with an occasional award winner *(Writers Foundation, Writer Digest, Mississippi Valley Poetry Contest*, Plainsongs Award), volumes of stuff for the United Nations and for the New York Board of Trade, and great cisterns full of marketing/promotional/educational materials for entities alive and dead.

William Ellis teaches at Simon Fraser University. He is the author of *The Theory of the American Romance*, nominated in 1989 for the John Hope Franklin Prize. He has published fiction and poetry in a number of journals, and is currently Poetry Editor of *Mala Literary Journal*.

Robert Evory is currently a PhD candidate in Creative Writing at Western Michigan University where he is the Poetry Editor for *Third Coast*; he is also the Managing Editor of *The Poet's Billow*. His poetry is featured in: *Baltimore Review, Natural Bridge, Nashville Review, Wisconsin Review, Ghost Town, Madison Review, Water~Stone Review*, and elsewhere.

Aly Wright Fields is a 20-something tattooed techie and punk rock poet based out of Boston. Besides writing, Aly's other interests and activities include listening to/composing music, engaging in political activism, cat wrangling, studying philosophy and the social sciences, and practicing a vegetarian, straight-edge lifestyle.

Linda Nemec Foster is the author of nine collections of poetry including *Amber Necklace from Gdansk* and *Talking Diamonds*. Her work has been published in such journals as *The Georgia Review, Nimrod, New American Writing*, and *North American Review*. She has two new collections forthcoming: a chapbook from Cervena Barva Press, and a full-length book from Wayne State University Press.

Christina Frei grew up in Nova Scotia, Canada and has lived in Senegal and currently in the Netherlands where she rides her bike everywhere and teaches writing workshops. She gets her best ideas while walking her dog, Stella, and her poetry has appeared in numerous journals.

Teresa Gilman has poems in *The Comstock Review, Peregrine, Kalliope, Lake Affect, Co-evolution 2*, and other journals. She has won first prizes in the National Penwomen poetry contest, the Abacus and Rose poetry contest, and in 2008 was nominated for a Pushcart. She lives in Syracuse, NY and would rather spend time with dogs than just about anything else.

Jonathan Greenhause was the winner of the 2015 Editor's Choice Poetry Award from Kind of a Hurricane Press and the second-place prize winner in the 2016 Gemini Magazine Poetry Open. This is his fourth time appearing in *New Millennium Writings*.

Lisa Gundry is an artist, writer and avid motorcyclist. She enjoys making new things out of old. Her book of poems, *A Crowd of Sorrows*, was published by Caffeinated Press in 2015. She lives in Grand Rapids, MI with two kitties and two motorcycles.

Juli Anna J. Herndon currently lives in Providence, RI, where she teaches writing to homeschoolers and tutors high school students. She works as a poetry editorial assistant for *Literary Mama*, and her work most recently appeared in the anthology *Missing Providence*.

Marilyn E. Johnston is the author of two full collections of poetry, *Weight of the Angel* and *Silk Fist Songs*, both from Antrim House Books. Her poems are widely published in periodicals and have garnered six Pushcart Prize nominations.

Marilyn Kallet is the author of seventeen books, including *The Love That Moves Me*, poetry from Black Widow Press. She has translated Paul Eluard's *Last Love Poems*, Péret's *The Big Game*, and co-translated Chantal Bizzini's *Disenchanted City*. Dr. Kallet is Nancy Moore Goslee Professor of English at the University of Tennessee. She also leads poetry workshops for VCCA-France in Auvillar. She has performed her poems on campuses and in theaters across the United States as well as in France and Poland, as a guest of the U.S. Embassy's "America Presents" program. The University of Tennessee lists her as an expert on poetry's role in times of crisis.

George Keenen is 74 and lives in Alameda, CA with his wife, Susan. He has Parkinson's Disease.

Joyce Kessel has three chapbooks: *Secret Lives* (2011), *Describing the Dark* (Saddle Road Press, 2014) and *Classroom Quixote* (The Writer's Den, 2015), and is included in the WNY Peace Center's *Poets Waging Words for Peace and Nickel City Nights* anthologies. She is a member of Earth's Daughters. She teaches literature, and creative writing at Villa Maria College Buffalo NY.

C. Ann Kodra works as an independent editor in Knoxville, TN. Her poetry and short stories have appeared or are pending in various journals and anthologies, including *Birmingham Arts Journal, Blueline, Cavalier Literary Couture, Common Ground Review, Cutthroat, drafthorse, Now & Then, Peacock Journal, Prime Mincer, Roanoke Review, RHINO, Still: The Journal, The Saranac Review, Yemassee,* and others. She is a contributing editor for *New Millennium Writings* and an associate editor for MSI Press (California). Medulla Press published her chapbook, *Thin Ice*, in 2011. Her first full poetry collection, *Under an Adirondack Moon*, is now available from Iris Press (October 2017).

Danny Kossow is an AmeriCorps member serving in Washington, D.C. He teaches first grade at Stanton Elementary School, where he spends most of his time peeling six year olds off walls. He spends most of his spare time fine-tuning his MFA applications and, when he can, driving down to Virginia for a taste of nature.

K. T. Landon is the 2013 winner of the Arts & Letters PRIME Poetry Prize, runner up for the 2015 Elinor Benedict Poetry Prize from *Passages North*, and a two-time Pushcart nominee. Her chapbook, *Orange, Dreaming*, is available from Five Oaks Press. She serves as a Poetry Reader for *Muzzle*.

Christina Lovin is the author of *Echo, A Stirring in the Dark, What We Burned for Warmth, Little Fires*, and *Flesh*. Her writing is widely published and anthologized, and is supported by Elizabeth George Foundation, Kentucky Foundation for Women, and Kentucky Arts Council. She collects wool, dust, rejection letters, and shelter dogs, and teaches writing at Eastern Kentucky University.

Alison Luterman is the author of three previous collections of poetry: *The Largest Possible Life, See How We Almost Fly*, and *Desire Zoo*, which was published by Tia Chucha Press. Her poems have appeared in *The Sun Magazine, Rattle, Nimrod, Prairie Schooner*, and elsewhere. Her poem, "Lady," was a finalist in last year's *NMW* contest. www.alisonluterman.net

Bernadette McComish earned an MFA from Sarah Lawrence, and an MA in Teaching English as a Second Language from Hunter. Her poems have been published in *The Cortland Review, Sunday Salon, Hakol, Hospital Drive, Slipstream*, and *Storyscape*. She teaches High School in Los Angeles, and performs with the Poetry Brothel.

Carol D. Marsh   See page 68.

Ed McManis is the Head of a small school in San Francisco for students with learning differences. He and his wife Linda have two sons, Jamie and Sean. His most recent chapbooks include *Sister Mary Butkus* and *Working For My Old Man*. His work has appeared in *The Blueroad Reader, Natural Bridge, Rhino, Colorado North Review, California Quarterly, Mudfish*, and others.

Barbara Mossberg is a poetry activist in the civic ethos ("no place safe from poetry"), President Emerita Goddard College, City Poet Emerita, Pacific Grove (CA), cultural diplomat, dramaturg, playwright, actor, literary critic, and professor (University of Oregon), and is founder and host of the weekly Poetry Slowdown podcast (BarbaraMossberg.com), poetry slams ("old lady moxie, strutting her poetic gear"), flash mobs, blogs, crawls.

Robin Myers   See page 12.

William Polsgrove   See page 28.

Julie Rochlin is doorperson to two tiger cats and the mother of two young adults. She's no longer grief-stricken and still deeply in love. She has a practice in Massage Therapy, and is devoted to her friends, community, and poetry. She attends poetry workshops, including Marge Piercy's juried intensive, and recently had a poem in the 2016 edition of *Chautauqua*.

Michael Rowe   See page 110.

Ed Ruzicka has published one full length volume, *Engines of Belief*. His poems have appeared in the *Atlanta Review, the Xavier Review, Plainsongs, Big River Poetry Review* as well as other literary journals and anthologies. Ed lives in Baton Rogue, LA and is an occupational therapist. edrpoet.com

JL Schneider is a carpenter and an adjunct professor of English at a small community college in upstate New York. Winner of the 2015 Prism Review Poetry Contest, his poetry collection, *It's Strange Here*, was recently published by Vine Leaves Press. www.schneiderjl.com

Carol Smith is a Seattle writer whose work led the anthology, *The Best Creative Nonfiction* (W. W. Norton, 2007). Her poetry, fiction and essays have appeared in *Signs of Life, Mississippi Review, Pooled Ink, The New Guard, Hippocampus Magazine, Oberon Poetry, The Florida Review, The Southern Indiana Review*, and *Travelers' Tales (to Go)*. She is currently working on a novel.

Victoria G. Smith is the lawyer-turned-author of the award-winning novella, *Faith Healer*, and the Kirkus-acclaimed poetry collection, *Warrior Heart, Pilgrim Soul: An Immigrant's Journey*. Her poems were recently chosen as finalists in the 42nd New Millennium Poetry Awards, the 2016 Knightville Poetry Contest, and the 2016 Edwin Markham Poetry Award. She writes a poetry column for *VIATimes Magazine*.

Laura Still is a poet, playwright, writer, and teller of local history stories for her tour business, Knoxville Walking Tours. Her poetry collection, *Guardians*, was released in 2009 by Celtic Cat Publishing and was followed in 2010 by *Acts of the Apostles, Vol. I*, a book of children's plays.

Armin Tolentino received his MFA at Rutgers University in Newark, NJ. His poetry has appeared in *Literary Laundry, Blue Earth Review*, and *Backwords Press*. He was a 2014 Oregon Literary Arts Fellowship recipient and lets the New York Knicks break his heart every year between October and March.

Barbara Ungar's latest book, *Immortal Medusa*, was one of Kirkus Reviews' Best Indie Books of 2015, and won the Adirondack Center for Writing Poetry Award. Prior books include *Charlotte Brontë, You Ruined My Life* and *The Origin of the Milky Way*, which won the Gival Prize, and several other awards. www.barbaraungar.net

Cady Vishniac   See page 34.

Oscar Wilde (1854–1900) was an Irish author, poet, and playwright. Notable works include *The Picture of Dorian Gray* (1890) and *The Importance of Being Earnest* (1895). He died in Paris at the young age of 46.

Kirk Wilson   See page 86.

Barbara Zimmermann's fiction, essays, and poems have been published in numerous literary journals and anthologies including *New Millennium Writings* (in which two separate issues contained her first- and second-prize winning flash fictions), *Rockhurst Review, Pleiades, Earth Daughters #72, Kaleidoscope, Out of Line*, and *The Deadly Writers Patrol*.

Lucia Zimmitti hails from central Connecticut and now lives in Austin, TX, where she's determined to eat at every single food truck at least once (perhaps an unrealistically low estimate), and to fill her ears and heart and head with more music than they can hold. She works as a copywriter, editor, and ghostwriter in several different genres.

20+ YEARS

EST. 1996

CONSECUTIVE WRITING CONTESTS	WRITERS AND POETS PUBLISHED	ANTHOLOGIES DELIVERED	AWARDED TO WRITERS AND POETS
45	1,800+	50,000+	$360,000+

BOTH ONLINE SUBMISSIONS AND MAIL/POSTAL SUBMISSIONS ACCEPTED

NEWMILLENNIUMWRITINGS.ORG

SUNSHOTS.ORG   MUSEPAPER.ORG

New Millennium WRITINGS

$360,000+ IN CASH PRIZES AWARDED

◊ Poetry, Fiction, Flash Fiction, Nonfiction

◊ No restrictions on style or subject matter

◊ $1,000 award plus publication for each category

◊ Anonymous and blind judging

◊ Every submission gets *at least* one full read-through

◊ Multiple and simultaneous submissions welcome

◊ Online *and* mail/postal submissions are accepted

→ **Write more. Hone your craft with monthly writing prompt/topic contests of 1,000 words or less (musepaper.org)**

✓ *Review this anthology on Amazon or your blog and send us a link to it!*

☼ **Visit the Sunshot Press when your poetry, short-story, or essay collection is ready for the world (sunshots.org)**

↔ SAY HI, ASK A QUESTION, OR SHARE SOME GOOD NEWS: HELLO@NEWMILLENNIUMWRITINGS.ORG

NEWMILLENNIUMWRITINGS.ORG
SUNSHOTS.ORG   MUSEPAPER.ORG